THE NUNAMIUT ESKIMOS: HUNTERS OF CARIBOU

THE NUNAMIUT ESKIMOS

HUNTERS OF CARIBOU

Nicholas J. Gubser

Yale University Press: New Haven and London 1965

*To the Great-Grandchildren of the Nunamiut Eskimos
of Anaktuvuk Pass, Alaska*

Contents

Foreword

George Peter Murdock

THE most striking fact about this substantial book is that it is the work of an undergraduate. As such, it should provide a source of encouragement and inspiration to college students everywhere, for it demonstrates that their potentialities for productive and creative work need not always remain latent.

Mr. Gubser took a seminar course with me in 1959–60, when he was a junior in Yale College. He had spent two months the previous summer in north Alaska as an assistant to John M. Campbell on an archaeological dig, during which he established personal contacts with the Nunamiut. In my class he distinguished himself by his enthusiasm and by a degree of sophistication, rare among undergraduates, derived from his field experience. In 1960–61 he revisited the Nunamiut for fourteen months of intensive ethnographic research.

Returning to Yale in 1961–62 for his senior year, Mr. Gubser, as a Scholar of the House, devoted himself to writing up his field results under the tutelage of Professor Leopold Pospisil, who had himself worked among the Nunamiut in 1957. The result was the first draft of the present volume, presented as an honors thesis when Mr. Gubser received his A.B. degree *summa cum laude* in 1962. He then entered Oxford University as a Rhodes Scholar to pursue his studies toward the Ph.D. degree, and he has subsequently prepared himself in languages at Rome and Paris for an intensive field investigation of the Galla of Ethiopia.

Most of the voluminous descriptive literature on the Eskimos has appeared in paperback numbers of such scientific series as the *Bulletins of the National Museum of Canada,* the *Meddelelser om Grønland,* and the *Reports of the Fifth Thule Expedition.* This book stands almost alone in being substantially bound in cloth and thus technically suited for use in the classroom. It is unique in that, being written by an undergraduate, it reflects the kind of interest in anthropology prevalent among intelligent college students. It is a straightforward account, enlivened by anecdotal material and by the obvious enthusiasm of the author, of the social organization, supernatural ideology, and economic activities of the Nunamiut in the setting of their history and geographic environment. Mr. Gubser may ultimately concern himself with such issues as "segmentary lineage structure" or "prescriptive matrilateral cross-cousin marriage," so common in the works which senior scholars address to one another, but this book shows no trace of such jargon or theoretical preoccupation. It is completely comprehensible to any layman.

This does not mean—I must hasten to add—that the book is in any respect superficial or "written down" to an immature audience. On the contrary, it presents, in simple, declarative prose, practically all the precise information which the most demanding professional scholar wants to know about the Nunamiut. Its seeming simplicity is as deceptive as it is ingratiating. Mr. Gubser writes with sympathy and humor. He makes his people come alive to us in every aspect of their traditional thought and actions and of their formal and informal social interaction. One could scarcely ask more of him.

Preface

THE Nunamiut are a group of a hundred Eskimos, the remnants of a large inland population, who live in Anaktuvuk Pass in the central Brooks Range of northern Alaska. They are primarily dependent on the migrant caribou for their existence in the mountains and on the north slope of Arctic Alaska. The purpose of this monograph is to examine an ecological problem—how the Nunamiuts' conceptions about the elements of their environment, set in a social context, enable them to perpetuate themselves as a society. The hunting of caribou is an essential factor in their survival, but this alone does not suffice; the exploitation of other elements of the environment is also necessary. Hence, while the fullest attention is given to the caribou, the total environment is considered as well.

In order to understand how the Nunamiut think of and exploit the elements of their environment, a broad historical background, from the points of view of both the white man and the Nunamiut, are developed. The outlines of their social life are presented, especially emphasizing the organization and activities of the two basic groups in their society—the household and the community. We then consider the ideas of the Nunamiut and the cognitive processes by which they become aware of their environment.

During the summer of 1959 I spent two months in northern Alaska assisting John M. Campbell on an archaeological project. At that time I met most of the hundred people of Anaktuvuk Pass and was able to collect some few data about folklore and religion and to establish an initial rapport. I had the good fortune to find, among others, an informant who spoke moderately good English and had had previous experience with note-taking biologists and geologists. Following a common ethnographic procedure, I hired various persons for their time, using interpreters when necessary.

In June 1960 I returned to the village and pitched my tent beside the family with whom I hoped to live. Simon Paneak, the man of the family and my principal informant of the past summer, was communicative, highly intelligent, and willing to talk about his culture, indeed, proud to do so to a sympathetic listener. In exchange for certain trade items such as tea, coffee, sugar, and condensed milk, I ate in the family's tent. The people had killed a large number of caribou in the course of the recent spring migration, and during the resulting summer leisure I conducted intensive interviews in an effort to familiarize myself with the elements of the Arctic environment, the organization of Nunamiut bands, and the nature of social life, supplementing the data I had collected the summer before.

During the latter part of August, the meat ran out, and the family began to prepare for a three-week hunt. As a novice ethnographer not quite certain of himself, I stood by my tent, gear readied; a few minutes later, five of us with thirteen heavily loaded dogs started moving slowly out of camp. From that day on, the whole tenor of my activities was altered.

In September and October I helped the family build a sod house. Just before we finished it I left on a short trip. When I returned, the house was completed. While I was sitting inside the new house drinking tea, the head of the family turned to me and said, "You better put your sleeping bag over in that place." Simon Paneak, his wife, six children aged 4 through 23, and myself in a one-room sod house, 16 feet by 24 feet, constituted the household. An old man in his early eighties lived with us for two or three months in the winter.

During the fall and early winter, my time was spent learning to speak the language, to hunt, to build moss houses, to gather and cut firewood, and to handle dogs. I became a full-time hunter, as a young man in his early twenties ought, taking frequent trips of one day to three weeks by dog sled and by foot in search of game. During the hunts, often with only one other person or a small group of four or five, I was able to learn a lot about the hunt: techniques of utilizing the fauna and of adapting to the climate, the division of the catch, and individual attitudes toward the hunt itself and toward the environment. At home I learned to make and repair things designed for the hunt.

In learning to speak Eskimo I made slow but steady progress; after two months I really knew very little. The written materials I had were meager but at least indicated that verbs are very highly inflected and that the noun paradigm contains eight cases. Because the phonemic shapes of suffixes vary according to the phonemic shapes of noun and verb stems, I had to learn the principles of phonemic alternation in Eskimo before I could assimilate new words into actual usage.

After five months of language study, I fished for two weeks with a family who spoke no English. I was able to get along all right but could not yet freely discuss ideas or fully express my own thoughts. During the period between the sixth and eighth months I finally felt the exhilaration of being able to understand and to express myself about probabilities, moral problems, desires, and jokes.

Toward the end of my stay I was able to understand when the Eskimos discussed certain matters among themselves, such as gossip (about myself sometimes when they thought I could not understand), hunting and traveling, and memories of past years. I had difficulty understanding certain technical discussions about making implements and about distant relatives of whom I knew nothing. The daily conversation, say, that would occur between two hunters over morning coffee, I came to understand with considerable ease. When I did leave, of course, I had the feeling that I could still have learned more about the language, but I had achieved, for my purposes as an ethnographer and as a human being, the desired end of meaningful communication.

Two or three older persons I never learned to understand very well, having very little contact with them and, indeed, particularly in my social position, not much to talk about. I could actually understand them better when they talked to other Eskimos rather than to me. One old man had an unmarried daughter about 25 years old. As a young, unmarried hunter, three or four years younger than the daughter (for the Nunamiut, the wife should be older than the husband), we came to be considered an ideal match. Thus, in order to keep gossip at a minimum and to prevent any difficulty, I tried to avoid contact with that family. Whenever I met the old man, I felt a little ill at ease. He had asked another young man to "go down the trail and meet his daughter" and marry her, and people joked with me about his obvious approach. The old man once heard such a joke but merely grinned knowingly at me. When another old man did offer me the old man's daughter, I sat frozen, not saying a word until the subject of the conversation changed.

As the year progressed and I was better able to communicate, I conducted fewer formal interviews. Rather, I would from time to time write up information at home after conversations. Eskimos respect industry of almost any kind, and thus I was able to sit in the corner of the house writing, assured that the family appreciated the vague relationship between the tea, coffee, sugar, etc. I was able to provide and the physical act of writing. I refrained from taking notes during conversations or giving the impression of asking structured questions about such sensitive matters as sex, religion, Alaskan game regulations, and gossip.

Living as I did, I was able to observe very intimately, and in fact to participate in, the arising and settling of disputes, the training and care of children, gossiping, carrying out kinship obligations, visiting from house to house, dancing, joking and becoming the butt of jokes, discussing religious and superstitious matters, and so forth. Listening to and participating, as a matter of course, in conversations and daily activities is perhaps the best ethnographic method and probably the most difficult, not only because of the requirements of language but also because the ethnographer must create a social position for himself that does not hinder the spontaneity of the people. This is a delicate and rewarding task.

The following incident is an example of the "informal interview." During the early winter I spent seven or eight days hunting alone with Simon Paneak. Every day we would walk 15 or 20 miles over the countryside, returning in the evening to a small hunting hut. On the seventh evening we had finished dinner early and would not go to sleep for another two hours so as not to awaken too early in the late dawn. We had not seen an animal all week, and we started talking in a melancholy way; it was —30° F and there was no door on the hut. For two hours we sat in our skin clothing, talking about him and his early life, his first sight of a white man, his first love, and the death during childbirth of his first wife, his ensuing despondence of several years, his encountering white men as an adult, his falling in love again, his father's advice against the marriage, and finally the choice of his present wife. One rarely hears such a sensitive expression of a human self as I heard that night.

There were many, many months during the winter when I was primarily concerned with the job of living. During the late spring and following summer I began taking more notes, rounding out my data; for one thing, I had a much clearer conception of my problem and, second, I would soon have to return home. I left Anaktuvuk Pass in August 1961.

My research among the Nunamiut Eskimos was supported by a contract with the Arctic Institute of North America in Washington, D.C., and the Arctic Research Laboratory of the Office of Naval Research at Point Barrow, Alaska. Dean William De-Vane, of Yale College, also provided support through the Dean's Discretionary Fund. I wish to thank Paul Pickrel, chairman of the Scholar of the House Program, for providing the opportunity during the academic year 1961–62 for me to prepare the first draft of this monograph.

I should like to express an especial appreciation to Professor John M. Campbell, now at the University of New Mexico, for first arousing my interest in the Arctic. To Max C. Brewer, Director of the Arctic Research Laboratory, I am indebted for confidence in and support of my work in the field. My grateful thanks go to Professor Leopold Pospisil, of Yale University, my advisor during my senior year (1961–62) in Yale College, whose carefully considered advice and constructive criticism were invaluable in the preparation of the first draft. He took the photograph of the Nunamiut family that appears on the dust jacket, which I use with his kind permission. During the summer of 1962 I was fortunate to be encouraged and advised by Professor William Davenport, now of the University of Pennsylvania. My grateful appreciation is due to Dr. Rodney Needham, of Oxford University, whose precise criticisms were very helpful in preparing the final draft during the academic year 1962–63. To Anne Wilde I express my gratitude for her painstaking editorial assistance.

I convey my humble and lasting appreciation to Simon and Susie Paneak and their children, Robert, Raymond, Mabel, Roosevelt, George, and Alan, for their generous hospitality during my stay in their home; to Elija Kakinya, one of the best traveling and hunting companions I have ever had the pleasure of knowing; and to the other villagers of Anaktuvuk Pass for their innumerable gestures of kindness and instruction.

New Haven, Connecticut   N. J. G.
January 1965

1. Historical Background

Russian Fur Trading and Exploration

IN the early 1500s Russia had shaken off the domination of the Mongols, and during the following centuries Russian Czars sought to expand their influence to the west and east. Since much resistance was encountered in the west, Russian power developed largely in eastern Asia, and the Russians spread into Siberia in the early 1700s as part of the general eastward expansion of their empire. By the early 1700s all of Siberia was under Russian political and economic domination. In those days no one knew of the geographical relationship between Siberia and America.

In 1741, Vitus Bering became the first white man to set foot on Alaskan territory. Bering, a Dane in the service of the Russian Imperial Navy, was commissioned by Peter the Great to determine whether or not Asia and America were connected by land. Bering did not accomplish the immediate purpose of his voyage, but he did arouse the attention of Russian fur traders in Siberia when he brought back a number of sea otter pelts from the Aleutian Islands.

The first fur-trading expedition was sent to Alaska from Siberia in 1743; many valuable pelts were brought back, and from 1743 to 1770 the Russian fur interests in Alaska grew steadily. By 1770 they were well entrenched and, during the next two decades, the Russian fur trade reached a peak. In 1784 the first permanent Russian settlement was established on Kodiak Island, and in 1799 the Russian American Company was chartered. By 1820, Russian trading posts extended up into the Bering Sea. During the early 1800s the Russian administrators in Alaska had intended to explore the Arctic, but lack of home support prevented extensive travels. A few geographical surveys, however, were supported by the Russian Imperial Navy and the Russian American Company (Hulley 1953: 30–69).

In 1815, Otto von Kotzebue, a German in the service of the Russian Navy, discovered Kotzebue Sound, just north of Seward Peninsula. He established contact with the Malemiut Eskimos there, who reacted initially with distrust, curiosity, and astonishment. Kotzebue reported that the Eskimos had already obtained some trade items but had never seen white men before. The Eskimos did not seem to comprehend firearms at all; while in kayaks well within the range of Kotzebue's guns, they shot an occasional arrow at Kotzebue, displaying their hostility. He did not reply with force but presented gifts of tobacco, beads, knives, and scissors. On receiving these gifts the Eskimos became friendly and offered furs in exchange for goods. Kotzebue observed that the Malemiut Eskimos were very shrewd traders (Kotzebue 1821: 192–251).

Before 1900, a few Nunamiut Eskimos traveled as far as Kotzebue Sound to trade, and it is possible that some of them saw Kotzebue. In any case, there is no doubt that very shortly after 1815 the Nunamiut heard many stories about Kotzebue from the Eskimos who had seen him, and they probably traded for items obtained from him.

Another Russian exploration effort ended rather unsuccessfully in 1838. Soon after Simpson's important trip (see below), the Russian American Company outfitted the ship *Polyfem* to explore the Arctic coast as far north of Kotzebue Sound as possible. The skipper of the ship, a Russian named Chernof, was under the command of Alexander Kashevarof, born on Kodiak Island. Kashevarof spoke several Western Eskimo and probably a few Aleut dialects. Many of his party were Aleuts and Russians, possibly of mixed blood, born in Alaska. North of Kotzebue Sound, Kashevarof met opposition from the Eskimos living along the coast. Finally, a hundred miles west of Beechey Point, a group of Eskimos armed with bows and arrows, outnumbering the Russians twenty to one, confronted the *Polyfem* and it was forced to turn back. The Russians continued to meet attacks but managed to return safely to Norton Sound (Bancroft 1890: 552–53).

After 1820, explorers began penetrating the Yukon River valley, and in 1842 Lieutenant Zagoskin of the Russian Navy traveled 56 miles up the Koyukuk River from its confluence with the Yukon. Zagoskin encountered the Koyukon Indians, who traded regularly with the Kobuk Eskimos and occasionally with the Nunamiut. Zagoskin's trip was possibly a subject of some discussion among the Nunamiut. As a navy man, Zagoskin traded very little, although he did hire a few Koyukon Indians to work for him. He tried to persuade them to guide him from the Koyukuk River to Kotzebue Sound, but the Indians turned back in fear of the Malemiut Eskimos (Allen 1887). His trip did not constitute a source of major contact and provided few trade items.

By 1840 only slightly more than twenty permanent Russian posts existed in all of Alaska. For years the Russians had taken furs out of Alaska, giving no thought to conservation and displaying little concern for scientific exploration. After 1840 the Russians made less and less money. The British were moving into the upper Yukon territory, and the Americans were beginning to dominate the Alaskan whaling industry. Russia finally sold Alaska to the United States in an effort to drive a political wedge between Great Britain and America by confounding British economic interests in the Alaskan Arctic (Hulley 1953: 193–212).

British Exploration

In 1778 Captain James Cook, on his famous third and last voyage to the Pacific Ocean, explored parts of the Alaskan Arctic coast including Icy Cape, halfway between Wainwright and Point Lay. Although he encountered no Eskimos north of Cape Prince of Wales, the westernmost extension of Seward Peninsula, he did meet Eskimos in Norton Bay. There he traded knives, chisels, pieces of iron and tin, nails, mirrors, and buttons for furs, native clothing, weapons, carvings, and human skulls. The Eskimos rejected cloth of any kind (Cook 1784, 2). The Nunamiut apparently were never aware of Captain Cook, although some of his trade goods may have reached the Brooks Range.

Captain F. W. Beechey made a significant voyage of discovery in 1826, exploring the Alaskan coast up to Point Barrow. At Kotzebue Sound, Beechey was offered ivory figures, wooden bowls, dolls, clothing, and weapons in exchange for beads, knives, files, scissors, tobacco, and buttons. While there he found a small Russian coin with an image of Catherine the Great on it. The Eskimos were very happy to trade and Beechey, wisely for his security, followed a policy of extensive and generous exchange. Traveling north of the sound, Beechey continued to trade with the Eskimos and maintained good relations; he demonstrated the use of firearms in a friendly way, but the Eskimos were afraid to shoot a gun themselves. Beechey ventured beyond Icy Cape into unexplored territory. He managed to keep the Eskimos well disposed by attending dances and trading, although he admitted expressing displeasure about Eskimo hygiene.

Beechey decided against sailing his entire expedition up to Point Barrow. Instead, he appointed Elson to go on in a smaller boat. When Elson reached Point Barrow, he made the mistake of not trading immediately; an Eskimo offered his lance for some tobacco and Elson refused. The Eskimos then became overbearing and stole from him. His trouble was obvious: the Eskimos at Point Barrow had of course heard of the white man and his goods and they were extremely, almost compulsively, desirous of trading. When Elson refused to trade items that the Eskimos could see in his boat, they could only interpret this as dishonest and unfair. Finally Elson did trade for some waterproof sealskin boots, and he reported that there were moments of friendliness. He visited the village at Point Barrow but could not stomach the food (Beechey 1831).

By 1826 the British had reached Point Barrow from the south. British influence came in from the east in 1770, when a ship sponsored by the Hudson's Bay Company reached the Coppermine River. In 1789 and again in 1793, Mackenzie reached the mouth of the Mackenzie River. Soon after, the Hudson's Bay Company followed and set up trading posts. While these early posts did not provide immediate, direct contact with the Alaskan Eskimos, the Company did support the exploration of the north Alaskan coast and established trading posts in the interior along the Porcupine and upper Yukon rivers.

In 1826 the famous Sir John Franklin, under the sponsorship of the Hudson's Bay Company, traveled west from the mouth of the Mackenzie River. Franklin reached Herschel Island in Canada and, being able to speak a little Eskimo, he picked up vague information about a series of rivers and broken mountain ranges in the interior of northern Alaska. Franklin distributed gifts and traded with the Eskimos camped along the coast west of the Mackenzie River, many of whom were Nunamiut.

Franklin noted that these Eskimos had Russian but not British trade goods. He learned that the Nunamiut obtained iron, knives, beads, and tobacco almost exclusively from the Point Barrow and Kotzebue Sound Eskimos, who lived farther west. The Eskimos on Alaska's north coast told Franklin they did know of the Coppermine Eskimos but had no dealings with them. The Alaskan Eskimos said the Eskimos to the east were bad people with crude and disgusting habits. According to Franklin, the Eskimos did not have firearms but knew and feared them, particularly since the Kutchin Indians who came to Barter Island had guns. The Eskimos told Franklin that they were happy to have finally become acquainted with white men, would try to be friendly, and looked forward to further trading in the future. Reports about Franklin ran west ahead of him. Occasionally, in approaching a village, Franklin noted a great wave of fear, but as soon as he began to trade, the fear subsided. He said that the Eskimos always asked a visitor's name and told their names in return, a custom persisting today. They were extremely curious about material things, particularly Franklin's boats and implements, and seemed to understand very well how they were made. Franklin also noted their keen sense of trading.

Franklin's destination was Point Barrow, where he hoped to rendezvous with Captain Beechey, but ice forced him to turn back at Return Reef just east of Beechey Point, some 146 miles short of his goal (Franklin 1828).

It was not until 1837 that Thomas Simpson, another of the explorers sponsored by the Hudson's Bay Company, closed this last gap. He set out from the Mackenzie River to chart the coast to Point Barrow. Although trading was not his purpose, he did trade "to quiet the Eskimos." Simpson thought highly of them, praising their appearance. He spoke a little Eskimo, to their surprise and delight. The Eskimos had seen the white man's books and declared that the books spoke Eskimo to white men, enabling them in turn to speak. Simpson presented gifts, exchanged dances now and then, and even once held a jumping contest; he felt that the Eskimos were almost overbearing in their friendliness, but he was tolerant. Some Eskimos even laid down their Russian long knives when approaching Simpson.

Just east of Dease Inlet, Simpson could travel no farther in his boat, and he started walking west. He came upon a small village where he was overpowered by caresses; there he chartered two Eskimo skin boats. The Eskimos then declared that Simpson and his men were true Eskimos and not unfortunate whites, a compliment given to this day.

Simpson finally reached his destination, Point Barrow. At first, the Eskimos were afraid, but he opened trade and soon established friendly relations. Simpson noted, as did Franklin and Beechey,

that the Alaskan Eskimos had Russian trade goods; one iron
bucket sold for two wolverine skins (Dease and Simpson 1838;
Simpson 1843). (In 1960 a good wolverine skin sold for $50 in
northern Alaska.)

In the 1840s the Hudson's Bay Company extended trading posts
into the upper Yukon territory, from northwestern Canada into
Alaska. In 1847 a Company man named McMurray descended the
Porcupine River to its confluence with the Yukon River. There he
established a trading post, Fort Yukon, which has come to be the
largest village in northeastern Alaska. Other posts were established
south of the eastern Brooks Range, but the Hudson's Bay Company
traded almost exclusively with the Kutchin Indians. Not until after
World War I did any Nunamiut come down to Fort Yukon to trade
furs for "white-man" goods.

In 1847 Sir John Franklin and 134 men were lost (on King
William's Land in the Canadian archipelago) in a search for the
Northwest Passage. In the twenty years after Franklin's disappear-
ance, over forty expeditions carried on the search for him, which
resulted in the exploration and mapping of a vast part of the Arctic
as well as providing sporadic white contact with the Arctic Alaskan
Eskimos. Point Barrow was rounded time and again.

The *Plover,* commanded by Maguire, was the first ship to spend
a winter at Point Barrow (in 1852–53 and again in the following
year). After some initial skirmishes, Maguire managed to establish
friendly relations for most of his stay. John Simpson, the ship's
surgeon, made extensive ethnographic collections and noted many
of the Eskimos' habits.

Simpson reported that while many Arctic Alaskan Eskimos had
never seen white men before 1837, they used the word *tannik* for
white man (still in use today), which came from the Eskimo word
tannikhlugo (to wash). The Eskimos of Arctic Alaska had heard
of white men (Russians) who had regular bath days at their fur-
trading posts far to the south.

Although most of the Russian trade items reached the Arctic
Alaskan Eskimos via Siberian Eskimos and other Alaskan Eskimos in the 1700s and 1800s, the news of Alaskan Russian fur traders and a few trade items very likely reached the Nunamiut by way
of the Western Alaskan Eskimos before 1800. Simpson mentioned
that, by the middle of the 1850s, the Eskimos had learned very
little English, but that sexual intercourse between white sailors and
Eskimo women was becoming frequent (Simpson 1855: 917–42).

American Contact

For several decades before and shortly after 1900, American contacts with Arctic Alaska included whalers, geological explorers, military patrols, prospectors, trappers, traders, and missionaries.

WHALING. The first American whaling ships entered Russian–American waters about 1820. In 1826 the Russian governor of Alaska requested the director of the Russian American Company to send whaling ships to Kodiak Island and the Aleutians. The Russians made only belated attempts to develop their own whaling industry and took few steps to protect their interests. In 1835, Americans heard of opportunities for whaling off Kodiak Island, and by 1842, thirty Yankee whalers were operating near the Aleutians. In 1848 an American whaler ventured past the Bering Straits, and the Arctic was opened to whaling. Each year between 1850 and 1860, as many as 300 foreign whaling ships plied Alaskan waters. The whaling ships carried rowdy crews. Ignorant and illiterate New England farmers, convicts, Fijians, and Kanakas were typical of them. A few whalers leaving from New England engaged in slave trading en route to Alaska.

As whalers worked their way up the Alaskan coast to Point Barrow, they brought large quantities of such trade goods as flour, molasses, tea, coffee, sugar, tobacco, liquor, needles, guns, and ammunition. American trade goods largely replaced the Russian goods which came to Arctic Alaska via Siberian Eskimos. Whalers also carried measles, influenza, tuberculosis, and venereal diseases; in addition they upset the economic balance of many indigenous Alaskan communities by hiring hunters at very high wages (usually paid in kind) for short periods of time. In a year when few whalers came north, some Eskimos and whites thought starvation would ensue. Few people went hungry as a direct result of less employment, but many Eskimos experienced the insecurity of the irregular demand for labor by the whalers. The intensive hunting pressure created by whalers resulted in a reduction in the numbers of whales, walrus, seals, and caribou by the late 1890s. Many inland Nunamiut starved before they could migrate to the coast.

During Lieutenant Ray's expedition (see below) in 1881–83, a Captain Herendeen acted as his hunter and assistant. After Ray left, Herendeen convinced the Pacific Steam Whaling Company that Point Barrow would be an excellent site for a permanent whaling station. Charles Brower joined Herendeen in 1884 and immediately became involved in the whaling industry. In 1886, Brower himself took charge of the station. At first he adopted the Eskimo whaling methods but soon introduced such techniques as the use of metal in place of flint and ground slate for harpoon heads. Brower also de-emphasized Eskimo taboos and other supernatural restrictions which cut into the number of chances at whales during the short season. By using the best of both white and Eskimo whaling methods, Brower and other white whalers were soon outstripping the Eskimos at their own game. Brower observed that 1888 was the last year in which the Point Barrow Eskimos relied exclusively upon their own techniques. Year by year Brower thought to take a long, perhaps even permanent, vacation; but the 1890s proved to be very profitable.

Despite their long contact with whites, the coastal Eskimos did not learn to make whiskey until the winter of 1888–89. By the early 1890s, liquor had become a real problem, seriously curtailing the Eskimos' own whaling activity. During the winter of 1893 there were three killings due to liquor. By the middle 1890s, many Eskimos were hiring out to white whalers as their own whaling declined.

Just before 1900, the Point Barrow Eskimos enjoyed a particularly successful whaling season, and the Nunamiut were invited to attend a huge feast at Point Barrow. All in all about fifty *umiat* (open skin boats) appeared, carrying Nunamiut families and their belongings. Many of the children had never seen white men before. After setting up camp, the Nunamiut very easily won the usual footrace. The Nunamiut and the Point Barrow Eskimos then danced together, showing off their best clothing and exchanging gifts. Next, inland goods were traded for coastal products. After the Nunamiut finished trading, a few ships arrived at Point Barrow loaded with trade goods. The Nunamiut immediately traded their possessions for liquor. The ships also brought influenza. According to Brower, the Nunamiut shamans encouraged the inland people to return to their own country in order to escape this horrible coastal disease. The Nunamiut packed up their umiat and started back, but Brower estimated that some two hundred Nunamiut died en route to their homes. How many, if any, actually survived was not known (Brower 1942).

Brower continued to operate a successful whaling business until 1908, when whalebone suddenly became unsalable. Brower went broke and he turned to the fur business.

Not until 1890 did the whalers reach Herschel Island in the Beaufort Sea, 450 miles east of Point Barrow. By that time the total number of whaling ships in Alaska had declined considerably from the peak in the middle 1800s, when about thirty whaling ships cruised in Alaskan waters each year. By 1900 the number was down to ten, and in the winter of 1913–14 only two whaling ships visited the Arctic coast of Alaska. Although fewer whaling ships plied northern waters after 1890, those Nunamiut traveling to the coast found considerable opportunity to hunt caribou for the whalers in exchange for trade goods.

The whalers largely replaced what influence the Hudson's Bay Company had built up in the fur trade along the Alaskan coast and damaged the Company's position in parts of northwest Canada. The massive killing of caribou encouraged by the whalers reduced even further a caribou population which was already declining in the late 1800s.

As has been typical of American expansion, entrepreneurs moved in ahead of the government. Toward the end of the 1800s, however, the United States military began to exert its influence in the administration of Alaska and, along with the United States Geological Survey, in exploration and mapping. During the late 1800s and early 1900s, many American geologists and other scientific explorers traversed several routes on land and sea in Arctic Alaska.

In 1881 the Chief Signal Officer of the United States Army organized the United States International Polar Expedition to Point Barrow, 1881–83, one of several expeditions sent to the Arctic by different countries to investigate problems of terrestrial magnetism. Lieutenant P. H. Ray was in command, and among the members of the expedition was John Murdoch, naturalist and observer.

When Ray and his party landed at Point Barrow, the Eskimos expressed surprise that the white men wanted to live there for the whole winter. They soon became friendly and helped unload the ship. Ray quickly checked a few petty thefts and had no more trouble. The camp was pitched at a distance from the village to prevent friction, and Ray hired Eskimos to perform odd jobs, to hunt, and as travel aides.

Ray journeyed up the Meade River with a party of Point Barrow Eskimos, who told him that the country had been inhabited three generations ago (possibly around 1800 or earlier). Either a decline in the caribou population or a shift in their migration had forced these people to immigrate to the coast and to the Colville River. Because geographical exploration was secondary to his investigation of terrestrial magnetism, Ray traveled little beyond the Meade River and did not meet the Nunamiut in their home environment.

According to Ray, the Eskimos had changed very little from their indigenous cultural state. Ray (1885) mentioned the contacts of Beechey, Dease and Simpson, Maguire, and the subsequent whalers but felt as of the early 1880s that the Eskimos had been little affected except for a few trade goods.

Murdoch, the observer, stated that since the 1850s, when whaling ships began to frequent Point Barrow, white contact had resulted in traffic in guns, ammunition, limited quantities of foods, tools, and some lumber from wrecked ships; a few oaths and such songs as "Shoo Fly" and "Little Brown Jug"; liquor; and gonorrhea and other diseases. Murdoch felt that the guns, food, and tools were of positive benefit to the Eskimos and that liquor, diseases, and sexual relations were harmful. Murdoch obtained ethnological specimens in barter and maintained that the expedition's relationship with the local population was very friendly. Because of the pressure of duties at Point Barrow, he did not visit the Nunamiut, although he was aware of them and their trading with the coastal Eskimos at the mouth of the Colville River and other sites along the Arctic coast.

Murdoch, like Ray, asserted that as of 1881–83, the Alaskan Arctic Eskimos were essentially very little changed from precontact days except for the results of white contact mentioned above (Murdoch 1892).

The next two decades were to see the beginning of the real changes, the changes which the Eskimos themselves were then aware of, which are still talked about, and which are continuing today.

In 1885, Captain M. A. Healy, commander of the revenue marine steamer *Corwin,* visited several villages along the Arctic coast. American revenue cutters patrolled Alaskan waters every summer from 1880 in order to curb the traffic in liquor and to offer help, especially to whalers, in emergencies. Although Healy traded very little, he maintained friendly relations with Eskimos. He noted that the early days of extensive gifts and massive demonstrations were past, and he saw little evidence of liquor, although Eskimos did use tobacco extensively and often begged for trade goods. The work that the Eskimos could now obtain from white men was simply not adequate to satisfy their demand for trade items.

Captain Healy instructed Lieutenant John L. Cantwell to explore the Kobuk River. Cantwell hired several Eskimos, many of whom he felt were very industrious. By 1885, Eskimos from the Noatak, Kobuk, and Selawik rivers, Point Hope, and up on around the coast had become familiar with white men and often associated very easily with them. While Cantwell generally praised the Eskimos, he criticized their hygiene, but said hopefully that they were beginning to imitate the whites.

Lieutenant S. B. McLenegan was charged by Healy to explore the Noatak River. McLenegan's experience was similar to Cantwell's. Interestingly enough, McLenegan speculated that no Eskimos were living on the other side of the Brooks Range from the Noatak, that is, on the northern side (Healy 1887, 1889; Cantwell 1887, 1889a, 1889b; McLenegan 1887).

In the winter of 1885–86, Lieutenant George M. Stoney and his men explored the Kobuk River country and other parts of the western Brooks Range. Stoney traveled up the Kobuk, established a winter camp at Fort Cosmos, and explored the surrounding country. In December, Stoney and Howard, his most trusted assistant, and four Eskimos reached the upper Noatak River and established contact with the Eskimos there. He wanted to cross through the Brooks Range and descend the Colville River to the coast. The Eskimos refused, however, to guide him to the coast, saying at that time of year (December) the northern Brooks Range was too desolate for travel. Stoney was upset by frequent demands from native villages for "tribute" as he termed it. He became anxious when a whole village beat drums and sang in apparent threat, and he suspected the Eskimos of petty theft. He saw army blankets, overcoats, and buttons presumably obtained in trade from the 1881–83 International Polar Expedition at Point Barrow. Stoney journeyed to the head of the Kobuk River and over to the Alatna River. Running short of firewood at Chandler Lake, he purchased a sled from a Nunamiut camped there and used it as fuel for cooking, which upset the sled maker very much, but Stoney maintained that the sled belonged to him. The Nunamiut told Stoney that no natives were camped beyond the head of Chandler Lake. Stoney urged the Eskimos to guide him down to the Arctic coast but they refused; in March of 1886 he returned to his Kobuk camp.

Stoney considered the Nunamiut, many of whom had never seen white men before, to be ignorant. He made a cairn at Chandler Lake and put a written message in it. He then performed a number of antics calculated to awe the Eskimos and told them if they touched the cairn their hands would rot off.

Stoney instructed Howard to make a third attempt to reach the Arctic coast by land from the Kobuk River. In the late spring of 1886, because it was the custom for many Nunamiut families in spring to travel down to the coast to trade, Howard was finally able to accomplish with relative ease Stoney's ardent desire to push across the Brooks Range. Howard encountered hundreds of Eskimos as he traveled up the Kobuk River, across the Noatak River, through Howard Pass, and down the Colville River to the Arctic Ocean. Howard sent Eskimos ahead to announce his arrival at villages and encampments along the way; he saw many trade items including guns, knives, a few articles of clothing, and even an ordinary pack of cards used for Russian card games (Stoney 1900).

In 1897–98 the United States revenue cutter *Bear* cruised in Arctic waters and supported a winter land expedition for the relief of Arctic whalers. The expedition started south of Seward Peninsula and followed the coast for the most part up to Point Barrow. The report of the cruise of the *Bear* stated that by 1888 the Eskimos had learned to make a whiskey from flour, molasses, and water, which were readily obtained from whalers. Flour was also used for making gravy and eventually for biscuits. The coastal Eskimos suffered more from liquor than did the inland Eskimos, who used up their supply of flour and molasses before returning home. When an Eskimo got drunk, he usually became quite happy and only occasionally caused trouble. The older natives were concerned about this new debauchery and wondered why the whites did not control the trade (Jarvis 1899).

In 1899 the United States Geological Survey supported Frank C. Schrader in a reconnaissance of the central Brooks Range. At Fort Yukon Schrader noted a steady trade with the Indians and occasional marriages of white prospectors with Indian women. On the Chandalar and Koyukuk rivers, small Indian villages seemed far removed from the main stream of Yukon River life. Missionaries were active in Nulato, Fort Hamlin, and Fort Yukon. Prospectors could turn up anywhere. Malemiut Eskimos from south of Kotzebue Sound crossed the Brooks Range, ascending the Koyukuk and Dietrich rivers to the divide and descending the Itkillik and Colville rivers to the north coast on trading expeditions (Schrader 1901).

In the summer of 1901 Schrader, again supported by the United States Geological Survey, traveled up the John River from Bettles to the summit of Anaktuvuk Pass and then descended the Anaktuvuk River to the Colville River on down to the coast; from there he went to Point Barrow. Schrader estimated that about a hundred Indians lived in the upper Koyukuk region in 1901; they traded frequently with the Kobuk Eskimos but he mentioned no contact between the Nunamiut and the Koyukon Indians. In fact, Schrader stated that the Indians rarely traveled north of the timberline in the Brooks Range, and the Nunamiut rarely, if ever, penetrated into the timbered regions.

During his geological exploration, Schrader met a few Eskimos but did not encounter the large numbers which Howard, under Stoney, did. Along the John River, Schrader counted some thirty Koyukon Indians hunting and trapping in the timber. While descending the Anaktuvuk and Colville rivers, he visited a few Nunamiut families briefly and then passed on. Schrader saw several Eskimos in the Colville River delta, but did not try to communicate much with them.

As he was traveling west along the Arctic coast, Schrader joined a native party in *umiat* (skin boats) and reached Point Barrow (Schrader 1904). There he met about a dozen white men associated with a trading post, mission school, and whaling station. Whalers, as many as ten a year, were still operating in Arctic waters in 1900. Schrader noted that in 1901 a Japanese tried to establish a trading post on the Staines River 50 miles west of Barter Island. A Nunamiut told me of this Japanese, who later married an Eskimo woman, moved to the Yukon River, and set up a hotel there. The Nunamiut have seen pictures of Japanese women and consider them to be very attractive because they look like Eskimo women.

At the time of Schrader's exploration, the Nunamiut were still numerous enough to travel down the Colville River annually to trade with the Point Barrow Eskimos at Negalik. The United States census recorded 200 residents at Negalik in 1900; the population of the Nunamiut had declined considerably since Howard's time.

In 1901 another United States Geological Survey man named

Mendenhall made a reconnaissance from Fort Hamlin on the Yukon River to Kotzebue Sound by way of the Dall, Kanuti, Allen, and Kobuk rivers. Mendenhall noted the large number of trade items which the Indians and Eskimos in these regions had and mentioned that the Eskimos on the Kobuk River were very anxious to learn English (Mendenhall 1902: 52).

Ernest Leffingwell, at his own expense, conducted a series of expeditions for the United States Geological Survey. In 1906 he explored the Beaufort Sea, living in close contact with Eskimos. In 1909 and again in 1913 he stayed on Flaxman Island, mapping the Canning River and surrounding territory. Leffingwell reported about a dozen white men living along the Arctic coast from the mouth of the Mackenzie River to Point Barrow between 1900 and 1920. At Herschel Island, two or three Canadian Mounted Police maintained a post, and an occasional missionary visited there. Mail service reached Herschel Island twice a year from Fort McPherson, on the Peel River near its confluence with the Mackenzie River.

At Point Barrow, traders, missionaries, a government school, and a whaling station provided constant contact with the whites for coastal Eskimos. Around the turn of the century, however, the Nunamiut had experienced little direct white contact in their homeland except for Howard, Schrader, and an occasional prospector or trapper. Most of the trade goods obtained by the Nunamiut in the early 1900s came by way of other Eskimos.

In 1906 there were about 50 Eskimos at Herschel Island and 300 to 400 at Point Barrow. Between Point Barrow and Herschel Island, Leffingwell reported only two or three families living on the coast. By 1913–14, only one family was living on the Sagavanirktok River and a very few families on the Colville River. Leffingwell knew that large numbers of Nunamiut had earlier lived along rivers of the northern Brooks Range (as Howard and Schrader reported and as the Nunamiut themselves corroborate). Leffingwell (1919) attributed this population decline to the diminished numbers of caribou.

Between 1923 and 1926 Philip Smith and J. B. Mertie surveyed northwestern Alaska for the U.S. Geological Survey and found no settlements or evidence of recent occupation in the northern Brooks Range and Arctic slope. They did note, however, that some time in the past there had been inhabitants (Smith and Mertie 1930).

Prospectors and Trappers

During the latter half of the nineteenth century, hundreds of white men came to the Yukon basin to search for gold. Many were successful and, as more and more men came to Alaska, prospectors turned to new areas. In the late 1890s, gold was reported in the upper Koyukuk River territory. In the fall of 1898, over a thousand white men rushed to the new area only to leave again the following spring. The population of Bettles jumped to nearly 1,500 and then dropped to almost 100 in one year. Some gold was found, and from 1900 to 1904 the population rose to 350. Many Indians were hired to handle boats and sleds but did little mining themselves. Several Nunamiut drifted down to Bettles to work for the white men and one, to my knowledge, married an Indian woman. By 1910 a few Nunamiut families still traveled down to Bettles to trade but did not stay long in Indian territory.

Ever since 1900, occasional prospectors and trappers have wandered through the Brooks Range. Schrader mentioned two prospectors who journeyed along the rivers of the Arctic slope between the mouth of the Colville River and the Canadian border from 1901 to 1903 in an unproductive search for gold. In 1903 two other prospectors crossed the Brooks Range, traveling up the Kobuk River, over to the head of the Noatak and Alatna rivers, and down the Killik to the Colville. Leffingwell mentioned two prospectors who worked out of the Sagavanirktok River in 1913–14. During the summer of 1959 I met a gold prospector who eked out a bare living from an unproductive creek in the southern Brooks Range. These men usually see the Nunamiut only briefly and often have assimilated more from the Eskimos than the Eskimos from them. While they are very interesting characters, they are in fact a very small part of the white contact.

Missionaries

During the late 1800s and early 1900s several Protestant denominations in Alaska effected an agreement by which they agreed not to proselytize in one another's territory. Accordingly, Point Barrow and several Arctic coast settlements went to the Presbyterians; the Episcopalians were granted the Yukon River and Point Hope; Anglicans were active in northwest Canada and occasionally supported the Alaskan Episcopalians. The California Society of

Friends (Quakers) established a mission in Kotzebue Sound and claimed the Kobuk River. The Congregational Church moved into Cape Prince of Wales, the Swedish Lutherans into Norton Sound, and the Moravians into the Kuskokwim area. Russian missions were widespread in southern Alaska in the 1700s and early 1800s and, although there are Russian Orthodox churches in Alaska today, I encountered no evidence of any Russian Orthodox missionary influence in the far north.

ANGLICAN AND EPISCOPALIAN. Anglican missionaries reached the upper Yukon territory by the late 1840s but did not extend far into the Brooks Range. Although the Nunamiut are aware of the Episcopalian churches among the Indians on the Yukon, Porcupine, and Koyukuk rivers, no Episcopalian influence has reached the Nunamiut by way of Indians. The mission at Point Hope had little or no contact with the Nunamiut. Today an Episcopal church is active on the Kobuk River, but the Nunamiut and the Kobuk Eskimos meet so infrequently that no Episcopalian influence has as yet reached the Nunamiut via Kobuk Eskimos.

The Anglicans entered northwest Canada as the Hudson's Bay Company was establishing itself. Nunamiut traveling to the mouth of the Mackenzie River were exposed to Anglican missionaries and by 1910 many Nunamiut went to live there. Stefansson remarked that the Anglican missionary considered that most of the Mackenzie River Eskimos had been converted by 1909. The Nunamiut heard of the Anglican success among the Mackenzie River Eskimos and were anxious to obtain prayers from them. Several Nunamiut asked Stefansson to teach them new prayers, during one of his visits near the mouth of the Colville. Stefansson had not learned any, but an Eskimo assistant taught them an Anglican prayer which they used for a brief but unknown period of time. At present in the Brooks Range, I encountered only awareness of the Anglican missionaries' work along the Mackenzie River.

QUAKER. In 1897 the California Society of Friends sent three missionaries to the Malemiut Eskimos at Kotzebue Sound. During the early 1900s the Friends established stations at Deering, Kivalina, Shungak (on the Kobuk River), Noatak, Buckland, and Noorvik (Kelsey 1917). Many Quaker ideas, notably of not working or hunting on Sunday, washing the hands and face before eating, and frequent and intense praying, spread up along the coast to Point Hope and beyond. The Eskimos from Kotzebue Sound and the Kobuk and Noatak rivers greatly influenced the Nunamiut. The Nunamiut, in turn, told the Point Barrow Eskimos about the "new religion," or Eskimo-Quaker Christianity. By 1909, many Point Barrow Eskimos were observing the work restriction on Sunday, to the detriment of their whale hunting. Quaker influence motivated Nunamiut to ask Stefansson for new prayers in the incident mentioned above. According to Stefansson, as of 1907–12 the Presbyterian missions had had no effect on the Nunamiut, who were under the Christian influence emanating from Kotzebue Sound. Stefansson mistakenly referred to the mission at Kotzebue Sound as Moravian. No Moravian missionary publications refer to Kotzebue Sound, and the work of the California Society of Friends there is amply documented (American Friends Board of Foreign Missions 1912; Kelsey 1917; Stuck 1920).

PRESBYTERIAN. While the Presbyterian influence on the Nunamiut in the late 1800s and early 1900s was negligible, it is well to consider the effect of the missions on the Point Barrow Eskimos because the Nunamiut have always maintained close ties with the coast, and recent Presbyterian missionary efforts stem from Point Barrow.

Spencer (1959) has described the effect of the Presbyterian missions on the Point Barrow Eskimos, which will be summarized briefly here. The first Presbyterian missionary came to Point Barrow in the early 1890s but was not very successful. Later in the same decade, a medical missionary arrived, learned to speak a little Eskimo, and introduced Eskimo hymns from Canada. Christianity was haltingly accepted, marked by occasional setbacks. Stefansson told of an incident in 1909 in which a Presbyterian missionary attempted to counteract the feeling instilled by the Quakers against working on Sunday, since the Point Barrow Eskimos were not hunting whales on Sunday during the short, intensive season. The missionary advised them to hunt on Sunday for their own good. The Eskimos countered by asking him to pray to God not to let whales pass by on Sunday. The missionary refused to do so. He was then compared to inefficient shamans of the past, and ultimately the Eskimos wrote a letter to the missionary's home office requesting his removal.

Although Presbyterian missionaries met with such difficulties as the lack of communication, the resistance of some shamans, and the conflicts ensuing from Eskimo-Quaker Christianity, after 1910 the mission began to grow. Physical benefits such as clothing, food, medical attention, and housing materials impressed the Point Barrow Eskimos, and the opportunity for socializing and hymn singing attracted many of them. According to Spencer and one or two of my informants, the missionaries and their teaching fulfilled a "native prophecy" called *oivaksat,* which foretold the coming of strangers. The ethnographic data are contradictory. Some informants saw little if any relationship between the concept of oivaksat and Christianity. Others suggested that, after Christianity had become the dominant religious influence, oivaksat was used as a rationalization to support the feeling that the prophecy of the arrival and success of Christianity among Eskimos was essentially an Eskimo concept.

Spencer feels that the most important factor in the success of Christianity at Point Barrow was the undermining of shamanistic power. Although shamans caused a great deal of anxiety and fear, they also provided a sense of security in fighting for survival in a difficult environment, curing sickness, and encouraging unsuccessful hunters to try again. A few shamans sought to use Christianity itself to their own ends by purporting to have visions of Jesus Christ and God.

As the Presbyterian missionaries gained in Point Barrow, the Church maintained its interest in the north Alaskan Eskimos, and the influence of the mission has grown. At present the Presbyterian church at Point Barrow is very active and is the dominant church there.

During the early 1900s, the Nunamiut living in the Brooks Range retained Eskimo-Quaker beliefs and practices. As Nunamiut were forced out of the mountains, they came under Presbyterian influence. Although many of them never met a missionary, Presbyterianism had become so much the prevailing religious "fashion" that friends and relatives urged them to become Presbyterians. By 1920 the last Nunamiut family left the Brooks Range, and Eskimo-Quaker influence has survived only in a few short songs, a few prayers, and in a feeling that working or hunting on Sunday is tinged with a lack of grace.

In recent years, since World War II, Presbyterian missionaries have conducted services at Anaktuvuk Pass and have appointed an Eskimo lay preacher. Because of the early, but not sustained, influence of the Quakers, the religious void left by the almost complete suppression of shamanism, and the indirect contact on the coast with the Presbyterian Church, the Anaktuvuk Pass people have been very receptive to Presbyterian mission efforts. No permanent missionary lives at the Pass, and the present Point Barrow pastor visits only briefly. Slightly more than half the village were members of the church in 1959. In the middle 1950s the Nunamiut, with Presbyterian encouragement, dragged logs up from the timber to Anaktuvuk Pass and constructed a log church which serves important social functions such as hymn singing, communal eating, and (now) council elections, as well as providing a place for religious services. Since 1960 the resident lay preacher of Anaktuvuk Pass has become less active, but during the summer of 1962 (Hall, personal communication 1962) Eskimo lay religious leaders from Point Barrow have, with increasing frequency, visited the village.

FUNDAMENTALIST AND/OR EMOTIONALIST. Such fundamentalist churches as the pentecostalist Assemblies of God are very active on the coast but have had as yet little impact on the people of Anaktuvuk Pass. Many Nunamiut feel that physically pounding the Bible with the hand, shouting, wailing, and sobbing are undignified. Some Eskimos on the coast, however, feel that fundamentalist churches are friendlier and offer a more meaningful religious experience than more traditional churches. The one or two attempts of an Assemblies of God missionary to proselytize at Anaktuvuk Pass have reportedly (Hall, personal communication) been thwarted by the villagers themselves.

During part of my stay at the Pass, a schoolteacher, who is a member of the Free Methodist Church and an exponent of emotionalism, exerted informal influence on the young people by holding frequent Sunday school classes. The villagers consider her a very good schoolteacher, and by and large she is pleasantly received.

Within the past decade, Jehovah's Witnesses have distributed literature in the Pass. Occasionally a pilot has brought in a Jehovah's Witness who has tried to influence a Nunamiut to become a local exponent with, as yet, little effect.

The success of any attempts of the fundamentalist, emotional churches to proselytize at Anaktuvuk Pass will depend on the personality of the missionaries and the Presbyterian pastor's ability to hold and expand his position. Eskimos are very impressed by honesty, successful prediction, concrete results or material benefits, opportunities for socializing, and a man's personality.

We have seen that in the last half of the 1800s and the early part of the 1900s the principal white contact with Arctic Alaska occurred on the coast because, of course, transportation into the interior was a problem. As late as 1920, very few white men had penetrated the Brooks Range. Although a few Nunamiut experienced direct, prolonged association with the whalers, most other contact was sporadic and limited, and the Nunamiut received more white-man goods and ideas from other Eskimos than from whites.

As Nunamiut emigrated from the mountains to the coast toward the end of the century, they became intensively exposed to whalers, traders, and missionaries. These emigrants, while attempting to maintain their identity as Nunamiut, emulated the coastal Eskimos' way of life. The Nunamiut who continued living in the Brooks Range—in 1900 about 300, and by 1920 only 20 or so—on visits to the coast met such men as Stefansson, Jenness, and Rasmussen, as well as the occasional whaler, trader, missionary, and very few white trappers, prospectors, and traders who traveled into the Brooks Range after World War I.

In 1920 or very shortly thereafter, the last Nunamiut families moved to the coast. Many Nunamiut have become assimilated into such population centers as Aklavik (Inuvik) in Canada, Barter Island, Point Barrow, Wainwright, Point Lay, Point Hope, Kotzebue Sound, Fairbanks, and other towns in Arctic Alaska. Several families, however, remained on the Arctic coast away from these "fleshpots" of civilization as they are sometimes considered by the hunting and trapping Nunamiut.

In 1938 three families returned inland and were followed in 1939 and 1940 by several others. Before World War II, fewer than 50 Nunamiut were living in the Brooks Range. By 1961, the population had increased to 100. Now let us consider the nature of white contact with the Nunamiut from the early 1900s to the present day.

Vilhjalmur Stefansson made three long trips to the Arctic, in 1906–07, 1908–12, and 1913–18. He first learned the techniques of Arctic living from the Mackenzie River Eskimos during the 1906–07 trip. He felt that from 1890 to 1906 the whalers had made a greater impact (not necessarily beneficial) on the Eskimos in Alaska and northwest Canada than the Hudson's Bay Company had made in a century. Stefansson met a few Nunamiut families briefly while they were hunting caribou inland east of the Firth River and again near the mouth of the Colville River. At first the Eskimos could not believe he would become an effective hunter, but gradually Stefansson won their confidence and went on in later years to gain absolute praise from many Eskimos.

In 1908 Stefansson returned to the Arctic and stayed until 1912, traveling and hunting with many of his Alaskan friends. He felt that he could learn more about the Nunamiut by living with them on the coast where so many of them had gathered, but he did not stay long, for lack of food forced him to leave. Stefansson spent most of his time to the east in the less explored parts of Canada, returning to Point Barrow in 1912 by way of the Alaskan coast.

Dr. Anderson, a biologist who accompanied Stefansson, spent the winter of 1908–09 south of Barter Island in the Brooks Range mountains collecting zoological specimens. Anderson hired several Nunamiut to help him in his biological work; like Stefansson, he used many Eskimo methods in living off the land.

In 1913, Stefansson again returned to the Arctic and remained until 1918. He abandoned the ship *Karluk* when it became stuck in the ice and made his way to the mouth of the Colville River with Diamond Jenness, an anthropologist, and others. Later the *Karluk* sank. He left Jenness with a group of Nunamiut families living on the coast and went to Point Barrow. Stefansson's main desire was to explore geographically the Beaufort Sea and the area to the north. He made several significant discoveries while basing his work out of Herschel Island, where he met many Nunamiut as well as other Eskimos. Two Eskimos, Jessie Ahgook and Elija Kakinya, now living at Anaktuvuk Pass, worked for Stefansson and speak with admiration of his feats of travel and his ability to work with both whites and Eskimos. Many Eskimos, as well as whites, thought Stefansson was foolhardy to venture out over the unexplored Beaufort Sea ice. But Stefansson, marshaling the experience of many years in the Arctic and the calm that knowledge can give, succeeded and won the admiration of many Eskimos for his survival on the open sea ice far from land.

Although Stefansson did not substantially affect the Eskimo mode of life, he demonstrated that, by respecting and utilizing Eskimo methods of adaptation to the Arctic, he could live with them. Stefansson illustrated that some white men are in fact sympathetic (Stefansson 1919, 1922, 1943).

Diamond Jenness remained on the north Alaskan coast near the mouth of the Colville River, living with several Nunamiut families there in order to learn their language; he observed their customs, made ethnological collections, and took somatological measurements. The wife of the family he lived with in 1913–14 had never been to Point Barrow.

Jenness learned that, although a few families were still living on the upper reaches of the Colville River and its tributaries, most of the Nunamiut had moved to the coast and were being assimilated into various coastal groups. In 1914 the remaining inland Nunamiut continued to come to the coast to trade. Jenness (1957) remarked, interestingly enough, that the caribou herds were beginning to increase as the Nunamiut left the Brooks Range.

Jenness was very friendly with the Nunamiut, and some remember him today. His effect was, of course, much like Stefansson's in promoting mutual understanding and respect. An anthropologist has the enviable position of not having to convert or exploit the people with whom he is living, but he must remember that he is essentially a guest and refrain from meddling in their affairs. Even when a native is having difficulty in using a white man's device, unless he is specifically asked, silence is the best policy.

During the winter of 1917–18, Hudson Stuck, an Episcopal archdeacon from Fort Yukon, circled the entire Brooks Range by sled. He traveled from Fort Yukon to Kotzebue Sound by way of the Yukon and other rivers that drain the southern Brooks Range. From Kotzebue Sound he went to Point Barrow by the coast and then on to Herschel Island. He returned to Fort Yukon by the Firth, Coleen, and Porcupine rivers.

In the spring of 1918, Stuck noted that Brower sent guns, ammunition, and food supplies to the mouth of the Colville River to trade for the furs the Nunamiut had trapped the previous season. A few Nunamiut traded at Demarkation Point and occasionally at Herschel Island, where the Canadian Mounted Police maintained a post. The Hudson's Bay Company had a store there, and an Anglican missionary was in residence.

In 1924 Rasmussen traveled along the Arctic coast of northern Alaska from the Mackenzie River to Point Barrow in the last leg of The Fifth Thule Expedition–Danish Ethnographical Expedition to Arctic North America, 1921–24. He noted scattered encampments of Eskimos and a few white men, mostly Scandinavians, trapping or prospecting. Rasmussen knew that Stefansson and Jenness had previously studied many Eskimos in Alaska and felt justified in hurrying on to Point Barrow (Rasmussen 1927). Some older Nunamiut still remember Rasmussen and commented that Alaskan Eskimos easily understood his Greenlandic dialect.

THE FUR TRADE. In 1908 the fall in demand for whalebone forced Charles Brower out of the whaling business, but he turned immediately to fur trading. He outfitted many trappers, and those Nunamiut living inland brought their furs to Brower in exchange for supplies. Before World War I, Brower's fur trade at Point Barrow became so profitable that he opened stations at Wainwright and Beechey Point. By 1920, the last Nunamiut had moved to the coast where trapping was good and trade supplies easy to obtain. The decline in caribou population added to the impetus to leave the Brooks Range.

After 1920, many Nunamiut continued to maintain a group identity as they gathered along the north coast of Alaska some distance east of Point Barrow. Brower, occasional fur-trading schooners, and the Hudson's Bay Company constituted the trade contacts. During the 1930s the fur trade along the north Arctic coast deteriorated, and Brower slowly pulled out. Jack Smith, a white trapper from Bettles who crossed the Brooks Range to the north coast about 1920, was encouraged by the Eskimos to go into the trading business. Smith acted as a go-between for the Eskimos and the schooners that came about once a year to the north coast. Ship captains suggested to one or two Eskimos that they attempt to trade, but they lacked the business sense to keep out of debt—the market for furs was falling, and the Eskimo traders could not refuse requests for credit from hungry relatives and friends.

THE REINDEER INDUSTRY. In 1898, 1,280 reindeer were shipped to Alaska from Siberia. For many years federal law had prohibited white men from entering the reindeer business. The regulations changed, and by 1920 the Lomen brothers had purchased several thousand reindeer. For years the Lomens expanded the industry and by 1929 they employed nearly 600 Eskimos and Lapps in northwestern Alaska (Lomen 1954). Carl Lomen felt that Eskimos were fairly good herders when properly trained, but if not, were haphazard in their work. The relationship between the reindeer industry and the Eskimos has been widely publicized. Because most reindeer were herded west and south of the Brooks Range, the Nunamiut were only slightly affected, since only Nunamiut emigrants came into direct contact with reindeer husbandry. Many Laplanders were hired by the Lomens to help teach Eskimos how to herd. Today in Anaktuvuk Pass, the children play a ball game in the summer called "Lapp game" learned from the Kobuk Eskimos who in turn learned it from the Lapps.

By the late 1920s, the Canadian government negotiated with the Lomens to drive 3,000 reindeer 1,200 air miles from near Kotzebue Sound up through Howard Pass along the front of the Brooks Range to the Mackenzie River delta. The drive began in December 1929 and lasted until March 1935. Lapps were in charge, assisted by Eskimos. While the Nunamiut were living on the Arctic coast, the drive passed along the north slope of Alaska. Several Nunamiut were hired to transport supplies by dog sled to the men working on the drive. One Nunamiut at Anaktuvuk Pass told me he had tried herding when all the Nunamiut were living on the coast, but he did not care for it much.

During the 1930s the Lomen brothers began to find it difficult to market reindeer meat. This, in addition to pressure from Washington, caused them to sell their interests in the reindeer industry to the government in 1940.

As the fur business grew steadily worse, many Nunamiut moved to Point Barrow or other population centers (including Fairbanks). By 1937, the possibilities for making a living on the north Alaskan coast became so poor that several Nunamiut families decided to return to the Brooks Range. In 1938, three families proceeded by umiak up the Colville River to its tributaries to hunt and trap. In the spring they came back to the coast to trade for supplies. They returned, and several other families joined them in the home country where they have remained until this day.

After the Nunamiut returned to the Brooks Range, they resumed a seminomadic life. One group of families settled in the Killik Valley and another in the Chandler Lake area. Frequently two or more families trapped for a season in a nearby valley. To obtain supplies some families traveled to the north coast. By 1940, however, there was no trading to be done on the north coast, and the Nunamiut turned to the south. Once a year several families journeyed to Bettles or to the small villages on the Kobuk River.

By 1930 a few pioneer bush pilots were beginning to venture over the Brooks Range. Shortly before World War II, Sig Wein, one of the most famous Alaskan pilots, landed in the Brooks Range and visited the Nunamiut. For several years thereafter, Wein or one of his pilots flew up to the Nunamiut and traded supplies for wolf hides and other furs. Occasional passengers, including military personnel during the war years, visited briefly with the Nunamiut. Especially during the war, Wein tried to help the Nunamiut by supplying them with ammunition, but it was so scarce that one Nunamiut finally made a kayak for spearing caribou in Chandler Lake, and many Nunamiut came to rely on snares for caribou and sheep. One man even snared a moose in the timber.

In 1947 the Nunamiut were living in two groups: five families at Chandler Lake and eight families on the Killik River. In 1949 the Chandler Lake families moved to Tulugak Lake in the Anaktuvuk Valley near the northern mountain line. Very shortly thereafter the Killik River families also moved to Tulugak Lake. In 1951, mail service was established on a regular monthly basis, and most of the families moved to the summit of Anaktuvuk Pass. In 1960 the last family joined the village at the summit.

Since 1947, various white men including geologists, archaeologists, ethnologists, botanists, zoologists, limnologists, soil scientists, sportsmen, oil field crews, and tourists have visited the Nunamiut, and especially since 1955 the traffic has increased.

Several scientists have established close relationships with Nunamiut families. Such contacts improve their economic status and provide a source of pride and self-respect for the individuals with whom the scientists work. Many highly educated white men have visited Anaktuvuk Pass in the past decade and have treated the Nunamiut with respect. The primary negative aspect of this contact is that many Nunamiut have difficulty in understanding how white men acquire such apparent wealth with so much less effort than the Eskimos must make. Many Nunamiut see the glory of being a pilot but fail to comprehend the effort and training behind such a job. A few, however, do appear to understand the nature of the white man's work.

Before 1949, the Nunamiut encountered few white men in the Brooks Range. During the winter of 1949, Helge Ingstad, a Norwegian, lived for eight months with the Nunamiut. His book, written in a popular, occasionally sensational style, contains many valuable data.

In 1949 an ex-trapper, who lived for a while in Bettles, decided to set up a trading post among the Nunamiut. He did not live continuously with them, observed them only superficially, and learned very little of their ways. This trader attempted to gather the Nunamiut into one village so he could carry on his business more easily and, as he once commented to me, to feel the effects of exerting his own power. He was generally successful: with the establishment of a regular monthly postal service by bush plane in 1951, the building of a log church four or five years later, and the increased traffic of white men who might purchase items and offer temporary employment, most Nunamiut have gathered at the summit of Anaktuvuk Pass. Two families chose to live twenty miles to the north until the fall of 1960. A white teacher began conducting a school under Alaskan state auspices, and the last of the independent Nunamiut moved to the summit for the benefit of their children. In the fall of 1960 the ex-trapper-turned-trader finally left Anaktuvuk Pass for good. Several Eskimos have attempted to go into the trading business, but as of 1961 there was no stable source of imported supplies for the Nunamiut.

In the summer of 1960, employees of an airplane company drove a caterpillar tractor from Umiat to Anaktuvuk Pass and dragged out a landing strip in a creek bed. In the spring of 1961 a large, permanent school building was constructed at a cost equal to about ten years' gross cash income of the village. The Nunamiut are extremely proud of these new developments. Nurses, doctors, Alaskan health officials, and other state employees visit Anaktuvuk Pass with increasing frequency and a variety of purposes.

In just over a decade the economy of the remaining mountain Nunamiut has been converted from one of mobile hunting and trapping to an economy of localized sporadic hunting, trapping, and odd jobs. The demand for employment and tourist items fluctuates erratically. The year I lived at the Pass, several families were still attempting to trap but with only moderate success. Because all the Nunamiut now reside most of the year in the one location —the village of Anaktuvuk Pass—health problems have greatly increased. Respiratory maladies such as colds, influenza, pneumonia, and tuberculosis are a constant threat to the well-being of the villagers. The local willow supply has been gradually depleted and villages are beginning to complain about the difficulty of securing fuel.

The Nunamiut continue, of course, to hunt caribou extensively, and many native crafts have survived unchanged. Much of the current process of change is taking place within the framework of traditional Nunamiut culture. In twenty-five or thirty years, I doubt this will be so. A generation hence, most Nunamiut activity, including future change, will take place in an already acculturated context. The Nunamiut of Anaktuvuk Pass will become another typical small north Alaskan native town. Alcohol has not yet been introduced nor is sexual promiscuity yet a problem, but time and the white man will probably change that.

2. Ethnohistory

ETHNOHISTORY is taken to mean that part of the verbal tradition which the Nunamiut consider to be a historical account of themselves from their creation to the present day. The Nunamiut distinguish between what they consider to be true history (*koliaqtuaq*) and imaginary folklore (*unipqaq*). By complementing the documented history with their ethnohistory, we hope to offer a more accurate background in which to examine the Nunamiut relationship to their environment.

In discussing the past, the Nunamiut make a threefold time distinction. The earliest period is *itchaq imma* (very early days). In response to questions about when itchaq imma began and ended, no time or number of generations can be given. Many of the events of itchaq imma are shrouded in myth. The second period, *iŋilagaan* (early days), starts from the end of itchaq imma. Although no time can be specified for the transition, the relative sequence of events within these periods will emerge from the following narrative. The third period is *ipani* (personal remembrance). At the age of four or five, a person's brain "solidifies" and he "begins to remember" all the events of his life. From that time, he may speak of ipani. An older person, however, may refer to events in his youth as iŋilagaan for rhetorical or emphatic purposes. When referring to events of the past three years or so, one does not speak of ipani; rather, the specific terms *ukiuk* (last winter), *ukiutqiq* (winter before last), and *ukiutqitqiq* (two winters before last) are used.

When discussing events in itchaq imma, the Nunamiut make a distinction between *unipqaq* (story), from the verb *unipqaqtoq* meaning "it seems like [the antecedent]," and *koliaqtuaq* (history or, literally, "it has been told"). In most instances there is no difficulty in distinguishing between unipqaq and koliaqtuaq. Several stories in itchaq imma are obviously unipqaq but have historical references. Likewise some accounts are obviously koliaqtuaq but have a fictitious tinge. The Nunamiut occasionally discuss this distinction, which is by no means completely resolved. The primary

concern here is *koliaqtuaq,* Nunamiut ethnohistory; fiction, unipqaq, will be included only when informants so indicated.

Aiyagomahala and the Creation of the Nunamiut

In the beginning of itchaq imma, Aiyagomahala created
the Nunamiut in the region of Survey Pass at the head of the
Alatna River, a tributary of the Koyukuk River that flows
into the Yukon.

Aiyagomahala, a giant and a great man, created the people
smaller than himself. He taught them how to hunt and to make
clothing, tools, and traveling equipment. He also created one
giant white dog which could pull several sleds carrying all
the persons and the camping gear of the whole village. Aiyagomahala and his people lived for a long time at the head of
the Alatna River.

One of the men that Aiyagomahala created was a bad person. He stole, murdered, committed adultery, and continually
made arguments and trouble for people. Aiyagomahala killed
this troublemaker but he came back to life and stayed with
the created people. He did not like to ride on a sled pulled
by the giant dog; rather, he always ran next to a sled. He never
married, liked to be alone, and always made a lot of trouble.

Finally, late one summer, after the fur of animals changed
color and became good for clothing, Aiyagomahala told his
people to hunt as much as they could and collect all kinds of
inland animal skins. Caribou, mountain sheep, wolf, wolverine, lynx, grizzly bear, black bear, beaver, marmot, and otter
were always around camp, and the people collected a large
number of summer skins. Aiyagomahala told his people that
he might call another people to come and trade. In those very
early days of itchaq imma no one knew about trading. After
freeze-up, the fur of animals grew longer, and the people continued hunting and drying skins. The animals were never
frightened, and the people added many fall skins to their summer collection.

In the fall, some time after freeze-up, Aiyagomahala told
them that he would call another people to come and trade. He
left the head of the Alatna River, and as he walked along, he
said to himself, "I think I should build a snow house [*aputyaq,*
not "igloo" as is commonly thought] so that people will re-

member me from generation to generation." About five or six miles above the confluence of the Itkillik and Colville rivers, Aiyagomahala built a snow house in the evening of his first day of walking. He stayed overnight there because he wanted to be remembered, it was said, from generation to generation. Aiyagomahala told his people that his snow house turned into a small knoll with a hollow on the top where he had left his pack. Today the knoll is called *puviksuk* by the Nunamiut.

The next day, Aiyagomahala walked over to Point Barrow. When he arrived, no one knew him. He stood in front of the *karigi* [communal or ceremonial house]. Someone inside the karigi heard a funny noise outside. Two men coming inside reported the presence of a giant; they were sent out to investigate and ask his name. "Who are you, what is your name?" they inquired. "I am Aiyagomahala; the inland people [the Nunamiut] always call me Aiyagomahala." The two men returned to the karigi but could not remember his name. They were sent out again to inquire about it. Once more the giant answered, "I am Aiyagomahala; the inland people call me Aiyagomahala." The two men returned to the karigi but again forgot his name. A third time they were sent out and finally managed to remember his name. Aiyagomahala was invited to come into the karigi. He tried to crawl in, but the tunnel was too small. The people almost rushed out to meet him, but they decided to take several spruce logs out of the tunnel. When he came in, they told him he was a big fellow and gave him something to eat. He was very nice, smiling at everyone. After he had finished eating, he told everyone in the karigi at Point Barrow about the people he had created inland. He said that they had collected a large number of inland animal skins and inland food, such as dried meat, caribou back fat, some plants, and so forth. Then he told the Point Barrow men that they should travel up to the inland people with seal and whale blubber and sea animal skins which would be a good exchange for the inland products.

At this time, however, Aiyagomahala asked each family to bring him a piece of whale blubber with *muktuk* [whale skin —one of the finest delicacies] on it. Everybody went home, got a piece of whale blubber with muktuk and brought it to the outside of the karigi. Aiyagomahala had a huge sack filled with blubber, but he was a big, strong man—a giant. He then said, "I will pay you with my own created animals; I will call the inland animals to come, but if any of you run out of arrows, don't say, 'I am out of arrows.'" Everybody believed Aiyagomahala and all the men with bows and arrows went over to a nearby creek. Aiyagomahala waved both hands inland calling the caribou. Suddenly, a huge herd of caribou appeared in the distance coming toward the creek where the men were waiting. The herd of caribou was like a sandy beach, nobody could see the end of it. The men were very happy and excited about shooting so many caribou. Finally the end of the herd came and the caribou passed on out over the sea ice.

Aiyagomahala then called wolves. As he was watching the exhilarated shooting of wolves, one man cried out, "My gosh, I am out of arrows." The wolf pack turned back inland and disappeared. Aiyagomahala called no more animals, saying that everybody had enough for a while.

After all the shooting, Aiyagomahala explained the best route to the head of the Alatna River where his people would be ready with a feast. He assured them that he would teach his people how to use blubber in shallow stone lamps.

Aiyagomahala walked back home, carrying a large sack of blubber. The Point Barrow people left shortly afterward and followed Aiyagomahala's trail in the snow, bringing more blubber with them. When they all came together, Aiyagomahala explained that they should hold a footrace. If the Point Barrow people won, the created people would give them many furs. If the Point Barrow runners lost, they would receive no prize but would have the opportunity to trade. Aiyagomahala's people could run faster and won the race. Everyone had a good time, making much happiness. Aiyagomahala showed his people how to built a karigi and how to play such games as jumping, wrestling, tug-of-war, and juggling.

Before the Point Barrow Eskimos left for the coast, Aiyagomahala advised them to prepare a feast the coming year; they should send two men as messengers to the head of the Alatna River to announce the feast. The next year, the inland people traveled to the coast in sleds pulled by the giant dog.

The bad man stayed with them, running alongside a sled all the way down to the coast.

After the inland people learned about the exchange of goods and feasts with the Point Barrow people, Aiyagomahala showed them how to trade with people from other regions. [Although the account is not specific, storytellers assume that the "other people" included the Eskimos on the Kobuk, Selawik, lower Noatak, and Mackenzie rivers, Kotzebue Sound, and other places on the coast. No mention was made of Indians.]

Aiyagomahala told his people that every family, as well as unmarried men, should have a partner in each of the other groups and that nobody should trade with anyone else. From that time on, the Nunamiut greatly enjoyed giving and attending feasts.

After Aiyagomahala had taught his people all these things, he told them he was going to leave forever. He admonished them never to be angry, to love each other, to be kind, and to help each other. He said he would go to a different country. Before leaving, he took his mitten and stuck it in the ground at the head of the Alatna River and the mitten turned into a mountain called Arigaruitch by the Nunamiut. He told his people to remember him whenever they saw that mountain.

Then he left, never returning, and no one knew where he went.

To the Nunamiut, Aiyagomahala is a very important figure; many Nunamiut have discussed him and his creation of the original Nunamiut band at the head of the Alatna River. Several Nunamiut have felt that Aiyagomahala also created the Point Barrow Eskimos and other Eskimos in northern Alaska, but this speculation has never been widely accepted. Many Nunamiut think that Aiyagomahala created the inland animals because he could command them. The karigi and its related behavior as well as many other aspects of Nunamiut culture are attributed to Aiyagomahala.

The Great Earthquake, the Great Flood, and the Story of Light

According to my informants there is no story about the creation of the earth itself. The Nunamiut have speculated about the origin of the mountains (the Brooks Range) and make the analogy that, like the sea ice crushing up to form pressure ridges, the land, pre-viously flat, crushed up to form mountains.

During Aiyagomahala's time, it is believed, the weather was obviously cold because his people traveled by sled. But some time after Aiyagomahala—during the middle phase of itchaq imma—the weather became warmer. Spruce forests extended over the Brooks Range and down into the Colville River. One informant has seen spruce logs as large as a stove pipe in cutbanks in the Col-ville River, substantiating to his satisfaction the accuracy of the account.

Mammoths, giant elk, giant bears, and giant shrews lived in the spruce and surrounding area. There was even, they said, a giant flying whale with holes in its wings which made noise as it flew. One day it landed on a mountain, and the people living nearby col-lected a large quantity of fresh muktuk and blubber. Many Nuna-miut have speculated that the people living in this warm period of giant animals must have been Aiyagomahala's created people, that is, the Nunamiut. They had difficulty hunting the mammoths at first, but finally managed, as told in the following episode.

> A man was hunting alone, far away from home. Suddenly he heard a loud noise like a thunderstorm. He turned around and saw a huge animal, a mammoth, running in the air. It did not land but was not far from the ground. Several men with dogs were chasing it; they called to the lone hunter to join them and share in the kill. Soon they all speared the mammoth. After skinning the beast and cutting up the meat, the lone man was told to collect firewood. He gathered a big pile of dry wood, but the hunters told him to go back and gather only green willows. They made a large fire and cooked several large pieces of meat. The hunters left the lone man with a share of the meat and told him that a great many giant animals might come to land soon. Afterward, several giant animals did land. From that time on, people hunted giant animals with dogs and spears. Also, from that time on, green willows were good enough to burn.

After Aiyagomahala, not only did people have giant animals to hunt but they also were constantly threatened by the people-killers.

> A typical people-killer was the giant shrew which lived in a lake at the mouth of the Killik River. When travelers passed

by, the shrew lay very quiet and seized them for its food. People tried to kill it with arrows but to no avail. At last two brothers, Ilyaganik and Kovavuk, killed the giant shrew, possibly with a large flint sword. They found several arrowheads stuck in its skin. The brothers killed a few other people-killers such as a giant fish living in a lake in the upper Colville, a giant bear, and a giant bird. Many people-killers, nevertheless, survived to menace the people.

Some time during this warm period, a gigantic earthquake was supposed to have shaken the country. The whole earth turned over "like a hot cake," killing the giant animals and the people. A few Nunamiut have speculated, however, that the people who were living in the Brooks Range after the earthquake were the same as those before. The turning over of the earth is viewed as "starting all over again," rather than the extinction of Aiyagomahala's people—the Nunamiut Eskimos. The weather was still warm after the earthquake, and spruce continued to flourish in the Colville River. Many giant animals and people-killers also survived. Several years before World War II, some Nunamiut travelers saw a dead Nunamiut family, fully clothed, in a defrosting cutbank on the Colville River. They were extremely frightened and fled immediately. The Nunamiut consider this family to have been victims of the huge turning-over of the earth.

Some time after the great earthquake, the water in the lower Colville began to rise. Most of the Nunamiut were living on the river some fifty miles southwest of Umiat near the mouth of the Killik River. Others were living elsewhere in the northern Brooks Range and north slope of Alaska. As the water rose higher and higher, they all gathered on the bluffs near Umiat where only a small island remained when the water stopped rising. At the time of the flood, the people noticed that the days were becoming darker and shorter. Nunamiut informants have heard reports of similar floods in the Kobuk River country, the Noatak, and elsewhere. The Nunamiut account, however, concerns only Umiat. People were able to hunt seals and whales from their small island. One Nunamiut has seen a large whale bone on the bluffs at Umiat. A giant man was living with the Nunamiut and he was friendly to the people, even after the flood.

Mr. Raven, a famous hero of many a story, especially fictitious ones, brought back the land. The people knew if they could spear one of the tussocks (popularly known as "niggerheads" in Alaska) floating by the island, the land would return. One day, Mr. Raven picked up an *itkilligruaq* (old Indian plant) and, as a tussock came floating by, he took a deep breath and speared it. The water gradually began to subside. Land began to appear everywhere, and all the sea animals left. Many fish, however, remained in lakes as the flood was draining, and thus we have fish today. As the water fell, a few very large sea animals crawled down to the coast, cutting the channels of Colville River and its larger tributaries as they traveled. Many Nunamiut seemed to think, however, that the land was essentially the same before and after the flood. Aiyagomahala himself walked down the Colville River before the flood, but the depiction of sea animals making rivers by crawling down from the mountains to the coast makes a good story. At least that is the impression I gained from storytellers.

The spring after the earth flood drained, the inhabitants at Umiat saw a group of travelers coming toward their camp in a skin boat. Everybody was very excited and the giant too was very happy, jumping and running. His tracks may still be seen today. After the flood the Nunamiut lived just north of where the Killik River joins the Colville, about fifty miles upstream from Umiat.

According to my informants, the story of "Mr. Raven Brings Light to the People" should now be related. This is a good example of the blurred distinction between story and history. Informants expressed varying degrees of belief in the story of Mr. Raven and the light, unlike the account of Aiyagomahala, which is emphatically stated to be true, and several stories about Mr. Raven which are considered pure flights of fancy.

> MR. RAVEN BRINGS LIGHT TO THE PEOPLE. The people were living just north of where the Killik River joins the Colville in two villages, one on top of a hill, the other near a creek. In the village on the hill lived an *umialik* [rich man], who was the richest man in the community. He had one very attractive daughter who refused to marry any of the young men who sought her. The umialik asked her to marry because he was getting old and soon would not be able to hunt; but his daughter said no.
>
> In those days it was very dark, but the umialik owned two

balls of light, both about the size of a basketball. One was
very bright and could be taken outdoors and used for hunting; it was bright enough to furnish light over a long distance.
The darker ball of light was sufficient only for collecting dry
wood and fetching water. Both balls of light were hung from
the ceiling of the house on loops. In those days in the creek
village, when the women went out to collect firewood, they
could not see the difference between green and dead willows.
They had to lick the willows to see if their tongues stuck or
not. This was a cold thing to do in the winter.

Mr. Raven, as known by all, is very tricky. All the
people were forced to wait until the umialik went hunting
with his light before they could go out. They hunted musk ox
in those days. The people became very tired of waiting for the
umialik to go out hunting. Most of the people wanted to buy
the brilliant light, but the umialik would not sell. They got
together and offered him a big price for only the darker one,
but he refused to sell it. A wise man was said to have given
the balls of light to the umialik.

In those days, Mr. Raven could talk like a human being and
lived among the people. Several persons wanted to fool the
umialik, so that everybody could use the light. One day Mr.
Raven said, "I think I can do it; I think I can fool the umialik
and bring out his light. If anyone has gifts such as parkas,
pants, food . . ." The people believed what he said, and they
gave him what he wanted; for *Mr. Raven, as known by all, is
very tricky.* Mr. Raven was so happy because he was going to
bring the light for everybody.

Near the village on the hill was a small lake where people
fetched water. Mr. Raven studied the situation, thinking how
he could steal the light; he knew full well that the umialik
was conscious of his crafty reputation. Some way he had to
fool the umialik. At last Mr. Raven said to himself, "I think
I will turn into the feather of an eagle and when the umialik's
daughter takes a drink of water from the small lake she will
swallow me." Mr. Raven believed his idea would work. That
evening he went to the lake. He made himself look like an
eagle feather. He looked at himself and was pleased with his
success. Then he made himself smaller and smaller. Soon he
was as small as a real feather.

Shortly afterward, the beautiful daughter walked slowly toward the lake so the young men might catch a glimpse of her provocative womanhood. She carried the darker light in one hand and a wooden pail in the other. Mr. Raven thought to himself, "I hope she takes a drink with her dipper before filling the pail." When she reached the lake, she lowered her dipper to the water and Mr. Raven stealthily slipped into it. The girl swallowed the water in the dipper and Mr. Raven sneaked into her womb; she felt nothing. She filled her pail and went home. Shortly after returning home she began to feel funny. Mr. Raven was growing fast. That same night, she appeared to be very pregnant. Her father asked her if she had been trysting with a young man near the lake. She said she had not. Presently she was ready to give birth. Mr. Raven was born with no difficulty; both the mother and the baby were in fine condition except that the baby had a small lump on its forehead. They could not see that the baby was Mr. Raven. The umialik was very happy to have a baby boy, "He may hunt for me; it is good to have a grandchild." The umialik believed that the baby would grow up to be his helper. Maybe he would grow up to be a wise man, maybe it was in fact the same wise man who gave him the light.

The baby grew very fast. Soon he was strong enough to sit up and look at the light hanging on the ceiling of the house. He began to talk. At first he could not say some words right because he was too young. Before long, the little boy, Mr. Raven, wanted to play with the light. "No, you are too young, it is too easy to break the light," his grandfather told him. The little boy cried and cried, exclaiming that he wanted to play with the light. His grandfather made him several toys but he refused to touch them. Finally his grandfather let him have the darker one. *Mr. Raven*!! He stopped crying and became a nice boy holding the light, tossing it gently up and down. His grandfather warned him not to throw it. The umialik and his daughter watched him, but Mr. Raven played very carefully with the ball of light. He played with it for several days.

In the village on the hill, no one knew where Mr. Raven was. The people in the creek village knew of course, but they said nothing because it was a secret. They expected the light any time. They heard that a boy with a lump on his forehead was born to the daughter of the umialik.

After playing with the darker light for some time, Mr. Raven got tired of it. He grew faster than a normal baby. He began to cry for the brilliant light but his grandfather said, "I will never give you that one." He encouraged his grandson to play with the darker light but to no avail. The umialik examined the boy's forehead. He thought the lump looked like a raven's beak, but it did not grow. He asked his daughter if she had met with a raven. She did not know. The umialik began to tire of the incessant crying. He was getting very little sleep. Finally the umialik gave the bright light to his grandson. How nice the boy was! The umialik cautioned him not to throw the light because it would break easily. Mr. Raven tossed it gently in his hands and smiled at his family. His mother and grandfather were happy to see the boy smile so nicely. Mr. Raven was still young, "I wish I could grow up and use this light to hunt." His grandfather understood him and felt he would become a good hunter. Mr. Raven knew in his own mind that he was going to break the light but he did not tell his grandfather. The old man was happy to hear his grandson talking about hunting. "But I am growing so slowly," complained Mr. Raven. "Stretch your arms and legs, and you will grow faster," his grandfather told him. After putting the bright light beside him, Mr. Raven stretched his arms and waved his legs. His family did not bother to watch him any more.

Suddenly Mr. Raven jumped out of the house with the bright light, and his mother jumped out just behind him. The moment he was outside the house he broke the light with his beak, turned into a raven, and flew away. His mother could not catch him in time. She began to cry because Mr. Raven had fooled her. And then there was light everywhere just like in the spring. The daughter cried and cried and said, "I hope the light will be divided into two parts; one should be called day, the light one, and the other should be called night, so people can rest." The umialik was upset and very sad, but everyone else was happy. As soon as Mr. Raven came to rest, the people gave him all the gifts they had promised, laughing, shouting, and jumping up and down in joy. The clothes were very fine—shiny and black for Mr. Raven. Now no one had to wait for the umialik to go out hunting because Mr. Raven brought the light out for all the people. The umialik kept the darker light but even in the night there was enough light to see without it. Finally he broke the darker one because he was so sad to have lost the bright light.

Some time after Mr. Raven brought the light to the people, the people-killers and other enemies forced the Nunamiut to flee to the coast. While living at the mouth of the Colville River, the Nunamiut fought the Point Barrow Eskimos and just managed to win the battle.

Kayaktuaguniktuu

In the last phase of itchaq imma, after the flood and the story of the light, an important giant, Kayaktuaguniktuu by name, came to the inland country. His stature in the annals of Nunamiut ethno-history is almost as great as Aiyagomahala himself. To tell the full story of Kayaktuaguniktuu takes a month; a brief summary is given here.

Kayaktuaguniktuu helped the Nunamiut in two major ways: first he killed the last of the people-killers and, second, he taught the people and animals how to live better, showing them how to protect themselves from enemies, how to defe-cate, how to eat the best food, how to give birth to children without the death of the mother, how to run faster, and so forth. As a background to Kayaktuaguniktuu's association with animals, it should be noted that during itchaq imma ani-mals lived like people, hunting and talking with normal hu-man beings. Animals could become human beings but retained their animal noses on the forehead. Animals had families and possibly lived in the karigi. By the end of itchaq imma ani-mals could no longer talk with people, nor were they able to turn into human beings.

The parents of Kayaktuaguniktuu were normal persons who lived on the Kobuk River. The father of Kayaktuagun-iktuu attempted several times to kill him. Finally he had to leave his family. Before he left, his mother made him some akutaq [Eskimo "ice cream," commonly made from caribou fat and ground meat]. When he approached a group of people

he would lick the ice cream four times, and then the people
he met seemed like himself.

One time Kayaktuaguniktuu was traveling through the
country and found a herd of caribou (he did not know, of
course, that they were caribou after licking the akutaq). He
joined the herd and married a caribou woman. They trotted
through the deep soft snow looking for food, but his wife,
possessing only two joints in her legs, was having a difficult
time. It snowed and snowed. The couple came to a lake, and
Kayaktuaguniktuu's caribou wife was very tired. "Come on,
cross the lake," he told her. "We need to travel. Don't be
frightened or sad," but the caribou woman began to cry.
Kayaktuaguniktuu became angry and started beating his
wife; suddenly she bolted across the lake, running like the
wind. Kayaktuaguniktuu had given her leg a third joint so
caribou could run fast enough to escape from the wolves. He
thought she was a human being before beating her.

Another time Kayaktuaguniktuu came upon a large village.
[No animal was specified to me for this incident.] Kayaktuaguniktuu heard that when a woman in that village was ready
to give birth, her belly had to be cut open for the baby to come
out and the mother died. Kayaktuaguniktuu married and his
wife soon became pregnant. Shortly before she was to have
her belly cut for the birth, her father and other relatives began
to cry. The woman herself was crying. Kayaktuaguniktuu
loved his wife and he knew in his own mind that he had a
secret. The moment before the baby was to come out, he
saved it. All the people in the village started crying about
their previous losses. Soon, however, they learned to deliver
babies without killing the mother and everyone rejoiced.

One day Kayaktuaguniktuu was wandering over the countryside and joined a group of muskrats, marrying one of the
muskrat women. The muskrat people would only suck meat
juice; they did not swallow the whole meat. Soon after joining
the muskrats, Kayaktuaguniktuu swallowed several chunks of
meat. They began to cry, saying, "This man will surely die because he swallowed meat. He doesn't have any way to throw it
out." Kayaktuaguniktuu knew better and told the muskrat

people that he had a way of throwing out the meat. He soon felt like defecating. He told everybody to follow him and learn. Kayaktuaguniktuu dropped a big pile of feces. He told the muskrat people to lick and taste the feces so they would acquire an anus and learn how to defecate. One by one, they tasted the feces and from that time on, everyone had an anus.

Not only did Kayaktuaguniktuu teach the animals (and consequently people) how to live better, but also he killed the last of the people-killers. In the full narration of the account of Kayaktuaguniktuu, the encounters with various animal people and people-killers are interspersed; but because none of my informants knew the whole story, I do not have an accurate sense of the sequence of events. At least the significance of Kayaktuaguniktuu for the Nunamiut can be demonstrated even though the full esthetic and epic qualities are missing.

After leaving one of his animal wives, Kayaktuaguniktuu was making his way through a mountain valley when he saw a group of people in the distance. He thought he would join them and have a good time. As he came near he recognized that they were rock ptarmigan [he apparently became a rock ptarmigan immediately], who suddenly began taking turns shooting arrows at Kayaktuaguniktuu. But he was very agile and hard to hit. At last one of the ptarmigan hit Kayaktuaguniktuu, hurting him badly. Instantly he turned into a human being, grabbed a bow and arrow from a ptarmigan, and killed them all.

Shortly after Kayaktuaguniktuu left his parents, he was drifting down a river in a kayak [Kayaktuaguniktuu means "clever at handling a kayak"] and briefly visited several persons. One day he encountered an unfriendly giant—a people-killer. The giant threw a large slate *ulu* [an Eskimo woman's semilunar knife] at him, trying to kill him. The ulu was very sharp and almost hit him. Kayaktuaguniktuu picked up the ulu and threw it at the giant, cutting off his right arm. The giant threw back the ulu with his left hand and this time narrowly missed Kayaktuaguniktuu. Again he threw the ulu at the giant, cutting off his left arm. The giant ran over to the ulu and, picking it up with his teeth, threw it at Kayaktuagun-

iktuu, wounding him on the side. Kayaktuaguniktuu then hit
the giant in the neck, finally killing him. When Kayaktuaguniktuu examined the ulu he found dried human blood on it, not
animal blood. The giant had killed many people, but now he
could no longer terrorize anyone.

Kayaktuaguniktuu kayaked on down to the coast. He followed the shoreline until he saw a large piece of driftwood.
As he came closer and closer he saw a large pile of human
bones beside the huge driftwood log. Kayaktuaguniktuu got
out of his kayak and cautiously approached on foot with a
bow and arrow. He thought someone might be hiding beneath
the log. Many of the human bones were very old; a few were
fresh. When Kayaktuaguniktuu was quite close, the big log
lunged at him. Kayaktuaguniktuu dodged to one side and shot
an arrow into the log. It began to bleed. The log continued
lunging at him, sometimes hitting and hurting him a little. But
Kayaktuaguniktuu was very intelligent and he kept shooting
the log with arrows. The log began to weaken and eventually
it could not move.

According to the rest of the account, Kayaktuaguniktuu killed
the remaining people-killers. Because of Kayaktuaguniktuu, the
state of the Nunamiut and the animals was considerably improved.
The people-killers were gone, and the animals and people knew
how to live better.

Some time after Kayaktuaguniktuu, toward the end of itchaq
imma, the summers began to shorten. The sun could no longer melt
the ice and snow. Ice started to grow and extended from high places
in the mountains down into the valleys. Before the earth flood, the
weather had been warm, and living was no problem for the people.
As the weather grew colder, the Nunamiut experienced increasing
difficulty in making a living. Little by little, by "studying the situation," they learned how to make good skin clothing, skin boots,
sleds, and snowshoes. Before the glaciation, people used slate for
their tools and only gradually learned to chip flint. After learning
to make flint implements, they were able to live much better. In
the very early days of itchaq imma people used only spears in hunting. Shortly before the glaciation, they also learned to make bows
and arrows. The Nunamiut say that young children playing with
animal ribs gave some smart person the idea for a bow.

The ice continued growing and filled all the major valleys of the

Brooks Range. The glaciation did not extend all the way to the
Arctic coast but did force the Nunamiut to leave the mountains.
All the giant animals died because they had no place to live. The
spruce gave way in front of the ice and cold. Many people died.
Only those living on the coast where they could hunt sea animals
managed to survive.

After the glacier receded the Nunamiut returned to the mountains, and all the animals we know today were living in the inland
country. After the glaciation a new ethnohistorical period called
iŋilagaan comes into being.

The Iŋilagaan Period

From the beginning of iŋilagaan to the late 1700s, I have little
ethnohistorical information and was unable to elicit any real sequence of events. The kind of remarks about early iŋilagaan are as
follows:

> After the Nunamiut returned inland at the end of the glacia-
> tion, they fled again to the coast in fear of enemies said to be
> lurking behind every knoll. When their fear subsided, the
> Nunamiut returned inland once more. Some time later, the
> Nunamiut and the Point Barrow Eskimos fought near
> the Colville River delta. An informant's great-grandfather saw
> a pile of human bones left from this battle and said that when
> he saw them, the bones were already very old. Another ac-
> count tells of a family traveling by umiak in the spring during
> breakup. They lost their umiak and all their possessions in the
> mushy, deep snow of a small river. I once heard a comment
> that marmots were numerous in such and such a place before
> anyone's great-great-grandfather's time.

These fragments are typical of the verbal record describing early
iŋilagaan—the period between the end of itchaq imma and the late
1700s. When I asked my informants why they knew so little about
this part of Nunamiut ethnohistory, they answered that when they
were children they had heard of one or two forebears before their
great-great-grandfather. My informants further stated, however,
that few people ever remembered incidents before that time. This
apparent gap in their ethnohistory poses no doubts in the minds of
the Nunamiut concerning the validity of their tradition. A Nunamiut knows that his great-grandfather knew of his own great-grand-

father's life and so on back to itchaq imma. How else could the
very careful delineation of the events of itchaq imma possibly survive all this time had the Nunamiut not maintained a continuous
tradition? In short, the Nunamiut feel that they are one people,
distinct from the coastal Eskimos of Alaska, the Mackenzie River
Eskimos to the east, and the Eskimos living in the timbered regions
of the Kobuk and other nearby rivers, and that they have had a
very long history in the northern Brooks Range mountains and the
north slope of Alaska.

The most frequently discussed subject of the 1800s is the relationship between the Nunamiut and the Indians. The Nunamiut
recognize two groups of Indians: the Koyukon, living mainly in the
drainage of the Koyukuk River, and the Kutchin (often called
"Chandalar Indians"), living in the upper Yukon, Peel, and lower
Mackenzie river territories. A few Nunamiut are aware of the Tanana and other Indians, but this knowledge has been recently acquired.

The Nunamiut and the Kutchin Indians

The Chandalar or Kutchin Indians are called *uyagamiut* (literally, inhabitants of rocks) by the Nunamiut because they often
lived in stone houses. While the present-day Kutchin Indians whom
the Nunamiut are aware of live in the southeastern Brooks Range
and on the Yukon River (see map in Appendix A), the first accounts concerning the Kutchin refer to a village of a hundred persons or more between the heads of the Kobuk and Noatak rivers
around Walker Lake, or perhaps a few miles to the north. According to the Eskimos, some of whom knew the Indian languages, these
uyagamiut spoke a language different from that of the Koyukon
Indians.

The Kobuk Eskimos and the uyagamiut began to quarrel and
fight before 1800. The Kobuk Eskimos felt that the Indians were
intruders in their territory, hunting and trapping where they had
lived for generations before the Indians. Sometimes the Eskimos
won a skirmish, sometimes the Indians; even women and children
were killed. In one fight all the Eskimos were killed but one man
named Sikirigaurak. He escaped over a willow wall surrounding
the Eskimo houses. Sikirigaurak went down to the lower Kobuk
and recruited a gang of men. He returned to the upper Kobuk and
killed a great many Indian men, but no women or children. The

Indians decided they had to leave after losing so many men, and they moved up into Howard Pass, near the head of the Nigu River. My informants did not know of any living person descended from Sikirigaurak, but from other evidence the Indians probably moved from Walker Lake to Howard Pass between 1800 and 1820.

The Indians lived for a number of years in Howard Pass, where Nunamiut also lived. According to the Nunamiut, the Indians learned many things from the Eskimos about building moss houses, trapping, hunting, and making implements. Although the Indians traded occasionally with coastal Eskimos, they usually obtained common and bearded sealskins and rawhide lines from Nunamiut, Noatakmiut, or Kobukmiut. The Indians did not care much for blubber.

At Howard Pass, trouble arose between the Indians and the Nunamiut. Like the Kobuk Eskimos, the Nunamiut considered the Indians as trespassers on their hunting and trapping prerogatives. There was sporadic raiding and fighting.

After a few years the Indians were driven from Howard Pass. They moved east along the northern Brooks Range and at various times settled in the Killik, Okokmilaga, Chandler, Anaktuvuk, and Itkillik valleys. According to the Nunamiut, the Indians lived much like the Eskimos, following the caribou herds and trapping the fur animals. One group of Indians lived for a time in the Anaktuvuk Valley near Tulugak Lake and traveled south on the John River as far as Hunt Fork and the Allen River. After the fighting at Howard Pass, the Indians and Nunamiut lived together peacefully for many years, perhaps just less than a generation. They lived together for so long that everyone almost forgot the blood spilled at Howard Pass. Many Nunamiut and Indians managed to become close friends. They learned each other's language and danced and played games together. One Indian composed a Nunamiut song which a few Nunamiut still know, but they say it is not a very good song. The Nunamiut reportedly did not learn anything about Indian kinship terminology or social organization, although Indians learned to use the corral for taking caribou during a migration.

Gradually the relationship between the Indians and the Nunamiut again deteriorated. Several small clashes brought the mutual hatred to a feverish pitch. Jealousy over women ultimately forced the Nunamiut–Indian conflict to a showdown.

At Chandler Lake, the Indians made a karigi of stone with a

caribou-skin roof. One day three Nunamiut travelers were invited inside to visit. While they were eating, they heard the Indians talking among themselves about killing those Nunamiut. They could understand the Indians, however, and one Nunamiut suddenly flew out through the top of the house like a bird. The other two Nunamiut remained in the karigi but the Indians were too frightened to kill them.

Once several Indians mortally wounded a Nunamiut, but he killed two or three of them with a flint knife before dying. Another time a group of Indians was following several Nunamiut families down the Colville River. The Indians had put one old Nunamiut to death, and finally the Nunamiut killed one of the richest Indians who owned many beads. The Nunamiut did not recognize any real chief or formal leadership among the Indians. On one occasion, several Indians surrounded a house where a Nunamiut man was alone with his old parents and sisters. The one man is said to have shot thirty Indians before running out of arrows. Then the Indians murdered him, his parents, and his sisters.

At last one fall at Kongumavuk, about five miles north of the summit of Anaktuvuk Pass, two Indian women were taken as wives by the Nunamiut, not by force. One of these marriages broke up quickly, and the other woman bore no children. The Indians expected to receive two Nunamiut women in exchange, but the Nunamiut, being proud of their women, refused to comply. The Indians and the Nunamiut almost came to arms. All winter the Indians stayed near the Nunamiut in the Anaktuvuk Pass region, trying to obtain two Nunamiut women. In the spring the Indians followed the Nunamiut to Tulugak Lake, some sixteen miles north of the summit of Anaktuvuk Pass, near the range front of the Brooks Range. The Nunamiut had become tired of the whole affair, the individual fighting and killings over the years, the intrusion on hunting and trapping prerogatives, and now the attempt to take two of their women. Nunamiut warriors held elaborate shamanistic séances in preparation for the fight that was bound to come.

On an April day, the Nunamiut started north down the Anaktuvuk River. When they reached the confluence of the Itigamalukpuk and Anaktuvuk rivers, about seven miles north of the range front, the Nunamiut took up a stand. The Indians advanced to meet them. As an Indian drew back his bowstring, a Nunamiut waited until the Indian's fingers turned white just before releasing the arrow, and then jumped aside. Before the Indian could nock another arrow, the Nunamiut would shoot at the Indian, giving a loud whoop if he killed him. Over twenty Indian men were killed, and only two Nunamiut were wounded. The Nunamiut immediately left for the coast, and the Indian women and children buried their men in a small knoll about a mile north of Tulugak Lake. The fight at Itigamalukpuk turned the tide of the decades-long conflict. One old Indian woman followed the Nunamiut down to the coast and, since her relatives had been killed, asked the Nunamiut to spear her which they did.

Two things, according to the Nunamiut, accounted for their victory. First were the secret shamanistic preparations, the lack of which would have resulted in a Nunamiut defeat, and second was the trick of watching the Indians' fingers when they drew back their bowstrings. An older informant's great-grandfather took part in this battle, and we could thus speculate that it occurred some time before 1850.

After the Itigamalukpuk fight, the Nunamiut fled to the coast while most of the Indians gathered in the Killik valley. The Nunamiut expected the Indians to offer determined resistance, but only minor incidents, as recounted in the following tales, occurred.

Shortly after freeze-up in the fall after the battle at the mouth of the Itigamalukpuk River, a Nunamiut shaman decided to ascend the Colville River to retrieve a sled he had left at the mouth of the Anaktuvuk River. People warned him to remain on the coast and stay away from the Indians. The shaman claimed he was unafraid, and that indeed he would kill any Indians he encountered. He started walking up the Colville River with two dogs. Before he reached the mouth of the Anaktuvuk River, he came face to face with several Indians who recognized him as a tough fighter. They surrounded him in a willow patch. He turned into a pigeon hawk and flew out of the thicket. The Indians saw the pigeon hawk but continued to beat the brush. When they realized he had escaped, they tried in vain to kill his two dogs with arrows.

The shaman [apparently] resumed his human form and proceeded up the Colville. The Indians followed him at a respectful distance. The Nunamiut shaman became very tired and knew that he could not elude them this time. He came to a U in a river and went out on the point of land encompassed by the U. He began taunting the Indians, bow and arrow in hand, challenging them to come near and fight. He told them to chase him all the way to the mouth of the Anaktuvuk River and then mutilate his body; he would not care. He waited but they did not approach. The Indians withdrew and the Nunamiut shaman retrieved his sled.

Later the following spring, the Nunamiut encountered the Indians and saw that they looked very weak and thin. The Nunamiut did not take the offensive. They said a "big hello" to the Indians, wrestled, and competed in other games. That summer the Indians traveled east across the north slope and passed through the Brooks Range by way of the Itkillik or other nearby valley to the southeastern Brooks Range, the Chandalar Lake country. There they joined Indians who spoke and lived like themselves. The remnants of the uyagamiut now live in Venetie, Arctic Village, and Christian Village in the southeastern Brooks Range north of the Yukon River.

After leaving Nunamiut territory, the uyagamiut did not mobilize for a pitched battle of retaliation or vengeance. They left the Nunamiut alone. According to the Nunamiut, Indians (including both the Koyukon and Chandalar Indians) have occasionally forayed into their territory, raiding trap lines and even threatening the Nunamiut themselves.

Some five or ten years after the Indians had left the northern Brooks Range, the Nunamiut shaman mentioned above was snaring mountain sheep at a salt lick in the mountains about fifteen miles west of Tulugak Lake. He slept in a cave each night after checking his snares and skinning his sheep during the day. One night his spirit helper came to him in a dream and warned him to ready his bow and arrow in the face of impending danger. Suddenly he heard a man climbing up the rocks approaching his cave. As the stranger appeared in the doorway, the shaman shot him. With a terrific shout, the intruder rolled down the mountain and the next morning, the Nunamiut shaman found a dead Indian lying at the base of the mountain. He immediately searched for some Nunamiut and told them about the Indian. Everyone came to see and, true to the shaman's word, found the Indian lying at the base of the mountain shot through with his arrow.

One Nunamiut hunter, perhaps fifty years ago, claimed to have shot two or three Indians and appealed to his relatives and friends to investigate. All those he told, however, were so frightened that no one ventured to look for the dead Indians and the report remains unsubstantiated.

Even to the present day, many Nunamiut are easily frightened by imagined Indian attacks. Shadows seen in the willows at night, foot tracks observed away from the beaten path, or an eerie laugh heard in the dusk of an Arctic winter night will give rise to much discussion. I saw no such evidence myself and, in view of the limited trapping today, a raid would hardly be worthwhile. Still, as a disciplining device for children, a subject of frequent conversation and occasional dispute, and as a source of fear supporting in-group feeling, the Indians are very much on the Nunamiut mind and are frequently discussed.

Although the relationship between the Chandalar Indians and the Nunamiut has involved constant conflict, they did trade to a limited extent. When most Nunamiut were trading with the Point Barrow Eskimos at Negalik, an island in the Colville River delta, a few Nunamiut traveled east to Barter Island and met the Chandalar Indians, who came by way of the east fork of the Chandalar River, through the Brooks Range, and down the Hulahula River to Barter Island. Furs and a few white-man goods were the main objects of trade. The atmosphere was always strained. The men on both sides often left their women and children behind and violence frequently threatened. On one occasion an Indian and a Nunamiut grabbed each other, each shouting how little he was hurt by the other. This incident went no farther. As far as I know, no full-scale battle took place at Barter Island between Indians and Eskimos.

At Barter Island the Nunamiut also traded with the Mackenzie River Eskimos, who carried such items as leaf tobacco, Siberian wolverine pelts, knives, and riveted iron pots from Siberia across Alaska to Canada. A few Nunamiut encountered Coppermine Eskimos but regarded them as strange people with disgusting customs. One Nunamiut family did travel as far east as the Coppermine country but did not mix freely with the Eskimos there. The Nunamiut family tended to keep to itself, hunting and trapping and eventually returning to the Brooks Range.

The Nunamiut and the Koyukon Indians

The Koyukon Indians live primarily in the Koyukuk River drainage, which lies mostly south of the Brooks Range, and are called *tagagavik* (travel by canoe) by the Nunamiut. While the Koyukon are considered *itkilluich* (Indians, generally) just as the Kutchin are, the Nunamiut's relationship with the Koyukon has been quite different. Although the Nunamiut regard the Koyukuk as inferior, there is little antagonism and violence between them. Even before the migration of the Kutchin Indians through Nunamiut territory, the Nunamiut were aware of the Koyukon Indians and where they lived.

The Kobuk Eskimos maintained a much closer relationship with the Koyukon Indians than did the Nunamiut, who in fact sometimes refer to the Kobuk Eskimos as *itkilliruich,* which is almost the same as calling them Indians. The Nunamiut usually obtained Koyukon Indian trade items through the Kobuk Eskimos. On rare occasions the Nunamiut and Koyukon Indians did exchange feasts. Shortly before 1880 two Nunamiut, one of whom could speak the Koyukon language, traveled by foot down the John River to the Koyukon Indians and invited them to Hunt Fork, about forty miles south of the summit at Anaktuvuk Pass on the John River, for games and trading. The Indians came up the river, and a footrace from Kolutak to Tulugak was held, some twenty-five or thirty miles. The Nunamiut won. After trading, the Indians left with the understanding that the Nunamiut would come south to the Koyukuk River the following year. That next year, the Nunamiut decided not to go; they were too busy trapping and hunting.

Such an incident is typical of the relationship of the two groups over the years. There is little marked hostility or vitriolic derision; mild disdain best describes the feeling the Nunamiut have for the Koyukon Indians.

The Introduction of Trade Goods

The historical evidence in Chapter 1 indicates that the Nunamiut had most certainly heard of white men and had received at least a few trade items before 1800. Jenness estimated that the Nunamiut received tobacco from Siberia by the early 1700s, a speculation I would support; it is unlikely that tobacco reached the Nunamiut much earlier because the Russians were not economically dominant in Siberia until the late 1600s and early 1700s.

The comments of Nunamiut informants give evidence to a constant trade in specific items between the Nunamiut and Siberian Eskimos (via two, three, or more groups of Eskimo middlemen) from the late 1700s until the early 1900s. Jenness (1957) stated that the last trade contact across the Bering Straits occurred in 1926. The Nunamiut traded inland furs (including fox, which previously had been considered worthless) for Siberian wolverine, green leaf tobacco, riveted iron cooking pots, knives, beads, reindeer skins, and reindeer leg skins. (The Siberian Eskimos were required by supernatural rules to cut the leg skins off the reindeer hide; the Nunamiut felt the Siberian Eskimos were merely trying to increase the trade value of the skin by making it into two items.)

By the early and middle 1800s, trade goods like knives, pieces of metal used for arrowheads, riveted iron buckets, and beads began reaching the Nunamiut with increasing frequency. These early items were not introduced as a result of direct white contact; all such goods obtained by the Nunamiut before Beechey, Franklin, and Simpson (1826–36) came by way of one or more Eskimo middlemen. A particular item was already well assimilated into established Eskimo patterns of usage by the time it reached the Brooks Range. From hearing Nunamiut talk about the early days, these articles merely supplemented their own technology. Another factor in the acquisition of trade goods was prestige. Nunamiut individuals are exceedingly prestige conscious and very quick to adopt a fad or novelty that might be paraded before others.

According to the Nunamiut, the first flintlock and cap and ball rifles came to Point Barrow along the coast from the east, originally from the British, and were then traded inland to the mountains. A very few flintlock and cap and ball rifles most probably reached the Nunamiut between 1850 and 1875. With the coming of whalers, high-quality breech-loading rifles became available as well as cartridges by the case. From 1890 to 1905 or 1910, the .44-40 and the .45-70 were very popular until replaced by the .30-30 and .25-35; modern high velocity rifles did not replace the .30-30 and .25-35 until after World War II.

Tea and coffee reached the Nunamiut through the Kobuk Eskimos, possibly around 1840. Flour was first traded in from Kotzebue Sound by way of the Eskimos living on the Noatak River, who held a feast in the Howard Pass region for the Nunamiut; they made large quantities of flour juice (water, grease, and flour boiled to make a gravy). Unfortunately for the prestige of the Noatak Eskimos, the Nunamiut did not like the flour juice.

Although the first introduced foods reached the Nunamiut from southwest of the Brooks Range, it was not until a steady supply became available from the whaling ships operating along the north Arctic coast that these foods became a regular part of the Nunamiut diet. Several Nunamiut first encountered onions in a stew at Point Barrow, possibly in the 1880s, but thought they smelled like dog urine. In spite of the initial dislike for many of the new foods, they were soon accepted and then desired for the novelty and variety they offered.

Before 1890, and especially among those families who rarely traveled to the coast, the Nunamiut obtained trade goods only sporadically. A century's acquaintance with even a few trade items, however, prepared the Nunamiut for the great flood of goods which arrived with the whalers in 1890. Despite initial hesitance on occasions, whalers had little difficulty in hiring Nunamiut hunters in exchange for white man's goods.

Changes Effected by the Whaling Industry

Documented history gives evidence that whalers were responsible for providing the Eskimos with large quantities of trade goods and upsetting local economies; introducing disease, whiskey, and sexual abuses; and so forth. Here I would like to consider a few aspects of the changes which the Nunamiut say were brought about by the whaling industry.

In the early 1880s a Nunamiut woman estimated that about seven thousand Nunamiut Eskimos camped at Negalik in the mouth of the Colville River one summer. This number also included Eskimos from the Noatak and Utukok rivers as well as the Nunamiut who lived primarily on the Colville, its tributaries, the valleys of the Brooks Range drained by the Colville tributaries, and a very few rivers to the east of the Colville. This number seems inordinately large in light of archaeological (Campbell 1961), historical, and ethnological evidence. There is no question that before 1900 many more Nunamiut were living in the Brooks Range than the hundred-odd who live there today. Before 1885, parents of my informants stated that the Nunamiut were more numerous than coastal Eskimos. This could easily be possible, although a coastal Eskimo might deny such a statement. Speculating from the archaeological, historical, and ethnographic data, I would venture to guess that in 1880, just over a thousand Nunamiut were living in the northern Brooks Range. This figure probably represents the peak of Nunamiut population in the past hundred years.

In the late 1880s, when most of the Nunamiut were living in the Brooks Range, they were threatened with famine because too many people were hunting the caribou herds. Since the Nunamiut did not strive to build up food surpluses, when the caribou herds decreased or altered their migration habits for a year or two, most Nunamiut were forced to leave the mountains or die of starvation. Moose, bear, mountain sheep, other mammals, birds, fish, and plants do not occur in sufficient quantity to support a large population in the Brooks Range. Only isolated families, or very cooperative small groups of families, can possibly subsist there on food resources other than caribou.

Not only did the Nunamiut suffer from hunger in the late 1800s but also from epidemics of influenza, fever, and measles. In the very late 1880s or early 1890s, a flu and fever epidemic killed over a hundred Nunamiut at a feast at the upper Noatak River where Nunamiut, Noatak, and Utukok Eskimos were trading.

Just as the Nunamiut were experiencing severe adversity, the whalers appeared on the scene. The main impact of the whaling industry, according to the Nunamiut, was felt between 1890 and 1905 when, in one year, as many as twenty ships wintered along the coast from Point Barrow to the mouth of the Mackenzie River. Many of the remaining Nunamiut flocked to the coast to trade their furs directly to ship captains and to hire out as hunters. In exchange for caribou meat and skins, hunters received large quantities of rifles, ammunition, knives, tobacco, flour, tea, coffee, sugar, butter, molasses, and whiskey. The persistent if sporadic flow of trade goods to the Nunamiut over the previous hundred years had aroused a strong curiosity and created a ready acceptance for the flood of supplies from the whalers. Hunters were encouraged to kill all the caribou they could and, being an easy animal to hunt, caribou were greatly reduced in number from 1890 to 1905.

As Nunamiut encampments sprang up around whaling ships, the captains often attempted to exert authority, occasionally with the help of a missionary. The following incident exemplifies the conflicts that arose during the period of intensive whaling.

A Nunamiut shaman moved to the coast with his family and hired out as a hunter to the captain of a whaling ship. The shaman was a good hunter, honest in his dealings, but he soon began drinking whiskey. He had adopted a little girl, and

one night while he was drunk he took her by the legs and
bounced her on the ground on her head. Soon afterward she
died.

When the captain heard about the killing, he seized the
shaman and, stripping him of most of his clothes, tied him to
the mast of the ship and beat him with a dog whip. The first
and second mates took their turns; then the missionary on
board took the last turn, beating the shaman the hardest and
the longest. The shaman was still alive when they took him
down from the mast and returned him to his family with a
swollen, bloody head and body. If he had not been a shaman
he would not have lived, but with his power and his wife's
care, he recovered.

Since the shaman was employed by the captain, he had
received a large stock of trade goods which the captain took
from him, leaving only a rifle, a few shells, a tent, and traveling equipment. After the shaman recovered, he and his family returned to the mountains to make a living, primarily by
hunting sheep. From time to time the shaman would rave
about being beaten. The following spring one of the ship's
crew died, and then, one by one, several others died, but not
the missionary. The shaman reportedly tried to kill him also
with his power but was not quite strong enough. The shaman
continued to dwell on how horrible it was to be beaten and
began imagining that the members of his family were turning
against him. Eventually he killed his own family and then
later killed another family. How the shaman himself met his
end, I do not know.

The period of intensive whaling (1890–1905) was a time of
major cultural change for the Nunamiut. Many new items were introduced and accepted. The old technology suffered only slightly
since many material needs could be met only by Nunamiut implements. Guns and food were the two kinds of goods which have
most affected Nunamiut life. As large numbers of guns became
available, they quickly replaced spears and bows and arrows and
modified hunting methods. White man's food has gradually fur-
nished the variety which the Nunamiut used to seek in their diet.

The organization of family life underwent little change, although
the tumult of change would often accentuate any stresses already

present in a family. This was especially true of liquor. The direct hiring of hunters and paying in kind, however, greatly affected traditional hunting patterns, and ultimately the organization and activity of the band. Since the whalers provided only sporadic employment, the Nunamiut continued to snare and corral caribou during the late 1800s. Relying on their keen knowledge of animals, now reinforced with the long-range firepower of guns, Nunamiut hunters could be independent of a group hunt. With a gun and many bullets, one man could guarantee for himself enough meat for the year. Thus he might tend to pull out of a communal hunt which, if it failed, would mean real hunger. The growing demand for furs, replacing the employment offered by whalers, encouraged this tendency to split up. Trappers could do much better alone, widely spread out over the country.

By 1905 the influence of the whaling industry had diminished considerably. By this time, only 150 to 200 Nunamiut were still living in the Brooks Range; some had remained in the mountains all through the period of whaling, others had returned from the coast to their home country. The rest of the Nunamiut either had died from starvation or disease or had emigrated. In 1905 or 1906, most of the remaining mountain Nunamiut came together at Okooluk, a tributary of the John River, for the last large-scale cooperative corralling of the caribou during a spring migration. Afterward, most of the Nunamiut scattered out over the Arctic coast from Fort McPherson on the Mackenzie River to Point Barrow, to Kotzebue Sound, and even to Fairbanks. The Nunamiut era of large-scale cooperative hunting and trapping in the Brooks Range and annual trading to the coast, which flourished from the 1700s or earlier, had by the first decade of the 1900s come to an end.

After 1905, most Nunamiut were under the direct influence of coastal missions and commercial activity. Yet a core of families remained in the Brooks Range to eke out a living until 1920 when the last Nunamiut left the mountains. Although most Nunamiut had either died or been assimilated into other population centers, a few families clustered together on the Arctic coast, some distance east of Point Barrow. Here the Nunamiut could trap white fox, make occasional forays inland for caribou, and obtain trade goods. Most of the last families to leave the Brooks Range between 1900 and 1920 went to the Arctic coast to join the small, resilient band of Nunamiut that was eventually to return to the Brooks Range.

The Impact of Christianity

The first wave of Christian missionization reached the Nunamiut in the form of a concept called *oivaksat*. There is disagreement among Nunamiut informants about the nature of oivaksat. Spencer (1959) observed similar disagreement at Point Barrow. The three basic versions I received are as follows.

In the late 1880s or early 1890s, according to one informant, an Eskimo from the Nome area traveled to the Noatak River for trading and proclaimed a new doctrine called oivaksat. The trader-preacher told the people that if they did not live right or if they lied, they would have to crawl forever on their hands and knees even after the skin had been worn off. Living right was explained to mean being pleasant and nice to other people. Several Eskimos (including a few Nunamiut) who heard this man took up the cause and on trading expeditions spread the doctrine of oivaksat as far north and east as the Mackenzie River before white missionaries arrived. According to some informants, after the Nunamiut encountered the missionaries, they stopped talking about oivaksat.

Other informants asserted that Nunamiut have talked about oivaksat for generations and that it means after death a person will meet all his deceased relatives coming around a corner or point (of land). As a person's relatives die, they begin to follow the oivaksat trail, and when he meets them coming around a big point they will all rejoice and be happy.

A few informants told even a different story. They said oivaksat used to mean that soon everyone would have plenty of material goods; that everything would increase. As white men, white man's goods, and missionaries reached the Nunamiut, a few persons thought the prediction of oivaksat was validated.

Spencer (1959: 257–58, 296–98, 380–81) collected data about the concept of oivaksat from informants at Point Barrow; the data I collected agree with his. Spencer maintained that oivaksat was not shamanistic, which I found also to be the case among the Nunamiut.

The remaining problem is to resolve the contradictions in informants' statements and to explain how the notion of oivaksat reached the north Alaskan Eskimos. I would argue that the doctrine of oivaksat in its diverse forms stems from Quaker and Moravian missionary work at Kotzebue Sound, Seward Peninsula, Norton Sound, and elsewhere south of the Arctic Circle in western Alaska. Those few Eskimos who traveled far on trading expeditions brought their concept of Christian ideas to the north before the arrival of white men. The first notions of oivaksat are most likely those expressed about the Eskimo trader from the Nome region. After the idea spread among the Nunamiut, the other variations developed.

Oivaksat was followed by the development of another religious phenomenon among the Nunamiut called the "new religion," also traceable, by way of other Eskimos, to Christian missionary effort. Just as the arrival of trade goods through Eskimo middlemen during the 1800s prepared the Nunamiut for the later flood of goods, similarly, the diffusion of oivaksat and the "new religion" among the Nunamiut prepared them for direct contact with white missionaries.

In the late 1890s and early 1900s, after the idea of oivaksat had reached the Nunamiut, a native religion based on elements of Christianity sprang up in the Brooks Range. It was drawn from Eskimo travelers and traders who had been in contact with Quaker missions in Kotzebue Sound and perhaps occasional missionaries aboard whaling ships. The "new religion" was preached by Eskimos. Shamans and would-be shamans reacted to early agents of Christianity in two ways: with marked hostility and an effort to preserve their own tradition and position in it, or with an attempt to mold fragments of Christianity into a new form of Eskimo religious behavior. A shaman, or other person seeking prestige in the tumult of change, would hold regular meetings based on the seven-day week. The following incidents concerning Eskimo preachers illustrate the nature of this brief, intense, transitional phase of Nunamiut religious history.

> CASE 1. One Eskimo preacher conducted a service by placing several persons in a circle. Everyone sang, danced, and shuffled around the circle clockwise. The preacher and the people beat their hands in the air, trying to knock everyone's sins to the ground. When all the sins were knocked down, the preacher shouted, "You shall now hear directly from God. God has come into my body and you may now hear of the 'new religion.' " Then the preacher told everyone that God had come down and taken his *iñua* (soul) up to heaven. His body felt dead while his iñua was in heaven.

When his iñua returned to his body, he came to life and was able to tell all the people what he had learned directly from God. Now everyone could hear the true words of God. The preacher told the people that they were almost free from sin, that maybe by the next service, they would be entirely free.

Several Nunamiut believed this Eskimo preacher but others doubted him. Many Eskimos felt that only white preachers were real, because they had books. This preacher was said to have been a shaman, but he refused to give up his shamanistic power after the advent of missionaries. Instead, he tried to fool people into thinking he was a true exponent of the new religion. Many people believed that the preacher did have a real experience with God. Before long, however, everyone lost faith in him, and his quickly won prestige disappeared.

CASE 2. A shaman heard about the new religion from a well-established Eskimo preacher and decided to become a preacher himself. He did not have visions nor did he tell anyone how to induce a vision. He spoke only about God and respecting the Sabbath. He admonished people not to work on Sunday, but only to rest. People should not even pull plants out of the ground on Sunday. Women should not sew or cut firewood. On Saturday people should cut enough firewood to last until Monday morning. Only cooking, eating, visiting, meditating, and praying were permissible. This preacher finally became tired of suppressing his shamanistic power; he gave up preaching and became a shaman again.

CASE 3. One of the most dominant Eskimo preachers held services at the mouth of the Colville River when the Nunamiut traveled from the Brooks Range to trade. He composed his own hymns and also dissuaded people from working on Sunday. This one said that just before every Sunday, his iñua ascended to heaven to receive the "news" and then returned to his body so he could tell everyone about religion. A few shamans watched the preacher carefully and wondered why he never moved or quivered during his vision like other shamans.

The preacher often sang his favorite song, which said in effect, "To the highest mountain peak, God will clean you up [spiritually]." Once a little boy died and the preacher comforted the relatives by singing this song.

CASE 4. One of the Eskimo preachers who failed tried to

convince everyone to take a bath on Saturday. He also exhorted the people not to steal, murder, or commit adultery. One woman listened to what he said about religion. One day when the preacher was walking alone, he saw this woman lying on a skin like a *tunagaq* (devil) and he slept with her. Then he recognized her as one of his listeners and felt that he had been fooled by the devil. After that no one listened to him.

In addition to incorporating elements of shamanism into the "new religion," a few shamans attempted to incorporate elements of Christianity into their own traditional religious system. In doing so, some shamans claimed to have visions of Jesus Christ and even of God himself, which supported their assertions of power in healing and bringing good luck. Many shamans were greatly impressed with the new dimension of a Supreme Being in the previous fractional universe of many individual spirits. A few shamans attempted to resist the use of animistic power and to seek power only from Jesus Christ or God. Some shamans returned to their individual helping spirits; others successfully focused their visions only on Jesus Christ and God.

As quickly as the Eskimo preachers rose, they fell, primarily because they demanded frequent and time-consuming services from the Nunamiut, whose increasingly difficult struggle for survival allowed them little time for such nonproductive activity. Many Nunamiut were already dispersed to different parts of the Arctic where they became subject to more established forms of Christian missionization.

After the dramatic religious flurry of the late 1890s and early 1900s, the more stable elements of Quaker Christianity became the dominant mode of Christianity among the Nunamiut, with a gradual diminution of traditional shamanism.

Eskimo-Quaker Christianity was characterized by a strict observance of the Sabbath, frequent washing of the hands and face, and intense praying. God was considered a very personal Supreme Being capable of intervening directly in sickness and luck in hunting (which were precisely the two major areas of beneficial shamanism). Jesus Christ was a vague figure—the Son of God living in heaven. God, however, appeared to be dominant, and people explicitly sought his help. The Holy Spirit apparently was not considered.

By 1920, when Presbyterianism became the dominant source of Christian influence, coastal Eskimos were often the agents of Christian influence to the inland Eskimos. Only those Nunamiut living in Point Barrow or other large permanent settlements, or who visited Point Barrow frequently, were exposed directly to white missionaries. Not until the late 1940s did Presbyterian missionaries reach the Nunamiut in the Brooks Range. Needless to say, with the demise of shamanism and the extensive indirect exposure to Christianity, many Nunamiut were receptive to Presbyterianism. To this day, however, several Nunamiut are not members of the church. A Point Barrow Eskimo has conducted services for several years and, with varying frequency, Presbyterian missionaries have visited the Nunamiut. With the institution in 1960 of full-term schoolteachers at Anaktuvuk Pass, informal white Christian influence now depends on the convictions and activities of the resident teachers. Shamanism as an active force is dead, although several Nunamiut are very aware of its form and content, since they have seen or been treated by shamans. The subject is a delicate one, and listening to Eskimos discussing shamanism among themselves proved the most effective method of learning about it.

3. The Family and the Household

THE household and the community are the two fundamental groups in Nunamiut society. Other social groupings are variations, parts, or extensions of these two basic units. In addition to membership in a household and a community, each Nunamiut stands in a variety of relationships with a large number of people—blood relatives, relatives by marriage, and non-kin—which support the ongoing activity of the household or the community or both.

The Nunamiut place an extremely high, perhaps the highest, value upon membership in a family. People talk of the need for cooperation within a family. A person joining a household for any length of time is expected to perform the role appropriate to his age, sex, and marital status. A smoothly functioning family is considered a joy—a supreme pleasure to be part of. Fulfilling one's role, the resulting attainment of prestige, the performance of expected obligations, and the reciprocation of them constitute the principal ingredients for a happy life within a Nunamiut household.

In the fall and spring of the year, all Nunamiut households join together to form bands in anticipation of the seasonal migration of the caribou. In the old days the formation and dissolution of bands was more pronounced than it is now. Today, with a variety of white influences impinging upon the Brooks Range Nunamiut, they have settled into a permanent band or village. Many families leave the village for months at a time for hunting and trapping, but they always return to the same village.

The primary function of the band was economic—the exploitation of the migrant caribou and the organization of trading expeditions—or defensive. Today, in the village of Anaktuvuk Pass in which most households reside most of the time, trade and economic cooperation, although practiced in different ways, are still primary functions. As in the old days, the band offers people a chance to visit other households, gossip, discuss and settle legal disputes, and, after the construction of a communal house, to sing and dance.

The Family

THE NUCLEAR FAMILY. The family composed of the mother, father, and children is the basic structural unit in Nunamiut social organization and is the essential constituent of a household. To maintain well-being and, indeed, to ensure survival in the Arctic, an individual's first claim for support and foremost responsibility are directed toward the members of his nuclear family, whether he is a child and sibling or spouse and parent. Several informants explained that a nuclear family which leaves the community and isolates itself in a distant valley can amass considerable wealth. Living in a household apart from other people, the father and eldest sons are able to run extensive trap lines. Few travelers frighten the animals and, in the absence of diverting company, a man and his sons may spend many hours tending the traps and searching the country for game. The mother and daughters can collect firewood with no competition from other women. The long hours of isolation give them a chance to prepare numerous hides and to make clothing, boots, and other items.

One informant told me that as a little boy his parents used to travel alone with their children far from concentrated settlements of families. In the evening his mother built a house by constructing a frame of willows and covering it with large pieces of moss dug from the tundra. The main skill needed here was to find moss that was not permeated with frozen water or soil. His father in the meantime scoured the countryside for caribou and signs of fur-bearing animals. On rare occasions his father walked so far from home that he was forced to spend the night huddled over a little fire which he fed every few minutes with willows. He drank water from puddles in the ice.

Although informants praised families that struggle to go it alone, they pointed out the boredom resulting from such isolation, economically rewarding though it might be. In actual practice most nuclear families are, and desire to be, part of a larger residential group—a household in an extended family or in a community with immediate relatives living nearby.

In educational matters, the function of the nuclear family varies according to the residential arrangements. In general, the mother and father are the primary sources of instruction for their offspring; grandparents, aunts, and uncles play important secondary roles.

Regardless of residence, a young boy learns from his father the elements of traveling by foot and by sled, trapping, and hunting. If a nuclear family alone constitutes the household, a boy also learns from him how to manufacture all kinds of tools, weapons, and traveling equipment. In a larger household grouping, such as an extended family, a boy usually learns much traditional lore and how to make things from a grandfather or an uncle and from men in the communal house. A very young boy learns a few things from his mother, such as how to cross streams and to maintain balance walking across a talus slope, but I rarely saw a mother advising an older son. Even in repairing clothing, a teenage boy will seek help from his sister or some close male relative.

Very young girls are instructed by their mothers in such outdoor activities as collecting firewood, berries, roots, ice, snow, and water. Before she is twelve a girl learns to handle two or three dogs on short trips for firewood and ice. Men do most of the house building today, but women often make small repairs which a young daughter, stimulated with praise, learns by imitation. Raising dogs is largely a woman's job, and a girl is taught to feed meat broth to a newborn litter. If a nuclear family lives alone, a daughter learns from her mother how to prepare skins and sew, but if an older, more accomplished woman, such as a grandmother or aunt is co-resident, she frequently listens to her advice and follows her example.

In the nuclear family the husband and wife are the primary reproductive unit, although in the old days socially approved spouse exchange included the possibility that an exchange husband would become the genitor of one or more children; the permanent husband, however, was socially recognized as the father. In the event of adultery, the biological father may or may not be considered the genitor. Adultery is not socially condoned, and a man seeking recognition in the eyes of others, especially if he has no children by his own wife, might brag about being the father of such a child only in the company of one or two other persons; others never admit it.

MARRIAGE AND INCEST. Young men do not consider marriage until their late teens and early twenties, but girls, often encouraged by their mothers, begin to think seriously about a spouse shortly after puberty. A boy and girl who are courting may exchange articles of clothing, skins or furs, and other small items. There may be sporadic sexual contacts at any time, but an affair of several months' duration signifies a mutual interest in marriage. If both sets of parents approve, the young people establish a common residence, usually in the household of the girl's family. If either person's family objects to the marriage, the father or mother will tell the son or daughter to stop the affair. Ideally a son or daughter should heed the admonitions of his parents, and a young person does in fact frequently respect his parent's advice.

A parent often suggests a mate for his child, the most common instance being the mother who singles out a strong young hunter for her daughter. The mother may present gifts to the boy and talk to his parents about marriage. If everyone agrees, including the boy and the girl, the marriage takes place. The boy or girl is certainly able to exert his will, and many attempts at arranged marriage have failed. I once heard an older Nunamiut say that his parents wanted him to marry when he was very young, but he was shy and refused. He reminisced nostalgically about missing all those years of sexual intercourse before he did marry at the age of twenty-two.

Marriage by force or capture was very rare and resulted either from warfare or uncontrolled lust. On occasion, a girl desiring to marry a certain young man may virtually seduce him and become pregnant by him. When she is obviously pregnant, she will appear in his tent or house; few Nunamiut men would turn down the mother of their child.

Among the Nunamiut, incest restriction has two aspects. One is the psychological repugnance to sexual intercourse within the nuclear family—mother/son, father/daughter, brother/sister. Of almost equal emotional horror is sexual contact with lineal relatives such as a grandparent or grandchild. One informant told me of an incident of father/daughter incest many years after it had taken place. Among Eskimos, this seems to be the most likely kind of incest to occur within the nuclear family. Although I obtained no verbal confirmation, mother/son incest seems to be the most abhorrent, and sister/brother more like father/daughter. I once heard several comments, uttered tensely, about the sexuality of a sister, but never about a mother.

Sexual intercourse and potential marriage with collateral relatives, excluding one's own siblings, are thought of differently from sexual relationships with lineal relatives and siblings. According to informants and a few situations I was fortunate to observe, a person should not propose marriage to or sexually approach any

collateral relative who is normally recognized as an *ilya* (consanguineal relative) and called by a consanguineal term of relationship. In contrast to the underlying, unexpressed psychological
aversion to sexual contact with members of the nuclear family and
lineal relatives, informants gave two reasons for the restriction on
sexual intercourse and marriage with collateral relatives (excluding siblings). One is the notion that a person should not be so shy
that he has only enough courage to engage in sexual relations with
and marry a collateral relative with whom he is intimate by nature
of the relationship. One should not feel ashamed to have sexual
contact with a nonrelative and should express his self-confidence
by seeking sexual relations outside the kindred. The second reason,
frequently mentioned by informants, is that it is advantageous to
have in-laws "from a different country" to create opportunities for
economic exchange, hospitality in time of emergency and travel
and, importantly, someone new to visit.

One informant could recall only one incident of first-cousin marriage, which occurred in the late 1800s. The respective relatives
discussed the matter exhaustively, but the marriage was permitted.
Second- and third-cousin marriages were very rare but did occur
as exceptions and in conflict with Nunamiut ideals. Today at Anaktuvuk Pass, owing to reduced choice, several second-cousin marriages have taken place. After much discussion and concern, the
final rationalization was that sexual intercourse was such a good
thing that to marry a second cousin was better than not to marry
at all.

RESIDENCE AFTER MARRIAGE AND THE EXTENDED FAMILY.
Upon marriage, a young hunter is supposed to join his wife in her
household. He is obligated to bring home all the animals he kills
and to assist in traveling and performing male chores around the
house. In return he receives weapons and good advice from his
father-in-law and new clothes from his mother-in-law. The relationship between a new husband and his parents-in-law is often very
close. A few men live near their wives' parents for decades. The
family I lived with had been living with the mother's parents for
over twenty years—not under the same roof but in a separate house
or tent nearby. The man frequently hunted with his father-in-law
and they constantly vied with each other in trapping, shooting, and
making implements. He also enjoyed a pleasant relationship with
his mother-in-law, bringing her occasional delicacies from the hunt

and chatting in a very relaxed way with her. The mother of the younger family enjoyed the security of living near her parents for many years, talking and working with her mother and presenting food and clothing to her father. The children, of course, basked in the affection of their grandparents.

Although this is the stated ideal, many variations occur. After a year of marriage, the newly formed extended family and the son's parents discuss future residential possibilities. The wife's parents might argue that the duty of a son-in-law is to help them—his wife's parents. The husband's family could counter this idealistic argument by expressing their own need for a young hunter and a seamstress in a large family, particularly if the wife's family is already well-off. If the young wife is the eldest daughter, the husband generally feels compelled to remain with his wife's family. If an elder daughter is already married and living there, he feels freer about returning to his own family or possibly joining a married brother.

Personality is an exceedingly important factor in any household arrangement. Cooperation and industry determine the success or failure of a new household grouping or cluster. It is a source of great happiness for two families to live together in harmony and a source of utter misery if even one person causes trouble. Lack of cooperation and the headstrong behavior of one member of an extended family was the most frequent cause of suicide—to spite the troublemaker as well as to end one's own grief. The idea of suicide because of unrequited love was considered very amusing by my informants—plenty of young girls and boys are always to be found.

Because of the significance of personality in determining residential arrangements, not a single son-in-law in Anaktuvuk Pass was living under the same roof with his wife's parents. Several people cited personal factors as the reason why the cultural ideals about marital residence were not being followed, even when this would have been the most feasible economic arrangement. Several sons-in-law lived near their wives' parents and cooperated with them. One daughter-in-law actually lived with her husband's parents and a few other daughters-in-law lived near their husbands' parents. While young or middle-aged couples often value association with their parents and parents-in-law more highly than association with siblings and siblings-in-law, because fewer parents are available, alignments based on siblingship occur more frequently.

Some form of the extended family used to be widespread among the Nunamiut. Two, or very rarely three, nuclear families—parents/married daughter and families, parents/married son and families, sister/sister and families, or brother/brother and families—often lived together under one roof. Nowadays, as the remaining Nunamiut have settled into a permanent village, most nuclear families have built their own winter houses and live in separate tents during the summer. A small cluster of two or three households is now very common. (Detailed information on residence and alignments will be found in Appendix B.)

THE POLYGYNOUS FAMILY. In the past a good hunter and successful trader sometimes took a second wife and, rarely, a third. Polygyny was considered an expression of lust and an attempt to solidify or expand a position of wealth and political influence by establishing a new series of kinship ties. Both wives lived under the same roof, and although the first wife considered that her seniority gave her authority over the newcomer, the second wife's youth and sexuality often resulted in favoritism from the husband and consequent jealousy and domestic trouble. Jealousy is very common among Eskimos, and two women sharing the same man was, and is, a prime cause of envy. Sororal polygyny was considered almost as bad as incest.

In the old days, a widow or widower was not supposed to marry his deceased spouse's sibling. Today, however, a man has married the widow of his deceased brother with at least tacit social approval (see Household 8 and the information about the parentage of one of the members of Household 6 in Appendix B). I recorded no incidents of polyandry, although the idea did not seem immoral to informants. One Nunamiut woman laughed and said that one woman with two husbands would have a terrific amount of sewing to do. A man, however, countered her argument by pointing out how much meat and skins the one wife would have. Today no polygyny occurs. In discussing the matter, older Nunamiut advised me as a young bachelor that one wife would be the best; two would lead only to trouble.

EXCHANGE OF SPOUSES. While socially condoned and very much desired by all parties concerned, the exchange of spouses was frequently a cause of jealousy. The most common pattern was for two men who had established a trading partnership to exchange wives. Usually one man was an inland Nunamiut and the other a coastal Eskimo. When several Nunamiut families arrived at the coast, the wives of partners were exchanged for one night or perhaps for a week. My informants indicated that longer exchanges did not occur because jealousy could, and did, result in murder. In addition to increasing the bonds of a trading partnership, the exchange of spouses was regarded as a vacation—a source of diversion and relief from the ennui of months of trapping and hunting, or sewing and collecting firewood.

The terms for spouse-exchange relationships are:

> *nuliaqkatigik,* the two couples involved in spouse exchange
> *aŋutauqkatigik,* the two co-husbands
> *aŋutauqun,* co-husband
> *aipagik,* the two co-wives
> *aipaq,* co-wife
> *uixaraq,* husband-by-exchange
> *nuliaxaraq,* wife-by-exchange

Among the Nunamiut themselves, spouse exchange was rare. Once, many years ago, two Nunamiut families decided to travel down the Kobuk River to trade. The men exchanged wives but, it should be noted, they traveled by different routes. Although all four spouses wanted to exchange, none of them wanted to camp each night in a tent next to the other couple. Some time before 1900 an unusual form of exchange happened between two families who were isolated from other people during an entire winter of trapping. The four men and women became so bored with the sameness of their daily work that they decided to exchange sexual partners in spite of their common residence. No violence ensued.

Even in this century a very nebulous form of spouse exchange has occurred. For two persons married to other persons to sleep together is considered adultery and may result in death for the offenders or very heavy public censure. But if a woman takes a lover and her husband, out of spite, sleeps with his wife's lover's wife, a not publicly recognized or a tacitly approved spouse-exchange relationship might be set up, which is not punished. The spouse-exchange terms given above are not used, and the two sets of children are not affected.

In a socially recognized spouse exchange, the two sets of children came to be related as *qataŋun* (step-siblings). Because spouse exchange normally occurred between communities, the primary benefit of this relationship was the extension of hospitality during travel in strange territory. One could always rely on a qataŋun for help. I observed a claim on hospitality resulting from a spouse exchange that had occurred two generations back, in which the husband-by-exchange was not the genitor of any of his exchange-wife's children. One informant laughed, as only a Nunamiut can laugh about such matters, and said that in the old days sexual intercourse was sufficient "to make relatives," that is, to establish some of the economic obligations which result from socially recognized marriage. When a person acquired step-siblings as a result of his parents' exchange, he generally was not restricted from marrying one of them. Qataŋun is also the term for the children of one's stepfather or stepmother by a former marriage (for an example see Household 4 in Appendix B). Such persons are restricted from marrying each other even though they are not biologically related. Step-siblings may come to regard each other as siblings.

The Household

LIVING QUARTERS. The composition of a household group and the anticipated length of residence determine the type of house to be built. The materials needed for various house types are usually readily available. For a nuclear, polygynous, or small extended family the caribou skin tent was the house most frequently built by the Nunamiut before 1950. According to Ingstad (1954: 38), this tent was dome-shaped, with an oval ground plan. When a family decided to build one, they selected a site that provided water, willows for firewood, and protection from the wind (primarily the north wind, secondarily the south wind). Husband and wife worked together and were often helped by close relatives or friends. If one spouse was busy with other tasks, the other could build the entire house. A level area about 15 feet across was selected and cleared of snow and other cover. The builder cut 23 willow poles, 12 to 13 feet long and as thick as a man's wrist or slightly larger; these were forced into the ground by hand, evenly spaced in an oval ranging from 12 to 15 feet in diameter.

The workers bent the poles toward the center, leaving approximately vertical walls 4 or 5 feet high. They tied several poles together with rawhide line at the apex of the dome, and some to other poles as they criss-crossed on the roof. The woman sewed 20 to 23 caribou hides together, usually 3 in a unit. The workers then stretched the hides over the walls and the roof with the fur out. An opening for smoke and excess heat was left at the top, and the woman often sewed a bear gut window into the roof or wall. The door was a grizzly bear hide which hung down from the top and was thrown onto the roof and then pulled down behind one as one entered or left. The woman, sometimes helped by her husband, cut several bundles of fresh green willow shoots the size of a man's thumb or smaller, about 3 feet long, which she laid in the house for a floor; several stones were set in the center of the floor for a fireplace.

Sleeping bags were sometimes made from caribou, sheep, or other light skins, but these were generally used by men when they were trapping or traveling. Normally, a person would place two or three bull caribou skins on the willow floor and cover himself with other skins or, if he were wealthy enough, with a marmot or rabbit blanket; today he might use a commercial sleeping bag. Bearskins can be used for sleeping but are heavy for traveling and the hair mats easily. A good bull caribou hide has no peer.

After the basic structure was completed, the workers packed sod, moss, and snow around the edge of the tent to keep out drafts and hold in the heat. In the old days the Nunamiut stretched caribou hides, with the hair removed, over the first layer of skins and then, if the weather was really cold, they piled snow on top. In the summer, the caribou skin with the hair removed protected the tent from rain. In the early 1900s, canvas replaced the outer layer of caribou skin. Commercial tents stretched over a spruce log frame for summer use became popular about 1950. Women often line the tent with caribou hides to give it added warmth.

The caribou skin tent comfortably accommodated a nuclear or small extended family of up to ten persons. The parents slept together on the side of the fire opposite the door. The youngest children slept closest to their parents and the older ones farther away. When two married couples slept in the same house, they stayed on opposite sides with the younger children in between; one mother would often comfort the other's children. In the summer, nowadays, teenage children usually sleep nearby in their own tents, either alone or with one other sibling. The tent in which the parents sleep, however, remains the family center where they eat, work, receive most visitors, and discuss any problems.

Nunamiut considered the caribou skin tent ideal shelter for many reasons. The primary materials—caribou skins, rawhide line, sinew, and willows—could be readily obtained in the Brooks

Range and the tent was easy to construct, requiring little time. Its main advantage, according to some informants, was its lightness and transportability. All the caribou hides necessary for a skin tent were only part of a sled load, and willows were likely to be available anywhere.

Today, because of reduced mobility, the need for the skin tent has lessened. As commercial tents have become available in exchange for furs and other objects, and since a family derives prestige from owning something new, especially if it comes from the white man, the old-style dome-shaped skin tent has disappeared. The technique, of course, is well known to most adults, and many canvas tents are lined with caribou skins, representing a carry-over from the old days.

Nunamiut families often built other types of houses. If a family planned to remain in a region for an entire winter, and possibly return in winters to come, they built a more permanent sod house, which was the forerunner of the most common house built today. Especially if the household was an extended family, a large, comfortable moss and sod house was desirable.

After a site was selected and the help of close relatives and friends recruited, several large willow poles were cut and spruce logs obtained, if possible. Subterranean houses are rare among the Nunamiut but, if the builders had time, they cleared away the moss and dirt where the house was to be built. They put in a layer of rocks and then a layer of moss. After the house was completed, a willow floor was laid down. A large extended family built a sod house with an elongated oval floor plan with sleeping areas at either end. The fireplace was laid, as usual, in the center. A tunnel entrance was built into the side of the house midway between the two ends. Meat, clothes, snowshoes, and other articles were stored there.

The frame of a sod and moss house was sturdier than that of a caribou skin tent. Spruce was used when possible. As soon as the workers thought the frame was strong enough, they dug up moss and sod from the tundra with shovels hewn from spruce wood and tipped with caribou antler. The walls were one to two feet thick, and the roof one half to one foot thick—a sturdy, warm structure. Today, because the Nunamiut have settled in what appears to be a permanent village, all families have built sod and moss winter houses. Men construct the frame of spruce logs, placing them side by side, vertically or horizontally; they haul the logs up forty miles from the timber, and logs large enough to hold the heat well are difficult to transport. Following the method of the old days, they enclose the log frame in a solid layer of sod. Most families use willow floors or, when available, lumber. Today, the men make stoves from sheet iron or oil drums and install them near one wall, using a stovepipe. The snow-block house was built only as an emergency one-night shelter. Occasionally a traveler might plan ahead to spend a night in a snow house. During the second night, however, after the snow house began to melt from the heat of the lamp, it became very, very cold.

In the old days parturition huts were constructed of a small willow frame covered with moss and snow. On rare occasions an old person, who knew he was going to die, built or had built a small hut so that his death would not affect the family house.

HOUSEHOLD COMPOSITION. The basic members of a household are the nuclear, polygynous, or extended family, but it is by no means exceptional for some other person to join a household for varying periods of time. An old, unmarried, or widowed person not only may live with a married son, daughter, or younger sibling but also may stay with an unrelated family for a season or part of a season. Such was the case in the household in which I lived. An elderly widower, who normally lived with a married son or daughter, lived with us for two or three months during the winter. He contributed meat, firewood, and other economic support to the household in exchange for several articles of clothing, meals, and other household services. The fur animals he trapped belonged to him. A distant relative who is poor and has no close relatives nearby may join a household. He would contribute the labor appropriate to his age and sex and receive the customary household services. A lone traveler, especially a friend in need of aid, may join a household for a while. Such was my position. A long-term residential guest is also expected to contribute labor, according to his age and sex. In a Nunamiut household, everybody works.

Thus, while we regard the family as the basic structural unit— the raw material in the formation of households—the household is the primary social group in Nunamiut society (see Appendix B for evidence supporting this distinction). Many households, of course, are composed exclusively of a nuclear or extended family, and the terms household and family may often be used interchangeably, as long as the conceptual distinction is held in mind.

DAILY HOUSEHOLD ACTIVITIES. Once a family builds a house, the members of the household must tend to a variety of daily tasks in order to exist. One of the absolute necessities for human survival in the Arctic is heat—heat to melt ice and snow for water (sucking below-zero ice and snow is not adequate) and to dry the perspiration in clothing (if it is allowed to accumulate, it will freeze solid). Every day, someone in the household, most frequently the woman of the house, must collect firewood.

When the members of a household are traveling or living away from concentrated settlements, gathering firewood is an easy task. The woman usually takes the initiative herself, in the morning or afternoon. If she is busy, her husband or another adult will sense, without conversation, that he should do it. If both man and wife are busy, the mother may ask a young daughter or son to gather firewood; even a child of ten or twelve can gather enough for a day from a good willow patch. In an extended family the older wife helps the younger wife to collect wood. When both women are otherwise occupied, the older husband is more likely to help with firewood because the younger husband is probably out hunting or trapping. Once the decision is made, the gatherer simply walks along, picking up dead willows; he usually ties them into a bundle for easy carrying. If it is dark he can distinguish the dead willows from the green willows by their lighter weight. Green willows do burn but very slowly, often allowing the house to chill. Once the immediate area is depleted, the gatherer must use a hand sled or dog sled.

When a household is part of a larger settlement, the immediate area is depleted of good firewood in a few days, unless people are camped in the timber. Longer and longer trips become necessary. Finally, in preparation for the second season, the older members of the household spend several days in May or June cutting green willows and piling them up to dry during the summer. Every two or three days during the following winter, someone hitches the dogs to a sled and brings in a load of the dried wood. In the old days, families were on the move so much that they were rarely forced to cut willows ahead of time. Today, after living more than a decade in the same locality, the several Nunamiut households are forced to plan ahead very carefully for firewood. Most of the spruce logs hauled up from the timber are used for house building and meat racks. A few logs are burned but constitute only a small part of the total amount of firewood needed.

In addition to the constant demand for willows, a household needs water for cooking and, especially today, washing. In the summer the woman of the house and the daughters carry most of the water in buckets from nearby springs, creeks, and lakes. When a woman is in the latter stages of pregnancy or otherwise incapacitated, her husband and sometimes her sons carry water. In the old days, pail-shaped buckets were made of slats and bottom pieces cut from spruce logs, tied together with baleen. Men hewed dippers from spruce roots, and even today they carve them from sheep horns. Nowadays, metal buckets and pans are widely used. In the winter, snow blocks are cut with a long knife (formerly of ivory or caribou antler) from the base of a hill or other snowdrifts and carried by sled to the house. If there is clear river or lake ice nearby, a woman usually chops out large chunks with an ax and transports them to the house by sled.

Although firewood and water must be brought in every day, there is no regular time for these chores. In the winter, most people work outdoors in the brief daylight hours from nine or ten in the morning until two or three o'clock in the afternoon. The main rule for bringing in firewood or water is not to let the current supply run out. The members of the household do not try to build up a surplus, which in general is contrary to the white man's notions—something I had to learn in practice as well as in the abstract.

Women do almost all the cooking. In the old days the Nunamiut used a bow-drill for lighting fires. A man made the bow from a strip of willow about a foot and a half long and strung it with a thin caribou rawhide line. The drill or shaft was usually carved from willow, with a cap of ivory on the top to absorb the friction, which was held either in a mouthpiece or in a receptacle placed under the knee. A man (usually) set the lower end of the shaft in a shallow cup of dry cottonwood or other wood and twirled the shaft with the bow. When the inside of the tiny cup began to smoke, any kind of fuzz, followed by wood shavings, soon produced a blaze. The fire was kept in a small ring of stones in the center of the house. To boil meat, women used to heat stones over this fire and drop them into wooden buckets filled with water and meat. Informants commented that this was a very effective way to cook meat. In the summer, a woman often used to build a fire outdoors and hang meat over the open flames, a method commonly used today. Nowadays matches are used to light the firewood in a sheet-iron stove, and a woman boils the meat by simply placing it in a large metal pot full of water on the stove.

A woman brings a large chunk of caribou meat into the house almost every day from the meat rack or from the permafrost cellar to let it thaw before cutting it up for cooking. Every Nunamiut eats some frozen meat, but rarely eats it thawed and uncooked. After the meat is boiled, the woman of the house sets the pot in the center of the floor, or sometimes, today, on a low table. When there are delicacies or a scarcity of meat, the woman doles out equal portions. Otherwise, each person in the house takes a piece of meat, eats it with a knife, then takes another until he is satisfied. Then everyone sits back, drinks large quantities of tea, and thinks how nice it is to be an inland Nunamiut Eskimo eating the best food in the world.

If all the members of a household are at home all day, they eat the principal meal at noon or an hour or two afterward. In the old days, breakfast consisted of a small piece of meat and fat left from the previous day, eaten from cups or bowls sewn from sealskin with a double stitch. Today, most Nunamiut drink coffee in the morning and eat sourdough hotcakes made of flour, water, baking soda, salt, and sugar. A few households can afford to have butter and syrup now and then. In the evening the woman of the household may fry caribou meat and boil rice if it is available. If a family is traveling or out hunting or trapping all day, the woman usually prepares the main meal in the evening. It is very common to skip a noon meal and eat only breakfast and a heavy, late dinner. When men are out alone hunting and trapping, they must of course do all their own cooking.

In return for the invaluable transportation provided by dogs, they must be fed every day except in cases of no meat or extreme laziness. This chore usually falls to the woman of the household, although the husband and teen-age sons often help. Toward evening she takes meat from the cache, cuts it up, and throws a portion to each dog. She may water them any time during the day. Once or twice a week, the woman or her husband boils a huge pot of entrails, meat, and grease and dishes it out to the dogs. This should be done a day or so after the dogs have had a strenuous trip, otherwise they will become very thin. Women also care for the puppies.

A constant task around the house is the disposal of waste. When a person makes a mess, either by working or by accident, he is supposed to clean it up, but he rarely does a thorough job. It is usually up to the woman to clean the floor of the house. A few women clean a little each day, others allow dirt to accumulate and clean it up all at once. Most trash is burned. After a person's hair is cut, all the hairs are gathered up very carefully and put into the stove. After my first haircut in the household, I grabbed all the hair and started to run outside up over a little hill and throw the hair to the winds. Two or three persons laughed and called me back to burn the hairs, or else, they said, birds would find them and put them in their nests. That would not be so good. There was no particular reason for this—just the thought of it.

One of the most regular daily tasks is repairing one's material possessions. Most adult members of the household are constantly repairing traveling equipment, clothes, and the house itself. A primary quality of Nunamiut Eskimo artifacts is lightness in weight. To achieve this, most items are made from a great many small, rather fragile parts. While an entire object may be very strong, its components are easily broken and have to be continually repaired or replaced—a few stitches on a pair of boots, a slat in a sled, or a string in snowshoe netting. One of the basic daily tasks is to keep one's material possessions in usable condition. Men used to carry their tools in a bag made from wolverine head skins.

It should be noted that most of the daily tasks are performed by the women in the proximity of the house. The women play a major role in their daily maintenance of the household; they provide a base from which the men are able to search the countryside for game and the highly valued fur-bearing animals.

SEASONAL HOUSEHOLD ACTIVITIES. Let us now consider how the household responds to seasonal changes in the Arctic climate and the concomitant alterations in the fauna (see Appendix C for seasonal calendar). For example, the description of hunting during the fall is concerned primarily with caribou. The exploitation of such animals as bear, moose, and mountain sheep and of birds such as ptarmigan during the fall will be found in a later chapter.

FALL. During September, October, and the first part of November the members of all Nunamiut households actively prepare for the coming winter. Many caribou must be killed. Large quantities of caribou meat and fat have to be cached against the possibility of a winter dearth of caribou and in hope of permitting some time for trapping and leisure activities. Skins are prepared and made into warm winter clothing. Any grizzly bears, moose, and mountain sheep which a man kills add to the winter supplies of meat and fat and increase the store of hides. The family house must be repaired and made ready for the cold winter winds. New sleds, snowshoes, and dog harnesses have to be made and old ones repaired.

During the fall, the primary responsibility of all able-bodied males in the household is to kill as many caribou as possible. Formerly all the households in a region banded together and cooperated very closely during the fall migration of caribou in a massive attempt to corral and kill huge numbers of them. Now, as pointed out above, the introduction of guns enables hunters to be independent; this, with the reduction of the Nunamiut population, brought cooperative hunting to an end. These cooperative hunts were essentially a group phenomenon involving organization among several households and will be described later.

Here we shall focus our attention on the household itself, the men of which today hunt independently during the fall migration, but usually in the same general area. Members of different households may hunt together, but they divide the kill equally among the hunters, each of whom brings his share back to his own house for its exclusive use. Each man is responsible for killing enough caribou for the winter supply of his own household. In cases of extreme need, when, for example, the man of the house is sick and no lineal relatives are living nearby to help, a close collateral relative such as a brother, uncle, or nephew may hunt for the distressed household. In return he is assured of hospitality whenever he visits. As a close collateral relative, he can of course expect hospitality, but offering to hunt for a household strengthens the bond.

In the early fall, most people are busy repairing the house, winter traveling equipment, and traps. The moment word of caribou comes, the men, in a turmoil of excitement, prepare themselves for the hunt.

In the old days an individual hunter carried a bow carved from a single strip of birch backed with hundreds of sinew fibers twisted and braided together, often by the women, to give it resiliency. A few bows were made without the sinew backing. A man twisted three or four strands of sinew together for a bowstring. A hunter made his arrows from spruce, feathered them with tail or wing feathers from a goshawk or any large bird, and tipped them with points of flint or caribou antler made in different styles for warfare, caribou, and birds. For protection from grizzlies and for killing wounded caribou, a hunter carried a birch-shafted spear with a point of flint, caribou antler, or bone from the forearm of a grizzly bear.

Before 1890, a few flintlock and cap and ball rifles were prized possessions. The blackpowder .45-70 (first made in 1873), the .45-90, and the .44-40 were the most popular rifles during the early days of whaling (1890–1900). These rifles were replaced soon after 1900 by the Winchester .30-30 (first made in 1894) and the Winchester .25-35.* Ranges on the tundra are very long; a man can go for months and never have a shot under 150 yards. Telescopic sights are desirable if the hunter can afford one.

Pistols are known but generally not thought to be of much use. Two or three Nunamiut own pistols and one man has killed a grizzly with a .22 pistol. He had four dogs which makes quite a difference; as one white man said, even a trained ground squirrel would help in hunting grizzly—anything to distract the bear's attention.

When caribou begin to migrate from the north slope through the valleys of the Brooks Range to the timber, the husband and elder sons of a household do not go out hunting because they think it is fun. Prestige is certainly to be gained from success, but a feeling of responsibility and obligation to the other members of the household is the most commonly expressed motive for hunting. For several weeks during the fall, the men take up their guns and teapots and walk out from the village up into the valley close to the mountains where caribou often travel. On any given day during the fall, not all households are necessarily represented by a hunter in the field. A few men hunt day after day, others hunt frequently but spend many days working on the house and equipment, and a few men hunt only sporadically because of laziness.

Although the men of a community hunt singly during the fall

---

* At present the .243 Winchester and the .270 Winchester are vying for popularity, followed by the .257 Roberts and the .222 Remington. Among the rifles found at Anaktuvuk Pass are the .22 Rimfire, .22 Special, .218 Bee, .219 Zipper, .22 Hornet, .22 Highpower, .222 Remington, .222 Magnum, .220 Swift, .243 Winchester, .244 Remington, .25-20 Winchester, .250-3000 Savage, .25-35 Winchester, .257 Roberts, .264 Magnum, .270 Winchester, .280 Remington, .30-30 Winchester, .300 Savage, .308 Winchester, and .30-06 Springfield. Most Nunamiut reload their own ammunition with good results. Only rarely does a gun explode.

migration, most of them do hunt in the same region and, as members of the same community, they try to avoid spoiling each other's chances. If one hunter walks up into the valley early in the morning two or three hours before anyone else, he and others in the village may feel that he is taking advantage of other hunters, in spite of the general sentiment that getting up and working early in the morning is a good thing. If a man situates himself ahead of all the hunters in order to have a first shot at the caribou, both he and the rest of the village may feel that he is spoiling other hunters' chances by making the caribou wary or possibly by scaring them up into the mountains where they are out of range.

If several men from different households spread out over a valley and shoot separately and independently at the same herd, each man claims and skins the caribou he shoots. If two or more men are standing together, they usually divide the kill evenly, but if one of the hunters had killed very few caribou in the season, and the other had already cached a large quantity of meat, the former may take a larger share of the kill. And if a more affluent hunter kills most of the caribou, he might decide to be generous and offer the others a larger share. While hunters voice the principle of equal division of a kill, the factors of need and the desire to be known as generous may affect the division of the hunt.

Caribou often come within a mile of the village as they migrate through the main valleys and on occasion may be shot from one's very doorstep. Most of the year, however, caribou rarely venture close to human settlements. When the fall migrations begin, excitement mounts to a fever pitch in the village. The more experienced hunters walk to one of several strategically located stone blinds in the morning and often stay there all day. Not infrequently, when the cry of caribou is heard or gunshots ring out from the hills, a younger man, sometimes encouraged by his mother, runs toward the herd, hoping to obtain a share of the kill. Caribou run to higher ground when frightened and a hunter running up from the village seldom has much luck. Although a young man will brag for days about how fast he can run up to a herd and shoot two or three animals, the conscientious hunter who walks up into the hills day after day is much more likely to kill six or eight caribou at a time and do so more often.

After a hunter shoots a caribou, he carefully removes the skin. If he has killed many, his wife and elder sons and daughters may help him skin, butcher, and transport the animals. In the old days men skinned caribou with knives chipped from flint, either single- or double-edged, but more commonly the former. Double-edged knives were generally used for killing people. Women's knives *(ulus)* were made in the well-known semilunar style. Occasionally slate was used. The Nunamiut believe that slate was used in an earlier historical period and that, as flint came into use, life became easier. Today, of course, jackknives and sheath knives are used. Women's ulus are usually made by a father, husband, or son, from old saws with antler handles.

To skin a caribou, it is placed on its back and a cut is made down the front of the front legs from the hoof to the sternum, down the back of the back legs from the hoof to the anus, and from the anus to the lower lip. The skinner peels the leg skins down as far as he can and pulls the head and neck skin back, making a cut around the antlers if required. He uses his knife to separate the skin from the flesh whenever necessary. He then pulls the skin from all four quarters and the stomach; from there it is easily pulled off the back toward the tail. The green skin is laid out carefully on the ground and allowed to dry or freeze.

After the skin is removed, the hunter cuts off the four quarters and the head and turns the carcass on its right side (because the stomach is on the left) to take out the guts. He carefully slits the abdominal muscles from just below the sternum along the left costal cartilages toward, but not all the way to, the animal's crotch. He then delicately slits the peritoneum, taking care not to puncture the stomach, and reaches into the cavity with his hands. First he loosens the stomach and small intestine from the inner side of the abdominal cavity. Then he grasps the esophagus just below the diaphragm where it joins the stomach and gives a mighty heave. The skilled or lucky workman pulls the intact stomach and small intestine from the carcass, but a novice may rip the stomach and spill the stomach contents into the abdominal cavity which then must be cleaned out by hand.

The butcher then severs the abdominal muscles from the rib cage. He removes the tenderloin strips by running his knife between the strips and the transverse processes of the vertebrae. He makes a small cut near the tail in the tough sinew (which is dried and used for thread) backing the tenderloin strips and pulls them out by hand toward the neck. He then cuts through the costal cartilages connecting the ribs to the sternum. After cutting the flesh attaching the first rib to the neck, the two rib sections are broken apart. The remaining connecting muscles are easily cut with a knife. The heart, lungs, bronchial tubes, and liver are removed in one piece. The neck and pelvis are severed from the main backbone. For easy carrying, the backbone may be cut into several pieces. The kidneys are usually left attached to the lower vertebrae and the tongue is sometimes removed from the head. Anyone planning to skin and butcher caribou would have to learn many other techniques, but to a person skilled in handling animal carcasses, this description will serve to indicate the method employed by the Nunamiut.

There are many variations in butchering caribou; the determining factors are how the meat is to be transported and how long it is to be stored. If it is to be stored for a long time, the caribou is not skinned but only quartered, deheaded, and eviscerated; then it is stacked up on a hillside. If, say, a woman is planning to carry the meat home by dog pack, she may even sever the meat from the legs and separate the leg bones from each other with her ulu.

After a man finishes skinning and butchering his caribou, he caches the skins and most of the meat right on the tundra for the moment; he usually brings some home to be eaten that night. At a later time—the next day or maybe several weeks later—the meat is brought to the house by sled or by dog pack. If the hunter is busy, his wife and elder daughters often bring the meat home. Women very frequently handle dog packs before freeze-up. Although men usually handle the sleds, some women are very able dog drivers.

Once the meat is brought to the household, the woman takes charge of the cooking. It is also her function to present gifts of meat and fat to other persons. During times of stress her first responsibility, beyond the members of the household, is to her parents and other lineal relatives. The second is to her siblings, especially if they reside close by or in the same village; the third is to her husband's parents. Beyond these persons the woman may distribute meat to such close relatives as cousins, aunts and uncles, and nieces and nephews of any member of the family, and to friends. No particular cut of meat or part of an animal is associated with or customarily reserved for any particular relative. A gift should be a good piece of meat with fat on it if possible. If a relative is known to relish a certain delicacy, a person often makes an effort to save it for him as an expression of affection. Once I obtained a green bearded seal hide from Point Barrow for rawhide line, which still contained the two front flippers. The household I was living in consumed one flipper and the woman of the house gave the other to her father. Another time the man of the house and I were hunting 25 miles from the village. We had the good fortune to kill a fat bull moose. My companion made a special point of saving the fat around the lower esophagus for his mother-in-law who, he knew, loved that kind of fat for breakfast. As his wife did not accompany us on this hunt, the man's daughter and sister-in-law (an adopted daughter of his mother-in-law) assumed the responsibility for handling the gift as well as the rest of the meat.

One of the most important tasks performed by the women in the fall is preparing hides and making clothing. Among the Nunamiut, the hair is almost always left on the hides; in preparing them, the method described here is the most common one.

Once a skin is dry, it may be either stored or worked on immediately. A woman does most of the work on hides, but a man does some scraping, either to prepare a hide for a dog pack or gun case he is making or just to help his wife if they have many children or she is ill. The first task is to remove the inner membrane and any particles of fat with a scraper. In the old days, men chipped scrapers from flint and hafted them in handles carved from the gnarled crotch of an alder tree. Now and again a woman sharpened the scraping edge by pressure-flaking it with a tool of caribou antler. Today scrapers are made from a two- or three-inch section of an old shotgun or other similar metal tubing. The handles are still made as in the old days, except that the method of hafting has been altered to receive a section of tubing. After the inner membrane is removed, the skin is allowed to dry for a day or two. The skin will crackle slightly if pinched, when it has become dry enough to be moistened. Today, most women rub Ivory soap and water into the skin. Formerly, a paste of boiled brains or liver and water was used. The woman folds the moistened hide with the skin side in and puts it under her sleeping skins. After two or three days the skin has thoroughly absorbed the moistening agent and is ready to be worked again with the scraper. The more the skin is scraped, the softer and more pliable it becomes. The woman usually scrapes a skin at least twice and often four or five times. For a particularly fine finish she uses flour or, in the old days, fine sand as a friction agent in the last scraping. The skin is then ready for use. Girls aged ten and twelve learn to scrape skins and help their mothers. Generally a teen-age girl scrapes skins for her own use and sometimes for articles for her father, brothers, and maybe a boy friend, but the mother of a household carries the main load of work on skins.

In the fall, women spend many hours making caribou skin clothing. A few men can make such simple garments as skin socks and mittens, but it is the responsibility of the woman of the house to clothe the members of her family. In an extended family with two competent women, each clothes her spouse and unmarried children. Even toward an older, unrelated man, a distant relative, or a guest who is living in, the woman feels a certain responsibility for his clothing needs. A widower might learn to sew boots, but he is likely to be scorned if he cannot find some woman to sew for him, although he may brag about his sewing ability. A teen-age daughter makes many items for herself, but her mother makes her parka.

Women used to carry their sewing things in a bag made from caribou leg skins. In the old days, needles were made from caribou bone, walrus ivory, and sometimes caribou antler. Thimbles were made from bearded sealskin. Today, of course, commercial skin needles and thimbles are used. Men remove the sinew from the back and legs of caribou and women hang it up to dry in the house. Sinew is used as thread for practically all kinds of sewing, as well as for removing particles of food from between the teeth. Mountain sheep sinew is also used but is less satisfactory than caribou for waterproof sealskin boots and kayaks. If no caribou or sheep sinew can be obtained, there is a little sinew along the breast bone of a ptarmigan. Women have sewn whole parkas with ptarmigan sinew. Moose and bear sinew are considered very poor.

In making a parka, a woman does not use a pattern. As a young girl, she watched her elders sewing and, as she herself began to sew, she was constantly instructed by her mother, grandmothers, aunts, and possibly mother-in-law. When a mature woman begins to make skin clothing, she has already had considerable training and experience. A woman looks very carefully at the person for whom she is making a parka (usually when the person is unaware!). She selects a well-scraped caribou calf skin and uses the head and neck skin as the base for the hood and the back skin for the back of the parka. For men the inner parka is short, cut just below the waist in a pullover style, loose fitting, with the fur side in. For women, the inner parka is much longer (reaching below the knees), is also a pullover, and is loose enough to permit her to carry a baby on her back or to nurse it inside the parka. The large, round, upright ruff for the hood is a combination of four strips of wolverine and wolf and is quite striking in appearance, complementing nicely the roundish face of Eskimo women. For men, the ruff is usually one strip of wolverine (sometimes wolf). In extremely cold weather an outer parka is worn; this is frequently made of caribou calf skin with the fur side out but fundamentally of the same pattern as an inner parka. An outer parka is often worn for appearance as well as for warmth. Both Eskimo men and women are extremely conscious of their looks and go out of their way to dress as well as their means permit. While little effort is made to beautify a dwelling, everyone carefully observes and comments upon the appearance of a person at a dance or on other occasions. If a woman is able, she will make outer parkas for her husband, herself, and her children from such furs as marmot, rabbit, ground squirrel, fox, wolf, or lynx. Even the neck skins of loons have been used for parkas. Nunamiut women greatly enjoy and take pride in trying out new materials and combinations for outer parkas. To-day, women make parka shells from calico in a variety of patterns and colors.

In the old days, and occasionally today, a woman made caribou skin trousers, with the fur inside, which came just below the knees. Men frequently wore only the inner trousers. Today a few women make ankle-length inner trousers, but most of them make trousers with the fur outside, using the zipper, pockets, and belt loops from a pair of old pants. Usually a man wears long underwear with these outer trousers.

A mature woman makes a variety of boots. The basic winter boot is made entirely from the leg and back skin of the bull caribou. Boot soles are cut from the heavy scraped back skin of a fall bull caribou. No pattern is used, but a woman with experience can easily estimate the size of sole necessary for a certain foot. She cuts the upper part of the boot, extending from either just below the knee or from just below the calf down to the top of the foot, from a scraped leg skin of a fall bull caribou, in a shape reminiscent of a gaiter. She then sews the uppers to the sole with a one-inch band of scraped caribou hide. The boot sole is always sewn with the fur inside. The band running around the edge is usually sewn with the fur inside, and the skin side is often dyed with alder bark. Women collect the bark in the early fall before freeze-up, grind it, soak it in hot water, and apply the mixture to a scraped skin.

The seamstress frequently turns the fur outside for the uppers of a boot; snow is easily brushed off the hair of a caribou leg skin and many Nunamiut like its appearance. For really cold weather, however, a boot is much warmer if the uppers are sewn with the fur inside. For early fall and late spring, boots are made in the same basic design, but bearded sealskin is used for the sole. The band connecting the upper to the sole is narrower, usually about half an inch. For a boot with a bearded seal sole, an insole of caribou skin, loon or duck skin, grass, or unbraided rope is needed. Waterproof boots for summer are made with a bearded sealskin sole with uppers of common seal. No band is used to connect the two parts; they are sewn directly together with two strands of sinew twisted together. The back skin of a bull caribou can be made waterproof by soaking it in water, scraping the hair off, stretching it out to dry, and then rubbing seal oil into it. A skin prepared in this manner may be used for the uppers in summer waterproof boots.

In addition to these basic items of clothing, a woman makes many other garments in the fall and throughout the rest of the year. She is constantly making skin socks from scraped caribou cow skin with the fur side in. The socks are simply made from a sole cut an inch or so wider and longer than a person's foot and an upper as described above. No band is used. As in the summer sealskin boot, the sole and upper are sewn directly together. Young bull caribou skin may be used for socks, and sheepskin is very warm. Mittens are best made from mountain sheepskin, although cow caribou is better than nothing. To make a mitten, a woman cuts two pieces of sheep or caribou skin slightly larger than an outspread hand. The two parts are sewn together with the fur out, and the fur side is then turned in. For very young children, socks or mittens are sewn onto the trousers or parka. Sometimes a woman makes fingered gloves from sheep or caribou skin. In the old days, a scarf made from the tail skin of a red fox was very much in style and was also very warm. Hats of almost any fur were valued for their appearance, although beaver, otter, marten, and mink were preferred. Belts were sometimes made from wolverine claws or porcupine quills.

Most indigenous clothing is still made. The main innovations are wool socks, rubber boots for summer use, pants, long underwear, shirts, and a variety of jackets, hats, and gloves. Many articles of white man's clothing, properly used, supplement skin clothing very well.

Men's main work with hides, other than skinning, is making rawhide line. For this task, a man selects a hide free from blemishes. He rubs water into the skin side until it is very wet and pliable. The hide is then wrapped very tightly with the skin side in and tied; the bundle is hung near the ceiling of a house where it is warm. After about two weeks, when the hide becomes rotten, the man takes the hide down and pulls the hair off by hand. After he takes a breath of air to recover from the odor, he washes the remaining hair off and pulls as much of the inner membrane off as possible. He makes a cut one third the length of the hide, equidistant from both sides, starting a third of the way from the end of the hide. Beginning from the inside of the skin, one person uses a knife and a U-shaped guide made from antler or ivory, with a slot to hold the knife across the legs of the U at a distance from the bottom of the U to give the desired width of rawhide line. Another person handles the skin and takes up the line as it is cut from the inside.

Rawhide line made from cow caribou is used for snowshoe netting and other light work. Line made from caribou bull is used like any heavy cord. The rawhide line made from bearded seal and moose is like rope and may be used for the towline of a sled pulled by as many as ten dogs. Young walrus rawhide is sometimes traded in and used for towing the open skin boats.

Aside from hunting and caching meat and hides, the main occupation of the man of the house during the fall is the manufacture and repair of winter traveling equipment. A father usually makes the snowshoes and sleds which a son in his late teens or even early twenties uses. A mature son-in-law and a father-in-law living in the same household normally make equipment for their own use. When a new couple joins a household, the father-in-law may present gifts of a pair of snowshoes and a sled to his son-in-law, but in a very few years it becomes a matter of pride for a man to make his own traveling equipment. Women rarely help in this work. A few women in the old days knew how to net a snowshoe, but none does today.

Before the first heavy snows of late fall or early winter, a man either makes a pair of snowshoes or repairs his old ones. The winter before, if he happened to travel down into the timber, he looked for a straight-grained birch tree. In the old days, trees were felled with an adz made of jade, if available (traded in from the Kobuk River) or, more commonly, flint or chert. The birch log is kept either frozen or soaking in water, because once dried out, it cracks and cannot be used for snowshoes. The first task in making snowshoe frames is to split the log into four equal pieces. If the grain is straight, the log will split easily. A man usually works from the base toward the smaller end. Even the straightest birch tree curves slightly, but after a little experience anyone can see the best way to split a log. After four nearly equal sections are obtained, the snowshoe-maker whittles them into narrow strips about an inch wide and an inch and a half high.

In the finished snowshoe, the bark side touches the ground. Each strip is shaped with the front and back ends thinner than the middle. Only experience with birch logs will enable a man to judge the strength and best contour of a strip. After the green strips are properly shaped, the worker ties two together at each end, pulls them apart in the middle, and inserts two sticks to hold them apart. He bends the front ends upward and ties them in place with heavy cord. Then for three or four days the frames are allowed to dry.

The Nunamiut make two basic types of snowshoe frames. One is pointed, with the front bent up four to six inches. Small pointed snowshoes have only two crosspieces; larger ones have three or four, according to the maker's idea of a good snowshoe. Men prefer pointed snowshoes because they can run faster on them. The other kind is the Loucheux-type or rounded-front snowshoe which is made by tying the front ends of the rims together and bending them around a pre-made form. Women prefer these because the pointed snowshoes catch on their long parkas. For walking in brushy country men also prefer the rounded snowshoes.

The length and width of snowshoes depend on the age, sex, weight, and activeness of the individual. A large man traveling in the timber might need snowshoes 6 feet long and 12 inches wide. A child's first pair is usually 1 foot long by 5 or 6 inches. The most common size is 4½ to 5 feet long and 8 to 9 inches wide.

Cow caribou rawhide line is laced in a triangular pattern for snowshoe netting. Bull caribou rawhide line is laced lengthwise and bearded seal rawhide line is laced crosswise for the foot. The foot binding is usually of bull caribou rawhide line, although bearded seal is sometimes used.

The Nunamiut have tried skis, but they have never become popular. Snowshoes, from my experience as well as from conversations with Nunamiut, seem much more satisfactory for hunting and traveling in the interior of Arctic Alaska.

Nunamiut men are very proud of their craftsmanship in making snowshoes. A few young men in their late teens and early twenties learn from their fathers to make snowshoes, but most boys will turn to a grandfather. Because a boy often lives with his father into his twenties, there is an unexpressed feeling of competition between the man of the house and the maturing son. Thus, although a son learns such things as hunting, trapping, fishing, and house building from his father by virtue of proximity, when he has a choice he usually turns to an immediate male relative living nearby. Grandfathers and uncles are favored for advice. During the early years of marriage, a father-in-law is a likely source of instruction although less desired than a blood relative. One informant learned how to make both snowshoes and sleds from an uncle.

Perhaps the most difficult job a man has to perform in the fall is to build a sled. Many years of experience are required to know at just what angle a stanchion holds up best, or just what kind of rawhide binding lasts longest. A man does not have to build a sled every year of course, but he has to make repairs based on the knowledge of the techniques of sled construction.

In the old days, the sledmaker split a long, straight-grained spruce log with an adz and spent several hours hewing the strips into runners which were later shod with whalebone or walrus ivory. The worker heated several shorter strips of spruce and bent them into upside-down U-shaped stanchions with the two legs lashed to the runners and the joining part of the U acting as a crossbar underneath the inside floor slats. A man usually built a sled with the floor about 9 inches from the ground, 18 inches wide, and 6 to 12 feet long. Sled rails, sometimes of birch, were held in place by spruce rail supports and sidepieces. These pieces were slightly notched and lashed tightly with bull caribou rawhide line, often through a hole bored with a bow-drill having a bit of walrus ivory or caribou antler in the perpendicular piece. The maker fastened the handlebars securely with the top crossbar, handle sidepieces, and a large X-shaped lashing. A sled constructed carefully from good materials will last for years, providing an excellent means of transportation over the tundra and requiring only occasional small repairs, such as a new lashing or a new rail support.

In recent years the Nunamiut have tried a variety of sleds. Many people like hardwood basket sleds of hickory (or other wood) and value them for their aesthetic appearance. They are easily damaged, however. A few Nunamiut have tried toboggans, but they break too easily on rocky tundra trails, although in the timbered regions apparently they are satisfactory. The most popular sled today is made from two long runners of spruce, about 2 inches thick by 8 to 10 inches high and anywhere from 8 to 16 feet long, nailed together with crosspieces 1 inch thick, 3 inches wide, and from 16 to 20 inches long. Runners are shod with thin strips of green spruce for the coldest weather and strips of steel for the early fall and late spring. Handlebears are fashioned as in the old days although with fewer and larger pieces.

In making traveling equipment today, the Nunamiut use a wide variety of imported tools such as saws, hammers, planes, files, grindstones, pliers, wrenches, screwdrivers, axes, chisels, and so forth in place of indigenous primary tools.

The description of the fall activities of the household, which emphasizes the exploitation of and adjustment to the environment and the sexual division of labor, is based on observation and participation supplemented by informants' statements. It is the typical pattern to be found among those Nunamiut living in the Brooks Range mountains. This is not to say there is no variation. In one household, the man and woman may well perform all the tasks indicated above in one season. A man in another household might have a pair of snowshoes and a sled in good repair; he will thus spend more time hunting caribou, trapping fur animals, helping his wife, or just doing nothing.

In recent years, all the Nunamiut living in the Brooks Range have remained there throughout the year. Before 1920, however, many Nunamiut in the fall were returning from trading expeditions to the coast. While these families were returning inland along the Colville River and its tributaries, the men and women performed many of the same tasks which the mountain-dwelling Nunamiut were tending to. After pitching camp in the evening, women were free to scrape skins and make clothing. During the day, men may have seen caribou and hunted them. Any surplus fat was saved for winter supply.

By late fall, in the old days, all the Nunamiut had returned to the mountains. The households which had been unable to obtain

caribou calf skins for making parkas traded for them from households having a surplus. In return, the mountain dwellers received
quantities of blubber and sea mammal skins. Today, of course, with
all households remaining inland, each family is responsible for obtaining its own calf skins, and products from the white man have
largely replaced the items traded in from the coast.

WINTER. By early November the temperature may drop below
−30° F for several days at a time. Usually the lower the temperature, the less windy it is. If a household fails to cache a good supply
of meat, fat, and skins during the fall, the winter months of November through February can be a long, cold, hungry struggle for
survival. The migration is over, and spring is a long way off. Most
of the caribou are feeding quietly on the south slope deep in the
timber where few Nunamiut dare to venture; a few feed in isolated
spots in the northern Brooks Range protected from the wind.

A household that is poorly prepared for the winter, either because of laziness or bad luck, has two choices. It may decide to
separate itself from a concentrated settlement of households and
attempt to find game on its own, or it may remain near more
affluent families and hope to be able to eat through kinship ties
and the desire of the wealthier households to be known as generous
and hospitable. The man, wife, and children all have a voice in
which alternative a household selects. Children complain that they
are very lonely living away from the community, and Nunamiut
fathers and mothers take their children's complaints to heart. The
man of the house, on the other hand, may feel a certain pride in
wanting to provide for his family. He may also want to try his luck
in trapping wolverine, wolf, and other fur-bearing animals.

A woman often supports her husband's desire to hunt and trap,
but she may have parents or a sister in the community near whom
she wishes to live. No one person or interest dominates exclusively.
I observed an instance in which teen-age children thwarted their
father's desire to trap far away from the community, a decision
detrimental to the household's economic condition although it increased their opportunity for sociability. Other examples attest to
the singular ambition of the man of the house to trap extensively.
On occasion a woman encourages and may even subtly ridicule her
husband into rousing himself to go out and trap. The determining
factors in a household decision are the personalities of those who
attempt to express themselves and the feelings of guilt (from lazi-

ness) or righteousness (from industry) felt by everyone involved.

During most of the winter, then, many households remain together, sometimes traveling as a group up and down the valleys of the Brooks Range in search of game, and sometimes camped in one spot for several months. How well a family prepares for winter determines its position and prestige within a community. If the autumn preparations have left most households well off, the winter may be a time of dancing, visiting, and intense sexual activity.

In times of plenty, the activity of a household living in a community settles down to a comfortable routine. Every day, of course, someone has to collect firewood and water. While the woman of the household is primarily responsible for these tasks, her husband, son, or daughter, if unoccupied, may hitch up the dogs and bring in a load of firewood or ice. On occasion, when a small herd of caribou wanders near the settlement feeding, the men rush out to shoot them and bring in the meat. When a household is well supplied with meat and the man decides not to trap extensively, he frequently occupies his time by making things. In the old days, a man carved sheep horn dippers or chipped implements to be traded to coastal Eskimos in the spring. Today a man with time off from hunting often makes such items for sale as ivory carvings, skin masks resembling human faces, miniature snowshoes, toy kayaks, and replicas of indigenous tools for museums. A woman, once she sees to her daily responsibilities, may spend her time making extra boots to trade to the coast or perhaps an especially fancy parka for herself or a member of her family. Many women now make boots and occasionally a parka to sell to non-Eskimos visiting or working in the Arctic. A few individuals with spare time merely do nothing.

One of the major activities of a good winter is visiting. Over several months' time, any single household will be visited by every person in a settlement. Older people talk quietly among themselves for hours about past incidents and occasionally about current gossip. When an older person stops in to visit, the woman of the house makes tea for him, and if he stays until mealtime, he is served as a member of the family. Active, middle-aged people tend to circulate less freely for purely social reasons, since they are primarily responsible for running the household; such persons are more frequently the hosts. Young, unmarried men and women visit most often. A boy visits a male friend just for the fun of joking and talking, or they may plan to go out hunting the next day. When a young man becomes interested in a girl, he visits the household on the pretext of talking with her brothers. He may not speak to her at all, but each carefully notes the other's presence and, most certainly, appearance to see whether there has been any special grooming.

Adolescent girls usually associate in pairs and constantly visit each other in their respective households. Girls do not visit as freely as boys but may take the initiative in visiting a household where a prospective suitor lives. If a young visitor remains for a meal, he eats with the members of the household. A teen-age girl may be expected to help wash the dishes and a teen-age boy to carry in a load of firewood or to perform other similar tasks. A frequent visitor accumulates an obligation over time and may discharge it by giving the family some meat or by helping them to build a house.

Young children visit very freely. Boys and girls of eight or ten years of age often carry such messages as invitations to a meal, a request to borrow a tool, any important news, and even certain items of gossip. Young children are given food when the household eats, just like any visitor. Sometimes as many as seven or eight visitors partake of a household's meal. When many visitors are present, the woman portions out the food equally, particularly if there is a scarcity of meat or if she is serving a delicacy. When there is plenty to go around, she merely sets the pot of cooked meat on the floor or on a low table and everyone serves himself.

At times a person may sense a feeling of guilt or irresponsibility. Just before the woman finishes cooking, a visitor may leave despite repeated injunctions to stay and eat. Such a person may know that he is lazy and is ashamed of constantly receiving what he is too indolent to offer. On the other hand, some member of a household may press hospitality on a visitor, hoping to curry favor or establish a claim on the recipient's generosity. Or a person may offer hospitality as proof of his hunting prowess and largesse.

An especially good winter may offer much leisure to a household and even to a whole community. Many long evenings and nights are whiled away by visiting, playing games, eating, gossiping, and engaging in sexual intercourse. A few persons become bored with their routine existence and long for the excitement of hunting, trapping, and traveling through the country. If such a person re-mains in a community, he accustoms himself to doing very little or submerges himself in social activity. But the desire for prestige does not allow some individuals to rest long. Driven by ambition to amass wealth and possibly a feeling of guilt from, or a fear of, too much indolence, a few households decide to go it alone despite the ease of community living. If the members of a household have worked hard during the fall and have built up a large winter supply of meat, fat, and skins, they are free to trap extensively. On the other hand, especially if the community as a whole is poor that winter, a household with few winter supplies may have no choice but to forage alone for itself.

While informants talked on and on about the good times of a long winter spent dancing, visiting, and eating, such prolonged conviviality was not, nor is, the norm by any means. The fauna of the Brooks Range is not plentiful year in and year out, as attested by the numerous stories of hunger and starvation. It is not unknown, in spite of hard work in all the households of a region, that winter may come before adequate supplies of meat and fat can be stored. Then if a winter dearth of caribou develops, hunger, starvation, and even death may ensue. In moments of crisis, families may band together in fear or spread out over the country in a last attempt to find game. Either course may end in death or bring salvation; there is no rule.

When a household is no longer secure in a large settlement, its most pressing need is to obtain caribou or other meat. Let us turn our attention to winter household activity as the families of a Nunamiut band separate into small groups wandering over the land in search of game and fur-bearing animals.

In the old days, before the advent of guns, hunting caribou in the winter with bows and arrows was exceedingly difficult. A very skilled hunter could shoot enough caribou without using other means, but often he had to enlist the help of other hunters to stampede a small herd of caribou up a small ravine or hill where he lay in ambush. When the caribou came into range, the archer loosed his arrows as fast as he could. Then he ran at full speed after the herd, trying to shoot more. If the snow was deep and he had good snowshoes, a hunter could sometimes kill several caribou before they escaped. If two or three runners on snowshoes cooperated closely, they could bring down many caribou with amazing feats of skill and endurance. Even with guns, caribou hunting on a still, crisp winter day requires careful judgment of the caribou's reaction to the hunter.

Before the Nunamiut obtained guns, most hunters relied on

snares to supply their families with meat. A caribou snare, typical of snares used for moose, mountain sheep, lynx, and other animals, was made from a strong piece of rawhide line 12 to 15 feet long and two willow poles 5 to 6 feet long. When possible, Nunamiut hunters traded bearded seal rawhide line from the coast, already cut into proper lengths for snares, and packed twenty to a bundle. A good bearded seal line could easily hold a bull caribou and was just under a quarter inch in diameter. If bearded seal line was not available, a man braided three or four strands of bull caribou rawhide line together. The man setting the snare tied the line to the base of a large trunk in a stand of willows in a creek which caribou were likely to cross. Two poles were forced into the snow or ground, about 2 or 2½ feet apart, one of which was near the large willow trunk. If possible, there were thick willows on both sides of the poles which would channel a caribou toward the opening. From the base of the large trunk, the man wrapped the line once around a pole, bringing it up to shoulder height. Then he draped the line across to the other pole and wound it down to knee height (for a cow). The line was then draped back to the first pole where a slipknot was tied, joining the line to itself to complete the loop.

When a caribou passed through the opening enclosed by the loop, its legs and chest pulled the line tight around its neck; it was usually killed by the hunter with a spear, or it starved or froze to death. In the old days the Nunamiut relied very heavily on snares during the winter months when caribou are difficult to approach. If a household moved into the timber, the men set much larger snares for moose. If they were near a region plentiful in mountain sheep, smaller snares were set high in the small creeks coming down between two mountains across which sheep tracks had been seen.

When a household camps near a lake, the man or woman sets a net of sinew or cow caribou rawhide line (or today, commercial gill nets of linen or nylon) across the open water of an outlet. Women or men check the nets twice a day. In places where fish are known to run, men chop holes in river or lake ice with ivory ice chisels. Single fishhooks are made in a teardrop shape about 1½ inches long, ½ inch wide, and ¼ inch thick. A second piece about ¾ inch long and 1/16 inch in diameter sharpened to a point was attached at about a 45° angle from the larger piece (a sharpened nail now replaces the smaller piece of ivory). The fisherman baits the hook with a small piece of meat and ties it to a short stick with a 1- or 2-foot length of sinew. He drops the hook 1 foot or 18

THE FAMILY AND THE HOUSEHOLD

inches into the water and jerks it slightly every few seconds to attract the fish. The moment a fish bites, he pulls it up through the hole and throws it onto the ice where it freezes in less than a minute.

Winter is the time for serious trapping. During much of the fall and spring, the fur of many animals is in good condition, but most Nunamiut are then too busy hunting caribou to run a trap line. When winter arrives and the household leaves the community, the man of the house sets out his traps.

A man usually concentrates his efforts on one kind of animal during a given trapping season. If he decides to pursue the wolverine, the household moves to a region they are known to frequent. The trapper roams over the region on foot or by sled in search of an area where wolverine tracks abound, and then he builds a rock deadfall. He may have to go to a talus slope a quarter mile away for rocks not frozen into the ground. A teen-age son might accompany him and help carry the rocks. The first task is to place rocks about 6 inches high and 2 or 3 inches thick upright in a rectangle (about 3 feet long and 2 feet wide) around a large piece of meat. The trapper then looks for a flat rock, 4 to 6 inches thick, large enough to cover the entire rectangle. Such a rock is so heavy that it must be transported by sled to the site. The hunter props it up with a trigger made from two long, slender pieces of rock, and places one rock vertically between the heavy cover rock and the midpoint of a short side of the rectangle to form a support. The cover rock is held about 9 inches to a foot above the ground. The trapper then lifts the cover rock and its support, and a helper places one end of the second rock, the actual trigger, horizontally under the support. Most of the trigger extends inside the enclosed area. As the wolverine reaches for the bait it touches the trigger and jars the very carefully balanced support, causing the cover rock to fall and crush the animal.

If a man is really in earnest about catching wolverines, he sets up several deadfalls and checks them every week or so during the winter. A story an informant enjoyed telling was about a trek several Nunamiut made in search of wolverines one winter some time before 1900 when a community was camped just north of the Brooks Range.

A small group of men left their families and, carrying only bows and arrows, spears, knives, extra boots, needles and sinew, and a few pieces of dried meat and fat, walked scores of miles into the Anaktuvuk Valley, across the divide, and down along the John River and its tributaries deep into the timber. The men huddled over fires in the night and occasionally built snow-block houses and willow lean-tos. Everywhere the men went, they built rock deadfalls for wolverines. In the old days, there was a supernatural restriction against catching more than five fur animals of a single species in a given trapping season. A few of the men caught their full quota of five wolverines, while others caught only three or four. After one and a half or two months, the intrepid Nunamiut trappers returned from the valleys of the Brooks Range to their homes, full of stories about their trip and enough prestige to last for months.

Although rock deadfalls and rawhide line and sinew snares were the most frequently used devices for catching fur-bearing animals, an imaginative trapper would experiment with various ways of catching animals. Constructing a small willow house with a triggered door, digging a pitfall under an animal trail, or freezing a coiled piece of baleen or a sharpened stick of green willow in a chunk of liver or blood were among the different techniques Nunamiut have tried over the years. Once, long before 1900, a Nunamiut developed a method of catching fur-bearing animals which made him an *umialik* (rich man) and won the respect of later generations for his ingenuity. He placed several old meat carcasses in a spot as bait and set up a fence of sinew and rawhide line around it. He left an opening several feet wide so animals could enter without having their suspicions aroused. He then constructed a small snow-block house on the leeward side of the enclosure. When an animal entered, the man pulled a section of fence across the opening and shot the animal with a bow and arrow.

Today Nunamiut trappers use commercial steel traps extensively. A very few rock deadfalls and rawhide snares are still in use. In one month during the winter of 1958–59, one Nunamiut snared four caribou and two mountain sheep. Sinew snares for ground squirrels and ptarmigan are commonly used. Most Nunamiut trappers set trap lines for wolf, wolverine, and fox. Occasionally an energetic man goes after marmot, ground squirrel, and sometimes beaver, marten, and lynx.

During some winters, February may be the hungriest month of

the entire year. Fall supplies have long been exhausted, and winter caribou usually have little fat. Many meals in February are nothing but lean boiled meat—a hunger diet. The winter I stayed at Anaktuvuk Pass, February was such a month. Every hunter searched the countryside by sled and on foot in search of caribou. Mountain sheep were skinny and hardly worth killing. Neither moose nor bear were to be had. Marmots and ground squirrels were hidden in hibernation. A few men and women snared ptarmigan in willow thickets. Every now and then some hunter killed a few caribou; his household was then besieged with visitors, and immediate relatives received gifts of fresh meat. The spring migration of caribou was many days in the future. All trade supplies any person could obtain were soon eaten but provided little satisfaction to people accustomed to a heavy diet of meat and fat. Usually no one dies as the direct result of a month's hunger and, although everyone lost weight, most people remained healthy. In early March when herds of fat caribou began to migrate from south to north, people gorged themselves with fresh meat and fat from their first kills.

During the long winter months the household responds to the environment more as an autonomous unit than at any other time of the year. During the fall and spring all households band together, and the community functions as the primary unit in exploiting the environment. In a social sense, the household is always primary; it is within the household that a person's rights and responsibilities to other persons are most keenly felt. When households come together, the group as such becomes important to individuals but never replaces the supremacy of the other bonds. Although a household may be part of a community during the winter, in terms of an active relationship to the environment it becomes an independent unit.

The Arctic winter can make life hard for a household, not so much because the weather is cold and snowy, but because the primary food animals are no longer as readily available. During the spring and fall, and less so in summer, a hunter usually has the opportunity to supplement his family's diet of caribou with sheep, moose, grizzly bear, marmot, ground squirrel, ptarmigan, ducks, geese, other birds, and a variety of fish. During the winter, on the other hand, caribou are scarce and thin, moose occur very rarely in the northern Brooks Range, and bears, marmots and ground squirrels are hibernating. A few ptarmigan are to be snared; ducks, geese, and other migratory fowl are far to the south; and only a few fish are available. It is difficult for a white man to imagine how still and silent the countryside can be on a calm winter day. At times there is not a sign of life for hundreds of square miles. A household that fails to make adequate preparations during the fall must hunt and snare the reduced winter food resources from day to day if it is to survive.

The families that have stored plenty of meat and fat during the fall are often free during much of the winter to trap and to make items for trade or for sale. A household that has prepared itself well in anticipation of seeking the highly prized fur animals is greatly aided by the seemingly inhospitable snow and cold of the Arctic winter climate. Fur-bearing animals leave evidence of every move. Changes in winter weather are only in terms of slightly differing degrees of coldness. Nunamiut clothing and travel equipment are better adapted to the Arctic winter than to any other season. Cold dry snow provides an excellent surface for travel by sled and snowshoes and is easily brushed off caribou-skin clothing. Nunamiut speak of winter as a difficult season, yet look forward to it as the time of greatest mobility and opportunity for trapping— if only there are enough caribou!

SPRING. In the first part of March, winter abruptly turns into spring. In early February, the sun first becomes visible over the horizon but only for moments at a time, with little effect on the weather. Not until March does one suddenly realize that the temperature is a little higher and that dawn and dusk are coming earlier and later. The weather is still very cold during March and April in comparison with more temperate climates, and the wind may blow for days at a time. But the Nunamiut welcome the light offered by the sun and begin to think of the coming spring migration of caribou.

In late February and early March, most families are scattered over the countryside. Several days before the migration, and certainly before break-up, all households return to the village (or, formerly, gathered together in one of the locations used in previous years for caribou corrals). In the old days the spring was almost exclusively a time of group action—caribou drives, communal eating, dancing, trading, and possible warfare. The household remained of course the primary social unit but, in response to the seasonal changes brought by spring, the group became the principal means of exploiting the environment. Especially after a lonely winter, most families are very happy to see each other again, and one hunter is very careful not to antagonize another by sloppy hunting practices.

In earlier times, after the members of the community had killed as many caribou as they could, and each household had received its share, the families which had trapped successfully during the winter usually journeyed to the north coast for trading. Other families remained in the mountains to make a living hunting caribou, marmots, ground squirrels, birds, and fish.

Today the Nunamiut do not drive caribou nor do they cooperate on a community-wide basis during the spring. In recent years the Nunamiut have split up into as many as five (and as few as two) small family groups spread out within a fifty-mile radius of Anaktuvuk Pass during the winter. When spring comes, however, all families return to the now permanent village to hunt and store away meat for the summer. As in the fall each household hunts as an independent unit. The men walk up into the valley each day and wait for caribou to pass by. Meat is carried by sled to the house. Much of the meat is hung up in strips on racks to dry, and some is kept in permafrost cellars for summer consumption.

In the old days, all those families planning to go to the coast for trading left before break-up in May. The families that had not collected enough animal skins to trade, did not possess an umiak or have ready access to one through a relative, or merely liked the inland life remained in the mountains. After the tightly knit group action during and shortly after the spring migration of caribou, the household regained a large degree of self-sufficiency. Today of course, because of the introduction of guns and other changes and the cessation of trading to the coast, all families remain inland and retain a considerable measure of autonomy. During May, then, both formerly and today, individual families living in the mountains continue to prepare for the summer.

One important source of food in the late spring and early summer is migratory birds. In the old days a man made a bolas by tying from one to five stones or ivory balls together with rawhide line. The hunter stationed himself on a lake shore or other likely place where he thought birds might travel. When a flock of migrating birds came near, he hurled the bolas into the air, trying to entangle as many as possible in the lines. Large birds could be snared at their nest or attracted to snares by feathers or other brightly colored objects. While snow was on the ground, a hunter could splatter fresh blood around to attract birds to pieces of meat bearing concealed hooks. Foot snares made of baleen were placed just under the water where waterfowl might feed or nest. Today the Nunamiut snare only ptarmigan and, in general, hunt fewer birds. Shotguns are highly valued for birds but are very costly, as is the ammunition. I saw only .410, 16, and 12 gauges at Anaktuvuk Pass. One old Eskimo tried out a 12-gauge for the first time on a flock of ptarmigan. He got five in one shot. He turned to his adult son and said, "My! . . . pretty good rifle." The son, now 65 years old, still laughs about that incident.

When the last of the snow melts in late May, the sleds can no longer be used. A living site for the summer must be selected where there is water, firewood, and (hopefully) an opportunity to hunt the occasional caribou, mountain sheep, moose, and grizzly; it is also wise to select a summer residence near a good source of fish. The Nunamiut used to make a fishnet from sinew, but it had to be kept in the water all summer and was good for only one summer. Men used a three-pronged fish spear (leister) made from caribou antler with a willow or birch shaft; they attracted the fish by a piece of bait or some brightly colored object. Men sometimes made small fish traps for use in creeks and small rivers. A fish trap shaped like the frustum of a cone was made from strips of willow tied with sinew or cow caribou rawhide line. The trap was about 24 inches long, the smaller diameter 12 inches, and the larger 18 inches.

Imported nets have replaced sinew nets. Some Nunamiut make their own nets from commercial thread. A few fishhooks, dry flies, and spinners are used, but older Nunamiut prefer their own fishhooks. I saw one fish spear and one fish trap in use.

The State of Alaska offers a bounty of $50 for a wolf. During the winter, of course, many men hunt and trap wolves when they can, but in the late spring wolf pups can be found if the hunter knows the location of the dens. Most or all the snow has melted in early June and a party of two to four hunters, aged 16 through 40, uses dog packs to carry camping equipment, meat, and other supplies. A few hunters stay out for more than a month, others return in a week or two. Wolf pup hunters usually walk at night because there is plenty of light, it is cooler, and wolves are up and about at night. When a party spots a den with a bitch and pups, they try to shoot the bitch and then capture as many of the pups alive as they can (to be sold for $100 or more to zoos or individuals); if a pup gets out of reach, the hunter shoots it. Sometimes hunters chase pups into a den and attempt to pull them out alive. Many wolves have been killed from airplanes and, since Nunamiut hunters have hunted extensively in their present region, fewer and fewer wolf pups are to be had.

Lineal relatives and siblings rarely hunt together—men prefer to hunt with such collateral relatives as cousins, uncles, and nephews. A man very frequently hunts with an in-law such as his wife's sister's husband, his wife's brother, or his aunt's husband. Unrelated friends also hunt together.

Household activity during the spring differs considerably from that of winter. The transition from the lonely, individual day-to-day struggle for existence to the exhilarating cooperative efforts of the community to exploit the dramatic spring migration of caribou is eagerly anticipated by the Nunamiut. Along with the caribou, other animals such as grizzlies, marmots, ground squirrels, and ptarmigan are suddenly available to hunters. Spring is a time of very hard physical labor. The hunting and processing of meat is only part of the work—spring is also the time when a family often moves all its household possessions to a new location. As the trails begin to deteriorate with the melting snow, each sledload of meat, logs, and supplies becomes more and more difficult to handle. By June, everyone welcomes the inactivity that summer offers.

SUMMER. This is a brief season in the northern Brooks Range. The Nunamiut consider the summer to extend from the latter part of June to the end of August. Summer activity is far different from the rest of the year. Mobility is greatly reduced with the absence of snow. For short trips and light loads, dog packs (made like saddlebags from a single bull caribou skin with the fur outside) are used. One man and several dogs might travel for days, but it is exceedingly difficult to move all of a household's belongings by dog pack.

Summer food resources are limited, and as a household usually spends the summer in one location, it must rely primarily on caribou killed that spring. Toward the end of a July I spent at Anaktuvuk Pass, a woman complained, "These days (July) all animals are poor" (i.e. have no fat). This reflects the major difficulty of summer even if hunters manage to find game. A few caribou remain in the mountains during the summer and occasionally wander close to camp. Singly, and in pairs of cow and yearling, moose travel up from the timber, through the valleys of the Brooks Range to the north slope. Many are intercepted by Nunamiut hunters. Ground squirrels, marmots, and mountain sheep are so thin that hunters seek them only in critical times. If several households are camped near a large lake, fish are available and may provide some fat, but most Arctic fish are very lean. Few birds are to be caught during the middle of the summer in the Brooks Range.

July can be the worst month of the summer. Mosquitoes are a constant pest. One summer many years ago they were so numerous that they killed a dog. Mosquitoes rarely disrupt household activity but may annoy people day after day and tend to keep them indoors. July is also the warmest month, with temperatures in the seventies and eighties; to a Nunamiut Eskimo, that is too hot to do anything.

During much of the summer, household activity is limited. Women must continue to carry firewood and water and to cook, but men often have little to do. They occasionally look for animals, which rarely are to be found. People visit, of course, and there is plenty of time for games. Children love the summertime when they are free to run and play over the tundra. Parents in their leisure frequently make toys for their children. Almost every material object that occurs among the Nunamiut can be made in miniature as a toy, and young children will play for hours with the simplest contrivance. Women sew balls from a piece of caribou hide with the fur side tucked in. A stick, preferably of spruce, is used as a bat for a variety of games. Dolls are made from caribou calf skins stuffed with clipped hair. Boys play at hunting with young ground squirrel skins that are stuffed with moss. Well constructed toy kayaks and umiat afford months of pleasure for the little ones. Tops, yo-yos, and a version of mumblety-peg are among the myriad of indoor games. String figures, or cat's cradle, are very popular and require real dexterity and originality. Playing string figures provides an opportunity for socializing, conducting races, and inventing new string forms or recalling almost forgotten ones. A good toy bow and arrows are the pride of any sturdy young boy. The skin of a moose leg that a thoughtful father carefully prepares and brings home serves as a sled on steep slopes near home for the children. Both men and boys love to contest their strength by a tug-of-war. The two contestants stand facing each other, each with a stick in his hands joined to the other by a piece of caribou leg sinew, 2 to 3 feet long. The first to pull the other across a line wins. Young men sometimes play tug-of-war with their fingers.

A multitude of trade toys have come to the Nunamiut in recent years, ranging from toy airplanes and space rockets to jack-in-the-boxes. A few precontact games, such as string figures, are played less often today because of the many substitutions. Nunamiut parents love to buy their children toys whenever they have a little extra money.

Russian card games seem to have reached the Nunamiut before 1900, followed by poker. The Nunamiut are impulsive poker players and a white man, accustomed to the slow, careful calling of another's bet, or the calculated bluff, has to change his style to the fast clip of an Eskimo game.

Today, the summer influx of white men considerably affects Nunamiut summer activity. Both men and women make a variety of objects to sell to visitors. Young men are anxious to secure part-time jobs as guides, handymen around camp, or unskilled workers, but the demand for work far exceeds the opportunities. A few young men stay around camp, hoping to find a job occasionally, neglecting less prestigious pursuits such as hunting caribou and wolves.

In August, in the late summer, life improves. Mosquitoes diminish, and mountain sheep are fatter and are no longer forced by mosquitoes to remain high in the mountains. Some bull caribou spend the summer in the timber and travel to the north slope in August. They are usually very fat. If a hunter is able to shoot several fat bulls in August, his family may eat well while waiting for the fall migrations.

In late August many plants are ready to be gathered. This is almost exclusively the task of women. The mother and elder daughters of a household walk out into the countryside, usually within hearing distance of the men in case a grizzly shows up, to gather berries and roots. Berries are simply plucked by hand and were put into the dried stomach or bladder of an animal; today a cloth bag or metal bucket is used. The berries are eaten raw or mixed with grease and meat and stored away for winter. If a woman collects a really large quantity of berries, she might put them into a sealskin poke along with blubber, roots, dried meat, and dried fish. Edible roots grow along gravel bars and riverbanks and are often grubbed up by a woman with a caribou antler or similar tool. After they are washed they may be eaten raw or, better, roasted over an open fire and served with blubber. That is good eating for a vegetable-hungry white man. Roots also may be stored with blubber, meat, and berries for winter usage.

The first cold wind of late August shakes people out of their summer ease and reminds them of the coming winter. Hunters begin to think of all the caribou they hope to kill during the fall migration and then how many wolves, wolverines, and foxes they will trap. The few households that have lived alone during the summer in an effort to catch fish, trap ground squirrels, and hunt in quieter regions join the more concentrated settlements in anticipation of the fall migration of caribou.

The summer, like the winter, is a time of relative household autonomy, whether a family lives in a village or not. Each household of course must see to its daily responsibilities of firewood, water, and cooking, and any hunting and fishing is exclusively an individual matter, except when two or three hunters band together. Making articles to sell to visitors and sporadic, temporary employment are also an individual matter.

4. The Individual

THE emphasis so far has been on the members of the household as the primary social group, the nexus around which revolves most of the activity directed toward survival and comfort. In order to see more intimately how a residential unit functions, let us examine the status and prestige of individuals within the household. I use here the biological factors of age and sex (and the concomitant expected marriage) as the dimensions for defining status and then describe each status in terms of the division of labor, the relationships with persons in one's own and other statuses, affection, and the gain and loss of prestige.

The term status may be used in several different ways: as a position in a behavioral pattern, as the sum total of a person's statuses in a society (Linton 1936: 113), and so forth. The consideration of status here, which uses only the dimensions of age and sex, is particularly revealing because no person in Nunamiut society is ever born into a position different from anyone else's. No person ever succeeds to a position by right of birth or by his relationship to a man who dies. In the broadest sense, all Nunamiut belong to the same status, namely, that of being *iñupiaq* (a real person or "Eskimo"). A treatment of status within the household will indicate, in most instances, the status of a person in the society at large. The bond of kinship, of course, affects the relationship of the member of one status with any person of the same or other status, but each status as defined by the biological dimensions of age and sex is supported in the society as a whole by a number of common behavioral attributes. There are two major exceptions.

The first is the *umialik* (rich man). In terms of several specific behavior patterns, such as certain aspects of economic activity, the settlement of legal cases, and the sparking of political activity, an umialik occupies a status different from that of other persons (see pp. 180–89). The position of umialik can never be inherited, succeeded to, or transferred to any other person; it can only be earned.

The second is the shaman. In terms of religious activity, he enjoys a distinct status. A shaman is not a full-time religious specialist and he must do his own hunting and trapping; in fact, he can ensure his status in religious activity and demonstrate his power by the success of his own hunting.

Thus, while it is appropriate to mention these two instances in which certain individuals enjoy a special status in a particular activity, the purpose here is to analyze the status determined by the age and sex of an individual within the household and the society at large.

One's prestige is a function of how one performs the role expected of him. If he does moderately well, his prestige is on the plus side and he is thought of as a nice person. If he performs his tasks particularly well, is generous and outgoing, his prestige increases; he strengthens the ties with the members of his own family and others consider him to be a very fine person. If he rebels from his role, is lazy and refuses to do what he really should, his prestige declines. His family may say nothing but he knows how they feel; he may sense that other people are talking behind his back. Whenever someone refuses to do him a favor or responds slowly and grudgingly to a request, he knows why. It is a painful retribution. A person not only avoids great pain by performing his role well but also experiences the pleasure of knowing that people are talking favorably about him, behind his back as well as to his face. When he asks a favor or is in need, people are more responsive.

Status and Prestige of the Individual Within the Household and Society

Infancy, male and female (*ilyiligaq*); birth to 1 or 1½ years; from birth until the baby begins to talk. I once heard a Nunamiut man remark that the most important thing in life is to have babies. Another Nunamiut made the flat statement that life is no fun without children. Such comments reflect the status of an infant, who enjoys the greatest attention he ever experiences in life, with the least effort. An infant is disciplined very little and is constantly rewarded with affection for being good or for any appealing behavior. It is constantly in the hands of a mother, older sister, grandmother, or one of the males of the household. Even young children of 6 or 7 care for an infant sibling for short periods of time with the greatest tenderness. An infant is expected to respond to the affection given by others. In a sense, an infant that cries all the time may be said to suffer a loss of prestige. One that does not cry, especially when a stranger enters the house, enjoys higher prestige.

Childhood, male (*nukatpiagaruq*); 1½ to 14 or 15 years; from the time a boy begins to talk until he reaches puberty. A child 1½ to 3 years of age is able to walk and talk a little, but not until it is 4 or 5 is it really considered a human being. A young boy is expected to contribute by helping his parents at small tasks. He learns to bring firewood into the house, sometimes as early as 5 years of age, and to put it into the stove. He is of course praised for helping, but he learns very soon that this is not idle play. Similarly, throughout the childhood years a boy is expected to absorb all the traditional knowledge he can as well as to develop and increase his craftsmanship and proficiency in making things. Only in this manner will he, as a young man, become capable of contributing to the welfare of his family.

Boys are often told to carry messages and news from house to house, which they are expected to do immediately and responsibly.

Young boys are very aware of sexual differences and occasionally tease the girls. Generally, however, boys tend to associate with one another; they consider themselves superior to girls, and vice versa. They dress differently from girls and are teased differently by their elders. Young boys kill mice and birds with sticks and rocks and engage in rough play, which young girls seldom do.

Parents rarely restrict what a young child does. In attempting to evoke response to a request, a parent or other relative may appeal to the importance of their kin relationship as such, offer praise to the child for responding to the request, or point out that performing the act is in the child's own best interest. Only when a child fights, or is selfish toward a sibling or very close relative, does a parent actually criticize him. Only once did I see a mother beat a child, which shocked everyone who saw her. A young boy does not receive the attention and affection that he did as an infant, but he knows he can always turn to his parents and relatives for help or sympathy. The affection of the family is normally focused on a newborn sibling, and a boy is encouraged and even praised for displaying affection toward it.

If a boy performs his role well, he wins the recognition of his family, older relatives, and others in the community. The more generous and persistant he is in learning and working, the more prestige he enjoys, but if he begins to fight, lie, or cry with little provocation, or is uncooperative and slothful in his actions around the house, word passes immediately among the members of the community. His parents and others scold him for fighting and constantly enjoin him to work or to make some effort. Such a child (and they are few in number) may become very withdrawn and flare out violently at times or turn into an ingratiating pest. But, it would seem, for some boys to enjoy high prestige, other boys must provide the contrast of suffering disgrace.

Childhood, female (*niviaksiagaruq*); 1½ to 13 or 14 years; from the time a girl begins to talk until she reaches puberty. Like the boys, a young girl learns to help with such small tasks around the house as bringing in firewood, cleaning up, and looking for lost articles. Girls often gather a few berries and roots near the house and now and then help their mothers to collect firewood; they usually learn to scrape skins and sew long before puberty. Unlike boys, girls are rarely asked to be messengers. During their childhood, the girls are expected to absorb as much as possible of the knowledge and experience they will need when they assume the role of a mature woman.

Girls too are aware of sexual differences and learn to be shy and demure at a very young age. They consider themselves superior to boys; one does not hear little girls say they wish they were boys. Girls under 12 sometimes tease young, unmarried men in their late teens and early twenties but rarely boys of their own age; they tend to associate with other girls and they stay closer to the house than boys do. A girl is expected to be a little less noisy and boisterous than a boy. Otherwise, the virtues of obedience, cooperation, generosity, and refraining from crying, lying, and fighting are the same.

The kind of prestige a young girl enjoys depends on her behavior around the house—how cooperative and generous she is. If she shows signs of becoming an able and interested seamstress and helps her mother willingly as a hostess to visitors, elders joke with her about how nice a wife she will make for some strong hunter. A young girl rarely, if ever, lies or fights, but if she is lazy or jealous, her prestige falls and people wonder what kind of a wife she will turn out to be.

Adolescence, male (*nukatpiaq*); 15 years until marriage (18 to 30 years or, rarely, later); from the onset of puberty until marriage. When a boy begins to grow tall and his voice changes, he is considered to be a young man. He becomes an economic asset to the household, compensating, hopefully, for his childhood years as a liability. A teen-age boy is capable of handling dogs and helps to bring in meat from the hunt, ice chopped from frozen lakes and rivers, and good-sized loads of firewood. A young man is expected to assume part of the work in managing the dogs, and he should learn to feel responsible for seeing that they are fed. As his interest and efforts increase in tending the dogs, he, as an emerging member of the adult group of a household, becomes a part owner of the dogs. This ownership is expressed by his saying "my dogs" when referring to them, which a child never does. Later, when he leaves the household for marriage or other reasons, he and his elders decide how many dogs he shall take with him.

When a father thinks his son is able and willing, he takes him along on short hunting trips and lets him shoot, pointing out his mistakes and praising him for his successes. When a boy has demonstrated courage, endurance, and skill in hunting with his father, he will go on short hunting trips alone or in the company of other young men. By the time he is 15 or 16, he has killed several caribou on his own and possibly has had a chance at moose, bear, marmot, and mountain sheep. For the Nunamiut, to become a man is to become a hunter. The comments and expectations of attractive young ladies, male friends, members of the household, relatives, and other people in the community build up in the mind of an adolescent boy, forcing him to do his best and to keep trying in the unending pursuit of caribou. By the time a boy has reached his late teens, his reputation as a hunter is established. If he is basically a good hunter, he is expected to continue being one; if his luck fails over a long period of time, people look at him askance. If a young man is actually a poor hunter, tiring quickly on the trail or unable to shoot accurately under pressure, he is expected to improve; if he does not, people may come to tolerate him, but he will never enjoy much prestige.

As a child, a boy makes a few things and possibly learns some simple stitches. As a teen-ager, when he begins to use hunting and traveling equipment on his own, he is expected to learn how to make snowshoes, sleds, dog harnesses, meat racks, traps, and snares and to repair clothing. Although a young man usually learns to hunt, travel, and trap from his father, he usually turns to a grandfather, uncle, father-in-law, or, in rare instances, an older, close friend for instruction in making things. Many teen-age boys develop a real interest in their technology and respond eagerly to their elders' advice. People soon notice an industrious young man and compliment him heartily, for example, on the first pair of snow-shoes he makes. A few teen-agers are indolent and careless about handicrafts—exactly why is hard to say. For whatever psycholog-ical reasons a young man fails to develop an active curiosity and positive approach toward making a living, as a member of a small community associating with the same persons day after day, it be-comes more and more difficult for him to alter his dilatory, apa-thetic ways.

In the old days when the men of the community maintained a communal house during much of the year, teen-age boys accom-panied their fathers in the evening when men gathered to work to-gether. Here they listened to the wisdom of their elders and re-ceived advice about all manner of practical things. Men exchanged experiences, told folktales, and recounted the historical legends of their people. Today, as a karigi is erected for only a few days four or five times a year for dancing and communal eating, most of this practical and verbal training takes place in the various households.

In listening to their elders today, young men learn songs and what legends and folktales are still told, and hear the personal ex-periences of mature men in recent years. With the absence of a written tradition, the spoken word seems remarkably important and powerful among the Nunamiut. In addition to the practical advice gleaned from listening, young Nunamiut learn to use their language in an expressive and compelling way. One frequently notices young men listening intently to their elders as they describe past incidents, attempting to impress their audience with their skilled use of language and their own courage in facing the harsh realities of the Arctic. In reply to a question about a sled trip I made with an older Nunamiut during the early part of breakup, I found myself using his colorful expressions in describing our fortitude in handling our sled in the rushing torrents of spring melt-water over the surface ice of a frozen river enclosed between the precipitous walls of a rocky gorge.

Adolescent boys enjoy great camaraderie; friendships between two and three boys are very close but generally not so close as be-tween two girls. Young men often hunt, trap, and travel together as well as visit and joke back and forth. At dances, boys wrestle stren-uously with each other to keep off the dance floor, but once a boy is pulled to the floor, he must dance. There is no homosexuality as far as I could determine, although there is a good deal of sexual joking and mild horseplay among boys. Adolescent boys are very shy in the presence of teen-age girls and tend to prefer and to feel more secure in the company of their own sex. As a young man nears 20, he comes under increasing pressure to look for a mate. He is expected to lose his chastity and he usually does.

The people of a community derive great pleasure in joking with teen-age boys about their incipient love affairs and their developing prowess as hunters. While parents rarely express overt affection for a teen-age son, they may brag about him to other people.

Young men gain prestige when they hunt extensively, help with male tasks around the house, work hard at learning the Nunamiut technology presumed of men, and listen closely to their elders. A teen-ager who does not lie or steal is talked about as an honest boy and a good prospective in-law. Should a teen-age boy fall into the habit of lying, the whole village finds out and he bears a mark for years, if not for life. He will have difficulty persuading a girl's parents to let her marry him. Even in the same family there is differential treatment between the son who is honest and industrious and the son who is dishonest and lazy.

Adolescence, female (*niviaksiaq*); 14 years until marriage (16 to 25 years or, rarely, later); from the onset of puberty until marriage. When a girl approaches puberty she also becomes an economic asset to her family. She is able to collect firewood, scrape skins, sew, help with the dogs, take a hand in building a house, and gather berries and roots. The most important ability for her to develop is her skill as a seamstress. As young children, most girls learn to prepare skins and to sew a little. If her mother has many young children, an elder daughter of 10 or 12 may even do most of the sewing on a younger sibling's parka. This is rare, however. More often, a girl of 10 or 12 has learned enough to sew herself a pair of boots under her mother's supervision. A young girl often turns to her grandmother or aunt for instruction; by the time she enters her teens, she may be capable of sewing mittens, caribou socks, and simple boots completely on her own. During her teen-age years, a girl gradually perfects her ability, but she may not make a parka until she is 20. The full range of Nunamiut clothing is so complex that a woman is often 30 or 35 before she can be considered an accomplished seamstress.

The most arduous physical task an adolescent girl has to perform is collecting firewood. In her childhood, a girl gathers some firewood, following her mother around, but as a young woman she is expected to gather enough firewood in one trip to last for a whole day. A teen-age girl often hitches up three or more dogs and drives them herself; she does not enjoy the same sense of ownership of dogs that her brother does, but she is supposed to assume part of the responsibility for feeding them and caring for pups. Upon marriage, some of the family's dogs may go to the son-in-law through the daughter.

Only a very few girls learn to hunt or trap, but they are greatly admired by men when they do. The women who hunt do so very seldom, and there is no feeling of the invasion of maculine prerogatives. I could not determine what women who do not hunt feel about a woman who does—probably a touch of jealousy among themselves, but pride in the face of men, in that one of their sex is capable of performing a masculine task. The oldest woman living in Anaktuvuk Pass is very skilled with a .30-30. At 150 yards I have seen her shoot a 3-inch group. In her earlier years she shot probably hundreds of muskrats, many caribou, moose, and about ten years ago at the age of 55, a grizzly bear. Although a few young women learn to shoot and hunt, most of them never fire a rifle. One older informant told me that in the old days most women could not paddle a kayak. Only during the adolescent years does a girl learn to handle men's implements, if at all. Once a woman marries and settles down to raising children, she rarely has the time or the inclination to "play" at learning these things.

Young girls visit frequently back and forth. It is common for two unrelated teen-age girls to form a very close friendship. They work together, sewing, collecting firewood and ice, joking with each other about boys in a fairly ribald manner at times, and even engaging in mild sexual horseplay, such as pinching each other's breasts. When a girl acquires a serious boy friend and marries, her relationship with her closest friend is greatly altered. The unmarried girl may regard the boy friend or new husband as an intruder into their special friendship. In such a close human relationship, strong feelings can be aroused. In a moment of jealousy, the ousted friend may even remark that the new husband has upset their friendship.

The girls are very shy in the presence of boys, often casting their eyes down when they pass on the trail. Girls begin thinking of marriage earlier than boys do, but they are rarely in a position to take the initiative. Once a young man begins to notice a young lady, she may easily arouse his interest by making boots for him, graciously offering him tea when he visits and, ultimately, making herself sexually available to him.

An adolescent girl gains prestige by her reputation as an industrious and skilled worker, and by her love and care for young children. The people of a community are quick to notice and to comment on a young woman who displays a sense of hospitality when visitors stop by the house and who is reserved and attentive to the advice of her elders.

A young woman suffers a loss of prestige if she becomes lazy or sexually promiscuous. A reputation for laziness spreads rapidly through a community, and young men are less desirous of a lazy girl even if she is good looking. The Arctic is a difficult place to make a living, and a man is less likely to think of a girl seriously who would not do her share in the work of the household. A girl creates a bad reputation if she engages in sexual affairs when very young, but a girl approaching her late teens is implicitly expected to have an affair or two as a prelude to marriage. She gains a certain amount of prestige by doing so—demonstrating her sexuality, as it were. Should a girl in her late teens or early twenties become promiscuous, it is considered likely that she would be unfaithful in marriage. And the people, knowing the power of gossip in a small community, greatly enjoy talking about promiscuous girls. The same feeling, to a slightly lesser extent, applies to young men.

There is less overt concern about a girl's veracity than a boy's. Perhaps girls just do not dare lie and I met no clear-cut case of a girl's doing so. Girls are not so able to roam and cannot leave home as easily as a boy (a very rare occurrence but the possibility, as an idea, does exist) should social pressure become too great. In this sense, a young man may be said to be more free to lie if he is so inclined. If a girl lies, the public censure and shame are very strong.

Among the Nunamiut a pretty young girl is a romantic ideal. Through the eyes of hard-working, mature men and women, here she is, unmarried and with no children, attractive to young men and teased by married men, often having a very close girl friend with whom many happy hours are whiled away, and proud of herself as a potential mother of children and of her developing ability as a seamstress. On the other hand, many young girls experience

insecurity in having to choose a husband and the sudden responsibility of being a major part of a household; having to care for
children brings their easy freedom to an end.

Husband and wife (*uii, nuliaq*), man and woman (*aŋuun,
aganaq*); from 16 to 25 years until 60 or 70 years; from marriage
until old age. When a young man marries, he is no longer called a
nukatpiaq (adolescent male), rather, he has become an *aŋuun*
(man) with the responsibility of making a major contribution to
the maintenance of the household. He is no longer as free as his
younger friends to "run around with the boys," although he certainly maintains close contacts with his male friends and frequently
hunts with them. When a young married man has only a child or
two, his responsibilities are not very great. He does not have to hunt
too much to support his small family. If he is living in an extended
family, however, he will be expected to work harder and follow the
advice of his father-in-law. As a man grows older and has more
children, he is expected to assume a greater responsibility for his
family and in the community as a whole.

When a man has worked hard in his teens and twenties, and has
learned all he can from his elders, he emerges in his late thirties
and forties as a highly skilled hunter, trapper, craftsman and, if
he is so inclined, story teller and songster. A man in his thirties and
forties is more stable and is able to endure greater hardships than
a younger man. The skills and psychological stability of men in
their forties carry them well into their sixties, when a few men are
still remarkably productive. A mature married man also has more
of a voice in community affairs, such as the organization of a group
hunt, trading expeditions, and the settlement of disputes.

When a young woman marries, her status is enhanced. She is
no longer the daughter of a family, responsible solely to it and
sought after by the young men of the community—she becomes a
wife, no longer beholden only to her parents and siblings. Frequently, of course, her new husband joins her in her household.
Before she has children, her position in an extended family is not
very important, but she gradually achieves the status and the responsibilities of a mature married woman as her children are born.
If a young woman leaves her parental household upon marriage
and establishes a residence either alone with her husband or in the
household of one of his or her blood relatives, she assumes a greater

responsibility at once in her new household for the simple reason that her mother is not there to direct her.

A mature married woman is a powerhouse of activity, a paragon of endurance. A good woman in her thirties, forties, or fifties is the main pillar on which the internal workings of a household depend. If a woman's efforts were not directed toward the maintenance of the household, some other form of social organization would perforce occur among the Nunamiut. Men, as hunters, trappers, and makers of equipment may range over the countryside from any suitable base, whether it be an individual household of one or two families, a compound composed of several males related by blood and their spouses (or any other principle of residence), or the entire community as a corporate group. The man as a hunter may leave and return to any place where he can obtain food, drink, clothing, shelter, warmth, and affection. A hunter supplies, of course, most of the raw materials necessary for the maintenance of any residential group, but the woman provides most of the labor that renders a place habitable. And among the Nunamiut, a woman —or two in the event of an extended family—is the focus of any residential grouping. This woman is the wife or mother—in an extended family, the junior woman is usually the wife or daughter— of the males living with her. Together, with an occasional outsider, they form the household group.

It is thus the woman who is primarily responsible for the ongoing activity within a household. To this end she does some work outdoors, such as collecting firewood, harnessing and on occasion driving the dogs, gathering berries, roots, and bark in season, and sometimes attending to fishnets. The largest part of her daily effort, however, is directed toward preparing skins, making clothing, stoking the stove, cooking, making tea and coffee, repairing the house, and caring endlessly for her children—making them toys, wiping their tears, and keeping them out of trouble.

During the initial stages of marriage, the relationship between a new husband and his wife is one of sexual cohabitation, common residence, and economic cooperation. There is an affective bond between the two young persons, but it is not so strong as it usually is in later years, especially after several children are born and their household becomes an integral part of the community. The idle chatter and frequent hyperbolean praise found between newly married white persons does not exist among the Nunamiut. One does hear a compliment for a young spouse now and then, but it is usually rooted in fact. The most important elements in a happy marriage are hard work, being faithful, and refraining from talking about a spouse's faults.

Small gestures of kindness, often reciprocated, private jokes, and occasional nostalgic talk reflect the deep sentiment and real attachment a few husbands and wives feel for each other in a way that is not readily noticeable to a white man. While a man and wife live in close physical proximity for many more hours a day than do most white couples, there is a great respect for mutual privacy and modesty. Middle-aged men often hunt together and visit as if women did not exist. When the men are out hunting, women come together for visiting as if men did not exist. By maintaining their own worlds, a man and wife are more able to tolerate each other.

Once a young man 18 or 19 years old was repairing a dog harness. As he was sitting on the floor working, he remarked how nice it would be to have a wife working by one's side (he avoided saying "my" side in order, as we all frequently do, to protect himself from being ridiculed too caustically). His comment reflects the feeling between many husbands and wives. This usually unexpressed sentiment of the pride of living and working together results from the Nunamiut attitude that marriage is the proper state for a mature person. The Nunamiut feel that a person should not live or work alone, and that people are happiest when they are able to respond to one another in a household situation.

The relationship between many Nunamiut husbands and their wives is very cordial. Sometimes a person irritates his spouse by periods of laziness, but only when a spouse becomes habitually lazy does the other complain. Frequently the hard-working spouse merely learns to work harder. As a result, there are rare instances of a father learning to sew parkas for his children. A woman with a lazy husband normally relies on a male relative or other person for meat and skins, but she may learn to hunt and trap a little herself. Laziness seldom causes a marriage to fall apart. An industrious spouse gains considerable prestige in the eyes of the community for carrying the bulk of the work load of a household.

The most serious obstacle to marital happiness is sexual jealousy —and this can be explosive. Living in a close, isolated situation for long periods of time, it is said, drives a person to seek a change or some source of excitement. And that source of excitement often revolves around sex. Among the Nunamiut, as the years go by, a spouse may come to desire an occasional change in partners. Eskimos, it would appear, seek sexual variations in partners rather than in practices. The slightest gesture between a spouse and a person of the opposite sex may be construed as the prelude to adultery. Frequently, however, when feelings of jealousy are aroused, there is little cause: a person, recognizing the longing in himself, can easily imagine that his spouse, being human, has fallen into an illicit relationship. Most persons suppress such feelings and avoid antagonizing their spouses; when jealousy does bubble to the surface, real trouble may ensue.

In extreme cases, a husband may strike his wife or leave her and go to another settlement. Reconciliation after a few months is not uncommon. Frequently the relatives involved tell the two separated spouses that they have a responsibility to their children. In one incident a woman reportedly hit her husband over the head with a log, rendering him unconscious, when he repeatedly accused her of adultery, which she said she had not committed. In rare instances, jealousy can drive a man to kill his wife's lover, resulting, in former years, in decades of feuding between the blood relatives of the husband and the deceased. Such an incident has not occurred recently. The most frequent kind of trouble arising from jealousy that I observed was incessant nagging on the part of the wife. It is difficult to describe the power of nagging in a small Arctic settlement, or perhaps anywhere.

In one case, a woman attacked her husband verbally for several months about an imagined affair between him and another woman. Over the months, the husband became exceedingly morose. He continued to do his work, checking his trap lines and so forth, but in a completely mechanical fashion. Feeling had left him. He lost weight and finally became very sick. His condition apparently made him realize the foolishness of his extreme self-deprecation, and he began to recover. Perhaps his wife began to relent. Although she had wanted to punish her husband, she did not want to lose him. And to show how wrong such jealousy can be, the villagers (on this subject their information always seemed to be very accurate) did not believe the husband had been guilty of any indiscretion.

Once a young man and woman establish a common residence, the people of the community regard them as a married couple.

Relatives and friends may drop in to visit, and the new couple is placed in the role of host. As children are born to them, their position as a mature couple, as an integral part of the community, is increasingly recognized by others, and eventually they become respected seniors. Middle-aged husbands and wives with several children are expected to show the greatest skill and industry in running their household and to exert the greatest stabilizing influence in community affairs. Young people turn to them for advice in organizing group hunts, rendering of legal decisions, and determining and enacting such political policies as intertribal trade and feasts, warfare, and the selection of important campsites. Older people rely on their middle-aged offspring for shelter and a steady supply of meat, hides, and clothing.

Young couples are judged by the standard of living they maintain. There is a certain period of grace during which a young couple with a child or two freely receives help from close relatives and friends, but within a very few years they will lose prestige if they do not become self-supporting or carry their full load of the work in a large household. When a couple has only two or three children, it is not too hard for the man and wife to support themselves in a respectable fashion. As more children are born, however, it becomes more difficult to maintain a high standard of living. Increased skill and work are constantly required. A woman in her forties with several children is incredibly busy; her job is truly never finished. Her husband must hunt continually to supply his family with enough good meat and skins. Should one or more of the responsible members of a household fail to perform his tasks, the standard of living of a family will plummet rapidly and a comeback is very difficult.

The capacity of a man to beget and a woman to bear children is greatly stressed by the Nunamiut and is an exceedingly important element in the prestige a couple enjoys. When a man and wife produce no children, the blame is usually placed on the man, unless he can prove otherwise. One man I knew had no children by his wife. He did claim, however, to have a daughter by a woman married to another man. One or two people did not believe him, to his private pain. When I accepted the man at his word, which did appear valid, we became good friends, and I wound up hunting with him more than with anyone else. It is extremely sad for a couple not to have issue. They often adopt children, and some couples in the early days raised dogs in the house and gave them human names.

Thus far in the consideration of mature men and women, I have dealt only with married persons. Most adults of course are married, and there is considerable social pressure on those who are not, aside from the sexual drive, to find a spouse, but a very few Nunamiut men never marry. I met none, but I did hear from informants of bachelors in previous generations.

A young bachelor usually lives near his parents, and during his later years near his siblings. He brings the animals he kills to the household of his mother or a married sister, who, in return, provides him with clothing. He may become very close to his nieces and nephews, sometimes treating them as if they were his own children, although usually in a joking manner. If a bachelor is hard working, contributes to the welfare of his parents and his siblings, and is honest, he attains a definite prestige. If he does any strange thing or develops a psychological quirk, the people of the community begin to say they knew all along that he was an odd person, since he had never married. An old white bachelor once visited Anaktuvuk Pass; he chain-smoked cigars and one Nunamiut remarked that his cigars "helped him out," that is, provided a sense of security for him that he lacked (as far as the Nunamiut was concerned) by not being married and having children.

In rare instances, Nunamiut women do not marry. I knew of only one spinster. She was the eldest sibling of a very large family. Following the example of her parents, and because she was the first-born child, she became very retiring. When her mother died, she became a mother-substitute for her younger siblings and assumed the role of the mature woman in the household. Although she almost married two or three times, her intense bashfulness inhibited her in her relationships with men, and her sense of duty to her father and siblings was another block to marriage. Although the people of the community enjoy joking about her, she is highly respected for her industry and devotion to her immediate family.

Among the Nunamiut, since early death is not infrequent, a few men become widowers in their late twenties or thirties. When a young man loses his wife, especially if a child or two has been born, his sadness may deepen into a melancholia lasting for years. He may lose all sense of drive and initiative. Frequently he returns to the family in which he was raised and merely hunts and helps enough with household chores to justify his presence. Any desire to trap or to make fine-looking traveling equipment and articles to trade or sell disappears. One informant who became a widower in his middle twenties decided not to remarry in memory of his wife. He told me of another man he had known years before, who became a widower in his late thirties or early forties and refused to remarry, saying that he could never find a woman as good as his deceased wife. People feel a great deal of sympathy for a widower and respect his wish not to remarry. Often, however, a young widower's father or mother will tell him that he should remarry, that he cannot spend the rest of his life alone. In most cases, an adult son responds to parental pressure and normally seeks another woman. Ultimately, because the Nunamiut regard the married state so highly, people feel it is right for a widower to remarry even though they would respect him if he did not do so.

Many of the same comments apply to a young widow. Somehow, perhaps because of my masculine bias, women did not seem quite so sentimental about remarrying, perhaps because of economic reasons. When a young wife becomes a widow, she returns to her family with her children and becomes dependent on her father and brothers for the products of the chase. A year or two after her husband's death, her family will urge her to become receptive to the bids of men looking for a wife: another hunter in the household would lighten the burden of her immediate male relatives. If the widow is much over 30 and has many children, her chances of remarrying are very limited; in this case she may become well established in the household of a brother or sister. If she is a hard worker, she will be able to attain prestige and the respect of the community for having overcome the formidable economic and psychological obstacle of not having a husband. Once, many years ago, a widow was so industrious that she produced a great number of parkas and boots to trade to the coast and came to be considered an umialik.

Old age, male and female (*aŋayukaxaraq, aganayukaxaraq?*); 60 to 70 years or older; when the hair turns gray, the face becomes lined, and the body is less agile. When both husband and wife continue living into old age, they remain as the senior couple in an extended household. If they have lived alone in their prime, with the coming of old age they are forced to join the household of a married son or daughter or, in rare instances, another younger family for at least the better part of each year. As the old couple become less able to contribute to the welfare of the household, their influence in making decisions diminishes, although a middle-aged person may ask an older person for advice now and then. Young people frequently visit with old people in a relaxed manner; it is not unusual to see a child of 5 visit alone with a person in his late seventies for some time.

Frequently, the person who reaches old age is a widower or widow, who then joins the household of a married son or daughter. Some old persons remain with the same family year after year; others move from house to house. On occasion, an old person joins an unrelated household for a while. He contributes the caribou he kills, but any fur-bearing animal he traps is his. One often hears comments from younger people evincing respect for an old person and happiness in serving him.

Many old persons are remarkably active; the toughness and ability of people in their seventies and older are sometimes commented on. While an old man's endurance is greatly limited, he is still able to trap and hunt a little. In particular, some old men are very effective as lookouts for animals; they have learned to be patient. Many times I have seen an old man select a spot he knew well and sit for hours waiting for caribou. When he saw a herd approaching, he would shout to someone in the village. A few old men have hunted for so many years in the same region that they know where caribou are likely to travel and in which direction they will run when frightened. An old man may bring down a considerable number of animals with slow, careful shooting.

The old women are still able to gather firewood and do extensive sewing, but they have to leave the heavy scraping to a younger woman. Young girls learning to sew often seek the advice of an old woman. Even a woman in her forties may ask her elderly mother about some little trick in sewing.

While old people are respected and their needs seen to, extreme veneration is absent. Owing to the small margin of survival in which the Nunamiut live, excessive attention to nonproductive or only nominally productive persons would lessen a household's and the community's chance to survive during a period of hunger or actual starvation. During normal times, an old person may be very much of an asset to a household, but when hunger strikes, and the family must suddenly range as far as possible in search of caribou, the older member cannot keep up the pace. He knows he faces death. If caribou are found, he may be saved. But as the hunger increases and game does not appear, an old person realizes that he faces death—he may even say so.

Apparently, in extreme circumstances, abandonment has occurred. This was a delicate subject and I obtained only vague comments about it. I did not observe an instance of abandonment and I felt at the time that I should not press for information.

In a sense, all old people enjoy a certain prestige merely because of their age. One does not think of an older person suffering a loss of prestige for lying or stealing. Such behavior is absent, or extremely rare, among them; if one is lazy or not very generous, he may be said to suffer a loss of prestige, but there is a tendency to excuse him for his age. If an old person is industrious and generous, his prestige is that much higher. Old men seem to enjoy more prestige than old women because they remain as active as possible until death. Old women sometimes are vaguely suspected of shamanism, only because they are old. Some informants seemed to feel that old women act "funny" at times and, widowed as they often are, they become sexually frustrated and the victim of jokes and folktales because they are unable to attract a man. Some old women may endear themselves to younger persons, however, by their many acts of kindness and their personal qualities.

Standards of Interpersonal Conduct

We have shown how the age and sex of a person determine his position in a household and in society at large, and we have discussed each person's responsibilities in contributing to the welfare of his household. In order to provide a sense of the tone or mood in which he performs his tasks, we shall consider the standards of interpersonal conduct—the general notions of propriety which influence the way people behave toward one another. To this end we shall examine how Nunamiut conceptions of such social qualities as obligation, reciprocity, competition, cooperation, industriousness, and generosity are exemplified in individual behavior.

OBLIGATION AND RECIPROCATION. Among the Nunamiut, in all the relationships a given person has with other people, there is an explicit sense of obligation and reciprocity. The purpose here is not to delineate the various obligations associated with each kind of relationship but to characterize the feeling and manner in which people fulfill them.

When a person enters a situation in which he is expected to make a gesture toward another person, whether it involves joking, presenting a gift, offering food, or rendering a service, several forces compel him to act. By responding to an obligation, he knows that his action will return to him in some way, whether in kind or not, and he can enjoy personal satisfaction and public recognition. In fact, most relationships are not maintained by reciprocating exactly in kind. Personal satisfaction and public prestige make up the difference, as it were. A person who extends himself more readily to others may claim more prestige than a less responsive person or one who does not take the initiative in a relationship. When someone feels in particular need of self-recognition he may openly claim prestige, but often he remains silent since he knows that other people are bound to notice his actions. Many people strive to build up a reserve of personal satisfaction for their own psychological well-being as well as a reserve of public prestige that may be extremely valuable in times of political crisis or personal need.

In addition to the personal satisfaction and public prestige which result from fulfilling an obligation, an individual is motivated to respond to the request or unspoken expectation of a relative, trading partner, friend, or namesake because that person may have helped him in the past, creating a social debt which he obviously should extend himself to repay. Thus, in discharging his debt, he satisfies his conscience and keeps the way open for future interchanges.

Concomitant with the notion of obligation is the expectation of reciprocity. By definition, in any given relationship, each person has obligations to the other. The moment one person fulfills an obligation, he expects the other to reciprocate eventually in some way. Likewise, when the second person does reciprocate, he feels his action not only clears his debt but he, in turn, expects the first person to carry the relationship farther by reciprocating. And thus social interaction continues, never quite in balance, always demanding action of some kind and enabling the person with initiative to amass prestige.

As might be expected, a few individuals do not respond readily to the obligations of their relationships, or they fail to reciprocate adequately when someone makes a gesture toward them. If a person fails to live up to expectations, people become aware that he is a slacker and they may respond to him with a minimum of decency and hospitality. Someone who is especially kind to him is either admired for his selfless actions or is ridiculed for putting himself out for nothing except a little prestige. If a person fails to reciprocate adequately, the person who proffers himself would feel slighted and hesitate before doing so again. Needless to say, complete failure to fulfill one's obligations or return favors rarely occurs because it would isolate an individual to an intolerable degree. The problems in maintaining equitable social relationships are relative matters and difficult to specify. One person may come to feel that another individual with whom he has cooperated in the past, say in hunting or building a house, is beginning to shirk his part of the work. One may carry the shirker along for some time, not quite sure if he really is failing to do his share in the relationship, or one may finally decide to withdraw, by claiming to be too busy to hunt this time, or to have made a prior agreement to hunt with someone else. Thus an informal hunting partnership may come to an end. A person cannot turn his back on a close relative, of course, but he can limit his dealings to a respectable minimum.

An individual is under very strong pressure to meet his obligations to the members of his family—pressures from within himself and the pressures of daily contact. From birth, every Nunamiut is inculcated with the idea that his involvement in his family is the source of meaningful existence and should he forsake his family, he would cut himself off from the joys of humanity.

The most obvious example of a person's desire to live up to his family's expectations is economic. He would suffer overpowering guilt for any failure to respond to the needs of his family for the essentials of life. When a 20-year-old son leaves his comrades in a distant trapping hut to bring home a sledload of meat, his explanation is that he is thinking of his family's meat supply. A woman never ceases to sew, that her husband and sons may be properly clothed. To do otherwise would hardly be conceivable for a sane person. While everyone owns the things he makes for himself and the gifts and objects he receives in trade, he must be ever mindful to loan them without comment to a sibling, parent, child, or spouse, should a request be made.

Sometimes a family's desire to keep together operates to their immediate economic detriment. If a man has been out hunting with no luck for several days, he begins to think of returning home. If a large herd of caribou suddenly appears, he will kill a few animals, but the desire to go home may have built up so strongly in him that he does not remain in the hunting area as long as he should. The older a man becomes, the more able he is to resist this impulse, and he will stay where he will, in the long run, be of most help to his family.

COMPETITION AND COOPERATION. Every Nunamiut loves to compete and enjoys bragging about his feats of endurance and skill and the superiority of his possessions. Men are perhaps a little more vocal than women, but women unquestionably compete, in their sphere, in as many ways as men.

A man brags constantly about his dogs, and will race almost anyone else traveling the same route. If there is no one to race, a man invariably makes some glowing comment about his dogs after any sled trip, no matter how short. Men compete strenuously in hunting and trapping to see who can catch the most fur animals in a season or who can shoot the most caribou during a migration. In making implements, a man not only strives for a functional article, but also one that looks better than anyone else's.

Although every woman has to make clothes for the members of her household, there is a strong undercurrent of competition. I have seen a woman carefully examine the stitches of an article made by another woman and comment that her technique was only so-so or that she did not even know the proper stitch to use. A woman with a large family complains about how much sewing she has to do but nevertheless brags about her capacity to work hard. Women also compete in maintaining clean houses and in preparing food for community feasts.

The most earnest competition occurs between members of the same status, with the notable exception of siblings. Although siblings cannot avoid competing in fact, one must never appear to compete or talk about competing in any way, nor must he ever evince jealousy when a sibling does something especially well. He is expected to be silent or to praise his sibling. Two persons of different status are not expected to compete openly with each other. A young man who brags that his dogs are faster than those of a 60-year-old man would be considered impertinent, whereas a young man may compete, and would be expected to do so, for all he is worth with the men of his age.

While a person can brag about almost anything he does, it is often in the realm of sports and games that the competitive urge is most freely expressed. This is as true of women as it is of men.

There is a great variety of physical contests among the Nunamiut, but the most important is long-distance running. Old men told me of footraces they had won forty years ago. Women also hold footraces, over as long a course as five or six miles. People do not feel that a race of under a mile or so is a fair test of endurance. By immersing himself in an effort to beat another person in a footrace or other endeavor, a man can work off much antagonism that might otherwise be directly expressed.

Despite the fact that the purpose of any competition is to win, there is a strong feeling among the Nunamiut against an individual who wins by too wide a margin or too often. Such a person soon falls into disfavor with the community. The principle has a parallel in those activities that enable a person and the family or community to survive. A woman who makes clothing, especially daily wear, more elegant than need be, would be talked about as extravagant, or even ridiculous. Once someone wins a game or makes a better pair of snowshoes, he should be content to sit back for a while and let someone else make the best drum, say. The two individuals can then admire each other, establishing, as it were, an approximate, though never quite complete, equilibrium.

It is on this note of qualified competition, within one's status, that the idea of cooperation appears. For an individual to achieve a sense of dignity and worth, he must develop a feeling of excellence in the eyes of other people. At the same time, as a member of a household and a community, a person must learn to cooperate to ensure survival. In a severe climate, wanton competition would result in extinction. The capacity to curb the competitive urge determines the extent to which a social group will be able to survive in a moment of crisis or great common need.

Cooperation within a family is often so taken for granted that there is little discussion or friction. In a few families, however, competitive impulses, feelings of personal pride, and rebellion against the demands and expectations of others cause a great deal of trouble. One member will sometimes argue on and off for days or months, attempting to assert the prerogatives he thinks he should enjoy. Such a conflict often results in painful loss of face, usually for an adolescent son.

Once many years ago two or three isolated families were threatened by starvation in the middle of winter. One of the young men had the good fortune to kill a caribou. Driven by hunger he ate the marrow. When he arrived home with the carcass, his mother asked him why he had eaten the marrow alone during a time of starvation. The young man became so ashamed that he left home and wandered around from camp to camp stealing food and destroying equipment that people had left outdoors. He was so completely disgraced by his failure to live up to the ideal of cooperation that he could not face his own family; his compunction was so compelling that he shuddered in the presence of society, yet lashed out against it.

In the old days, people used to cooperate at the community level to a much greater extent than today. Aside from the idea that hunters in the same area should not spoil another hunter's chances, some community cooperation still exists. During the 1950s the Nunamiut used an old army tent for a communal house for dancing in the summer; just before it was put up every year, most of the women of the community came together to sew up the rips. The men of the community maintain a footbridge over a creek running through the middle of the village, and almost every man contributed a log or two and can point it out. In building a small log church several years ago, each man carried as many sledloads of logs as he could; as each brought up his load of logs, he bragged about the strength of his dogs, his generosity, and his cooperative attitude.

Without doubt the most frequent compliment one hears about a person, both to his face and out of his hearing, is how industrious and hard working he is or what a good job he has done. Most of these compliments are given in earnest. Rarely does a person offer a compliment, except perhaps to a stranger, because he hopes to gain favor. In Nunamiut society, such a motive would be transparent and not respected.

A man who wakes up early every morning, and hunts and traps at every opportunity, or a woman who gathers large quantities of firewood, keeps the house in order, and sews continually, is considered an industrious worker. Every now and then such individuals say what a hard job something is, or how hard they have been working, and no one disagrees. Not only are there obvious material benefits to be gained from hard work, but a person also develops a sense of personal worth, feels that he is involved in his family, and enjoys the approbation of society at large. In the old days a hardworking person was considered immune from shamanistic attacks and disease (*nuvuq*).

Just as the highest praise concerns industry, the sharpest criticism is directed toward laziness; endorsing their own feelings of righteousness, the industrious do not hesitate to point out the shirkers, and to be called lazy is a real disgrace. One very well knows when he is being indolent and often he is the first to call himself an idler. But, unpleasant as it can be, a few people continue being lazy year after year.

Because hard work is so demanding, once an idler is subjected to public pressure he can seldom avail himself of new stimuli—the psychological inertia seems difficult to overcome. The Nunamiut are very explicit about the psychological dangers of being lazy. As the years go by and a lazy person fails to change his ways, he may indulge in self-pity and assume a couldn't-care-less attitude. In a small community where hard work is praised, no one can escape the pressure. Just as a hard worker is considered normal and immune from disease, a lazy person is thought more likely to fall ill and to become emotionally upset. A habitually lazy person often behaves in mildly neurotic ways, especially by talking in a strange or queer manner at times or by making needless blunders during a hunt.

Although a hard worker is praised for his industry, he is also expected to share the fruits of his labor with others. If a diligent worker is not generous with his wealth, his industriousness is recognized, but he will also be called stingy. In the Arctic, where a person never knows when he may desperately need help himself, stinginess is dangerous.

The child is taught early to be generous with everything he collects, makes, or is given. From learning to share his possessions with siblings, a person learns to be generous with other relatives and non-kin. One is hesitantly generous to a stranger, who might be an enemy or a friend; he might reciprocate an act of kindness or not.

A generous person has the pleasure of knowing that he is responding to what is expected of him and of seeing other people happy with a gift or well fed as a result of his efforts. The more possessions a man acquires, the more he is expected to share with his relatives and friends. In doing so, he achieves a position in which many people are obligated to him—for material goods and services if he should need them or for backing in a social or political controversy.

Some persons with few possessions may become in a sense over-generous. A person might be lazy, but if he shares everything he does have, little though it may be, he knows he can never be accused of being stingy and can expect handouts from other people. A lazy but generous individual will never starve as long as there is food in the village. Once, while I was hunting with an older man in February (frequently a hungry month), we were discussing a lazy, unmarried man who was always generous in his way. My companion's final observation, after bitterly complaining about him, was, "He will never die [from hunger]." Any man, by virtue of his proximity, must at least be offered something to eat.

External Relationships of the Household

In social and economic affairs concerning outsiders, the members of a household act independently, but in the event of malicious gossip or a physical attack on any person in a household, the members unite to form a single front against an outsider. Let us consider a few examples of individual autonomy in social and economic activities and how household membership affects these matters.

One early afternoon, a man and wife were walking back to their summer tent after working all morning on their winter house. As the couple passed one house, the woman there called to the wife to come in, to eat and visit; the two women were distant kin. The husband continued on alone to their tent.

A married granddaughter of the man with whom I was living once invited both of us (but not the man's wife) to eat the evening meal in her household. His wife (his second) was not the woman's grandmother. The ostensible purpose of the visit was to see the granddaughter's newborn son, my companion's great-grandchild. I was invited because of my close association with the proud great-grandfather and because of friendliness on the part of the host.

Any member of a household would not hesitate, should he be so moved, to leave his house and visit an individual living in the community. Likewise, a visitor might come to visit with only one or two persons in a house, and simply be silent, or pleasant to other members of the household.

Thus we see that social interaction outside the household is based upon individual kinship ties and contractual relationships such as friendship and partnership. There is a limit, of course, to the extent of social circulation outside the household; one does not neglect one's family. The demands of seasonal activity usually determine how much free time a person has for visiting, and the amount of food in a household may determine how welcome a visitor is. The point here is that in the course of normal visiting, whatever it may be, a person's membership in a household does not force him to respond only as a part of that social group.

Except when trading with members of households in other communities, an individual's economic activity outside his own household is also based upon his own ties of kinship and friendship. In helping another family, for example, an individual represents his own interests, not those of his household as such. The following paragraph is an illustration.

The family I lived with built a winter house in the fall of 1960. An unrelated young man helped in the work with the sod and moss for two or three days. In return he ate with us while the work was in progress. But, more important, as he had been a frequent visitor in the past, he sought to maintain a friendly welcome for himself in the future by helping the family in a time of need. It was his affair. This welcome, which he successfully maintained, was only for himself and did not include any members of the household from which he came. In fact, he was much more welcome as a visitor than some of his lazier brothers. Only if his own family had seriously needed him as a hunter or worker would they have objected to his devoting two or three days of work to another household.

Young men often help unrelated families with no expectation of payment, because they have been a frequent visitor or are interested in one of the daughters of a household. When the members of a household embark on a major project such as building a house, hauling logs, or digging a permafrost cellar, they may offer a strong young man a pair of white man's boots, a knife, or even a rifle in exchange for his labor. While these articles have to be purchased with money earned by trapping, working at odd jobs, and making things to sell to white men, I never encountered an instance in which one Nunamiut hired another to do a given job for a specific wage.

On occasion, a commodity such as meat, a strip of fur, or an article of clothing is transferred from one person to another, or from one person to a household, without an explicit agreement to trade. Such a presentation is of course a "gift" and is usually given for social reasons, for example to ensure hospitality when the giver visits, to express or sustain a bond of kinship, or to curry political favor.

These external contacts are indispensable in enabling persons to pay and create social debts, to express and maintain bonds of kinship, and to keep up with news and gossip. They provide opportunities for young people to visit and select spouses and for old people to maintain and occasionally change their alignments with other households; and they are effective in creating and sustaining a community feeling. Everyone is free and is in fact expected to respond to the individual human bonds of kinship and friendship outside his family, but in the total social and economic life of an individual, his involvement in his household is still dominant.

When any member of a household is threatened from the outside, the people co-resident with him are bound to come to his defense and support him in any action he might take. When a person is confronted with malicious gossip about a member of his household, he is bound to defend the honor of his family and the people with whom he is living. Even in minor disputes over lying and petty theft, the co-residents of the accused band together behind him. In general, one feels that a very close relative, particularly a co-resident, cannot do wrong. After all, other people associate an individual with those persons with whom he is living. If a man is prone to lie or steal, his siblings or other members of his household may also be so inclined. Thus, from the inside, i.e. as a member of a family, one defends his family as himself. In more serious disputes, such as feuds, the members of a household are forced to act very closely as a unit in seeking retaliation.

One of the most important aspects of the external relations of a household is the formation of a household cluster. Since the cluster has largely replaced the extended family, a cluster is usually composed of two or three households in which closely related persons live. In joining an encampment or building a house for the first time, the primary consideration is where the parents of the husband or wife are living. There is a tendency for a family to live with or near the wife's parents. If these live elsewhere or are deceased, or if there is a severe personality conflict, the family will tend to set up camp or build a house near the husband's parents. I saw both alternatives in practice. If neither set of parents is living, the most common solution is to live near a sibling. Two sisters, with their husbands and children, who live close to each other is a very frequent combination. Such an alignment is very close because women stay at home most of the time in order to maintain a base from which their husbands may hunt over the country for long periods at a time. Brothers and their families are not so likely to live close together because the bond between the two wives is not necessarily intimate. Among the Nunamiut there is a term for one's spouse's siblings' spouses, but the obligations commensurate with this relationship do not demand cooperation or mutual support. Although I observed married brothers hunting together, the only instances I saw of married brothers living near each other were those in which the two wives were related either as sisters or collateral relatives. There are several instances in which a married brother and his family live near a married sister and her family. In such cases the brother and brother-in-law often associate closely, hunting and visiting together, and the sister and sister-in-law work together in one or the other's household. Nunamiut highly esteem the sibling-in-law relationship and say that it provides a good base for a cooperative living arrangement.

When two or more households form a cluster there is little trading among the people concerned. But they do cooperate economically—the men hunt and trap together, women collect firewood and sew together, and everyone pitches in when traveling, moving camp, and building houses. While I was living at Anaktuvuk Pass, several babies died, and members of an associated household helped in digging the graves—a difficult task in the permafrost.

Aside from the material benefits to be gained from association, over time, a very strong feeling of mutual accord, good will, and happiness in living and working together develops. The whole may be said to be more than the sum of its parts. The stimulation created by two or three families living together evokes a greater response from each person than if one family remains alone. Any one person enjoys a greater sense of well-being and "togetherness" in a lonely, hungry country when he is a member of a complex of two or three households. Lest the writer be considered sentimental, let me say that the foregoing sentences are based upon frequent comments by many Nunamiut. This is the reason, I believe, that people prefer to live in association with other households even though an isolated family can amass greater wealth. Strong ambition is required on the part of a potential umialik to overcome this psychological desire for security in his drive for wealth.

Characteristic of the emphasis on small mobile groups in the organization of Nunamiut society, the obligations of a household to the community as such rarely impinge on any household's desire to be autonomous. When a household joins a particular community, however, certain obligations come into force. In the old days, each household was expected to contribute so many caribou skins and so much labor for the construction of the communal house and was expected to work very hard during the seasonal caribou drive. Of course, all had a share in the kill. Each household also functioned as a unit in communal eating. Today the Nunamiut eat together four or five times a year; each household prepares and carries as sumptuous food as it can manage to the communal house. A household sits together as the unmarried young men and women serve each person—man, woman, and child—with equal portions of each dish. In the old days, a community ate together in this fashion for weeks at a time, especially after a successful caribou drive.

Formerly, and to a limited extent today, most Nunamiut men had partners among the coastal Eskimos with whom they traded in the spring when Nunamiut families traveled to the coast. In a sense, the two households from which the partners came assumed a certain relationship to each other. The two partners carried on their trading with the wants of their respective households in mind—the need for such staples as blubber, skins, furs, and sinew; and, later, guns, ammunition, needles, flour, tea, and coffee. Two partners might exchange wives for a short while, strengthening the bonds of the partnership. The man of the household, who conducted the trading, was supposed to trade with only one person in another band. Thus over time, each household came to regard the other as its source of staple trade goods and its companion in fun and merriment in the spring.

5. Kin and Non-Kin Relationships

Various classes of relatives have been mentioned in our discussion of Nunamiut social life but, although they are exceedingly important, the kinship system does not provide a sufficient or total reference for the formation of the household and the community or for most activities. Friendship and partnership are obvious examples of the important role of contractual relationships in Nunamiut life. Despite the fluidity of social groupings and the lack of exclusive kin groups, the Nunamiut kinship system provides the individual with a specific set or, more precisely, a set of sets of potential relationships. The individual, with varying degrees of choice, exploits the socially defined potentialities of a given relationship when such a factor as residence, locality, economic exigency, or political crisis brings them into play.

By considering the rights and duties which a person acquires during his life as a result of culturally recognized cognatic and affinal relationships, as well as the sentiments, expressions of affection, and the customary behavior accompanying these relationships, we can more readily see how order is achieved in an important aspect of Nunamiut social life, which is not so obviously manifested as the organization and activities of the household and the community.

The Structure of Kinship Relations

By virtue of being the legitimate child of his mother and father, a person stands in a variety of relationships with certain other people—a specifiable range of consanguineal relatives and their spouses. When he marries, he acquires additional relationships with his spouse's consanguineal relatives and his spouse's siblings' spouses. And subsequently, with the birth of his children, their marriage and production of offspring, the marriages of certain consanguineal relatives and their production of offspring, the individual acquires many more relationships. During his lifetime he may be related to very many people as a result of cognatic and marital links, but the nature of these relationships varies greatly, dependent on the type of relationship and, importantly, whether a certain related person is living in the individual's household, near him in a complex of two or three households, in his community, in another community where he might be seen two or three times a year, or in a distant region where he might never be seen.

Ego is the natural point of reference for discussing kinship relations among the Nunamiut, especially since there are no social groups based exclusively on kinship. In using ego as the point of reference, however, we must be conscious of ego through time and ego in space, particularly when we consider specific instances of behavior based on kinship ties. In terms of the people to whom he is related, a Nunamiut passes through three distinct phases: (1) as an infant, child, and adolescent, the period during which ego lives in a household as a member of his family of orientation; (2) as a married person, husband or wife, the period during which ego lives in his household as a dominant partner of his family of procreation; and (3) as an old person, the period in which ego is usually a widow or widower and largely dependent on a married son or daughter. In space, ego lives with a person to whom he is related in the same household, near him in the same community, or knows of him living in a different community. Thus, while it is useful to think of "ego" in an abstract sense, we must keep these three phases in time, set in space, constantly in mind. This will become more obvious as particular situations involving kinship are examined.

In order to illustrate how ego categorizes his blood relatives, a summary of Nunamiut terms of consanguineal relationships follows.

amauluq, great-grandparent, includes FaFaFa, FaFaMo, FaMoFa, etc.; FaFaFaBr, FaFaFaSi, FaFaMoBr, etc.

tata, grandfather, includes FaFa, MoFa; FaFaBr, FaMoBr, MoFaBr, MoMoBr; FaFaFaBrSo, FaFaFaSiSo, etc.

ana, grandmother, includes FaMo, MoMo; FaFaSi, FaMoSi, MoFaSi, MoMoSi; FaFaFaBrDa, FaFaFaSiDa, etc.

apa, father

aka, mother

apiaq, older brother

atauraq, older sister

nukatchiaq, younger sibling

nukaxalik, youngest sibling, includes youngest Br *or* youngest Si (not the youngest siblings of both sexes) *igniq,* son

paniq, daughter

aŋaluq, uncle, includes FaBr, MoBr (for exception, see *akaka* below); FaFaBrSo, FaFaSiSo, etc.; FaFaFaBrSoSo, FaFaFaBrDaSo, etc.

akaka, mother's brother (only one informant gave this term for mother's brother; he said this term was rarely used and only in the old days, but that he himself had used it)

atchuq, or more affectionately, *achaluq,* aunt, includes FaSi, MoSi; FaFaBrDa, FaFaSiDa, etc.; FaFaFaBrSoDa, FaFaFaBrDaDa, etc.

aganaqan, cousin, includes FaBrSo, FaBrDa, FaSiSo, etc.; FaFaBrSoSo, FaFaBrSoDa, FaFaBrDaSo, etc.; FaFaFaBrSoSoSo, FaFaFaBrSoSoDa, FaFaFaBrSoDaSo, etc.

ainyaq, cousin, in the following instances: for all the specifications listed under aganaqan, when both ego and referent are female, the term *ainyaq* is used reciprocally, although some informants asserted that aganaqan could also be used. If ego is female and older than a male referent, the term ainyaq is often used, but it was stated that aganaqan is also correct. If ego is male and older than a female referent, the term aganaqan is used, although I noted once that the term ainyaq was used by two cousins of opposite sex of whom the boy was the elder. Aganaqan is by far the most common term for cousin.

uyuro, niece and nephew or "nibling," includes BrSo, BrDa, SiSo, SiDa; FaBrSoSo, FaBrSoDa, FaSiSoSo, etc.; FaFaBrSoSoSo, FaFaBrSoSoDa, FaFaBrSoDaSo, etc.

tutiq, or more affectionately, *tutichiaq,* grandchild, includes SoSo, SoDa, DaSo, DaDa; BrSoSo, BrSoDa, BrDaSo, etc.; FaBrSoSoSo, FaBrSoSoDa, FaBrSoDaSo, etc.

ilyulik, or more affectionately, *ilyuligaluq,* includes SoSoSo, SoSoDa, SoDaSo, etc.; BrSoSoSo, BrSoSoDa, BrSoDaSo, etc.

The more important combined kin terms referring to the family are:

aŋayuqaak, both parents collectively

nukagitch, all children collectively

kitunagat, all children collectively

kitunagarit, a nuclear family of mother, father, and children; from the term *kitunagat*

ataatak, extended family, a term used by the offspring of a married child living in the same household with the latter's parents (from the term *tata,* grandfather)

Since a half-sibling is considered an *ilya,* consanguineal relative, the following terms are pertinent:

apiaxaraq, older half-brother, includes FaWiSo and MoHuSo when the referent is older than ego

atauxaraq, older half-sister, includes FaWiDa and MoHuDa when referent
is older than ego
nukaxaraq, younger half-sibling, includes FaWiSo, FaWiDa, MoHuSo,
MoHuDa when referent is younger than ego

Other than half-siblings, there are no separate terms for those
consanguineal relatives with whom ego shares only one ancestor.
Such persons are fully recognized as consanguineal relatives.

Although stepchildren and stepparents are not considered *ilyap-
iat,* "real" (consanguineal) relatives, because they often live in the
same household they may come to regard one another as true relatives. Hence the following terms:

> *apaxaraq,* stepfather
> *akaxaraq,* stepmother
> *ignixaraq,* stepson, includes HuSo, WiSo
> *panixaraq,* stepdaughter, includes HuDa, WiDa

Having defined Nunamiut terms of consanguineal relationships,
we may advance to the most important rights and obligations (economic support, economic cooperation, hospitality, moral and political support in disputes and feuds) and the sentiments, expression of affection, and other aspects of customary behavior which
these terms imply for the Nunamiut, with reference primarily to
ego's kinship ties within the family and the kindred.

Because the terms economic support and economic cooperation
are frequently used, it seems appropriate to indicate what is meant
by them.

When ego is said to be obligated to support some person, he must
provide (in accordance with the latter's needs and his own capacity, age, and sex) meat, fat, skins, weapons, tools, traveling equipment, shelter, aid in traveling, clothes, cooking services, firewood,
water, roots, and berries; in other words, the necessities of life.
When support within a household is indicated, a person, within his
ability, must constantly and unstintingly provide all the goods and
services needed by the recipient. When economic support between
two persons of different households within a community is indicated, the person under obligation must offer support only in time
of need, such as hunger, bad luck, or illness, or when requested;
otherwise, he is free to contribute services or to share his material
wealth as gifts with the recipient in order to maintain pleasant relations or to secure political backing. When support between two per-

sons living in different communities is indicated, it usually involves offering complete hospitality to the traveler—providing him with shelter, a place to sleep, food to eat, helping him to repair his traveling equipment, and perhaps even giving him a dog.

When two people cooperate economically, they associate or work together in such undertakings as hunting, trapping, and making weapons, traveling equipment and other implements, transporting meat and skins, building houses, traveling long distances, scraping skins, sewing, cooking, and collecting firewood, water, roots, and berries. Cooperation within a household is obligatory. When cooperation is indicated as an aspect of a relationship between two persons of different households within the same community, it means that the two persons may or may not take advantage of this opportunity for economic association. When cooperation between two persons living in different communities is indicated, the host is generally expected to offer assistance to the traveler but not in the sense of full support. When two people cooperate, both receive the benefits of their labor, but they hope to produce more by working together than alone. I focus initially on these aspects of kinship relations—those affecting the exploitation of the environment—because our general concern is the relationship of the Nunamiut to their environment, because informants often talked about these matters, and because that is what I most frequently observed.

Within the nuclear family, relationships are characterized by complete support and cooperation, consideration but restraint in outward behavior, and feelings of strong sentimental attachment and affection. As a child, ego is economically dependent upon his parents, obedient, receptive and responsive to their fond gestures as an infant and very young child, but increasingly restrained and less outwardly affectionate toward them as he grows older. As a parent, ego is ultimately responsible, with his spouse, for his children's economic welfare, expects cooperation and obedience from them, especially when difficulties arise, is dominant over them but mindful of their feelings, rarely punishing them severely, very affectionate toward them as infants, but increasingly restrained in outward behavior as they grow older. As a sibling living in his family of orientation, ego is cooperative and willing to share without reservation with his siblings. A sibling of either sex must always be restrained in outward behavior toward his siblings, joking very little and never displaying jealousy or any sharp emotion toward them, although an older sibling, like a parent, may fondle a younger sibling. An older sister may assume some of her mother's responsibility in caring for her younger sisters and brothers. One 14-year-old girl who was especially attentive to her younger siblings was affectionately called *akachauraq* (cute little mother) by many people. *Apiaq* (older brother) is a diminutive form of *apa* (father) and most older brothers feel responsible for the welfare of their younger siblings. Younger siblings usually regard their older siblings very highly and try to emulate them. Sisters are often much closer than brothers, especially in their late teens and early twenties.

As a spouse, ego cooperates extensively with and fully supports his or her spouse in the many phases of economic activity. Regardless of sex, ego shares with his spouse in making decisions. A man and wife enjoy exclusive conjugal rights, except in occasional instances of spouse exchange, but they are very restrained in their outward behavior toward each other, especially in public. In the privacy of the household, however, spouses often display consideration, and they may talk and laugh together.

During his lifetime, ego is a member of two families—his family of orientation and his family of procreation. In some respects, the bonds that are developed with his parents and siblings in his family of orientation always remain paramount. Although nearly every person establishes his own household with his spouse and becomes deeply involved in it, he never relinquishes his ties with, and his emotional feelings for, the members of his family of orientation. Should a mature, married man learn that his parents are starving in a nearby valley, he may abandon his spouse to her blood relatives and rush to their aid. Usually, of course, a man and wife remain together in their household and try to help the set of parents that happens to be nearby. Geographical location, then, often determines which kinship ties are expressed, although conflict is always possible between a man and wife over which set of parents should receive support in times of stress. Likewise, in legal disputes or political moves, a married person must side with his parents and siblings, especially if they live nearby, even if it involves siding against his spouse. If a man has lived away from his close relatives for decades and if he and his wife have had many children, he is likely to enjoy a close association with her blood relatives and would support her in any conflict. If his parents or siblings should appear and demand hospitality, he would of course have to see to their needs and offer any support—economic, political, or otherwise—which they might require.

The commitment of an individual to his consanguineal family reflects bilateral or filial ties which are stronger among the Nunamiut than those commonly found in American society. From the point of view of many Americans, a person's commitment to his spouse gradually comes to supersede his obligations to his parents and siblings in terms of residential arrangement, support and cooperation in economic matters, and the expression of affection. Throughout his life, a Nunamiut is beholden first to his parents, second to his siblings, and third to his spouse. As children are born, they assume first place, with a person's parents, as lineal relatives. With many Americans, when a person is unmarried he is bound first to his parents and second to his siblings. But after a few months or years of happy marriage, the individual becomes committed first to his spouse, second to his parents, and third to his siblings. In many marriages, as children are born, they come to supersede siblings and parents. Children, however, rarely supersede the regard of one spouse for another. Although exceptions occur, the ideal of many Americans is that their closest relationship be with their spouses.

After the death of a spouse, an American may return to his siblings for emotional support, cooperation, and assistance in time of need, but Americans, nowadays especially, try to avoid becoming a burden to their married children. They are more likely to rely on siblings or friends of similar age for companionship and sympathy. Old Nunamiut parents, widows, or widowers readily look to their children for support, economically and emotionally. Most Nunamiut rarely experience actual conflict between their relationship to their spouses and their latent feelings of ultimate commitment to their parents and siblings. Only in a crisis are these sentiments likely to boil to the surface. Let us consider an interesting example.

A young man and wife were living as the junior couple in a household with the husband's parents. The senior couple had no children of their own and had adopted several children, all now grown, one of whom was this husband. Both his foster siblings and natural siblings live in the village. The husband and wife quarreled now and then and at one period their arguments became exceedingly bitter and violent, accompanied with shouting, screaming, and crying. There was talk that the wife might leave her husband's household and return to the household where her own father and an elder, unmarried sister lived. A foster sister of the recalcitrant husband took upon herself the responsibility of informing the husband's biological siblings (both natural parents having died) of the trouble and the possibility of an open break. The natural siblings were ultimately responsible for their trouble-making brother, and the older siblings especially were in a position to be morally suasive and contribute to a reconciliation or force an open break.

In this instance, the real siblings did nothing beyond commenting that it was unfortunate, partly because of their antipathy toward the senior couple and partly because they were waiting to see if a separation would actually occur. A reconciliation of sorts was achieved and the husband and wife did not separate. In listening to people discussing this incident afterward, I was impressed by the strength of, and the high regard for, bilateral ties, which superseded marriage and even adoption in a really severe dispute. There was no doubt, however, that the fact of the existence of the household was a major force in holding it together. The household was a very productive one; the father- and mother-in-law and the daughter-in-law worked very well with each other and had achieved a very high standard of living. The things they did together, the ongoing activity of the group, held it together in spite of the marital conflict. The daughter-in-law could be happy except in her marriage. Many readers have probably observed similar situations in which the fact that a household exists acts to hold it together.

When a person leaves his family of orientation and establishes his family of procreation within the same community, he can maintain a pleasant relationship with his parents and siblings in normal times by helping them in housebuilding and traveling, by cooperating in hunting and trapping, by visiting frequently, and by presenting them with meat, fat, or articles of clothing now and then. When the families of orientation of both spouses live in the same village, the man and wife have a full job in keeping both their parents and siblings and their parents- and siblings-in-law well disposed. But having several very close relatives in one community can be a real advantage when hunger or illness strikes. On the other hand, if a person leaves his family of orientation in one valley and joins his spouse and family in a distant region, locality will impose itself on Nunamiut bilaterality.

When a Nunamiut speaks of the members of his kindred, he says *ilyatka* (my relatives) meaning all those consanguineal relatives whom he recognizes as such. The plural form (inflected only for plurality) is *ilyagitch* and the uninflected singular form is *ilya*. The word ilya also means "an (entangled or involved) part of something." An informant saw a picture puzzle and said that one interlocking piece of the puzzle would be called ilya in Nunamiut Eskimo. When a Nunamiut says *ilyatka,* the plural form of the word, we translate it with the singular noun "kindred" or "personal kindred." This is unfortunate semantically because, in English, the term kindred as a singular collective noun has a certain suggestion of group-ness and corporate-ness about it which is inapplicable to Nunamiut social organization. The use of the term *ilyagitch* (kindred) among the Nunamiut cannot be construed to indicate a corporate social group of any kind. The members of any person's kindred never come together all at one time for any purpose. The members of any person's kindred never own goods, tangible or intangible, as a group, nor is a person ever considered to stand for or represent the members of his kindred as a whole in any way. Among the Nunamiut, the members of a kindred can be defined only in reference to one person, or in the case of identical twins, two persons. A person's ilyagitch is a category of people cognatically related to him within the ranges of generation and degrees of collaterality which we have defined above (pp. 135–37).

Before discussing sociological aspects of the personal kindred, we must consider how some of the terms of consanguineal relationship may be extended beyond the range indicated. I recorded instances of a person learning about a great-great-grandfather and referring to him as *amaulutqiq;* the suffix *qiq* means "one more." Reciprocally a great-great-grandfather may refer to his great-great-grandchild as *ilyulitqiq*. When ego either knows or knows of a member of the fourth ascending or descending generation, he considers him to be an *ilyapiaq,* a "real" relative, that is, a member of his kindred. In response to questions, informants said they could double the suffix to say *amaulutqitqiq,* great-great-great-grandfather, but beyond that additional suffixes did not "sound right." Thus we may see how the range of ascending and descending generations which is normally recognized may be exceeded. It should be noted, however, that this happens only occasionally for the simple reason that few persons ever know or hear of an ancestor beyond the third ascending generation.

In considering the range of the degrees of collaterality of consanguineal relatives which ego normally recognizes, let us suppose that two third cousins who know they are cousins have lived together in the same community for many years. They call each other *aganaqan* (cousin), never indicating in their terminology the degree of collaterality, and otherwise behave as cousins. If both cousins marry and produce children, a child learns to refer to whomever his parents call aganaqan, as *achaluq,* aunt, or *aŋaluq,* uncle. The children would then call their parent's third cousin achaluq or aŋaluq; he would call them *uyuro,* "nibling," and they would otherwise behave as aunts and uncles and nieces and nephews extending collaterality to the fourth degree in the first ascending generation. Furthermore, if the two third cousins lived in the same community, their children would refer to one another as aganaqan, cousin, and behave as cousins extending collaterality to the fifth degree in the same level of generation. One 60-year-old informant knew a woman living in Fairbanks who is his FaFaBrSoDa, whom he calls aganaqan. She has a young son whom he calls uyuro. When I asked him what he would call his uyuro's children when he married, my informant answered *tutichiaq,* grandchild, without hesitation. Here is a very explicit case in which a FaFaBrSoDaSo would be called tutichiaq, extending collaterality to the third degree in the second descending generation. There are few instances, however, in which the range of collaterality we have indicated is exceeded. A person seldom knows a third cousin, and few people ever have the opportunity to recognize relatives beyond the normal range given for collaterality. Not only that, but locality may actually impinge upon the recognition of those persons who are fairly closely related to ego. Some informants did not know of a grandparent's brother or a great-grandparent's brother's son. There is no compulsion on the part of a Nunamiut to find out who and where an unknown person is who theoretically could be reckoned as a member of his kindred.

What is important to a Nunamiut is not so much the abstract idea of a term of consanguineal relationship or the usual limits of the kindred, but rather those members of his kindred whom he knows personally as a result of proximity, those he has met on his travels, and those whom he has heard about from his known relatives. A man, say, travels to a distant region and encounters a family. If a man and one member of the family can establish a relative whom they both know and recognize as a member of their respective kindreds, then they can call each other by a kinship term, even if they have to exceed the normal range of the kindred. But two strangers cannot establish a relationship unless they are able to relate themselves through a link known and recognized by both of them. This fact acts as a convenient check against falsehood and possible treachery. When two strangers meet and are both able to recognize a third party as a blood relative, they are no longer strangers but relatives themselves. Thus they know they can trust each other and exchange hospitality.

The Nunamiut gossip so much about their relatives and everyone they know, and each personality is so distinctive and so important to a Nunamiut, that a stranger could hardly convince another that he was related to a man he did not know. And the sense of hospitality is so strong among relatives that no person in his right mind would risk creating a reputation as a bad host. A Nunamiut is quick to learn the names of all the relatives he meets and hears about, and remembers for life through what links they are related to him; he follows the principle that if he calls a blood relative by a certain kinship term, then he calls that relative's children by the term used for the next descending generation and recognizes them as relatives. Likewise, a Nunamiut knows that if his father calls a man *aŋaluq* (uncle), then he (ego) calls his father's uncle's children by the same term, and so on at any generation level.

Now an interesting speculation comes to mind. The ranges of the degrees of collaterality in various generations which define the consanguineal relatives whom a person normally recognizes have been suggested, and we have seen how a person outside this limit may be recognized by extending the use of a kinship term. We have indicated that such extensions are rare because of longevity in the case of generation level, because of locality in the case of degree of collaterality, and because in Nunamiut society a person is not expected, nor does he desire, to know about relatives who are long dead or who live far away. This is not to say that locality caused, determined, or gave rise to the range of the degrees of collaterality normally recognized, but the factor of locality—the size and distribution of settlements—does at least act to encourage the continued existence of the way in which a person reckons who his blood relatives are.

In youth, a person lives with his parents and of course regards them and his siblings as his closest relatives. It is very likely that a child lives with or near some grandparents and some of his parent's siblings and their children. Thus most people know very intimately and associate closely with their lineal grandparents, their aunts and uncles, and their first cousins. A young child frequently knows and lives near one or two of his lineal grandparent's siblings, who are his "classificatory" grandparents; their children, who are his aunts and uncles (in the Nunamiut sense of these terms); and their children, who are his second cousins. These consanguineal relatives are certainly the ones a young child knows best. As a child, a person may know his lineal great-grandparents and their siblings, his classificatory great-grandparents. At least, as he grows older, he usually hears stories about them. Over the years, in traveling thousands of miles, a person may encounter and recognize his classificatory great-grandparent's children who are his classificatory grandparents, as well as their children who are his aunts and uncles, and their children who are his third cousins. Ego usually knows people in this last series only slightly, primarily because of lack of contact. Because Nunamiut bands must remain relatively small and scattered, usually between 50 and 150 people for any period of time, a person has little opportunity to recognize and become familiar with distantly related consanguineal relatives.

In earlier years, when a band grew too large for the region in which its members were accustomed to hunt and trap, thus restricting their opportunities of making a good living, several households left the community and formed a new band in another valley or region. When a band split, the two resulting groups were composed for the most part of closely related persons. Distant collateral relatives tended to separate. Only people in bands which were located nearby saw each other very often. The more distant bands saw each other only once or twice a year when several bands came together for trading. The effective range of the kindred was thus limited by settlement patterns.

Now let us consider the dimension of consanguinity—certainly the strongest aspect of Nunamiut kinship relations. Aside from a specific kin term, when a Nunamiut refers to a consanguineal relative, he says *ilyaga* (my relative). When he wants to be positively understood that he is referring to a consanguineal relative, he will say *ilyapiaqka* (my real relative; the suffix *piaq* means "real," *ka* means "my"), which is equivalent to our saying "my blood relative," or technically "my consanguineal relative." The only modifications of the clarity and force of consanguinity result from adoption or illegitimacy.

When a person, at whatever age, is adopted, his natural father, mother, siblings, and other bilateral relatives are never forgotten or ignored by anyone. An adopted child is called *tiguaq* (in addition to the consanguineal term); from the word *tiguruni* (to take or grab). Many adopted children are continually reminded by their foster parents and other foster relatives of their adoption, usually in a joking way. Older adopted children sometimes told me of their adoption and who their natural parents were. An adopted baby does not remember living in his natural family, and his attachment to his foster parents and siblings becomes very strong. He enjoys all the rights and responsibilities of a natural child, including inheritance. For an adopted child, the incest restriction applies to members of his foster kindred, i.e. his kindred by adoption, as well as to the members of his natural kindred. How marriage between an adopted person and his foster third cousin would be regarded, I was never quite sure. It seemed that an adopted person would be advised against it for the same reasons given for not marrying a natural third cousin (pp. 64–65); but he could argue that his foster third cousin is not really his blood relative, and the marriage would probably be tolerated, at least to a greater extent than if two natural third cousins married. This argument, of course, would never arise in the case of foster siblings and first cousins.

Even if a person were a one-day-old baby when adopted, his natural family and relatives might claim his help in the event of a very serious blood feud in which every supporter was needed. Such a claim would create considerable conflict in the mind of an adopted individual, and he might or might not come to the aid of his real kindred. If both the natural and foster kin were adamant, only violence or exceedingly painful loss of face would resolve the conflict.

Sometimes a family adopts a child who has lived for years as a member of his natural family. In such a case, the adoption is as complete as possible; that is, the child is absorbed into his foster family with full rights and responsibilities. A young boy or girl who is adopted is much more aware of his blood ties than is a person who was adopted as an infant and, in a crisis, whether economic, legal, or political, the sentiments of the former would be severely divided. If a situation became extreme, he would be forced by the demands of his natural relatives and his own feelings to support them in any way he could.

I observed an interesting case in which a young boy was "adopted" for part of a year, returned to his original family for a while, and then adopted back again for part of another year. In such an instance, the rights and obligations associated with blood relatives operate only within a person's real kindred, although the rights and obligations a person has by virtue of living in a household would hold wherever the child might live. Informants indicated that this kind of arrangement was not true adoption and was made primarily for immediate economic reasons, the real family being burdened with too many children, the other family being able to support and wanting another child.

Informants discussed two reasons for adoption. One, already mentioned, is economic pressure. Sometimes a woman simply produces more children than she can adequately take care of, or a woman gives birth to a child ten or eleven months after a previous child. In either case, the mother tries to convince a sister, female cousin, or other close relative with a smaller family to take the newborn baby. The second reason is that a man and wife with few or no children might desire to "fill up their home" with a respectable number of children. A childless couple would feel uneasy with no offspring to support them in later years. They would be very receptive to any offers and might even ask a mother for her newborn child. Although a child is usually adopted by close relatives of the parents, this is by no means universal, as I knew from several instances. A third, but usually unexpressed, reason for adopting a child is that a man and wife acquire prestige by supporting a large family, and they are proud of their ability to take on an additional child that some other family cannot support.

When an unmarried woman gives birth, the child calls her mother and recognizes, and is recognized by, her consanguineal relatives. If the genitor is known and unmarried, the parents and relatives of the girl would create considerable pressure for him to marry her, in which case the situation would become normal. If the genitor is married and known in fact to be the genitor, he would not be recognized sociologically as the father. The child would not call him father, nor would any of the genitor's relatives recognize, or be recognized by, the child as a relative. Thus a bastard has a lopsided kindred, comprised, as a youngster, only of maternal relatives. An illegitimate child certainly does not suffer loss of dignity or his right as a human being to participate in the Nunamiut society just because he is a bastard. But when he marries, those relatives who would normally be reckoned through his father would be missing in the kindreds of his offspring.

If a married woman gives birth to a child which she conceived from a man who is not her husband, the child would nevertheless be recognized as the legitimate child of the married couple, as fully related to the members of his kindred as if his mother's husband were the genitor. The actual genitor would not be recognized as the father, the child would not recognize any of his genitor's relatives as his own relatives, and the genitor's relatives would have no obligation to or rights in the child.

Ego's relationships with the remaining members of his kindred, including his parents, siblings, and children when he is not co-resident with them, are as follows. As a mature, married son or daughter, ego is committed to support his parents should they ever need help, and they in return help him out when necessary, as far as they are able. If ego lives in a distant community, he would try to go to his parent's aid in time of crisis, but difficulty in traveling might prevent his doing so. Whenever his parents travel by, ego offers them complete hospitality, giving them any assistance they might need, which they would of course reciprocate should ego visit them. Only if ego's parents live nearby does he cooperate with them in economic matters. Ego is always very restrained in his outward behavior toward his parents, but he feels a real affection for them, manifested in an occasional very nice gift, an expression of thanks, and an infrequent but sincerely given compliment.

As a married person ego is bound to support in any crisis his siblings who live nearby. During a time of need he might also try to reach a sibling living far away. Married siblings often cooperate extensively in economic activities. Sisters especially work well together; brothers may associate well, but one sometimes notes tension and a hesitance to cooperate without reservation. Adult siblings are always very restrained toward each other, never showing overt affection, joking, or displaying jealousy or envy of any sort.

As a grandchild and great-grandchild, ego is not economically dependent upon his grandparents and great-grandparents but he is frequently given small presents, and is adored and praised by them. Ego behaves with some restraint toward his grandparents and great-grandparents and shares mild jokes with them occasionally. But the relationship is a very relaxed and friendly one and he readily turns to them for advice. A person's sentimental attachment for his grandparents and great-grandparents seems to be very great and is expressed in many gestures of courtesy, but never to the point of veneration. As ego grows older, if his grandparents and great-grandparents are still alive and live nearby or with him, he becomes increasingly responsible for supporting them.

Ego as a child is taught to share his possessions with his cousins, but not to the unqualified extent he does with siblings. When ego and his cousins become a little older, they may associate a great deal in learning how to hunt, trap, and make implements; to collect firewood, water, roots and berries, and to sew. Cousins of the same age and sex become great pals and joking partners. They often engage in mild horseplay and much ribald talk about sex. Two good friends who joke continually are said to behave like cousins. In later years, cousins continue to cooperate in economic activities, and in a crisis ego is obliged to support a cousin as best he can after seeing to the needs of his parents, siblings, children, and other lineal relatives. As a niece or nephew, classificatory grandchild or great-grandchild, ego is neither dependent upon nor obligated to support his aunts and uncles and classificatory grandparents and great-grandparents, under normal circumstances. In an economic crisis, however, ego knows he can turn to these collateral relatives for economic support to some extent and, when he is grown, he may be called upon to offer them support. As an adult, ego has learned that he can expect hospitality from his collateral relatives living in distant regions and vice versa.

As with cousins, ego usually enjoys a great joking relationship with collateral relatives of ascending and descending generations, especially those not too much older or younger. I have seen an uncle tease a young nephew and niece to the point of tears—something unthinkable for a parent to do to his own child. Collateral relatives often cooperate very happily in many phases of economic activity. In asking a young man of 17 why he often hunted with a man of another household who was in his thirties, he replied, "Oh, he's my uncle."

Although ego is bound to support and cooperate with those lineal relatives and siblings with whom he is living, he is able to exercise greater choice in economic matters with collateral relatives and even nonresident mature siblings. I observed married brothers who rarely hunted together, whereas others cooperated very closely in hunting, trapping, making implements, and so forth. Of the many possible combinations of consanguineal relatives, close associations develop largely on the basis of similarity of age and sex and on personal compatibility. Alignments shift from season to season; no one wants to be too exclusive—the wider the bonds of cooperation, the better.

Among the Nunamiut it is very common for two or more households to travel for several days together or to live together in an isolated valley for a season to hunt and trap. Such complexes of households are not necessarily organized on the basis of membership in a kindred alone, although many of the people in a traveling group are usually related by blood. The Nunamiut do not have closed kin groupings, and an unrelated family could easily join a small cluster of families who are related.

We have seen that the structure of the kindred, with possible extensions, provides ego with a set of potential relationships involving economic support and economic cooperation upon which residence (in terms of households) and locality (in terms of communities) act to select those persons whom ego actually does support, and those with whom ego does or may cooperate. We now turn to further sociological aspects of the personal kindred among the Nunamiut.

In legal disputes, those consanguineal relatives living with an accused person are especially bound to support him not only verbally but also in any action he might take, and they are bound to come to his defense with little or no reservation. Those relatives of an accused person who are less closely associated with him would tend to come to his defense verbally, knowing that they must support their blood relative if he is ever to come to their support. Another motive for supporting an accused relative is that people often compare morally, and identify together, two persons who are blood relatives. Thus, aside from the expectation of returned support, one defends an accused relative, at least verbally, in an effort to protect one's own character from blemish. On the other hand, of course, a conscientious man might feel that his accused relative has indeed committed a wrong. In most instances, especially in less serious cases, a person's sense of right and wrong about a particular action is likely to be absorbed into the more important sense of right and wrong of kinship relations.

Murder is a much more serious matter, and here the bonds of kinship are tested to their utmost. When a man is killed, the closely related members of his kindred do not rest until complete revenge has been achieved. The immediate relatives of the deceased, especially the members of his family of orientation and his children, if any, recruit as much support from other relatives as they can. Their first action, if possible, is to kill the murderer or maybe one of his closest kin. Then of course, the members of the murderer's kindred are brought into the feud. These two kindreds may snipe at each other for years, possibly extending the feud to the kindreds of all the people who are murdered. In a blood feud, the most closely related consanguineal relatives carry the brunt of the fighting and enlist the support of more distantly related consanguineal relatives when they are able. One individual may be a member of both kindreds. When kindreds overlap in this fashion, the closest relationship in collaterality and generation usually determines which side a person supports. When a man is only distantly related to both murdered men, however, his past associations of residence and friendship may well determine which side he supports.

Because no Nunamiut now living have been involved in a blood feud, I could obtain no clear-cut case of a conflict of overlapping kindreds, but informants were able to generalize about the nature of the commitments of relatives in such a crisis. In a recent instance of suspected shamanism, the accused man's children, grandchildren, nephews, and nieces (as well as a son-in-law and a brother-in-law) were quick to tell me that such gossip was meaningless. Only persons unrelated to the suspected man felt he possessed shamanistic power. A grandchild of the son-in-law who supported the accused felt the accused did possess shamanistic power. That grandchild was the son and nephew of persons who were most adamant about the accused's shamanistic proclivities.

Feuds can create very mixed feelings in an individual; a person directly involved in a feud may come to feel that a resolution must be reached. Many years ago a blood feud arose between the kindreds of two men on the Arctic coast. Several persons were killed. One man, after many weeks of emotional and mental anguish, killed his own brother, whom he believed to be the one really evil force in the feud. This was considered as extreme an action as a human being could possibly take (except for killing a parent or child), but it ended the feud and saved the lives of many people. This is of course an exception to the obligation of mutual support within the family but illustrates that individuals, when highly motivated by what they believe to be the proper course of action, are sometimes capable of taking initiative of the most extreme kind.

In concluding our discussion of the kindred, it bears repeating that every Nunamiut thinks of ilyatha as "my relatives" and not as "my group of relatives" in a collective sense. Rather, he regards the members of his kindred as a social category which presents him with a set of potential relationships. The Nunamiut kindred does not constitute a group. I would make the distinction in this way: A person's kindred constitutes one category of persons, i.e. all his consanguineal relatives whom he recognizes as such. The primary dimension of the definition of this category is blood relationship—a Nunamiut cultural notion. Thus it is a common quality or attribute that characterizes a category. The term group, on the other hand, implies an assemblage, cluster, or aggregation of persons (e.g. the household, the community) who explicitly undertake some common activity or behave in such a way as to exhibit their group-ness. All the members of one social category in a society may of course constitute a social group, but this is not imperative by definition and is not the case among the Nunamiut. Even in the formation of the household, although kinship is the primary consideration, I have maintained the distinction between the household as the fundamental social group and the family as the basic structural unit in Nunamiut society. Among the Nunamiut, social groups engaging in any activity for any period of time are formed by using the defining dimension of a social category to some particular extent and by invoking other considerations such as friendship, economic exigency, and contiguity.

In the discussion of consanguineal relatives, references have been made to those relatives who are related to ego by marriage either to him or to the members of his kindred. The relationships of husband, wife, father-in-law, and mother-in-law have for the most part been described. Here we consider affinal relatives more generally.

In order to illustrate how ego categorizes his in-laws, a summary of Nunamiut terms of affinal relationships follows.

uii, husband

nuliaq, wife

nuliaqpaq, the senior wife of a polygynous marriage

nukagaq, the junior wife of a polygynous marriage

tataruaq, father-in-law, includes WiFa, HuFa

anaruaq, mother-in-law, includes WiMo, HuMo

niŋao, the term used by ego to refer to those males married to his consanguineal relatives of the same and descending generations; in response to specific inquiries, informants hesitated to call male in-laws of ascending generations by this term.

ukuak, used by ego to refer to those females married to his consanguineal relatives of the same and descending generations; similar to niŋao, informants hesitated to apply the term ukuak to female in-laws of ascending generations.

sakiraq, primarily used to designate spouse's siblings, but is used more extensively. Spouse's father and mother, as we have noted, are called tataruaq and anaruaq respectively, but in discussing the relationship of ego to his spouse's kindred, I found that ego may use the term *sakiraq* for all consanguineal relatives of spouse of the same and ascending generations. These persons refer to ego as niŋao (or ukuak); he reciprocates by calling them sakiraq. This leaves one's spouse's consanguineal relatives of descending generations and the spouses of ego's consanguineal relatives of ascending generations without an in-law term. In the case of the latter, we should note that in practice, a Nunamiut child identifies the spouses of senior collateral relatives as blood relatives and usually calls them by consanguineal terms. Theoretically, however, they stand as niŋao and ukuak to ego. In the case of the former (spouse's consanguineal relatives of descending generations), we should again note that in practice a specific term is rarely used. Some informants said there are no terms for such persons. Theoretically, however, these affinal relatives stand as sakiraq to ego. In order to justify my inferential extension of the use of niŋao, ukuak, and sakiraq, consider the following information: I discovered that if I had remained among the Nunamiut and taken a wife, a situation which did not occur, I would have been called "niŋao" by every person in the village. In return I could have called every Nunamiut at Anaktuvuk Pass "sakiraq." I heard similar uses of these terms ignoring generation level and even subsuming the terms tataruaq and anaruaq (when father- and mother-in-law are classified with spouse's consanguineal relatives) within the broader category of sakiraq. Thus the ethnographer is presented with an interesting difference between informants' statements and their actual behavior. In the broadest sense, therefore, we observe that the terms niŋao and ukuak designate the spouses of ego's kindred, and sakiraq designates the kindred of ego's spouse.

nukonouruaq, wife of spouse's younger brothers *and* husband of spouse's younger sisters.

aŋayunoruaq, wife of spouse's older brothers *and* husband of spouse's older sisters (the age and sex of ego and referent do not affect the terms of these "in-law" relationships through two intervening marriages, only the relative age of the two links between ego and referent).

nuliik, coparent; i.e. SoWiFa, SoWiMo, DaHuFa, etc.

While Nunamiut terms of affinal relationships are more precise than our own rather vague "in-law," we have seen that there is nevertheless a certain flexibility in the Nunamiut use of these terms, which is also the case in the rights, obligations, and customary behavior implied by them.

As an in-law to the spouses of his kindred, ego is expected to extend only limited support in time of economic need. Since ego would try to help any of his own relatives who are in difficulty, their spouses would receive some help by virtue of their marriage and presence in a household. Just as ego has greater obligation to his lineal relatives and siblings than to his collateral relatives, so is he expected to offer more aid and feel a closer attachment to the spouses of his lineal relatives and siblings than to the spouses of more distant relatives.

A person often cooperates in many economic activities with his siblings' spouses of the same sex. When a sibling or close blood relative marries, an ego of the same age and sex of the new spouse is supposed to offer to cooperate—to show his approval of the marriage. If they get along well, they may associate for years. Ego is expected to be pleasant and hospitable toward the spouses of his more distant blood relatives, but he is not likely to go out of his way to cooperate with them just because of their relationship, or to present gifts to them. Ego may treat his more distantly related in-laws with minimal decency or, personalities and location permitting, he may associate very closely with them in economic and social matters.

The fact that persons married to one's blood relatives are reckoned as affinal relatives, involving the expectations we have indicated, presents an individual with an additional range, beyond his kindred, of potential relationships in economic matters.

In a legal dispute, a person may seek to enlist the support of the spouses of his kindred. He may appeal to the existence of their affinal relationship as such or he may point out how it would be to the in-law's advantage to identify himself with ego and his relatives in a given community. An in-law, especially if he has few or no consanguineal relatives living nearby, may seek to associate himself with a powerful or dominant person by voicing his support in a legal or political crisis. Even though none of an individual's consanguineal relatives is involved in a feud, he may support his spouse in seeking revenge, especially if his spouse is closely related to the murdered person.

One important function of an in-law is hospitality. A man and his family traveling in a distant region know they can rely on either of their kindreds for hospitality and aid for a few days. The spouse joins the host in making the travelers welcome and in seeing to their needs.

Although a stepfather or stepmother is an affinal relative, as far as I could determine ego usually treats a stepparent as a natural parent. I did hear of instances, however, in which a person asserted very emphatically that his stepmother was not in fact his mother. Still, by virtue of being in the same household, mutual support and cooperation are obligatory in spite of differences. If a child is very young when a parent remarries, conflict is unlikely.

When a person's child marries, the former acquires not only a son- or daughter-in-law, but also a set of co-parents. One's obligations to a co-parent are formally negligible. I observed co-parents visiting, and no doubt the marriage of their respective children brought them closer together for visiting and light joking, but I encountered no evidence that one was expected to offer support to a co-parent or felt compelled to cooperate with him. There might be an occasional gift exchange, but such an exchange was not one-sided, symbolic of the marriage, or formally required.

As an in-law to the members of his spouse's family of orientation, ego is expected to offer support and to cooperate on major projects. When a newly married man or woman joins the household of his spouse's family, complete support and cooperation is obligatory. If these closely related in-laws live nearby, ego presents them, especially the parents, with gifts of meat, fat, or articles of clothing now and then in order to maintain good relations. Ego offers his parents- and siblings-in-law whatever economic support he is able to muster after seeing to the needs of his consanguineal relatives living nearby. He most likely cooperates very easily with his in-laws (members of spouse's family of orientation) in the usual daily activities, especially since the tensions common between parent and child, and sibling and sibling, are absent, and he may come to regard them with real affection over a lifetime of close association.

As an in-law through two intervening marriages, ego is not obligated to support his spouse's siblings' spouses. He may join with them in some economic activities if they are living nearby and if they are compatible. Ego may joke with spouse's siblings' spouses of the same sex and similar age.

As an in-law to spouse's kindred (other than spouse's immediate family), ego is expected to offer only limited support in time of crisis. Ego may cooperate with in-laws in economic matters, location and personalities permitting, or he may merely treat them with minimal decency.

In legal disputes, a person may encourage his spouse's consanguineal relatives to support him. Spouse's parents and siblings may readily come to his defense, especially if co-resident or living nearby, but other members of spouse's kindred are more likely to be swayed by the accused's position or lack of position than by the fact of their relationship. In blood feuds, a member of spouse's kindred is likely to stay out of the fight unless he has associated with ego for many years.

In discussing kinship generally, Nunamiut informants differentiated very carefully between *ilyagitch* (consanguineal relatives) and *ninao, ukuak,* and *sakiraq* (affinal relatives). In blood feuds, severe legal disputes, and malicious gossip, this distinction between consanguineal and affinal relatives becomes sharply defined, but in other matters such as economic support, cooperation, and the expression of affection, once a relationship is established, either by blood or by marriage, many of the same obligations ensue, particularly when residence and locality bring people together.

FILIATION AND INHERITANCE. By virtue of being born to a husband and wife, a Nunamiut child is bilaterally filiated to them; that is, the connective bond of blood relationship between parent and child of either sex is reckoned equally with both the father and the mother. The relationship of ego to any relative is traced with absolutely no distinction between the maternal and paternal side of any link. Once consanguinity as such is established, the degree of collaterality and the level of generation are the only dimensions of relationships within the kindred.

Bilateral filiation is manifested in several ways. When a child is born, his parents give him one or more names, usually the name(s) of a recently deceased blood relative from either side, without favoring either side. Today children still receive their first names in this manner, although they now assume the last name of the father and, until recent years, neither spouse took the name of the other. For all consanguineal relatives of the same sex, of the same degree of collaterality and of the same level of generation, ego uses the same kin term irrespective of the sex of linking kinsmen, and no relative is favored on the basis of the sex of any intervening links.

Before a person dies, he distributes some of his possessions. He might give to a close relative or very close friend a small remembrance, such as a cup, a pair of labrets, or a knife. Nunamiut used to carry amulets, such as a small skin pouch filled with mosquitoes or a miniature *ulu,* which a woman wore on a string around her neck. An amulet was said to have great power in warding off sickness. Shamans and laymen could make amulets for their own use as well as for sale. Many years ago a woman was said to have killed a huge enemy with a tremendous blow from a miniature ulu. Before the possessor of an amulet died he usually gave it to a grandchild or, in rare instances, to an unrelated young child to whom the old person had taken a fancy.

A shaman occasionally decided to transfer some of his shamanistic power to a niece or nephew, grandchild, or perhaps an unrelated person, whom he had instructed. This might be done by instructing him for the last time in the methods of obtaining power from a helping spirit. Or the shaman might give his protégé an amulet he had used in securing power. After the shaman's death, the initiate might make a small sacrifice now and then, such as dropping a small piece of meat or fat near the shaman's grave, to thank him for the good luck brought by the power or to maintain the strength of the power.

After a person dies, his valuables are distributed. The surviving spouse receives most of them, such as the house, sleds, umiak (in the old days), dogs, harnesses, and stores of meat, fat, and skins. The surviving children according to sex receive such things as the weapons, kayaks, tools, tool bag, sewing kit, traps, snares, and other smaller items. Residence again is a factor. An adult child living near or with a parent at the time of his death is likely to receive more than one who lives in a distant community, unless he comes to claim his full share as a legal heir. A son- or daughter-in-law does not technically inherit anything, but through an heir (his spouse) an in-law may in fact acquire the use of a gun, or sewing kit, or kayak by virtue of his presence in a household. When a very young person dies, whether married or not, his parents and siblings are likely to take his material possessions. A surviving spouse of a short-lived marriage may receive only one or two small items. As children are born, a spouse gradually achieves the position of principal heir.

Non-Kin Relationships

STRANGERS. All the Nunamiut of Anaktuvuk Pass are known to one another. The older people living in the Pass come from several different regions (Appendix B), but of course have come to know each other very intimately, since everyone now lives in one village. In the old days, especially before 1900 when the Nunamiut population was much larger and people were spread out over a very wide geographical region (Appendix A), some Nunamiut living in the upper Colville River seldom encountered the Nunamiut living in the Itkillik River valley and valleys farther east. In addition to the distance between these two areas, the Nunamiut on the upper Colville River traveled down to Icy Cape or to Kotzebue to obtain blubber and sealskins, whereas most Nunamiut living along the Itkillik River traveled to the mouth of the Colville River for coastal supplies. Since all the links between two people who are distantly related must be recognized by both, the distribution of relatively small bands over a wide area often prevented a person from knowing all his consanguineal relatives. Furthermore, since Nunamiut population was expanding in the late 1800s before the advent of

whaling, many Eskimos from regions peripheral to the main territory of the Nunamiut joined established bands in the Colville River
drainage and over time were assimilated. Thus in the old days, it
was possible for Nunamiut, traveling to an unfamiliar region
within their territory, to encounter Nunamiut who were strangers.
On trading expeditions to the coast and elsewhere, a Nunamiut also
came into contact with Point Barrow, Point Hope, Kobuk, and
other Eskimos who were strangers to him.

A Nunamiut treated an Eskimo stranger initially with reserve.
A stranger could be a thief, rapist, murderer, or enemy or, more
likely, he could become a friend and a possible source of trade,
and he might eventually even marry into a band. Nunamiut frequently talk about how much they like to have in-laws from
different regions even though they are hesitant to let their own
women leave the Brooks Range. Only if gestures of friendship are
not reciprocated will a stranger remain a stranger or become an
enemy.

Indians were generally regarded as enemies and many first contacts were violent. In the old days, a few Nunamiut used to meet
Kutchin Indians at Barter Island and the Koyukon Indians at
various places along the John River for trading. Relations were
usually strained. An Indian stranger was regarded with suspicion
as well as reserve. If it became apparent that no violence was
going to take place, a Nunamiut would try to establish a trading
relationship, but rarely one of friendship or complete partnership
involving spouse exchange.

Nunamiut today meet many strangers, mostly white men, but
also an occasional Indian or Eskimo. In contrast to Indians, white
men are usually classed as potential friends who might furnish
employment or a trading relationship. The women, at least
initially, tend to be more reserved than the men with strangers.

ENEMIES. The conflict between the Kutchin Indians and the
Nunamiut was deep-seated (pp. 44–49). The Nunamiut gave the
enemy no quarter, even to the extent of cutting an Indian's body
open and placing his stomach membrane over his face so his iñua
(soul) could not depart. In warfare, every member of an Indian or
Eskimo community might be killed except for one man who would
be sent back to tell his people what had happened. As a magnani-
mous gesture on the part of the victors of a skirmish, the women
and children might be spared.

When two Eskimo communities came into conflict, shamans

might exchange power gestures, such as trying to make everyone ill in the enemy community. If a Nunamiut were visiting the coast and discovered that a small piece had been cut from his boot or parka, he would suspect that some coastal Eskimo, possibly a shaman, had attempted to make him ill or to kill him. In such an event, the only solution was to destroy the garment and seek the advice of a trusted shaman.

In blood feuds, a person usually attempted to kill only the murderer. Inland Nunamiut sometimes were drawn into a feud with coastal Eskimos over the abduction of a woman; her kinsmen and very likely the members of her community were obligated to demand her return. If she were mutilated or killed, they were compelled to seek to kill the abductors, but the feud could easily expand into a full-scale battle between communities.

PARTNERSHIP. Most Nunamiut adults had partners in the various groups of Eskimos with whom they came into contact. The term *niuvirik* means a partnership of two persons (*niuvik* is the singular uninflected form meaning "a partner," and *niuviga* means "my partner"). Today, some of the wealthier Nunamiut still maintain partnerships. Women as well as men had partners. Between inland and coastal groups, a partnership was primarily economic, secondarily social. A Nunamiut could obtain the blubber, muktuk (whale skin), and seal and bearded seal skins which he needed for food and clothing. A coastal Eskimo could obtain caribou, wolf, wolverine, and other skins for clothing and flint for implements. A great many other items were traded, but these were the typical, certainly the most important, ones. Socially, a partnership implied dancing, gossiping, fun, and occasional spouse exchange. A person was expected to be fair in his economic dealings, and a partnership might last a lifetime; it was likely to be abrogated only if one partner cheated or was no longer able to trade. A person was expected to trade only with his partner and not to intrude on someone else's relationship. Two persons of similar economic stature tended to pair off: a coastal umialik with an inland umialik, a coastal man of average economic status with an inland man of like status.

Partnerships between persons of different bands were exceedingly important to the Eskimos of northern Alaska. Most Nunamiut bands could not possibly have subsisted in the Brooks Range without trade from the coast.

Blubber and seal skins, now supplemented or replaced by trade goods, are the items the Nunamiut must have from the coast or other trade centers. Before the introduction of rubber boots, bearded sealskin was the only satisfactory material for boot soles for summer use. A few Nunamiut have tried to make summer boots from grizzly bear hide but reportedly without success. More essential however is blubber. Some years ago two families survived through a winter on ptarmigan and blubber when no caribou were to be had (p. 248). Ptarmigan alone would have been insufficient because of their low fat content.

The Nunamiut are able to obtain a fair amount of fat from caribou as well as from grizzly bears, moose, mountain sheep, and to a lesser extent from ground squirrels, marmots, ducks, and geese. But these sources are not constantly accessible nor do they occur in sufficient numbers to satisfy Nunamiut needs. Blubber, on the other hand, could always be traded from partners on the coast. The blubber of seals, bearded seals, and whales was packed in sealskin pokes, freighted inland by umiak and sled, and could be stored for months. Nunamiut rarely have difficulty in obtaining enough meat, but fat is a constant problem, in contrast to the Kobuk Eskimos who enjoy access to the fat-laden salmon resources. In a year when vegetation is scanty owing to light rainfall, caribou carry less fat than normally. And should the following winter be severe, caribou exhaust their limited fat reserves, leaving the Nunamiut in difficult straits, especially in December, January, and February. With a good supply of blubber (or present-day substitutes) obtained through a coastal partner, the Nunamiut can survive these months.

Within a band, a person who preferred to remain inland in the spring often exchanged late summer and early fall skins for coastal goods from a relative who frequented the coast. If a person who remained in the mountains had no close relative with whom he could easily trade, he often had a partnership with a nonrelative living in his band. Their relationship was much more informal than an interband partnership and did not imply spouse exchange. Often, as is the case today, two intraband partners hunted, gossiped, joked, and danced together. Such a partnership usually grows out of close friendship and is distinguished from friendship by the use of the term *niuviga* (my partner). An intraband partnership usually lasts more than a year but not necessarily as long as a partnership between the coast and the mountains.

FRIENDSHIP. In the band in which a person lives there are some people who are not relatives, partners, strangers, or enemies. If a person is cordial in his relationship with such people and occasionally exchanges gestures of friendship—presenting gifts or rendering services—they come to be known as friends. They might hunt and even dance together. The relationship of two friends of similar age and sex may become so close that they regard each other as partners. A young person often has an older friend, a nonrelative, from whom he might gain a few pointers in making a sled or setting traps. Friendship also implies joking. Sometimes two friends are said to joke "like cousins." In time of economic or legal crisis, a friend may be relied upon for aid and support, after he sees to the needs of his own relatives.

In a village also, a person may know a few people who are not relatives, strangers, enemies, partners, or friends. If two persons have lived for a long time in the same village with no evidence either of hostility or hospitality, they merely enjoy a relationship of cordial distance. They would share a feeling of common territoriality. Such a relationship is rare among the Nunamiut and is usually a prelude to friendship or enmity.

NAMESAKES. When two people who know each other happen to have the same name, they enjoy a namesake relationship. They use the term *atik* (my namesake) in personal address and referentially. If they are related, the kinship bond is that much stronger. If they are unrelated, they often dance together as namesakes and generally maintain a relationship of mutual trust and hospitality. They may hunt together and even offer support in time of need. Joking as such did not appear to be an expected part of a namesake relationship but might accompany it.

The Nunamiut of the northern Brooks Range indicated to me a feeling of identification as Nunamiut distinct from all coastal Eskimos, from the Eskimos living on the Kobuk and Selawik rivers, and from some of those Eskimos living in the lower reaches of such rivers as the Noatak, Utukok, and Kuk, although these last groups were considered to be very much like the Nunamiut. Some informants even referred to these Eskimos as Nunamiut, but they never referred to the Kobuk Eskimos as Nunamiut. The Nunamiut characterize themselves as those bands of Eskimos who camped during most of the year in that part of the Brooks Range drained by the Colville River and its tributaries (including the Itkillik River), those bands of Nunamiut who in the latter part of the 1800s and early 1900s were venturing into the Kuparuk, Saga-vanirktok, Ivishak, and Canning rivers to the east of the Itkillik River and, according to many informants, those bands of Eskimos living in the upper reaches of the Noatak, Utukok, and Kuk rivers.

The Nunamiut consider themselves to be dependent on the migrant caribou, and some Nunamiut assert that they could subsist on caribou alone without trade from the coast. But it appears to me that the Nunamiut are in fact dependent on the coastal trade (or the present substitution of imported goods) for existence. Only a few isolated families could go it alone without trade, for the Brooks Range is not rich in food resources. The Nunamiut further believe that they speak the natural or correct dialect of Eskimo. They are very aware of different coastal dialects and of the Kobuk Eskimo dialect; they also know that their kinship terminology differs from that of the coastal and Kobuk Eskimos, although the overall patterns are similar enough that a Nunamiut has no diffi-culty in learning them. The Nunamiut point out that their tech-nology differs from both coastal and Kobuk Eskimos because of ecological reasons. According to my informants, "tools [broadly] vary according to the [demands of the] country." The coastal Eskimos rely heavily on the exploitation of sea mammals. Kobuk Eskimos live along the Kobuk and Selawik rivers in the timber, where they rely on salmon and other fish, moose, and caribou. In the Brooks Range mountains north of the timber, the Nunamiut are singularly dependent on the caribou.

As pointed out earlier, all the Nunamiut share a verbal tradi-tion which they believe sets them apart from other Eskimos and illustrates that they are indeed a unique group. To a Nunamiut, the feeling that he is in fact a Nunamiut is all-important. When one meets a Nunamiut on the coast, and there is talk about the differ-ences between coastal and inland life, he is quick, emphatic, and nostalgic in stating that he is a Nunamiut, although he realizes he has become assimilated into another group and that properly speaking his children are not Nunamiut.

Many Nunamiut know that there are other Eskimos living in Alaska, Siberia, Canada, and Greenland. A few are aware of some affinity through language over this vast region, but the tie is very vague. They know very little of trade beyond the Siberian Eskimos to the west and the Mackenzie River Eskimos and perhaps the Coppermine Eskimos to the east. But the awareness of being a part of a larger northern world, so to speak, makes a Nunamiut feel a little more significant as he continues to encounter the economic and political power which the white men appear to possess.

Most Nunamiut are aware that they are part of Alaska. Several Nunamiut have been to Tanana, Fairbanks, and Anchorage for medical or other reasons. They know that they are a small, but perhaps well-known part of the state. Some of the young people are very curious to learn more about Alaska, but their role often seems to them to be undefined. Difficulty in communicating about goals, difference in goals themselves, and difference in methods of achieving them often confuse Nunamiut about their expected response and attitude toward the state.

Nunamiut conceptions about the United States are vague. In the 1960 presidential election they voted under the auspices of a school teacher, although there appeared to be little understanding of the issues involved. Very few Nunamiut have been "outside," down to the "lower forty-eight," as the first 48 states are known in Alaska. During the winter of 1961–62, four Nunamiut in their late teens attended Chemawa Indian School in Oregon, where they undoubtedly formed ideas about the United States as a whole which will greatly influence the conceptions of other young Nunamiut about modern American culture.

Some Nunamiut are nebulously aware that there are other countries in addition to the United States. A Nunamiut once heard an Englishman speak and, although he could hardly understand him, he could recognize that he spoke English. The Nunamiut are aware of Russia and have heard about the struggle between it and the United States. One Nunamiut said that Russia was trying to "grab all the countries," which he did not feel was right. In general, their conceptions of the world are very vague, and most Nunamiut know very little of it outside of northern Alaska.

6. The Band

IN the fall of 1960 the last Nunamiut family living in the Brooks Range joined the village of Anaktuvuk Pass and built a permanent sod house there. The Nunamiut community has thus ceased to be a band, which was essentially a shifting aggregation of households whose members identified themselves as the inhabitants of a region—usually a large valley or an area dominated by a lake or a major river junction. Although many Nunamiut families now spend several months of the year away from Anaktuvuk Pass, hunting and trapping, the households comprising the community no longer shift as a group either within a region or from region to region, and the settlement at the Pass must now be regarded as a village. Most of my discussion with the Nunamiut, and indeed much of my experience among them, concerned the community as a band. Many aspects of band organization still characterize the village, others have been slightly modified over the years, while some principles of band organization no longer operate in today's context. The following description of the community concerns the band; when appropriate, reference will be made to the village.

A band was composed of several households, the members of which resided together in a recognized hunting territory and traveled and camped as a group on trading expeditions to other regions. During the summer and winter months, the households that customarily composed a band usually dispersed in order to trap and to make a better living between caribou migrations. During part or all of the summer and winter, a band might stay together if there had been an adequate kill from the last migration.

When a specific band known to reside in a certain locality regrouped in the spring or fall, one or more households might decide to go elsewhere and join another band. Likewise, a few households from another area could decide to join a particular band. A Nunamiut band was a shifting aggregation of households that located itself in a region which offered good opportunities for exploiting the caribou and other elements of the environment. An additional feature of a band not found in, say, a small complex of households, was the construction of a communal house and its related activities, which we shall discuss shortly. The basis of the formation of a band was twofold: kinship and a sense of territoriality. Households that were linked by ties of blood or marriage naturally felt secure together. In any band, however, there were likely to be unrelated families, many of whose members had been born and had lived for many years in one region, who could therefore live in the same community in mutual trust and close association. Informants displayed a very strong sense of territoriality in relating accounts of battles and conflicts with the Indians. The Nunamiut felt that their country had been invaded and that the Indians had encroached upon their hunting and trapping prerogatives. The few white men who occasionally hunt in the Brooks Range near Anaktuvuk Pass give most of their meat to the Nunamiut, but, should many white men begin to take large quantities of meat, caribou hides, and furs out of the country, there is no doubt that strong sentiments of territoriality would be aroused. Similarly, when state and federal authorities try to tell Eskimos how, what, and when to hunt, they feel it a considerable imposition.

During the summer and winter months when a band dispersed, two, three, or perhaps four households clustered together to hunt, fish, and trap. Such a group was only a temporary cooperative complex of households with little or no continuity in membership or time. Such a cluster did not build a communal house but was formed usually to accomplish a specific economic purpose, such as a long trip or a season's trapping. An independent household cluster ceased to exist when it merged into a band.

Today, clusters of two or more families often establish temporary camps away from the village in order to hunt, trap, and fish. This is done mostly during the winter months when caribou are less likely to appear near the village. During the summer, because of the influx of white men and the difficulty of traveling when there is no snow, only an occasional family or two leaves the village, but individual hunters and small groups of men may leave any time for a day or two or as long as three weeks.

A band was, of course, larger than a temporary household cluster. The group was a recognized social entity persisting from year to year with a sense of membership, though flexible, and a definite sense of territoriality. The band engaged in such corporate activities as hunting caribou, constructing a communal house, communal eating, singing, dancing, traveling as a group during a trading expedition, and fighting as a unit in warfare.

Most bands ranged from 50 to 150 or so people. For two or three seasons, a band that had done especially well in corralling caribou might attain 300 to 400 members, but a band of that size was too large for the resources of the Brooks Range.

Whether precontact or present-day hunting methods are used (both are very effective), too many hunters in one region tend to alter the migration patterns of caribou and will, over time, deplete the caribou population. As we have noted this has been a problem for the Nunamiut in the past.

During this century the population of the Nunamiut in the Brooks Range has been so small and dispersed that not until recently has overhunting in one region been a problem. In talking with informants, it became obvious that overhunting was certainly a concern of the more intelligent Nunamiut decades ago, despite their inability to do much about it. Because there was neither a sufficiently powerful centralized leadership nor the means to control population growth, a thoughtful Nunamiut in the 1880s could only watch his people in silence as they sealed their doom. Even today with a population just over 100 some of the better hunters are beginning to complain that there are too many hunters in the field, that even a concentrated population of 100 is too large for the Brooks Range. But no one as yet has seriously contemplated forming another village in a nearby valley. Individuals may leave Anaktuvuk Pass, and with the increasing opportunities of temporary employment offered by white men, the reduced effectiveness of each hunter in a crowded field may not affect individual household economies for some time.

Because overhunting and the ensuing decline of caribou population occurred so long ago, I could not obtain reliable estimates of the populations and location of all the Nunamiut bands then in the Brooks Range. On the basis of informants' comments, historical information, and inference from the present situation, the estimate of 50 to 150 people for a stable band in one region seems justified. Appendix A gives some idea about the distribution of the more stable bands during the late 1800s and the formation of the temporary bands resulting from population increase. It should be emphasized, however, that a band could grow to 300 or 400, and one would expect archaeological data to confirm this.

The Communal House

When several households came together in the fall and spring to form a band, they contributed the materials and labor necessary to construct a *karigi* (communal house). The Nunamiut karigi was merely an enlarged caribou skin tent, a temporary edifice. The willow frame was larger than that of a normal dwelling, with more and larger willow poles and many more caribou skins. In any season, the karigi was constructed in the same fashion. A hundred or more people (admittedly close quarters) could gather in a Nunamiut karigi. Or, on short notice, the frame of one's caribou skin tent could be expanded, and as many as fifty or sixty people could gather for an evening of conviviality. There is an old Nunamiut saying: "An Eskimo's tent will never burst; there is always room for one more." On occasion, how true that seemed to be. Today the Nunamiut gather under one roof only four or five times a year for communal eating and dancing; in recent years they have used an old army tent for a karigi in the summer, and a large sod house in the winter.

When a band had especially good luck during a caribou migration, many of the member households might stay together for several months during the summer or winter. In this case, the karigi that was built when everyone first came together would be maintained and repaired as needed. Only when the several families decided to leave the community would they dismantle it and claim their skins.

In contrast to the limited use of the karigi today, it formerly served as the center of much community activity. As soon as the karigi was constructed, everyone came together for a communal meal, and continued to do every day as long as the band remained together. In the afternoon, the men gathered in the karigi to work and visit while the women prepared the food in their respective homes. At an agreed time, usually when the sun passed over a certain hill, all the women brought their wooden pots full of boiled caribou meat and any available delicacies to the karigi and set everything in the center of the floor. The men, women, and children of each household gathered together around the walls. The young men and women of the community served equal portions of each dish to each person, saving a fair share for themselves after everyone else had eaten. The good hunters enjoyed a rise in prestige and had the pleasure of seeing their surplus distributed to the families whose hunters had had poor luck.

During the first few days after the formation of a band, the hunters met in the karigi to discuss the coming migration of caribou and review their customary plans for corralling them. As soon as the first big kills were made and the meat, fat, and skins were divided among the households, the communal eating took on new zest, with huge quantities of freshly boiled meat and fat. The people in a band continued eating together until they split up to go their own ways.

After the evening meal, the men often brought out their drums and sang. The Nunamiut drum, still in use today, is made in the fashion of a tambourine, from caribou skin (with the hair removed) stretched over a thin, circular spruce frame, 2 feet in diameter. A water drum has recently come into use, and is made by stretching a wet caribou skin, with the hair removed, over a tub half filled with water. Slender, flexible willow sticks are used for beating the drums.

A song was, and is, composed in a few minutes. My chief informant once composed a song as he walked up to the karigi for an evening of singing and dancing. When he arrived, his song was not quite finished, so he walked around the karigi two or three times before entering. When the drums were ready, he announced that he had composed a song and proceeded to sing it, tapping the edge of a drum very lightly. At first it was wordless—only a melody with a definite rhythm and a variation of three or four vocalic tones. After singing it two or three times, the men who were sitting near the drums began to join the composer in certain passages they had learned. Before long, all the drummers had learned the whole song. The following day, the composer sang the song at my request a few times and spontaneously added a few words reminiscent of the dance.

Once, while we were sitting near a small boulder watching for caribou, a Nunamiut told me that many years ago an old Nunamiut was sitting alone where we were. As he (my companion) traveled by, the old man called out to him to hear a new song he had just composed about the coming new year. This song, the Happy New Year song, is one of the most popular now sung by the Nunamiut at Anaktuvuk Pass.

The creation of songs in this fashion is very common, and some

persons are especially noted for their talent. When a song acquires
words, they are usually descriptive, commemorating some occasion
—the coming of a new year, the first snowfall, the coming together
of everyone after a long absence, etc. Only the Kobuk Eskimos
reputedly compose love songs, some of which the Nunamiut have
learned.

After the drummers have sung several times, one or two people
stand up to dance—individual motion dances in time to the music.
Dancing is very important to the Nunamiut; this is one time they
say when everyone can be happy—no one is hungry or cold or
mad at anyone. Even a shy person is obliged to express himself
ecstatically in an acceptable and even expected manner. An out-
spoken, extroverted person looks forward to a few happy moments
of self-exhibition, also in an acceptable and welcome fashion.
When anyone finishes a dance, he may pull another person from
the wall of the karigi onto the dance floor. Young men who have
hunted together wrestle violently to pull one of their perhaps more
reticent friends to the floor. An ex-mistress may dance, even after
marriage to another man, with her previous lover. I have seen as
many as six adult siblings dancing together—individually, but at
the same time. At a dance a person has the opportunity to express
his affection for a number of persons.

In earlier days, when the men of a band had completed the
strenuous job of corralling and butchering caribou, they spent
many days in the karigi making implements and talking from
morning till night. As soon as a man awoke, he went to the karigi
and met the other adult men of the community. Soon afterward,
the women prepared a light morning meal, brought it to the men,
and then returned home to their own chores and the company of
other women. During the day, two or three closely related women
often worked together, as they do today, in one home, but never in
the karigi. As the men worked there, making tools and implements
designed for the chase, they freely exchanged ideas about making
things and practiced new techniques that someone might have
learned from another band of Eskimos or even, perhaps, from
Indians. A father often brought his adolescent sons along, to learn
the elaborate Nunamiut technologies. The young men were advised, and teased about all manner of things.

Sometimes a story teller was encouraged to recite legends and
folktales in the karigi. Here the young men learned the verbal tradi-

tion of their people. Men frequently recited accounts of strange experiences they had had while out hunting or trapping, trying to outdo one another with the drama of their narratives. The younger men listened in fascination, learning the ways of the land as well as how to use the language to convey their thoughts and impressions and to persuade and influence others.

Legal disputes that could not be settled by the individuals concerned or by members of the immediate families would often wind up in the karigi. It was an extremely serious and difficult moment when both the accuser and the accused were present to discuss a case in front of the men of the community. There was no previously agreed-upon procedure for the adjudication (or perhaps, more properly, the attempt at discussion and settlement) of a case, and threats of violence, even rarely violence itself, might flare up. We will subsequently discuss more fully the nature of legal disputes.

Shamanistic séances were often held in the karigi, since shamans preferred to conduct them in dimly lighted surroundings. They often worked in private homes, of course, but a respected or feared shaman usually performed in the karigi, especially when he tried to help all the people of a community. After singing, dancing, and beating the drum, the shaman worked himself up to a feverish emotional pitch, ultimately entering a trance, during which he might be able to foresee the future, or his *iñua* (soul) would visit the top of a mountain, some distant region, or the moon. The iñua would secure power from a helping spirit with which the shaman would try to improve people's luck in hunting and trapping or cure a disease.

An evil shaman rarely practiced in the karigi itself; he usually worked up his power alone, although he might run into a karigi to utter a threat to kill someone or to make him ill.

Before any warlike action, elaborate shamanistic preparations were considered essential to the successful outcome of the battle. The Nunamiut point to shamanistic preparations as the cause for victory in the long series of battles with the Indians. A Nunamiut warrior, it was said, felt more secure going into battle with the power of a good shaman behind him.

The karigi was often the site of political discussion. Before entering battle, the men planned their strategy there and worked up determination to vanquish the enemy. Although a feud started as an individual and family affair, the fighting might become so violent and far-ranging, that the men in the karigi would discuss it and its possible developments. In the spring, shortly before most of the households of the several Nunamiut bands went to the coast to trade, the men made plans for the trip, discussing the various routes that could be taken, the possible sources of food along the way, and the fun and games they would have with the other Nunamiut bands and with the coastal Eskimos.

The karigi is now used only for communal eating, singing and dancing four or five times a year. The making of implements, visiting, discussing plans, and settling disputes now takes place in households.

The Caribou Drive

The Nunamiut no longer corral caribou during the spring and fall migrations. Today every man hunts with a rifle alone or in very small groups of close relatives and friends. Each man in the field represents his own household. Much of the knowledge of caribou behavior needed for a successful caribou drive is still essential for the good hunter today.

The primary reason for the formation of a band was to exploit the seasonal migration of caribou. Just before a fall or spring migration, the hunters gathered in the karigi to review their plans, determining the number of snares people had, the most likely route the caribou would travel, how they would react to the terrain and the wind, and the most effective deployment of every person in the band. The following account describes a spring caribou drive, but was also typical of many fall drives.

During the winter, most of the caribou feed in small, widely dispersed groups throughout the southern Brooks Range and elsewhere. In the spring, the small groups begin merging into larger and larger groups until mighty herds are formed. Thousands of caribou head through the valleys of the Brooks Range toward the north slope where the cows bear their young. Cows and their not quite yearling calves make up the first several herds and then, during the ensuing weeks of migration, the young bulls come, followed in the early part of May by the mature bulls—"after a good trail has been made," said informants with a laugh.

A band usually established a camp late in February or early March near a large creek running down from the mountains across a wide valley to the major river below. A band always tried to camp near a creek with a heavy growth of willows, which was hidden from the view of northbound caribou by a high cutbank, bluff, or low hills. The Nunamiut knew the various locations which had been used successfully for corralling caribou in the past. One Nuna-miut told me of an umialik many decades ago who, while out trap-ping, found a new location which he thought would be ideal for a spring corral. The umialik told all the hunters living in his region and, since they respected his judgment, they decided to give it a try. The drive turned out exceptionally well, vastly increasing the umialik's prestige.

Once a location had been selected, all the able-bodied men from every household set as many snares as they could. If there were a very heavy growth of willows through which the caribou had to pass, two or three rows of snares would be set side by side, if pos-sible, for several hundred yards along the creek; but willows are rarely thick enough for this technique to be used. Usually, just beyond the creek, still hidden from view, the men set two, three, or four rows of snares side by side in a large U-shaped corral into which caribou could be driven. Often, especially when the band was small or when few snares were at hand, piles of sod, moss, and willows were interspersed with the snares to form a U-shaped fence; when a caribou attempted to escape between two piles of sod and moss, it ran into a snare.

While most of the men were setting snares, other men, and some-times a few women, walked south from the corral along the main valley, setting up *iñuksuk* (scarecrows) of stone, sod, and moss (literally translated, iñuksuk means "like a man"). The idea was that when the caribou had become wary at the presence of men several miles down the valley, they would easily be frightened by what looked like a man on top of a hill or on a ridge. When caribou mi-grate, they usually travel along a major valley near the mountains, away from the main river draining the valley. When frightened, they either reverse their direction or climb into the mountains. Thus with one line of scarecrows set very carefully between the moun-tains and (as nearly as could be judged) the path of the herd, Nunamiut drivers could keep hundreds of caribou moving along a valley for miles, neither turning back nor escaping up into the mountains, and ultimately into the open corral. Sometimes, de-pending on the terrain, two lines of scarecrows were set up along a valley in a wide V-shape which could be used to channel caribou into the corral.

Before the drive, lookouts climbed halfway up a mountain and scanned the countryside for twenty or more miles around. When the first caribou were seen, the hunters near the corral readied their spears and bows and arrows. The drivers—some men, and all the women and children—spread themselves along the valley near the line or lines of scarecrows, remaining silent as the caribou approached. As the animals passed by, the drivers howled like wolves and took off their parkas and waved them at the caribou. A high degree of skill was required to drive effectively. Each person had to time his whooping and shouting in such a way that the caribou were never frightened too much but were merely excited and made to trot uneasily along the valley. If a person shouted too early, he might cause the lead caribou to bolt, and the entire herd might reverse its direction—bringing the wrath of the whole community down upon his head. As the caribou neared the corral, nervous and restless from the noise and waving of parkas, the drivers suddenly increased their cries in a last effort to frighten as many caribou as possible into the corral. It was a tense moment. If the caribou suddenly became unmanageable and bolted, days and days of planning and hard work would have come to naught. If, on the other hand, the bulk of the herd charged frantically into the waiting hunters, there would be meat, fat, and hides for months to come. Once the major portion of the herd entered the corral, the drivers near the open end of the U closed off the corral as much as possible and began loosing their arrows. The hunters, until now hidden and silent behind the snares, leaped forward and quickly dispatched the snared caribou with their spears and then began shooting their arrows at the caribou milling around in the enclosure. When everyone ran out of arrows, the men relaxed, and the remaining caribou, if any, were allowed to escape.

After a few moments of rest, all the men, women, and children who were able, pitched into the enormous job of butchering the kill. The meat, fat, and skins were divided in the following manner. Three or four hunters, including the umialik, all of whom were respected for their judgment, assumed the responsibility for apportioning the animals. Each household as a unit received a part, but the size of a share varied on the basis of the number and ages of the members of each household and, in the judgment of the dividers, its need. A large household with two or three mature sons who had contributed importantly to the success of the drive, and which maintained one or two large teams of dogs would receive more than a small household with one or two children and a few dogs. A household that had run completely out of food would receive a little more than a household that still had supplies. Thus, while no person received a larger share because he was an umialik, shaman, or noted story teller, the division of the hunt was not exactly equal, either among individuals or households. There seemed to be little if any bickering or disagreement among the people about their share. One explanation may be found in hospitality. When one household ran out of meat, its members knew they could visit relatives and other people living nearby and get something to eat. As the welfare of the band went, so went the welfare of each member household. This does not mean that a household could not pull up stakes and seek a better living elsewhere.

In the fall, the caribou migrate from north to south, and different locations had to be used, but the method was the same unless a band happened to be camped near a large lake. If the caribou migrated before freeze-up, the band might try to drive a herd into the lake and spear them from kayaks, using the same techniques described above. Sometimes it was difficult at the last moment to force the caribou into the water, and on occasion a band sought the services of a shaman to ensure good luck. The moment the caribou entered the water, each man who owned a kayak paddled out into the lake, spear in hand.

Nunamiut kayaks were often 20 feet long, much longer and narrower than those of coastal Eskimos who needed shorter kayaks for the rough, choppy sea. In building a kayak, a man chose for gunwales two long spruce strips which he securely bound together at either end with rawhide line. He selected green willow shoots the size of a man's thumb for ribs, bent them into a U-shape, spaced them evenly the width of a man's hand apart, and mortised them transversely to the gunwales to form the bottom of the frame of the kayak. The builder lashed five or seven thin, longitudinal strips of spruce (or birch) with cow caribou rawhide line to the ribs, inside the frame. These longitudinal strips did not extend to the stem and stern of the frame but ended a rib or two short of either end. The two gunwales formed the stem and stern. The worker mortised slender deck-beams of willow to the gunwales, as he had done to the ribs, although these were much flatter in contour, leaving a deck that would hold a small caribou. Longitudinal strips were also used to reinforce and to stabilize the transverse members of the deck. The man built a round cockpit into the frame in the center of the craft, just wider than his hips. In front of the cockpit, he secured the crotch of a willow or alder tree on which to pivot the paddle while traveling through the water. The man's wife, or sometimes the man himself, removed the hair from three good bull caribou hides. Using a double waterproof stitch, the woman sewed the hides together to form the cover, leaving only the cockpit open. The man hewed the paddle from a spruce log almost as long as the kayak. A kayaker carried a spear made from birch, tipped with a flint or caribou antler point.

When a hunter paddled near the swimming caribou, he had to be very careful to spear the animal high in the rib cage just to one side of the backbone, puncturing either the heart or the lungs, so that the caribou would die quietly. He had to learn to jab the spear in very smartly and withdraw it just as quickly so that the animal would not overturn the kayak. If a beginner jabbed a caribou in the gut, it would thrash violently, possibly upsetting him, and very few Nunamiut can swim. Sometimes, when the caribou were crowded together, a kayaker might literally be borne along on the backs of the herd, stabbing caribou right and left. The last Nunamiut kayak was made during World War II, when ammunition ran short. The Nunamiut who used it said it was easy to kill a very large number of caribou. In the old days, several men in kayaks could kill all a band could possibly consume in a winter, sometimes more caribou than the whole community could skin and butcher, provided, of course, that sufficient caribou were to be had.

One of the most important functions of the community, both formerly and today, is the opportunity for enjoyment. Young men and women have a chance to visit different homes and flirt, and the older people have a chance to reminisce about the old days. After weeks and months of isolation, nothing is more pleasurable for an individual or a family than to become immersed in a band— laughing, joking, singing, dancing, exchanging juicy bits of gossip, and relating experiences of grandeur and endurance. In a community context a person is able to renew his bonds with his relatives and friends.

Today, the village of Anaktuvuk Pass is the only Nunamiut community in the Brooks Range, and the villagers must seek almost all their diversion among themselves, supplemented by occasional white and Eskimo visitors. Nunamiut visits to Point Barrow and other communities in the Arctic are rare, since a ride in a bush plane is expensive, and it takes two or three days or more to go by dog sled to the nearest village.

Formerly, when Nunamiut bands were numerous and encountered each other in traveling, they assumed a definite relationship as separate units. As an illustration, let us examine the activities of two inland bands during a trip to the coast.

In the spring before break-up, the Killikmiut (a Nunamiut band living in the Killik River valley) traveled by sled down the Killik River to the Colville River, then down the Colville to the mouth of the Anaktuvuk River. The Tulugamiut (or Tulugakmiut, a Nunamiut band near Tulugak Lake north of the Anaktuvuk Valley summit) traveled by sled down the Anaktuvuk River to its confluence with the Colville River and there met the Killikmiut. The two bands pitched their camps together, but each family clustered with its own band.

As soon as everyone was settled, a footrace was held between the young men of the two groups. The losing band had to build the karigi. That evening, all the people from both bands came together in the karigi to eat, each family bringing what it could manage. Two or three days later, after the men had had a chance to hunt and fish, the women prepared a more elaborate evening meal, and everyone came together in the karigi for a big dance. If the Killikmiut had lost the footrace and thus had to build the karigi, the Tulugamiut had to prepare the drums and start the singing. While the Tulugamiut were alone, sounding the drums and singing, the Killikmiut entered the karigi very quietly. Each person suddenly held up in full view a gift which he would soon give to a cousin, nephew, niece, uncle, or aunt, or even to a very good friend. One by one the Killikmiut danced, holding up their gifts, which might be a pair of gloves, boots, socks, or mittens, a caribou back or leg sinew, or some tobacco—anything, just so long as the gift was new. When a Killikmiut finished his dance, he threw his gift to the recipient whereupon the latter threw his own gift to the former and they danced together. Sometimes the dancing lasted until morning, so happy were the people to see one another after a long winter of hard work. The following day, provided that enough food was in camp, everyone continued to indulge in such sports as wrestling, finger pulling, jumping, and juggling. Both men and women participated. Again in the evening everyone ate and danced together.

The Tulugamiut and the Killikmiut did not trade very extensively with each other. They came from similar environments and thus had access to the same resources. Small luxuries such as furs or unusual items like porcupine quills might be exchanged now and then, but this kind of sporadic and occasional trading could take place between any two persons and was not restricted to partnerships.

After four or five days of fun at the mouth of the Anaktuvuk River, each household, or sometimes two or three very closely associated smaller households, rebuilt its *umiak* (a large, open skin boat). Its frame was built mostly of spruce, with joints notched and bound with rawhide line, and was much sturdier than a kayak. Either young walrus or bearded seal hides, traded in from the coast, were used for the hull. Very rarely, the Nunamiut would construct an open moose hide boat for descending rivers in the timber. Log rafts are known, and open caribou skin boats with a light willow frame have recently been made, for crossing rivers.

The Tulugamiut and other bands always cached the frames of their *umiat* (the plural of umiak) at the mouth of the Anaktuvuk River. Thus the communication and transportation center on the Colville River upstream from the mouth of the Anaktuvuk is called Umiat. During my last brief visit in 1961, no permanent residents lived there; the facilities were manned by temporary white and Eskimo employees. My older Nunamiut informants thought that the bluffs at Umiat would provide archaeologists with some very interesting digging.

As soon as the Colville River was navigable, some time in May, the men and women of each household, or small complex of households, piled their children and belongings into their umiat and started drifting downstream toward Negalik, a small island in the Colville River delta where the Point Barrow Eskimos and the Nunamiut had traded for decades, possibly centuries. The travelers kept their umiat together on the river from morning until the middle of the afternoon. The men visited back and forth, exchanging information about hunting and trapping in different regions and strange sights they had seen, and gossiping. The women were usually quiet, watching that their children did not fall overboard in their rollicking play. In the afternoon the people would start looking for a good campsite where they could dig edible roots and catch fish. Everyone ate together in the evening, sharing their catch for the day. They traveled leisurely on their way down the Colville River—there was no hurry.

Other Nunamiut bands (see Appendix A) joined the Tulugamiut and the Killikmiut at Negalik before the Point Barrow Eskimos arrived.

Many marriages took place among the Nunamiut at Negalik. There was no ceremony when the young man and woman took up residence together, but there was public recognition in that the new couple was referred to as a married couple, the woman as so-and-so's *nuliaŋa*, (his) wife, the man as so-and-so's *uiŋa*, (her) husband. Children resulting from the union were recognized as legitimate offspring.

Late in the spring, a large group of Point Barrow Eskimos left their homes, traveling by dog sled over the rough sea ice and by umiak over the open water. With them they carried whale blubber, muktuk, baleen, sea animal skins (common seal, bearded seal, walrus), and some manufactured items such as rawhide line and snares. In the late 1800s and early 1900s they supplemented or replaced these with such trade goods as flour, sugar, tea, coffee, baking powder, baking soda, oats, matches, gunpowder, lead, shells, and guns. The man, and sometimes the woman, of each household had a partner among the Point Barrow Eskimos with whom, and only with whom, he traded.

The months of late spring and early summer were happy months for the people camped at Negalik and elsewhere along the Arctic coast. They danced and showed off their best clothes. Footraces and other sports and games were conducted. The Nunamiut liked to spend the summer on the Arctic coast where they could catch all kinds of fish, shoot and snare large birds, collect eggs, and usually have a chance at an odd caribou.

Shortly before freeze-up, some time in September long after the Point Barrow Eskimos had left, the various Nunamiut bands began to repair their umiat for the return trip inland. Traveling upstream was much slower, especially with a heavy load of blubber and sea animal hides, and the umiat had to be pulled up the river by people and dogs. In September the Colville River was usually low for a few days, enabling the travelers to reach with little difficulty the mouths of the various rivers where the bands had cached their sleds the previous spring. After freeze-up, each family cached its umiak and headed back to its own territory by dog sled. At this time a family might decide to join another band for fall hunting and seek a new region for winter trapping. Or the reports of one man or family who had seen a new valley might draw a group of families to a heretofore unexploited region.

The Umialik

The word *umialik* literally translated means "having an *umiak*," implying its primary defining characteristic, namely, economic strength. While many Nunamiut used to own umiat, Nunamiut use of the term umialik differs from coastal usage. On the coast an umialik actually owned an umiak and was explicitly regarded as a leader in economic, political, legal, and other matters. While living with the Nunamiut, I heard the term umialik uttered every day. Whenever a person made any money, or made an item to sell, or trapped a wolf, or even shot a large number of summer caribou for their skins, shouts of umialik! or umialikpaq! would go up (the suffix *paq* is usually translated as big, actual, real, etc.). Most white men are considered *umialit* (the plural of umialik), but not all, because some Nunamiut have seen a few very poor white trappers.

In political affairs, an umialik held a position of power and influence in a very subtle, initially almost imperceptible way. The Nunamiut did not possess formal political organization in the sense of explicit and previously agreed-upon methods of handling political issues, but there were implicit patterned modes of political behavior, and the umialik played important roles in many aspects of political activity.

In one band, usually only one umialik was dominant. As his reputation became established, he would come to be known, for example, as the "umialik of the Killikmiut," although he never achieved formal leadership by such processes as election, selection, or succession. Such a man emerged as a dominant member of his community and gradually came to exert influence in all manner of things, but he never represented the community in which he lived.

Among the Nunamiut, the position and influence of an umialik has changed to some extent since precontact days. The primary change has been a decrease in the umialik's role in political and legal affairs. In recent years under white influence, a village council has been established, which attempts to discuss and settle disputes, with some success. Yet, the umialit of Anaktuvuk Pass still wield considerable moral power when issues arise. Both precontact and present-day umialit excel in economic activity, providing examples for other people, especially young hunters, to follow, offering aid to poorer people, and exerting informal influence as leaders. The following statements apply to the umialik and his position in the community before the full impact of white contact was felt. Many of these comments hold in modified form for the present day.

A man became recognized as a rich man by amassing wealth through his abilities as a hunter, trapper, and trader. An umialik was a man who had "more than he needs"; that is, he had a surplus of goods. He had plenty of good dogs, a constant supply of good meat and fat, and more skins and furs than he could use in his own household. Such a person was in a good position to obtain in trade not only products of the sea from the Arctic coast but also such items as black-bear meat, marten and beaver pelts, articles of clothing, and other luxury items from the Kobuk Eskimos living to the south of the Nunamiut in the timber, from other Eskimos, and occasionally from Indians.

Umialit were considered very intelligent men who carefully observed the habits of all the animals and the conditions affecting them: climatic, topographic, other animals, and the presence of man. They learned tricks from the old people, but mainly they had to learn for themselves by experimenting with different ways of catching animals as well as originating new methods and improving upon old ones. Some umialit were shamans, but not necessarily. If a person always worked hard, was never lazy, and tried to learn better ways of catching animals, he did not need the services of a shaman nor did he feel compelled to obtain shamanistic power for himself. In the old days, most people wanted to have a little shamanistic power in order to prevent sickness and to improve one's luck in hunting and trapping. But a successful umialik did not rely on it too heavily; he knew there was no real substitute for careful hard work.

The sons of an umialik did not necessarily become umialit. A person had to spend years learning how to catch animals and to trade effectively. He could learn what he needed to know from a close relative or even from a very good friend, but he had to implement what he learned by precept and go on to learn more through his own efforts. Some folktales extol a poor, abused orphan who becomes rich and more influential than a contemporary umialik through hard work, the kindly attitude of animals, and the care of a devoted grandmother.

One umialik many years ago gained such a reputation for wealth and successful trading that he came to be remembered as "having fat or blubber for eating most of the time so you became sleepy from eating at his house because he had so much blubber."

Shortly after flintlock rifles reached the Nunamiut in the 1800s, a rich man displayed the ingenuity and courage typical of umialit. During a caribou migration he spotted a grizzly bear sleeping in the willows. He could have shot it, but there was a supernatural restriction against using a weapon for four or five days after killing a bear with it, and the umialik did not want to miss the caribou. He therefore made a stone hammer and killed the bear by hitting it on the head while it slept.

An umialik's success in hunting and trapping earned him the respect of his relatives and friends. Only if a man really knew the animals and used good judgment could he always have such good luck. In the fall and spring, when people came together to form a band, the men from the various households would listen very carefully to anything an umialik had to say in the karigi. He could suggest a location for a caribou drive and recommend how snares were to be set. Other men would concur or offer some modification. After a few of the more respected men came to support the informal proposals of the umialik, then almost everyone else joined in, with little comment or reservation.

As the people worked on the corral, an umialik would labor side by side with them, occasionally offering advice about how best to set a snare or where to put a scarecrow. After the drive was over, an umialik was usually one of the men who determined the share each household was to receive. After a successful drive, people here and there would mention what good judgment the umialik had exercised. Thus he achieved prestige and gained the assurance of his position for another year. On the other hand, he could be held responsible for the failure of a group hunt and suffer a great loss of prestige. People would no longer consider him an umialik and they would refuse to listen to him about economic, political, legal, and other affairs. If his judgment had gone bad in one sphere, then it was assumed that it had gone bad elsewhere.

An umialik was the dominant figure in organizing a trading

expedition, and he was likely to be the biggest trader. When he returned inland, he frequently had more coastal goods than he needed, and he could trade with those Nunamiut who had remained inland. Through his generosity in trading with the people in his own community, an umialik could build up a considerable reserve of obligation and affection. The ideal of all little boys was to grow up and become an important umialik, a successful trapper, hunter, and trader, and to be called a good man for his generosity by the people around him.

In achieving and holding his position, an umialik had to be successful both in his own right and in his judgment during group activity; he could also maintain and expand his position through generosity. As a man with a surplus of goods, he was naturally expected to share with those who had less. When visitors dropped in, an umialik was expected to offer better food and more delicacies than anyone else, and he must always be responsive to the needs of relatives by blood and by marriage. It was common for an umialik to take a second wife, thereby increasing the number of his affinal relatives. Through generosity to unrelated persons, he could often draw other people to him. I have seen an umialik offer two or three out of several caribou he had recently killed to an unrelated person in need of meat. An umialik invariably created some envy and, along with his prestige and influence, he had to be ever mindful of his words and actions lest he provoke a verbal attack.

By means of a sensitive and dominant personality, an umialik could develop a real esprit de corps within a community when competing with another community in sports and games or in conflicts leading to warfare. In warfare itself, a shaman or two lent their aura of supernatural power in developing cohesion within a community, but an umialik could add his weight to a battle by committing himself to fight until death.

It was the umialik who could do more than any other single person to help promote friendly relations among the members of a band. His personality usually gave him a position of social prominence. People in the band visited his house frequently and ate there, talking about the trials of the day, their troubles and squabbles, their successes and future plans. An umialik always had a ready ear for other people and they listened carefully to any advice, moral, practical, or otherwise that he might have to offer.

The umialik often exerted informal authority in the settlement of legal disputes, which included stealing and the destruction of property for real or imagined causes, murder, adultery, and "making trouble," a catch-all category characterized by lying, spreading false or malicious gossip, making an agreement for an exchange of labor or goods and failing to live up to one's end of the bargain, etc.

A hypothetical case will illustrate the role of the umialik in the settlement of legal disputes. This case is based on two or three actual instances of theft and informants' discussion about the settlement of disputes.

A person takes some meat from a cache that does not belong to him and fails to replace it or inform the owner of his action. Several persons see him or see enough tracks and other evidence to convince them that he is guilty. The witnesses report the theft to the owner. The owner of the cache and his family then discuss the theft among themselves. Upon deciding the theft has in fact occurred, the members of the family inform their relatives living in the community of the matter, many of whom mention the theft to others, creating considerable social pressure. In many instances, the pressure aroused in this way is sufficient to discourage most persons from continuing their wayward behavior. In a small society, the power of unified public approval or disapproval can have devastating effects. I knew a man who stole some meat; after a few days of talk, the social pressure became so great that he developed a slight nervous twitch in his face and he would cast his eyes down when meeting anyone on the trail. He stopped stealing and after several months he appeared to have worked out his guilt. Once again he could look people straight in the eye with a happy, smiling face.

Initially, the plaintiff would avoid any confrontation with the offender. If the thief continued to steal, the owner, upon meeting him, might go so far as to accuse him openly of theft. Veiled threats of violence might follow, but rarely violence itself, at this stage.

If the stealing still did not cease, some night when everyone was in the karigi, the plaintiff, in the presence of the men of the community, would charge the defendant with theft. Again threats of violence might flare out. Then there would be much talk. All the evidence would be presented, all the witnesses for and against the plaintiff would be called upon to testify. The defendant might lash out at the plaintiff, charging him with perpetuating a falsehood to the detriment of his character.

This is where an umialik could make his power felt, although I received different responses from different informants. Some maintained that an umialik brought his influence to bear in every case, and was expected to do so, while other informants pointed out that even though an umialik has potential influence in any crisis because of his economic position, he might choose not to become involved in a particular case. Because an umialik is related to many of the people in a community either by blood or marriage, and is involved in binding economic relationships with many unrelated people, he would exert influence in a great many legal cases. It strikes me that an umialik becomes involved in most legal disputes because he is frequently the plaintiff; he has many blood relatives in the band in which he lives; he has many in-laws, often more than the average as a result of taking a second, and (rarely) a third wife; he has strong economic ties with many nonrelatives whom he has greatly aided in times of need; he exercises informal political leadership in group hunts, trading expeditions, and to a limited extent in warfare; and he commands respect for the advice he offers on all sorts of problems. It is not because an umialik is considered a "man of law" per se that he becomes involved in legal disputes: he is first a business man and, as the effect of this, he acquires a position of influence and respect and he assumes informal leadership in settling legal controversies.

The umialik by his presence (formerly in the karigi, today in a household where men have gathered either spontaneously or as the Village Council) is naturally drawn into the argument. As a perceptive man he often forms an opinion early in the discussion of the case, one which he can effectively support. As he senses the trend of the discussion, he gradually molds the opinions of the other men, some of whom may be older than himself, sometimes without their being fully aware of what is happening. Eventually the full weight of the umialik's influence is brought to bear as the core of older and reputable middle-aged men begin to express their opinions to the defendant. One man might cite the moral of a folktale, another man might mention the manner in which a past incident was settled. But among the Nunamiut there is no sense of a highly formalized, God-given law defended as the ultimate guide for human affairs, such as is found in the Constitution of the United States or the Declaration of Independence. Rather, the ultimate repository of legal power, short of violence, are those few moments in which the men of the community express their final opinions, molded to varying degrees by the umialik, in the context of the specific case. An older man, who was recognized by all to have lived a good life, who had been a good worker and hunter whether umialik or not, and who was known to have spoken wisely in the past, would command real attention when he appealed to the defendant's sense of shame and morality, calling upon him to rectify his actions. Should the defendant persist in stealing despite the injunctions of the men of the community, becoming a chronic, probably a psychologically disturbed criminal, the more responsible members of the community might discuss the matter among themselves and decide upon more positive action, such as killing him or banishing him from their territory. Sometimes the plaintiff might organize some of his relatives and other persons into vigilante action.

A legal dispute was frequently not brought out openly before the men of the community in the karigi. A controversy might continue for some time, especially when evidence was weak, and many disputes were settled exclusively by discussion among the relatives of the persons concerned. Sometimes an umialik could settle a case privately through the influence of his own moral admonitions.

An umialik was never secure in his position for very long. His judgments and opinions could be and were constantly challenged by other people. A well-established umialik could usually handle the barbs and caustic remarks of ordinary people, but his position might well be threatened by a younger man who aspired to become an umialik. Umialit rarely came into open conflict, unlike shamans. If a young man was to become an umialik, he had to learn to work with existing social conditions and to avoid antagonizing people. A young umialik usually waited quietly, building up his economic strength and developing a reputation for good judgment, then he gradually assumed the dominant position as the influence of the older umialik began to wane.

Today, as in the past, the Nunamiut community usually seems to be composed of two political factions. Among the Nunamiut living in Anaktuvuk Pass, there are two principal groups: the Tulugak Lake people, represented by the family names of Kakinya, Paneak, and Rulland, headed by the umialit Kakinya and Paneak who lived primarily in the Chandler Lake region and at Tulugak Lake before settling at Anaktuvuk Pass; and the Killik River people, represented by the family names of Ahgook, Morry, Hugo, and Mekiana, formerly headed by the umialik Old Morry and now, although loosely at times, by the umialik Mekiana, who lived primarily in the Killik River valley before joining the Tulugak Lake people at Tulugak Lake in 1949 and then settling at Anaktuvuk Pass in the early 1950s. (For reference to households, see Appendix B.) Generally the members of one faction share more ties of blood and marriage among themselves than with members of the opposing faction. At present in Anaktuvuk Pass, there are ten marriages among persons of the four family names within the Killik faction. There are two marriages (not including two other marriages of which both wives have died) among persons of the three family names within the Tulugak group. Only two marriages cross faction lines, one between an Ahgook (Killik) and a Kakinya by adoption (Tulugak) and one between a Hugo (Killik) and a Kakinya by adoption (Tulugak).

The existence of factions is further supported by strong undercurrents of gossip. In an instance of suspected shamanism mentioned above (p. 151), the accused was a member of the Tulugak faction, and his fellow members who are related to him by blood (or adoption) and by marriage asserted that he was not a shaman. Many members of the Killik faction, on the other hand, felt the accused did possess shamanistic power.

During the 1950s, a white trader provided the principal contact by which many Nunamiut obtained trade supplies in exchange for furs, some manufactured articles, and the bounty money for wolves. The Killik people tended to rely very heavily on him. The Tulugak people often spent whole seasons away from Killik settlements and maintained their own trade contacts by chartering a small airplane to bring up loads of supplies in exchange for their furs, bounty money, and manufactured articles. Needless to say, the Tulugak people inevitably got more for their money although, of course, they had to plan ahead more carefully and resist the temptation of becoming dependent on the white trader. The Tulugak people are a hard-working, intelligent group, and they have been able to maintain a higher standard of living than many Killik people, which has created jealousy at times, particularly when a Killik person has had to ask Tulugak people for help. White visitors, especially those seeking information about the Brooks Range, tend to align themselves with the Tulugak people, although never to the exclusion of talking and visiting with the Killik group.

Although the existence of these two factions may easily be rec-

ognized, it should not be considered a dominating force in Nunamiut life, either today or in the past. Nunamiut rarely speak of factions as such, and there is no competition in sports between them.
Some ties of blood and marriage usually crossed factional lines
and over time some persons changed their alignments from one
group to another; the dichotomy was never too pronounced. Only
in a scandal, political conflict, or economic crisis did the existence
of factions become noticeable. At a community dance and to the
face of a stranger, the Nunamiut appear as one.

In the old days, and often today, the members of one faction
were constantly checking on the actions of the other in matters
concerning the group as a whole. At best, two factions vying for
prominence resulted in the adoption of the most productive solution to an economic or political problem. In spite of internal tension, when a group effort was required or the group as a whole was
threatened, one would hardly know that two factions existed. At
worst, two opposed factions created so much tension and rivalry
within the community that people might fail to respond adequately
to the environment or to defend themselves as effectively as they
could from an enemy. This rarely was the case, however; a Nunamiut band was often too small to contain two factions large enough
to threaten its capacity to respond as a unit. Most bands appeared
to possess enough integration or internal cohesion to survive. When
starvation and emigration did occur, they invariably seemed to result from external factors such as disease, decline in the caribou
population, or the appeal of opportunities for making a better living elsewhere, rather than a breakdown in household or band organization.

Sometimes a band had exceptionally good luck for several years
in corralling caribou. Hearing of the band's success, friends and
relatives might join it, swelling its numbers. Newcomers would
tend to side with the faction of which most of their relatives were
members, upsetting the equilibrium that had existed in the smaller
band. If two large factions of similar size and strength developed,
both headed by powerful umialik, the political unity of the band
would be threatened. A large band with a population over 150
people became unwieldy and inefficient. When people began to feel
the pinch in their stomachs, households became receptive to following the leading members of a faction, sparked by an umialik, to
a new location, either forming a new band or joining another small

band. The only alternative was increasing hunger, leading eventually to forced emigration or starvation. While the precipitating cause of a split was economic, political differences and personality conflicts often supported it, and the split usually took place along factional lines.

Sometimes in a stable band of normal size, a young, restless umialik might decide that the band in which he was living was nevertheless too large, and the opportunities for hunting and trapping were too restricted for his boundless energy. He would then probably leave the band and seek to join and dominate another smaller band where he had relatives, or he might try to find a new region. By his success in hunting and trapping, he might encourage other people, both relatives and nonrelatives, to join him, ultimately forming a new band.

7. Nunamiut Ideas and Concepts

As every ethnographer soon learns, people often seem more interested, knowledgeable, and talkative about some aspects of their life than about others. Thus the following account of Nunamiut ideas lacks the balance that might have resulted from a more elegant literary effort, since it reflects the nature of the field situation and the imbalance, as it were, in my interests.

The Universe

TOTAL REALITY. Nunamiut children often bicker with each other about what is theirs. The most extreme claim a child can make is that *shulimauragatatpianigiluragatatpialaurat* belongs to him; in other words, total reality—the entire universe—is his. A literal translation would be "very much again, really extremely so, really to a very great extent." While adults are aware of this term, they rarely discuss it in as serious terms as some metaphysicians do. The term *supaiyaat* means "everything" and is used in such expressions as *supaiyaani* (everywhere), *supaiyaanik ilisamaroq* (he knows everything), and so forth. Within this notion of the total universe, vague as it is, the more reflective Nunamiut do not search for a primordial cause, a complete explanation of order, or the nature of ultimate destiny. The Nunamiut do have two words *ishuilaq* (without, or lacking, an end) and *ishuitchuq* (does not end, or unending) which mean "forever" or "for eternity," but there is little speculation or concern about the outer reaches of ishuilaq.

When an intelligent Nunamiut pauses to reflect about the nature of things, his mind is likely to turn either to unusual natural phenomena he has seen or the kind of life he has lived and how much he has helped other people. A man once said to me that for forty years he had helped friends and relatives as much as he could, but inevitably, he seemed to think, he had given far more than he had received. At times he wondered if it had been worth all the effort; but then, he observed, when a person works hard and has more meat, fat, and hides than other people, he cannot refuse their requests for help. In other words, when Nunamiut ponder the fundamental questions of their existence, their ultimate concerns revolve around their relationship to other people and natural occurrences which seem out of the ordinary or incomprenhensible.

TIME. The Nunamiut are very conscious of time; watches and calendars are today among their prized possessions. The white man's year, month, week, day, hour, minute, and second have been adopted with the partial loss of their own divisions of time.

There are terms for morning, evening, and night, as three parts of one day. By adding suffixes, early or late morning, for example, may be indicated. Before the use of watches, time during the day was only approximately indicated with such expressions as "a little while," "soon," "before the evening meal," and so forth.

Days used to be grouped into thirteen lunar months. The starting point for the year was (and is, for a few Nunamiut) based on the first appearance of the planet Venus above the horizon shortly after the first of January. Twenty-eight days per lunar month give only 364 days to a year, but, as no written records were kept, a discrepancy of one or two days was of no importance. According to my informants the most frequently used names for the months were as follows, beginning at the first of the year:

siqiŋñachuq, the sun begins to return
siqiŋñashugaruq, the returned sun shines even brighter
panikshukshivik, the time for drying caribou (and other animal) hides
qarigilikvik, the time of ptarmigan migration
sukloavik, the time when the rivers break up
ignivik, the time when caribou and other animals bear their young
itsavik, the time when (male) geese moult
niglaligitch, the time when (female) geese have their young and moult
amigitshivik, the time when velvet is lost from (caribou) antlers
shikovik, the time for freeze-up
nuliagvik, the time for mating (for many animals)
tagakshiovik, the time for (rams) chasing their own shadows
siqiŋñiglaq, lacking sun

All the names of months thus refer to an aspect of the environment—either wildlife or climate.

The four seasons are much more important in reckoning time through a year:

ukiuk, winter; the last of November, December, January, and February
upinaxaraq, spring; March, April, May, and the first part of June
upinagaaq, summer; the last of June, July, and August
ukiaxaraq, fall; September, October, and the first part of November

The division of time in the past was discussed in Chapter 2. For the future, the Nunamiut speak of tomorrow, the next day, and the day after that. In addition one speaks of the next winter, spring, summer, or fall, as well as the next year, and the year after that. There is a very general term for some time several years in the future. When pushed, a person can speak rhetorically of his great-grandchildren's descendants for all time to come, but there are no terms for century or millennium. As mentioned above, the term *ishuilaq* (without end) refers to time. An example of the use of this word is to describe a shaman who dies trying to kill another shaman; they will fight each other forever—ishuilaq.

The present, however, is the primary concern. It is good for one to think carefully about his needs for the immediate future, but people joke about a man who thinks so much about the coming season that he forgets what he is doing for this season. One knows he can never predict the future very well, but he is assured that he can rely on past solutions, with a little ingenuity now and then, to cope with almost any future problem. Nunamiut rarely worry about several years in the future, but a few thoughtful men and women are aware, for example, that in ten years or so a certain willow grove at Anaktuvuk Pass will be exhausted as a source of fuel.

Some Nunamiut are conscious of time as it progresses from generation to generation. Parents teach their children things they need to know for the future. They in turn will be able to pass their knowledge on to their children. When a person approaches death, he dislikes the thought that remembrance of him will soon vanish. A Nunamiut is aware that he himself knows of very few ancestors who died before he was born. Only those Eskimos who were outstanding Indian fighters, very successful trappers and traders, or famous shamans are remembered for more than a few decades after death. In an attempt to avert the anonymity of passing time, a dying Nunamiut often gives some small personal article to a lineal descendant or other closely associated person as a remembrance of him.

IMMEDIATE SPACE. In learning how to live in an unfamiliar country, the most important aspect of immediate space which Nunamiut emphasized to me is that a person has to see a region or locality or even the inside of a house before he can actually know it. It helps for someone else to describe, for example, the course of a river used as a travel route, but until an individual sees the route and travels it himself, he does not have knowledge about it; he has only heard what someone had to say. A Nunamiut usually describes a physical object, whether a house or a geographical region, in terms of a similar or analogous object with which the listener is familiar, using a variety of verbal devices to convey his message. One of the dimensions of the Nunamiut Eskimo noun paradigm is similitude, and may be translated as like, as, or similar to. The Nunamiut dialect of Eskimo contains many words, suffixes, and infixes which indicate whether a given subject is a little larger or smaller, higher or lower, nearer to or farther away, etc. than a particular object. Many of these words are reciprocal pairs, others are singular in definition, and others are multiple.

WORLDLY AND CELESTIAL SPACE. The Nunamiut thought both land and sea were flat, circumscribed with a kind of boundary or outer limit. If a person came to the edge of the earth and fell over, he would fall forever. When they first heard of a round earth, many of them pointed out that the water would run off if the earth were not flat. They said that deep in the ground itself burned an endless fire which only shamans could visit, and the earth was stationary; only the sun, moon and stars moved. They observe that the sun moves around the sky in a circle during July and June when it never sinks below the horizon. During the months when the sun sets, it was thought to travel all the way under and around the earth, since any other explanation would not make sense in view of what one could see.

The Nunamiut are more aware of the moon than of any other celestial body. The phases of the moon are recognized, but I never heard of any explanation for this. In early spring, when the first crescent appeared, if the moon was in first quarter, concave up, it was believed that hunger and perhaps starvation would ensue. If, however, the moon was in first quarter, concave down, caribou and other animals would be plentiful in the following months, just as if they were poured out of an upturned dish. One Nunamiut has watched for this relationship but has been unable to see any real correlation.

When the moon is full, the night is considered to be a little warmer. The Nunamiut rarely hunt at night, but when a full moon is up, the light is bright enough to shoot fairly accurately. When a faint circle appears around a full moon, a storm or a cold spell is said to be in the offing. Whenever the moon is seen to catch up with a star and envelope it, an eclipse of the moon is expected. In the old days, the Nunamiut believed that an eclipse of the moon occurred because the *tatqimiñua* (the man, or soul or spirit, of the moon) was ashamed and wanted to visit the earth. At other times, just after darkness fell and before the moon had risen in the sky, the tatqimiñua might come down to the earth, especially if he were angry, and steal meat, skins, snowshoes, and other equipment. To protect themselves from the tatqimiñua, people used to hide their goods and throw ashes into the air. Because all garbage and old clothes are burned, ashes are considered filthy, and any self-respecting person, including the tatqimiñua, would stay away from ashes scattered in the air.

Compared with the moon, there is little talk about the sun. People are aware of the variations in the appearance of the sun through the seasons but take them for granted. During the middle of winter when the sun does not appear over the horizon for several weeks, people do not seem unhappy about it. They talk occasionally about it, but only in a matter-of-fact way. Everyone is happy in late January when the sun shines on the mountain tops because he knows that spring is soon coming and, with it, the northward migration of caribou. Round whitefish are said to see the sunlit mountain peaks and begin to leave the lakes. During the months when it is visible, the Nunamiut use the position of the sun to tell the time of day. I never heard the Nunamiut speculate about how far away the sun is.

There is a story about the origin of the sun and the moon which many Nunamiut know, but they told me they learned it from coastal Eskimos living around Point Hope:

> A brother and sister were living alone in one house. The brother told his sister that she ought to marry and bring a hunter into the household to help out. The sister refused, saying they did not need help. She asked her brother to seek a wife, but he too refused, saying that he had enough clothing.
>
> In those days, there was no sun or moon.
>
> One night the brother sneaked over to his sister's bed and forced her to submit to him. The sister, wanting to find out who was violating her, marked the man's face with ashes. The brother awoke early and went to the karigi before breakfast. Shortly afterward, the sister went to the karigi and saw

the ashes on her brother's cheek. He was sitting alone looking very sad but his sister did not say a word. She left the karigi and walked home. As soon as she entered the house, she picked up an ulu and cut off her breasts. She then mixed her own urine and blood together with the cut-up breasts and made *akutaq* (Eskimo ice cream). She carried the dish to the karigi and gave it to her brother, saying, "Here, eat." She then told everyone what had happened the night before and announced that she was going to leave forever.

She went home, picked up an Eskimo stone lamp, and started to walk in a circle counterclockwise. Slowly she rose up into the air. The people shouted at her to come back, but she would not listen.

The brother was riven with sorrow. He picked up his tool bag and also started to walk in a circle counterclockwise. Soon he too rose into the air. As the sister continued rising into the sky, her lamp became warmer and warmer, giving out heat and light to the country. As the brother rose, he became bright, but he never became hot.

From that time on the moon, the brother, pursued the sun, his sister. But he never caught up with her, he was always behind. The heat from the sun comes from the Eskimo stone lamp, and the dark spots on the moon look like a man carrying a tool bag.

Once, some time in the 1800s, an eclipse of the sun occurred in the middle of the day, and the Nunamiut were greatly frightened; they thought the world was coming to an end. Everyone went outside to await doom. The sun, of course, reappeared, and people talked about the eclipse of the sun for many decades afterward.

During the winter, the stars are especially bright. The Nunamiut recognize several individual stars and constellations by name, but the Nunamiut say they rarely use stars as guides for direction. In crossing lakes and valleys in the evening in wind and fog, I often used a star or planet as well as the wind for direction, but Nunamiut rely more completely on the wind and occasional glimpses of the terrain. Toward spring the stars are said to rotate faster in the sky than in the winter. Individual stars were used to tell the season; for example, when a certain star first became visible over the horizon in late winter, spring was just around the corner. Sometimes a star was used to indicate bedtime. Planets as such were not recognized. Venus is called *uvluiaqpaq* (the big star) and is considered to be the only star that moves in the background of stars. Other planets may have been recognized previously, but I could evoke no knowledge to that effect. Shooting stars are called the feces of stars. Some meteorites were found by Nunamiut in the early days and were thought to result from thunderstorms. I heard no mention of comets. The Nunamiut are unaware of the difference in distance to various stars or the existence and distribution of galaxies. A few Nunamiut have speculated that perhaps there is land somewhere among the stars.

Northern lights or the aurora borealis occur throughout most of the winter. On a very clear night, the light can be bright enough to hunt by. Sometimes a noise like the wind in the mountains is said to accompany the aurora borealis. A band of northern lights dividing the sky in half means that many animals will be nearby the next day; when the whole sky is flooded, a storm is said to be in the offing. Sometimes the northern lights become bright red, like blood; even the snow may be tinted red or orange, but no special meaning was attached to it. Today, a few Nunamiut say they like the northern lights. Others appear only to be awed. I perceived no relationship between northern lights and shamanism. In the old days, it was thought that the people of the air took someone's head and kicked it around in the sky to cause the northern lights.

In comparison to the interest, knowledge, and speculation about natural phenomena, social relations, and human psychology, there is little discussion or awareness of the celestial world. Astronomy has very little appeal to a Nunamiut; he appears to take the universe for granted.

NUMBERS. The Nunamiut system of counting is based on the unit twenty because, I was told, a person has twenty fingers and toes. The word for twenty is *iñuinaq* which means "a whole man," i.e. all his digits. Within twenty, counting is done by fives because, it is said, there are five digits on each extremity. Forty is two twenties, 100 is five twenties, and so on up to 400, which is twenty twenties; 500 is twenty twenties [and] five twenties, 600 is twenty twenties [and] ten twenties, 700 is twenty twenties [and] fifteen twenties, and 800 is twenty twenties twice. There the numbers stop. Should there be more things to count, one starts over again and merely keeps track of how many times he counts to 800. In actual practice of course, there are very few occasions that require a Nunamiut to count to 800. I found that very few persons knew how to say the numbers above 400. When several thousand caribou appear to the eye at one glance, the Nunamiut say *tuttupauragatat,* which could be freely translated as "a hell of a lot of caribou." In response to a question about how many white men there are, I could only say more than all the stars one could see. Today our numbers are used extensively, but there is little if any awareness of how many ten thousand or a million are.

There is a specific term for a half, but no other fraction is precisely indicated. Using the root word for half, a little more or less than half can be indicated with suffixes. For an eighth or a sixteenth of something, only the term "a little bit" is used.

The addition of two figures is common but if, say, one is going to add five figures of three digits each, the first two figures are added, one digit at a time to arrive at a sum. The sum of the first two figures is then added to the next figure and so forth until the total sum is determined. Subtraction of two figures is done as we do it, taking the lower digit from the one above from right to left, borrowing when necessary. Multiplication and division, interestingly enough, are unknown. To determine how many snares there are in five bundles of 20 snares each, 20 is added to 20 to arrive at 40, the third 20 is added to 40 to arrive at 60 and so forth until the total sum of 100 is achieved. Division is accomplished rather by trial and error. If there are 47 objects to be divided among 6 persons, the man in charge begins conservatively by giving each person 5 objects, leaving 17. Two objects are then given to each person, leaving 5. The divider then takes a little piece from each object, gives them to one person, and gives the other persons the remaining partial objects. If the objects are indivisible, one person might say it is all right with him to receive one less. Should there be no volunteer, either scuffling, real violence (very unlikely), or the decision of the divider would settle the matter. In the division of the hunt, someone respected for his judgment looks at a pile of meat and portions it out as best he can. I never heard anyone say he had been cheated, even though an occasional discrepancy is bound to have occurred.

A few Nunamiut are able to use pencil, paper, and our numbers to add and subtract in the Nunamiut fashion. The younger Nunamiut are learning simple arithmetic by our methods.

MENSURATION. The parts of the human body are used for almost all measurements except travel distances. The distance a man can span with outstretched arms (a fathom) is a very common unit of measurement for cords, lines, and other long items. A kayak is usually 3½ fathoms long. An arrow should reach from the end of the outstretched arm to the breastbone—half a fathom. A snare for cow caribou is set with the lower part of the loop at knee height and the upper part at shoulder height. A piece of willow or baleen to be coiled up in a chunk of frozen liver for a wolf to swallow should reach from the base of the palm (where the palm-lines meet at a fork) to the top of the index finger. The openings in a sinew fishnet are usually two fingers on each (of four) sides, and three fingers for a gill net. The distance from the nape of the neck of a man's parka to the edge just over the forehead is measured by the length from the base of a doubled-up fist to the end of the extended thumb plus four fingers. Many Nunamiut consider the eye, or an unmarked stick or string, to be a more reliable measure for making a stove or a house than one of our rules marked off in inches and feet, probably because most Nunamiut are not yet skilled in the use of a rule.

A traveling distance is indicated by the number of days, or part thereof, required for the trip. If a person is trying to impress his audience with his strength and endurance, a distance could be "very, very long"; if he does not want to take a certain route, it is "very far indeed"; but if he wants to convince someone to travel with him, the distance is "not far at all."

The white man's measures of feet, yards, and miles for distance over the land have come into use, but few Nunamiut as yet are very accurate in their estimates. Exaggeration is common. If a man says he shot a caribou "a long way off," it was probably 200 to 400 yards. If a man actually says 700 or 800 yards, it was more likely much less, although so many shots are taken at 700 and 800 yards that I have seen an occasional, rare kill at that distance. When Nunamiut first started using rifles, they bragged a great deal about the distances at which they could kill caribou. A hunter would say that he thought he had shot a calf, but when he walked up to skin it, he discovered he had shot a bull. In telling an Eskimo about a long shot I had made one time, I used the same example; he laughed and told me that the same story has been used by generations of Nunamiut hunters.

Weight is relative: a large man is heavy; a moose is heavier than a caribou; when a person is tired, a given object may be very heavy. A person often brags that his dogs can haul so many caribou. Whether the caribou are bulls or calves is not always indicated. If a man says his dogs can haul five bull caribou, then one has an idea how much he means. The only notions of volume I recorded that were used in the old days, though still recognized today among young people, were the quantities a seal poke, caribou stomach, grizzly bladder, and other dried membranous sacs would hold. Today the five-gallon gasoline can is a common unit of volume. The degree of heat and cold is relative. "Very cold" is usually −30° to −50° F, "cold" but pleasant (if there is no wind) is from +10° to −20° (in the winter), and so on. On a summer day, +30° F is "cold." There are terms for angle, crooked, fork, point, etc., which are commonly observable in nature. I found that a Nunamiut could describe in great detail the size, shape, and nature of many, many elements of Arctic environment, whether they were of immediate economic concern or not.

The Supernatural

IÑUA. Almost every element in the universe has an *iñua* (soul or spirit). Most, or possibly all, animate objects (people, mammals, birds, fish, and insects) and most inanimate objects (lakes, mountains, the moon, directions of wind, and the atmosphere as a whole) have *iñua*. The Nunamiut word *iñuroat* corresponds to our term "animate." The possession or existence of a spirit, however, is not limited to animate objects. Nor is a spirit only the "animating" force of an object. The word *iñuk* means "person," and the inflected form *iñua*, which grammatically could be called possessive, genitive, or other arbitrary or descriptive term, literally means the person of (the antecedent), but not in the sense of a human being. An *iñua* is not the personality or even a characteristic of an object although an *iñua* itself may have a personality. The spirit of an object may be thought of as the essential life force, or in the case of inanimate objects, the essential existing force of that object. Without a spirit, an object might still occupy space and have weight, but it would have no meaning, it would have no life or real existence. When an object is invested with an *iñua*, it is a part of nature of which we are aware; but when the *iñua* of a fox leaves its body after the head has been cut off and the skin removed, it is next to nothing. The carcass is like the ashes of a log after it has been consumed by fire.

A person usually thinks of an iñua existing in the here and now. When thought of in time, it is believed to have always existed, or at least to have existed as long as anything has, and to exist forever (ishuilaq) in the future. In the old days, a few Nunamiut speculated that a very long time ago (in *itchaq imma*) someone may have drowned in a lake and had to remain there forever, living like a man. A shaman, or perhaps just his iñua, was able to travel to the bottom of the lake and obtain power from the *natavum iñua* (the soul or spirit of the lake). Only a shaman could see an iñua, most of which are thought to have distinct personalities. The following examples illustrate their characteristics.

The iñua of blowflies and mosquitoes could be very helpful. Many Nunamiut used to carry a small pouch filled with dead mosquitoes to ward off sickness but not necessarily to ensure good luck. The mosquito spirit did not like a man to use seal oil as a repellent until five days after the first appearance of mosquitoes in the summer. Blowfly iñua did not like a house with too much smoke in it. Many iñua were easily offended by any little thing; if one were careful not to insult them, they could be very helpful.

In the old days, when a person was sick, he might be placed on a grizzly bear hide. Since a grizzly bear iñua does not like to have a dead person lying on its skin, it would drive the sickness out of the person. A grizzly, however, can hear very well, and if a man bragged aloud that he could easily outrun or kill a grizzly, its iñua might hear him and would perhaps kill him some day. While a person was sick, everyone around the house should refrain from hammering anything so as not to anger the iñua of the grizzly.

If a woman scraped or sewed caribou skins near a fishing place, the iñua of the fish would be angered, and a fisherman would have bad luck there.

A woman should not boil seal and caribou meat together in the same pot, or else the seal and caribou iñua would become angered, and any person in the community might have poor luck in hunting.

In the old days, each direction of wind had an iñua. The north wind was a woman, the south wind a man. There is a story about the northwest wind:

Once the northwest wind was so strong and so cold that it killed a few people each year. A man named Shiokti decided to travel to the northwest and investigate this killing wind. After many days of traveling, Shiokti finally saw a man, the iñua of the northwest wind, chopping the snow with a flint adz. The wind was so strong and the snow so blinding, that Shiokti was forced to lie down from time to time. He finally managed to seize the adz and break it. From that time on, the northwest wind became weaker and weaker.

SHAMANISM. There are no explicit accounts of the origin of shamanism. The "bad guy" in the chronicle of Aiyagomahala and the creation of the Nunamiut is by no means to be equated with shamanism nor were Aiyagomahala and Kayaktuaguniktuu shamans.

Informants made the following speculations about the beginning of shamanism. Many Nunamiut feel that before the time of Mr. Raven, people did not know about shamanism. Since recent shamans have had the power to do things beyond the capabilities of normal or regular men, and since Mr. Raven also had this power (it was Mr. Raven who ended the great flood and brought the land back to the Nunamiut and brought the light out of the umialik's house and gave it to everyone), he must have been a very powerful shaman.

Aiyagomahala and Kayaktuaguniktuu, of course, performed superhuman deeds, but there is no history of shamanism after them. Furthermore, Aiyagomahala and Kayaktuaguniktuu acted autonomously, not under the aegis of external power as do shamans. It should be stressed that the Nunamiut as a whole do not point to Mr. Raven as the first shaman; this speculation is the result of the reflection of a very few philosophical Nunamiut minds. After Mr. Raven acquired shamanistic power, he passed it on to his close relatives. From that time on, power could be transferred to relatives or purchased by nonrelatives for furs or other valuable goods.

An example of the way in which a person could obtain shamanistic power follows. A well-established shaman might take an interest in some younger relative or, in rare instances, a young unrelated person, and might want to help him, for personal reasons, by transferring shamanistic power to him. An initiate responded by associating closely with the shaman and learning by precept how to obtain power and to use it to heal people and bring good luck in hunting. The initiate might have dreams about the acquisition of power and might ultimately have a vision. When he felt he truly was in possession of power, he would feel secure in trying to cure sick people and to improve his own luck in hunting and trapping. An old shaman could teach an initiate only so much; the novice had to acquire power and learn to use it on his own. As the young man succeeded in curing sick people and improving his own and other people's hunting, he gradually came to be recognized and perhaps acclaimed as a powerful shaman.

According to many Nunamiut the power of shamans was a good thing, and the shamans who cured the sick and brought good luck were reputedly the most powerful. If a good shaman felt his power beginning to ebb, he might become an evil shaman. In a futile effort to recover his power or to wrest power from another shaman, a declining shaman might lash out, making people sick or even trying to kill them. While many good shamans were respected, though held in awe, an evil shaman was a source of tremendous fear. It is interesting to note that while some informants characterized shamans generally as good people, in actual fact the accounts of shamanism and much of the ethnographic literature tend to present the shaman as a negative power. From what limited observation I could manage in the present ethnographic situation, shamanism seemed to loom larger as a source of fear than as a source of comfort and hope. Some very positive results must be credited to shamans, however, in curing psychosomatic illnesses and in persuading discouraged hunters to try again or to seek game in a new region.

A few individuals with little or no preparation came upon shamanistic power in a single vision. Such a vision might be interpreted by older people as the investment of power. The following incident is an illustration.

Shortly after freeze-up in the fall, a man was sitting alone on a hill watching for animals. In the distance, he heard several travelers coming with dog teams. He walked down the hill to meet the strangers, none of whom he had seen before. They were very pleasant to him and told him all about their recent trip. Finally the travelers invited the lone man to sleep with them in their camp that night. The men made overnight snow-block houses while the women gathered firewood. The women then built a huge outdoor fire and heated stones for dropping into wooden pots of water to boil meat. After everyone finished setting up camp, it was a good-sized village. The man ate, visited, and was happy. Late in the evening, a few of the travelers told the man that they were not regular people but that they would not reveal their identity until morning. They gave him a sleeping bag made of one caribou skin and one sheep skin sewn together.

In the morning, just as the man awoke, a great flock of ptarmigan rose into the air. The lone man looked down at himself and saw two feathers, one black, one white, which he thought had been the dark caribou skin and white sheep skin sewn together. Suddenly he realized that he had spent the night with ptarmigan. He immediately went home and told everyone about his experience. An older man told him that the ptarmigan iñua had come to him as his personal spirit helper and was to be the source of his shamanistic power. The man had already received a little power from his father, and now with the aid of the ptarmigan iñua he became a recognized shaman.

The following incidents illustrate the nature of shamanistic activity.

CASE 1. In 1900 or shortly thereafter, a Nunamiut boy 16 or 17 years old became paralyzed, unable to move. He was sick for a whole summer. About the time of freeze-up in early October, his parents called a shaman to heal their son. The shaman stood in front of the boy, sang a short magical song, and performed a dance. When the shaman stopped singing, he forced the boy to swallow a small piece of raw meat. In a short time, the young man became ravenous and he ate a terrific amount of meat. The shaman told him that he would get well, but not all at once; it was to be a slow cure. The shaman stayed with the family for two or three days, sleeping and eating as any visitor would. Then, after receiving a small gift as a token of appreciation and payment, the shaman traveled on. Several weeks later the boy had completely recovered his strength and was able to hunt and trap again.

CASE 2. In 1904 a whaling ship came to Point Barrow. One of the white men on the ship was said to be a magician who could make coins disappear and reappear again. A shaman saw this magician and decided to show him who was the more powerful. The shaman tied one end of a long rope onto a pair of gloves which he put into a small tent about 2 feet high. The shaman held the other end of the rope in his hand. Suddenly the gloves flew up in the air to the ship, got a bottle of whiskey, and returned to the little tent. The people opened the tent and the white magician was amazed to see the bottle there. He looked around to see if anyone was hiding inside the tent. He found nothing and returned to the ship.

CASE 3. Several Nunamiut families were gathered on the Arctic coast one summer in the early 1900s. A shaman was putting on a show in an attempt to convince the people of his power; he was not trying to cure anyone. The shaman beat a drum with two willow sticks and sang in a loud, tense voice. The shaman's wife came up to him and plunged a knife into his body, but he did not bleed or seem to feel the effects. The shaman told the people that he was very powerful; had they not just seen an example of his power? If any person would present the shaman with a gift, he could cure him.

CASE 4. Some time before 1890, several Nunamiut families were gathered at Chandler Lake in late summer. They were planning to drive a herd of caribou into the lake in order to obtain summer caribou skins for clothing. Three shamans were on a nearby hill competing with one another to see who could pull the caribou up from the north slope into the lake.

One shaman had a whole dried grayling and claimed to have power from the grayling iñua; he cut the grayling open and showed it to everyone; it was empty. He folded it together and told the hunters and their families that if his power was strong and true the grayling would fill up with lichens. If the fish remained empty, no caribou would come. The shaman put the grayling on his stomach under his parka and began beating his drum and shouting. He loosened his belt, allowing the grayling to fall onto the drum; it was full of lichens. Everyone was very happy because the caribou were going to come.

Another old shaman tried to call the south wind, because caribou travel into the wind to avoid mosquitoes. He made a small bundle of wood shavings and set it on fire. Then, while everyone watched, he swallowed the burning firebrand. Soon a warm south wind began to blow. Before long a good-sized herd of caribou began to head toward Chandler Lake from the north slope. Using two lines of scarecrows strung out in a long V, the drivers gently frightened the caribou toward the lake. But when the caribou got to the edge of the lake, they became restless and would not enter the water.

As the caribou were milling around in hesitation, a funny old shaman began beating a drum with all his might, trying to pull the caribou into the lake by sucking the air. From time to time he swallowed a small piece of chipped flint to demonstrate his power. His mouth started to bleed, but he continued beating the drum, shouting, and sucking air. Suddenly he spat a great glob of bloody caribou antler velvet onto the drum. Slowly but surely the caribou began entering the lake. The men in kayaks immediately paddled out into the lake and speared so many caribou that the people could not skin them all. When other Nunamiut heard of the successful drive at Chandler Lake, they came to visit their friends and relatives and everyone had a good time.

From these examples we can see that shamanism not only provided a means by which certain individuals could attain prestige in the eyes of their fellow men, but it could also help to bind the members of a community closer together in a common effort to survive. Especially in the last example above, one can easily imagine the tension in the moment before the caribou entered the lake. It is difficult enough for two or three hunters to exercise good judgment as they lie hidden behind a knoll watching a herd of caribou walking slowly toward them, offering weeks of food and months of clothing. But when a communal hunt involving virtually everyone in the community approached the final moments before the success of the kill could be known, the tension could become excruciating. Men in their kayaks, spears nervously in hand, waited anxiously as the drivers made their last attempt to force the herd into the water.

At times an individual might feel a terrific impulse to withdraw from the uncertainties of communal hunting and fly off by himself in a desperate effort to survive. In the company of other hunters, though, a man would reach out for any assurance of success. The sense of security and hope which shamans offered helped to integrate individuals with diverse impulses into cohesive, cooperative action. The knowledge that the shamans of the community were working themselves into a frenzy, beseeching their personal spirit helpers for aid in a crucial instant, could hold a person to a community until death overtook him.

NAMES. To a Nunamiut, a person's name is extremely important. When a Nunamiut meets a stranger, he asks his name and gives his own in return. Calling a person by name establishes his identity as a human being. It is impossible to think of a person without his name. After a visit to Fairbanks, one Nunamiut told me how odd it felt to see so many people whose names he did not know. It is highly improper to call someone by the wrong name, to mispronounce a name, or to forget a name. Nunamiut parents rarely seem to confuse the names of their usually many children. In the early days it was believed that when a child was named after a deceased relative, the iñua of the dead person helped the child by warding off sickness and bringing good luck in hunting and trapping. Shamans especially might call upon the spirit of a deceased namesake for help.

Most names are asexual; only a few are specifically for males or females. Over half the names of Nunamiut are words that occur frequently in the language. A plant, some animals, a phase of the climate, a part of the body of an animal or human being, or even a process such as "to sharpen a knife" may be a name. There seems to be no real restriction beyond common decency and something specific enough to be easily recognized. However, a word that is extremely common, e.g. *tuttu* (caribou) does not occur as a name.

DREAMS AND VISIONS. Great stock is placed in dreams. The meaningfulness of dreams is in prediction, usually for the ensuing day.

> One morning a man woke up and said he dreamed that a red fox would scream some time that day. His hunting companion told him he was crazy. Later that day, they both heard a red fox scream. Another time the same man dreamed that he could improve his luck in catching wolves by placing some woman's hair in his traps. He did not believe his dream at first, but it returned to him. The man then felt it must be true, so he placed some woman's hair in several wolf traps and his luck improved.

A dream of this nature could restore hope and a man would be motivated to try his luck again, probably in a more careful fashion.

One man said that when he dreams of a past umiak or sled he once had, he catches cold. If he dreams of shooting several wolves, then someone falls ill, but not seriously so. The same man said he always dreams of great herds of caribou just before the migration.

During an influenza epidemic, a woman dreamed that some person was going to die, but no one did.

On rare occasions I heard a person who was experiencing personal problems say how confused his dreams were. People do not worry or brood over dreams. If a man dreams that a herd of caribou is coming and no caribou appear, nothing is said. If a herd of caribou does appear that day, there might be a passing mention of the dream. When a man or woman has a dream, it is in the early morning shortly after awakening that he tells other people about the prediction. After that, no one is likely to mention the dream except in unusual instances.

Young children sometimes have nightmares. I could never discover the content but suspect that nightmares are usually about Indians or grizzly bears since parents often discipline their children by telling them that Indians or bears will catch them if they do not behave better. One night a 12-year-old boy sleeping next to me suddenly sat up in his sleeping bag and screamed in blood-curdling fashion. His older brothers and parents shouted loudly at him to lie down and go back to sleep. They did not offer to comfort him in the least. He did lie down but he wept and sobbed for some time, almost rising up to scream again even under the harsh injunction of his elders to be quiet.

Any person can have a dream. Visions on the other hand are much more powerful than dreams and are experienced by very few persons. In fact, informants asserted that only a shaman could have a vision. A very typical example of the first vision a shaman has concerned the ptarmigan iñua, described above. After his first vision, a shaman from time to time attempted to enter a trance in which he would again experience a vision. He would work himself into an intense emotional state by singing, dancing, shouting, screaming, breathing heavily, and making violent gestures. When the shaman entered a trance, his iñua flew out of his body like a bird and sought power from the iñua of an animal, his personal helping spirit, or gained insight into the future. When his spirit returned to his body, the shaman relaxed and regained his normal composure. After recovering from a trance, he could tell people what his iñua had experienced.

SUPERNATURALLY SANCTIONED RULES. The Nunamiut maintained a great many supernatural prohibitions and rules, most of which are no longer respected.

In responding to a question about them, one of my informants said, "Oh, you want to learn about *agliganaq* (Eskimo rules). " Agliganaq is related to the word *aglinigaqtuni* meaning to menstruate; it also means to begin to grow full or large.

In the old days, when a young girl began to menstruate, she was required, according to Eskimo rules, to drink only from her own skin cup for one month and not to touch anyone else's. She was not required to live apart from her family for any period of time. A girl should not have sexual intercourse or be approached until after her second menstruation. Sexual intercourse is then permissible and the conception of children is considered possible. Shamans formerly were very afraid of menstrual blood. If there were any contact, they might lose their power by alienating their personal spirit helper. Laymen, both formerly and today, do not fear menstrual blood, although sexual intercourse is normally avoided during menstruation for hygienic reasons.

Childbirth used to be considered risky and difficult, more so than it is today. Among other things, a pregnant woman was restricted from eating the meat from the front part of the legs of a mountain sheep, or else the man who killed the sheep would fall ill. When labor began, a woman was required to enter a parturition hut where women attended her. Today women believe if they work hard during pregnancy that the fetus will not grow too large and the delivery will be less painful. If a woman is lazy during pregnancy, the birth might not only be difficult but the child might also be lazy. Nowadays children are born in the home, and a few older men and women have become very capable midwives.

Although the term agliganaq is related to the word "to menstruate," it included rules for behavior other than those pertaining to menstruation and birth. In particular, there were several rules about the treatment of fur animals.

When a trapper caught his first wolf, wolverine, or fox of the year, he had to melt snow for his own water and drink out of a specially made cup for four days if the animal were male, five days if the animal were female. If the man drank water out of the family bucket, the animal's iñua would be angered. When the iñua returned to its own kind, it would tell of the trapper's disregard for the rules and he could never catch another animal of that species. After skinning out the animal, the trapper hung the skin up on a rack outdoors for one day for everyone to see. He told his family all the details of his first catch of the season and everyone hoped for a successful year. After four or five days, the trapper cleaned the pelt with a knife and sent the iñua of the animal away saying, "We want you back again."

Some time during the year in an attempt to improve his luck, a trapper might hang up a flint knife, a few beads, or perhaps an article of clothing and tell the wolf, for example, to take what it wanted. The object itself remained the same and could still be used, but the wolf had been induced to help the trappers by yielding itself to his traps. In the spring, a successful family carefully dried all their skins, cut a little piece from each one, and put them all on display. When a trapper had done well, he and his wife would feel that they could express their pride by giving food to several nearby relatives and friends.

When a hunter killed a grizzly bear, he could not use the weapon again for four or five days, dependent on whether the bear were male or female. After the bear was skinned and butchered, the meat could not be brought to the house but was left a hundred or so yards outside the camp. After all the meat was eaten, the pots used to boil the meat had to be thrown away.

The breaking of most supernaturally sanctioned rules resulted only in bad luck, but infractions of a few could result in death. If a person threw a dead eagle onto a freshly skinned grizzly bear hide, several people might die. Some 80 to 100 years ago, a man did just that and ten people died within two days.

The list of supernaturally sanctioned rules goes on and on. A few additional ones have been mentioned elsewhere. Most rules did not affect a person's chances to do well at hunting, trapping, and otherwise making a living or to repress individual behavior unnecessarily. Many rules seemed to make people more aware of what they were doing and, in a sense, to make them more serious about their daily tasks. Most Nunamiut now no longer adhere to the specifications of agliganaq, as a result of seeing whites and other Eskimos under white influence disregarding supernatural prohibitions with impunity. Also, missionaries spoke out against many of the rules.

One of the most elusive supernatural apparitions is *tunagaq*. Before missionary influence, this was considered to be a troublesome and bad force in itself but not evil in the sense of pervading man and nature in an effort to bring about a moral breakdown in society. Missionaries have translated the word devil by tunagaq and have given it a more evil connotation than existed originally.

In spite of missionary influence, many Nunamiut still indicated that tunagaq has a plural nature. Each tunagaq is an autonomous spiritual or supernatural entity and does not have a close relationship with any material thing or natural object. A tunagaq may appear almost any place at any time. Many years ago, several Nunamiut heard what they thought was a tunagaq in a willow patch. It sounded more or less like a raven. The next morning everyone looked for the tracks in the snow, but none was to be found.

Sometimes when a person finishes drinking a cup of tea, he turns the cup upside down, sets it on the ground and says, "Tunagaq will not bother us now. Tunagaq is weak." The Nunamiut are never very explicit about what tunagaq would actually do to a person if there were an encounter. Tunagaq always appear when it is dark or foggy and difficult to see. A Nunamiut places so much value on the sense of sight that he becomes uneasy whenever it is obscured.

Numerous stories exist about minor supernatural creatures. A miniature archaeological artifact that does not appear to be a toy is good cause for discussion about dwarfs. Even in recent decades dwarfs have been reported:

> In the middle of the 1800s, a family of dwarfs, perhaps 1½ or 2 feet tall, came down from the sky with a huge load of caribou skins and valuable furs. The dogs were invisible, but the harnesses moved as if pulled by dogs. Several Nunamiut saw this sled driven by the family of dwarfs. The sled stopped by a house and the dwarfs walked away and climbed into the sky, leaving the richly loaded sled behind.

Evil spirits, they said, often traveled behind a cloud or in a fog where they could not be seen. In the early days the Nunamiut were easily frightened by evil spirits or enemies, and an entire community might abandon a valley for fear of them.

The Nature of Individual Man

A Nunamiut does not think that a child is conceived from a single act of coition. The father "builds up" the fetus in the womb of the mother with several depositions of semen which "make the baby." A male adolescent engaging in a clandestine love affair figures that one sexual contact will not result in pregnancy, but that three or four might. When a couple is childless, the husband invariably bears the blame unless he happens to impregnate another woman.

During pregnancy, any number of behavioral traits may be transmitted to a child, and pregnant women are advised to lead a moderate life. Sometimes the fetus is said to get turned around and tangled up with the umbilical cord. One man living in Anaktuvuk Pass has become a very effective masseur and has "straightened out the fetus" of many women in the latter stages of pregnancy.

In the old days, a woman entered a temporary parturition hut to give birth and was usually attended by another woman. Today, women give birth in their homes, and both a man and a woman attend. At present in Anaktuvuk Pass, one woman attends the actual delivery and ties the umbilical cord, and one man relieves pain before the delivery by massaging. Often, a few hours or days after delivery, further massaging is needed "to put the womb back in place" and to stop any bleeding. Birth causes intense but momentary pain, but women do not seem to fear giving birth. As a 22-year-old bachelor, I did not feel it my place to intrude on an actual delivery, and thus relied only on informants' comments for information.

To a Nunamiut, a newborn baby can only eat, urinate, defecate, laugh, and cry, and it certainly cannot know anything, but they are enjoyable and loved even if they are useless. When a baby learns to walk and talk a little, it becomes a child. A very young child still cannot know very much, but at least one can see an incipient human being there. Even a child of 2 or 3 years of age is always forgetting; it cannot remember anything. A young child is unable to think because he does not have an *ishuma* (mind).

When a child reaches the age of 4 or 5, his brain grows thicker and heavier; he stops forgetting and begins to remember things when his ishuma has thus become formed. When a mature person speaks of his early youth, he refers to the time when he began to remember everything. From that time on, a Nunamiut can relate all the events of his life in sequence. The period of personal remembrance is called *ipani*. The Nunamiut think of the ishuma as the seat of memory. As a person's memory of past events increases, he develops a capacity to use his memory to solve problems of the day.

Many years of experience are required before a person can become effective in handling the great variety of problems he must face. In the old days, a person with a large head was thought to have a large ishuma, and to be more intelligent than other people.

The ishuma is also the repository of the emotions. When a person becomes angry, his ishuma feels the anger; it experiences the happiness a person feels when people come together for conviviality, or when a person has a love affair and establishes a household. The ishuma also experiences all the sadness in life, and at death, finally, there is no more sadness. The balance in most people is on the fun and happiness side, enough so that life is considered worth living. A few individuals do become so sad that they decide to end it all by committing suicide. The only trouble is that such a person's ishuma goes on killing itself forever.

There were, and are, a fair number of Nunamiut who might be called neurotic, some mildly so, some bordering on the psychotic and almost unable to take care of themselves because of mental and emotional disturbances. Such a person is not considered really sick, but his ishuma has become distorted and out of balance because he "thinks too much." His ishuma dwells incessantly on some past incident or personal conflict to the detriment of his ability to face daily life; he may flare out in anger with little provocation and is difficult to talk or work with in a reasonable, accepted fashion. Such a person finds little sympathy in Nunamiut society.

From about five years of age until just before death, a person's ishuma does not change, but it may become ill and leave the body; in fact, this is the cause of some diseases. Just before death, when a man or woman is very old, the ishuma can be lost. A few old people cannot talk straight or understand properly because this has happened. After death, the ishuma does not think any more and is no longer aware of the body or even of life.

While the ishuma of a person is considered to be his intellectual capacity, his iñua is considered to be his spiritual aspect. The iñua is more important to a person than his ishuma in the sense that without it, a person could not be alive, whereas without an ishuma, a person merely could not think straight. A person's iñua is the specific essence of the life force of that individual. A newborn baby becomes invested with an iñua with his first breath. The iñua is not known to grow or originate in any particular place. One informant, in admitted speculation, said that maybe it is inside the mother's body when the fetus begins to grow and passes into the baby when it begins to breathe. There is no specific location for the iñua inside the body. In the old days, when an elderly shaman's collarbones became very thin, they thought it was because the iñua grabbed the shaman's collarbones each time it climbed out of his body. Generally, one thinks that the iñua resides in the trunk of the body.

The iñua of a person lives forever; it may be said to enjoy a pleasant existence after death, and there is none of the sadness to be found in earthly life. Only in the case of suicide or when a shaman dies trying to kill another shaman is the iñua thought to suffer. There is no elaborate structure for afterlife. The iñua of all people exist in the same way on the same plane and are in communication with one another. Some Nunamiut think that iñua hover forever, just a little way above the ground, are able to travel anywhere any time with no effort, and never leave tracks.

As mentioned above, an iñua may help out its living namesake by warding off sickness and improving his luck in hunting and trapping. About twenty years ago a man died just before his wife gave birth to a boy. The boy was named after his father, and today the young man is considered to be the impersonation of his father. Some Nunamiut would say that the father's iñua entered his newborn son's body.

The most nebulous aspect of a man is his *taganiŋa* (shadow). This does not seem to play a significant role at birth or during infancy, and is not an aspect of the iñua or ishuma but is a vague sort of second self. It is described thus:

> A person is really himself, but there, in his stead, is his taganiŋa. Some time before 1900, an old woman was near her son when he died. At the instant he died she saw his taganiŋa rush from his body out of the house into the air. It is very rare for a taganiŋa to be seen. A taganiŋa is shaped like a person and looks perhaps like glass, but there is nothing in it. It has no substance. Sometimes a shaman hid his power in his taganiŋa where no other shaman could find it.
>
> While a person's taganiŋa does exist during his lifetime, it has a greater function after death. When it leaves the body, the person, in addition to the loss of the ishuma and iñua, is truly dead. A person's taganiŋa can never return to his body and give it life. After death the taganiŋa and iñua do not

necessarily do anything together, but they are aware of each other. A shaman could see a taganiŋa, and he could bring news of the dead to the living.

SICKNESS AND HEALTH. When a person's body is free from illness and his iñua and ishuma are functioning properly in his body, he is perfectly healthy. When he is healthy, working hard, and fulfilling his obligations to appreciative friends and relatives, he is indeed very happy. Life, however, is not always that easy. Bodily illnesses and injuries, conflicts of the mind, and unresponsive people unwilling to do their share of work may mar an otherwise pleasant existence.

In previous years seal oil was the great cure-all for minor physical ailments. It was applied to the skin for burns and frostbite; to the face, chest, and back for coughs or colds. For cuts, seal oil or spruce gum was used to prevent infections, and the inner membrane stripped from a caribou hide was used for a bandage. For a bloody nose, blubber was stuffed into the nostrils. For abdominal upsets of all kinds, seal oil was taken, and sometimes the stomach was massaged. These uses of seal oil have today largely been replaced by medicated petroleum jelly, especially among the younger people.

Snow or ice is rubbed gently on a bruise for a few moments to reduce swelling. Some people place snow or a piece of ice on the back of the neck for a bloody nose. Heated rocks are sometimes placed on the back to relieve stiff or strained muscles.

The Nunamiut are careful when they are outdoors, and severe sprains and fractures are very rare. When they do occur, anyone with experience can twist the limb back to its normal position and bind it with caribou hide (cloth is often used today) and a splint, if necessary, to keep it straight. A sprain or fracture that is not corrected will swell and "grow old" in a misshapen way.

Bloodletting was a common method in the old days of relieving aches and pains in specific parts of the body. For a headache, a small incision was made in the temple and the blood allowed to flow. Similarly, for a pain in the elbow, shoulder, back, or knee, an experienced person, not necessarily a shaman, could make the incision.

For a deep internal wound such as an embedded arrow, a shaman (usually) tried to enlarge the hole and pull the arrow out.

Because arrowheads intended for human beings were tanged, extraction was exceedingly difficult and painful. The shaman helped to alleviate the pain by singing and dancing, upon assurance of payment.

The Nunamiut have never performed internal surgery. One Nunamiut told me he thought he could learn a great deal about the human body and how to make it well if he could observe a careful autopsy. He has skinned thousands of different mammals, birds, and fishes and has an amazing sense of anatomy. But a Nunamiut's sense of physiology, of bodily processes, is very limited. Most Nunamiut have an idea of the passage of food through the digestive system and of the flow of blood through the vessels. During a time of hunger, the blood is said to become very thin, causing a person to lose his strength.

One of the most common sources of disease is *nuvuq* (phlegm). Any kind of mucus or fluid emanating from the respiratory system and eyes, colds, influenza, and other respiratory illnesses is generally referred to as nuvuq. This is considered to be dirty and contagious. A person should not cry too much or he will make his body dirty and he could become ill. When a relative dies, no matter how much a person cries, he cannot bring the deceased back to life again. So really, a person should never cry too much. He could even contaminate the dead body with nuvuq. Respiratory illnesses used to be very rare among the Nunamiut but were exceedingly contagious. Influenza could sweep through an entire village, killing half its members. In the old days, the affliction of nuvuq was considered to be the result of an evil spirit such as tunagaq or the work of an evil shaman. An epidemic could be counteracted only by large-scale shamanistic activities designed to protect and cure the whole village. Recently, respiratory diseases, including tuberculosis, have become the primary health problem among the Nunamiut.

Sometimes a person falls ill with a high fever and becomes unable to talk straight or make sense—in other words he is delirious. In such a case, a person's ishuma has become ill and left his body. If he is seriously ill but still retains his senses, then it is likely that his iñua has left his body. In the old days, only a shaman had the power to find the lost iñua or ishuma and return it.

The Nunamiut stress diet and hard work as the primary factors in maintaining health. The ideal diet consists of meat and fat, in whatever ratio a person prefers, usually from a quarter fat and three quarters meat to half and half. Caribou meat and whale blubber are considered by many people to be the best combination. Most Nunamiut regard caribou meat as the standard. After only a few days of moose or bear, they, especially children, begin to want caribou meat, although mountain sheep, ptarmigan, waterfowl, ground squirrel, and marmot are considered acceptable substitutes for a while and are even desired for their variety. Similarly, fat other than that of caribou, whale, seal, and bearded seal is greatly valued for novelty and change, but only for a short time. The most important requirement of a diet is that it contain both meat and fat, in any proportion a person feels like eating at the time. After a meal or two of nothing but fat, a person gets a "string around his throat" and cannot swallow more fat. A meat diet with very little fat is a hunger diet. Either meat or fat alone will make a man sick in a day or two. Plants and fish are much desired for the change in diet, but one rarely hears of the nutritional motive. It is good, solid meat and fat that are the healthy foods.

When a person is working hard, he not only keeps his body in good shape with the exertion but is also less likely to suffer from nuvuq and other diseases. If a person brags that he does not become sick easily, he will certainly fall ill some time. The hard worker who is also modest is the more virtuous person. In earlier days an industrious person was also considered much less susceptible to the attacks of evil spirits and malevolent shamans.

GROWTH, AGING, AND DEATH. Nunamiut comment that growing children eat ravenously at times, far more than is necessary to restore energy. It is thought that this extra food is used to make a person grow. When a girl's breasts enlarge and her hips broaden and fill out, she is no longer considered a child. Older men may joke with a young girl, pinching her breasts or commenting how nice her buttocks look nowadays, and warn her that young men are likely to pursue her. At the same time an older man may tell a young girl jokingly that she will never catch a husband unless she is receptive to the advances of young hunters.

Not until a woman is in her late teens or early twenties does she reach the height of her physical strength. Even then she continues to learn techniques and to develop a state of mind that enable her to perform amazing feats of endurance in house building, wood collecting, butchering, and traveling. After menopause, a woman is thought to deteriorate slowly, but Eskimo women even in their sixties can run a short distance with great speed.

When a boy begins to grow very fast in his early teens and his voice changes, he is no longer considered a child but a young man. The actual onset of puberty in males is not marked by any formal recognition. Formerly, when a young man killed his first large animal, he gave the meat to relatives and friends, eating none of it himself. Today, merely verbal note is made of his first major kill. A young man in his late teens and early twenties is considered to be at the height of his physical ability in terms of running and climbing mountains rapidly. A man in his thirties and early forties, however, enjoys much greater technical knowledge and superior mental conditioning which enable him to outperform his juniors in traveling and hunting for extended periods, when skill and endurance rather than mere power are needed. I often hunted and traveled with older men and never ceased to marvel at their persistence. One always had the feeling of greater accomplishment in their company.

At the age of 40 or 45, men realize they have to slow down or they will dangerously exhaust themselves. From then on, they feel themselves gradually declining in strength. A man does not like to be 65 or 70 because he can remember so vividly how little he used to tire as a youth. Many people are able to stay active until the age of 80 or more. Their activity is usually confined to the camp, but they may be very useful to a household. As far as I could determine, the killing of old people was not a common practice, nor is it practiced today.

Just before an old person dies, I was told, his body is worn out like an old tool; his bones soften, his blood becomes very weak and thin, and he just dies. His iñua, taganiŋa, and ishuma leave his body and he is truly dead. When a person stops breathing, his relatives wait for a while until they are sure he is dead, for no one would want to be near the iñua when it left the person's body, and the precise moment of departure seems undetermined. In earlier days, after a few hours, perhaps, the deceased person's relatives dressed him in fine clothes, handling his body very carefully. They placed him on high, dry ground, covered him with caribou hides, and put a knife or other small, useful object near his body to pay respect to his departed iñua. An umialik may have had a larger item such as a sled placed near his body. If there were time, his relatives might pile a few rocks over him.

After the death of a person, the members of his immediate family entered a brief period of mourning, four days if the deceased were male, five days if female. If possible (that is, if everyone were not desperately hunting for caribou), the bereaved worked very little during the mourning period. No one could sew, make implements, hunt, or trap. Only the collecting of firewood and water and simple cooking were considered permissible. No one visited the close relatives of the deceased unless necessary, although the house itself was not abandoned. After the period of mourning was over, the immediate relatives resumed a more normal life. Also, while a show of grief was allowed and expected during the period of mourning, it should end after four or five days. After all, no amount of crying would bring a deceased relative back to life and the tears could pollute a person's body and make him ill. No further observance or sacrifice was made to the deceased except that a shaman might drop a small piece of meat or fat near the grave of a relative whose iñua had aided him.

Today, graves are dug in the permafrost in a cemetery near the village. If a missionary happens to visit the village, he gives the deceased a Christian burial.

THE ETHICAL GOOD. Among the Nunamiut, ethics are primarily, but not exclusively, a social matter. The first reward for good behavior and the first sanction for bad is the response of nearby friends and relatives. I have dwelt at length in Chapter 3 on personal relationships and how one is expected to act. Here we are concerned with the more abstract aspects of ethical behavior which the Nunamiut express. It will be remembered in the account of Aiyagomahala and the creation of the Nunamiut that just before Aiyagomahala left the Nunamiut he told them "never to be angry, to love each other, to be kind, and to help each other." And in the final part of the story of Ikiashuruak and the caribou in Chapter 9, people are admonished to "stay clean, to avoid becoming angry, and to be helpful to others."

Some time after collecting these and other stories containing similar ethical statements, I was asking informants what it means to be called iñualautak (a good person). I received the following reply.

A good person never becomes angry; he works hard and is never lazy, helping friends and relatives in building a house or making clothes in time of need and giving them food, skins, and firewood; he does not steal; he does not lie; and he refrains from arguing or talking to people in a funny, affected, or "neurotic" way.

It is very interesting to note the similarities between the ethical values found in Nunamiut ethnohistory and folklore and in the statements of living Nunamiut. And the spontaneous comments made from day to day about other people's actions reflect the same ideals. Several Nunamiut are still aware of animals' sensitivity to the ethical behavior of human beings and speak of it occasionally. A person who makes a strong effort to live in accordance with these ethical notions is said to be free from disease, evil spirits and, in the old days, from shamanistic attacks.

> A bad person becomes angry with little provocation and is lazy and very sluggish in responding to other people's requests for help; he lies, cheats, steals, argues, acts strangely, and generally makes trouble with vicious gossip and impossible stories. A bad person usually manages to keep within the letter of customary law and avoids becoming labeled as a true criminal; in lying and refusing to help others, a clever person can wriggle around for years without being pinned down. Even minor theft may be difficult to specify when a person says he merely forgot to return a borrowed item or shifts the blame to someone else. Murder and adultery, however, are definite crimes, demanding clear-cut action on the part of society.

One trait that hovers between good and bad is pride. A Nunamiut feels that anyone should feel proud of a good job he has done. If a person cannot express some pride about himself, he becomes very quiet and ashamed. He gradually loses ambition, may cease to work hard, and may even become neurotic. One of the reasons given for the restriction against marrying recognized collateral relatives is that a person should not live under a sense of shame. On the other hand, if a man tries to make people think more highly of himself than he deserves, he and other people know that his pride is not real. Every person is so aware of what everyone else is doing that if one person works hard, the whole village knows immediately. For example, the day after a hunter has killed several mountain sheep, he may visit friends and bask in their admiration without a single word being said about the hunt.

One Nunamiut asserted that people should be good for the

sake of being good—a Platonist among savages, so to speak. He
constantly encouraged anyone to try to learn or to do something
new just for the sake of trying. He often said one should always
wake up early in the morning and work hard because that is the
best way to live as well as the best way to win the respect of people
and animals.

Alayanaitchuq and *koviashuktoq* both mean "to be happy."
Alayanaitchuq is negative in form, the morpheme -*nait*- being one
of the two negative infixes. When a person is having fun at a dance,
is joking or making love, he is not burdened at the moment with
any trouble or difficulty; the situation is alayanaitchuq. When a
person himself is a great source of laughter and merriment, he also
is described as alayanaitchuq. When he is forced by circumstances
to work harder and with greater difficulty than he normally should,
the situation is *alayanaktoq,* the positive or indicative form of the
verb. If someone should cause trouble for another, the former
would be described as alayanaktoq. We may thus think of alayanaitchuq in terms of fun and having a good time.

Koviashuktoq on the other hand connotes general happiness.
When a person lives in accordance with the ethical ideals expressed
in the above, he should be koviashuktoq. One can tell if a person
is koviashuktoq by the expression on his face, the manner in which
he performs his tasks, and the spontaneity of his relationships with
other people. Nunamiut, even when very young, are exceedingly
sensitive to the happiness of other individuals. There is little attempt to maintain a gulf between appearance and reality or to for-
malize relationships to the extent that frequently seems necessary
in more complex societies. Even though a person might be working
hard and fulfilling his obligations to other people, he might seem
unhappy at times, which a Nunamiut is quick to notice and comment upon. To be truly happy, a person, in addition to living in
accordance with ethical ideals, must laugh and joke freely and refrain from "thinking too much." When a person thinks too much,
he may become obsessed with some personal or future problem,
fancied or otherwise, and he may very easily undermine his happiness. A person in a quiet mood may even be told to visit people, to
laugh and to joke.

Aside from purely personal problems, the primary source of un-
happiness among the Nunamiut is a close relative who does not
perform his role very well. Within a household, an in-law who re-

fuses to cooperate or who openly foments trouble may cause another to become very morose. In the old days, especially when a family was isolated for months at a time, conflicts within the household might lead to a suicide.

Nunamiut sometimes become melancholy and talk of the anxiety and sadness of life: there is no relief from the day-to-day work required to maintain existence and a semblance of comfort; one never knows when caribou will be scarce for months on end; a lazy member of the household is a constant burden to a hard worker; other people may ask for help when they mean to give very little in return.

But life is not just a dull struggle for survival. Most of the Nunamiut have an insatiable zest for living. I have heard many of them, in describing their general condition to Point Barrow Eskimos and other outsiders, say *koviashuktugut* (we are happy). At least the people are happy enough to continue striving for the good life.

KNOWLEDGE. The Nunamiut consider knowledge to be the cumulative memory of each person. Synonymous with the awareness of one's experiences in the past is a person's capacity to apply his knowledge to a particular situation. The abstract interpretation of phenomena found in universities is little developed among the Nunamiut. Rather, the following example illustrates what a Nunamiut told me he considers to be a use of knowledge.

A man is sitting on a hill and sees two or three caribou in the distance. An intelligent person notes the direction of wind, the relative temperature of the air, the condition of snow if present, whether it is raining or not, the shape of the terrain, the appearance of the caribou (whether they are feeding, walking, or running), and the presence of other animals. After sizing up all these factors in a moment or two, he immediately recalls past situations having similar factors. Then the hunter decides whether to remain where he is or move to another location. If he shoots the caribou, then his decision was based on a knowledgeable use of past experience. If not, he either exercised poor judgment or was unable to observe some critical factor such as a wolf hidden behind a knoll. A few people make little use of their knowledge, because of laziness or obstinacy rather than innate inability. Some people simply do not look at a total situation very carefully and

decide on a course of action on the basis of only one or two
factors; they merely encounter problems as they occur rather
than planning ahead and trying to determine what the requirements of a situation will be. A knowledgeable person
always tries to remember how every experience took place. If
something strange, unpleasant, or unexpected happens, a
knowledgeable person thinks to himself that he will never do
that again and tries to figure out why it happened. A less intelligent person does not bother. He misses the significance
of an unfortunate event because of lack of attention and may
well cause or allow it to happen again.

The cognitive processes by which the Nunamiut approach their
environment are scientific empiricism, supernaturalism, and anthropomorphism. Let us consider how their conceptions are developed.

Many examples of Nunamiut empiricism are considered in this
monograph. As a child, a Nunamiut develops vague notions about
the environment from hearing his elders talk. When he encounters
the elements of the environment personally, he learns that many of
his pre-existing notions are false. For example, one young man told
me that he thought hunting wolves would be easy, similar to hunting caribou, until he tried it. For years he had listened to his elders
speak confidently about their successes in wolf hunting. As every
hunter soon learns, however, wolf hunting is an exacting test of a
man, mentally, physically, and emotionally. As a Nunamiut accumulates experience, he gradually modifies his conceptions about
the nature of the environment. The greater his ability to remember
past experiences and to compare them, the more closely his conceptions will approximate reality.

The test of this is the relative efficacy of specific applications de-
duced from general conceptions. If, for example, a young hunter
figures that caribou are easily frightened by the sight and scent of
man, but not by the sound, he may be perfectly successful in the
summer. But once cold weather sets in, the general notion that
caribou cannot hear well must be qualified if the hunter is to have
any luck. Most Nunamiut seem very quick to adjust their conceptions when new evidence so requires. Even Nunamiut in their fifties
and sixties willingly learn anew from experience. The techniques
for trapping beavers and river otters (see below) are examples.

Whatever the cause or the source of this empirical approach to the environment, if Nunamiut were not responsive to the details of their environment, they would not be able to survive.

There are a great many things, however, which a Nunamiut finds inexplicable on the basis of only his empirically derived knowledge. This is partially due to the limitation of his capacity to gather empirical data. Also the Nunamiut do not have a literary tradition, which might encourage the accumulation of information. Although some knowledge about the environment is passed down from generation to generation, the Nunamiut emphasize that each individual must learn from his own experience. No person is criticized for not knowing any given fact as such, but if he fails to learn fairly rapidly from his own experiences, people will begin to think his mind is very small.

One of the primary limitations of the explanatory power of empirically derived knowledge is the limited means of verification available to a Nunamiut. There are few tools or implements with which to measure things, and the Nunamiut system of mensuration is relatively unelaborated. When the sense of sight is distorted by fog, for example, a Nunamiut has little way of correcting a mistaken impression. Even comparison with other experiences may not fully clarify poorly conceived notions, because experiences in similar circumstances are likely to produce similar results. A Nunamiut interprets most experiences, even under adverse circumstances, at face value, since he has no means other than his human senses to investigate a problem. For the Nunamiut, supernatural and anthropomorphic interpretations provide explanations where empirically derived knowledge fails to elucidate something as he thinks it should be. The following example is based on the comments of an experienced Nunamiut wolf hunter.

> One time a hunter shot a wolf and he saw that it was badly wounded. He found a considerable quantity of blood splattered on the rocks where he had shot the animal. He followed the wolf for a long distance, but the wolf never seemed to lose its strength. Finally the wolf got away, apparently in good condition.

To a Nunamiut, only shamanism, the breaking of a taboo, or the action of the spirit of the wolf, the *amaugum iñua,* could possibly account for such an incident. An explanation in terms of chance or randomness is not permissible in Nunamiut thinking. On the basis of extensive experience and his sense of sight, the hunter knew he should have had that wolf, but the wolf got away. This is a dilemma. Such an experience is inexplicable in terms of physical reality as a Nunamiut conceives it. In the absence of a conviction that there may have been an unaccounted factor fully explicable in terms of observable reality, had fuller observation been possible, a supernatural interpretation completes the explanation of the experience.

Awareness of supernatural factors is a part of a man's knowledge but is distinguishable from that part of his knowledge which is empirically derived. The Nunamiut are not so explicit about this distinction as an inexperienced ethnographer might like, but there is adequate evidence to discern some order in the matter. Empirical knowledge derives from experience based upon the human senses, primarily sight, but also hearing, smelling, tasting, and feeling (in the kinesthetic sense), the memory of experiences, and the comparison (analogizing) of them. Traditional knowledge of a supernatural kind, such as the beliefs and behavior associated with an animal's iñua, contains some step or some action that cannot be verified by sight or other human senses. A Nunamiut admittedly cannot *see* a wolverine being propitiated, but he knows in his own mind that the wolverine has been propitiated because that is the way things operate by virtue of the nature of the wolverine. Here a Nunamiut assumes the inherent presence of a factor, which we call supernatural, that cannot be directly verified. An anthropologist, on the other hand, argues that such a belief and associated behavior has an arbitrary relationship to the wolverine, that there is nothing intrinsic in the nature of a wolverine which demands propitiation. The need for propitiation of the wolverine cannot be demonstrated, at least not to the satisfaction of the modes of demonstration that we normally accept.

Many supernaturally sanctioned rules do not involve a sense of awe—this is the way things work, and a propitiatory act is part of the whole process of bringing success, although not a part subject to step-by-step verification as is the setting of a rock deadfall. In an experience that contradicts what a Nunamiut thinks should have happened, he accepts a supernatural explanation with some wonder, but because supernatural explanations often seem to be very good ones, I never noticed a profound sense of awe associated with them.

In an experience that does not appear to contain a contradiction but has human-like aspects, a Nunamiut supplements his empirically developed conceptions by attributing human characteristics to an animal as part of the explanation of an incident. The following example is an illustration.

> In November 1960, a Nunamiut hunter and I were approaching a flock of five mountain sheep—one large ram and four smaller sheep. The ram scanned the countryside from time to time like a man. While we were still some distance from the flock, my companion said, "Really, that ram thinks we are just two other sheep feeding on the moss and maybe we are a bit lonely, looking for sheep company." In climbing up the mountain, we were out of sight of the sheep, but the wind was very erratic. When the sheep got away, my companion speculated on the basis of past experience that the sheep must have smelled us. The ram must have decided that we were not sheep after all and immediately had turned to the other younger sheep and told them to get moving.

Underlying these cognitive processes—scientific empiricism, supernaturalism, and anthropomorphism—is a general attitude toward nature. The elements of the environment may be considered fairly well disposed toward man: it is not actively benevolent but at least it is readily permissive. No part of nature may be said to be inherently hostile to man, although the grizzly for example may easily be irritated. A Nunamiut may complain about the north wind, for example, but he does not consider it to be a personal affront. By and large, man can wrest a comfortable living from his environment, but at times Nunamiut do have to endure hardships. Occasional starvation and disease have struck people down in numbers. While individuals strive to the best of their ability, still, people do die. In the face of impending tragedy, a Nunamiut often resigns himself to say *kanolaitchuq* (it cannot be helped). Things sometimes take place beyond man's control, although they may be perfectly explicable in terms of empirically derived knowledge. Once a Nunamiut's infant great-grandson fell ill with influenza. He commented how much he loved the baby boy, that he did not want him to die, and that he would do what he could to save him. But he knew well the inexorable course of sickness and if, he said, his great-grandson died, well, there was just nothing that could be done—*kanolaitchuq*. Happily, the little boy was not severely ill and he did not die. Even to a Nunamiut, the Brooks Range is a difficult region, and the acquiescence implied by the expression kanolaitchuq soothes a person when he encounters the harsher edges of reality.

LUCK. The Nunamiut do not think in terms of pure luck as many white men do. They characterize their territory as a hungry country and say, "We hunt to live." Heavy reliance on luck, supernaturalism, or the assumption that the world or somebody in it owes one a living is absent. *Pilyautaktuni* means "to have good luck," but it implies effort or involvement rather than success merely by chance. I have said that reflective Nunamiut do not search for the overall explanation of order in the universe. But, keeping in mind the particular ideas which Nunamiut express about what contributes to the success or failure of an attempt to exploit any one element of the environment, we may observe in general terms what appears to be a "fractionally organic" view of the universe, although I never evoked specific comments to that effect. By fractionally organic I mean a world view in which each part of the universe is thought to effect every other part, but in which each part is not considered to be so integrated that it is governed by the total scheme of interrelationships.

The validity of this notion is not our concern, but only its practical effect on Nunamiut efforts to explain things and to exploit the environment. There is no "whole-ness" about the Nunamiut world view. To a Nunamiut, the universe appears to be only a collection, not even a system (so far as I have been able to discern at this point), of parts, all of which stand or act in relation to one another, but not necessarily in any inexorably defined way. If there is any randomness in the world of a Nunamiut, it is in the modes of the interaction of parts; that is, that parts affect one another is assumed, but how they affect each other and which element affects another are not always specified, as far as I could determine. In such a world nothing happens by chance. In a given week, for example, one hunter may kill many more caribou than another hunter. At first it may be easily explained that the former had more opportunities to shoot. Anything can happen once, so to speak, although ultimately it is for some reason, even if it is unknowable. Over a period of several weeks, however, if the same hunter continues to shoot very few caribou, there must be some explanation. The universe as a whole is not affecting his success but, as one part reacts with other parts in this "fractional or-ganism," some thing or things about him or responding to him is the cause of his misfortune. He may be a poor shot, he may not be smart enough to place himself advantageously, he may be lazy or obstinate even if he knows what to do, he may be mentally dis-turbed and incapable of thinking straight, he may have aroused the resentment of the caribou iñua by some action, or (formerly) he may have incurred the wrath of a shaman.

Luck, then, can only be a function of the man, and never a matter of chance. Even a man's generosity can improve his success. In the early days, and to a lesser extent today, whenever a person enjoyed success in trapping fur animals, he was supposed to help poor people. When a poor person received aid, he was supposed to say, "Thank you very much, may you catch many animals." A benevolent man was, and is, truly thought to be helped by the good wishes of those whom he aids.

TRUTH. The Nunamiut are very concerned with truth, but not truth in the sense of an ideal abstraction. They are interested in the truth of a person's statement—the extent to which his statement corresponds with observable reality. The Nunamiut consider the eyes to be the most reliable means of determining the truth of a statement. Ears, it is said, lie very easily, but not eyes. If a hunter returns home from a day's hunting and says that he shot and skinned six caribou on a nearby hill, he will be taken at his word. But if another man should happen to pass by the hill and see only five caribou, and if other persons should substantiate the latter's observation by looking for themselves, people would talk with surprise and distrust about the former's lack of veracity. The next time he made a statement about what he had done, people would doubt him. In fact, eyes are trusted to such an extent that if a hunter sees a mountain sheep which he has just shot fall over a cliff, and if he cannot find it on the rocks below when there is blood on the cliff above, the only explanation is a supernatural one. The eyes do not lie, but supernatural phenomena take place be-yond the limits of sight. Thus a shaman could perform magical tricks, such as sleight of hand and feigned stabbing which the eye could not follow, and convince laymen of his supernatural power.

Making untrue statements is divisible into two categories: "black" lies and "white" lies. A black lie is a statement that does not correspond to observable reality, which a person does not admit as false or a joke and which he may have made with evil intent. A white lie is a statement that is untrue but which the speaker immediately calls a "joke" or "white lie" with a big guffaw, causing other people to laugh. Life is said to be no fun without a little white-lying or good spirited joking now and then. Most people tell white lies or jokes every day. A Nunamiut can make a joke out of anything. Once I returned home after hunting all day. When I entered the tent I saw a huge pile of freshly boiled caribou meat. When I asked if the meat were cooked, meaning was it all right to start eating, a young married woman said no it was still raw. She laughed and laughed, as though it were a great joke.

8. The World of Nature

The Land

THERE is no story among the Nunamiut about the creation of the earth as a whole. They believed the land was flat before the mountains came into being, and they make the analogy between sea ice crushing up to form pressure ridges and the land crushing up to form mountains. No time is specified, except that this happened a very long time ago (*itchaq imma*).

As might be expected, the Nunamiut have a great many terms for the physical features of the land, including mountains generally, an individual mountain, small mountains, hills, knolls, bluffs, cutbanks, ridges, river terraces, valleys, passes, summits, the range front, dry flat ground, swampy ground, tussocks, rivers, creeks, gravel, sandy and muddy creek banks, gravel bars, lakes, ponds, and on and on. Each term may be highly modified by inflection as well as by straight description.

Many features of the land are named. The major features (large mountains, rivers, lakes) bear the same names for generations and are usually based on some suggestive aspect of the locality or a particular incident: Raven Lake is so named because there are many ravens about; Mud Lake is a dirty color; Marmot River abounds in marmots. The names of minor features, especially small creeks, often change from generation to generation. I visited two small creeks some fifty or so miles from the village, which I was told were named after two young men who had recently set traps there. One summer, an older Eskimo and I shot a young grizzly near an unnamed creek. After that the creek was called *aklavirak* (crazy little grizzly).

A few Nunamiut are aesthetically sensitive to their countryside. One very striking mountain called Napaktualuit, at the northeast corner of the junction of the Anaktiktuak River valley with the main Anaktuvuk/John River valley about six miles northeast of the village, sometimes evokes comments from them. On clear days,

Napaktualuit may be seen from the village. One young man told me several times what a beautiful mountain he thought it was. Another young man commented how much he missed the mountains when he was away and how much he enjoyed being high on a mountain where he could see for miles around. One day I was walking up a small mountain with an older Eskimo; as we were enjoying a remarkably spectacular view, he mentioned aloud what an impressive sight we beheld.

It is exceedingly important for a Nunamiut to be familiar with the topography of his region. Many animals respond in fairly predictable ways to the terrain. Caribou in particular react to a certain condition in such a similar way that it is essential for a hunter to be fully conscious of the kind of terrain he happens to be in at the moment. The Nunamiut talk a great deal about the shape and condition of the land, commenting on a day's travel or describing the general lie of an entire valley. Young men listen carefully and discuss their first experiences in traveling and hunting in the country. It is recognized that physical features of the land affect wind and snow conditions as well as many of the actions of animals. A traveler learns quickly that large flat areas protected from the wind are likely to be covered with deep, soft snow toward spring.

Older, well-traveled Eskimos have memorized the topography of an amazing number of square miles. When an intelligent Nunamiut comes to a valley he has never seen before, he will often sit down and take a long look because the knowledge might be very helpful in the future. The Nunamiut had no maps of any kind; they kept their maps in their heads.

In traveling with Nunamiut, it is striking to observe how they take difficult terrain for granted. Rather than complain or think wishfully about how nice it would be to have an easier trail, most Nunamiut travelers reconcile themselves automatically to a difficult trail, even saying aloud at times that the going will not be hard forever. Hard work is almost placidly accepted as a necessary part of the job—once the decision to hunt has been made.

Because the Nunamiut spend most of their time in the mountains, they use familiar configurations of terrain to maintain a sense of position and direction. They emphasize the importance of knowing the small knolls and ridges along a trail, especially when mountains are blanketed by heavy fog. Sometimes a traveler cannot see ten feet in front of him. Then even the smaller features of the land are obscured, and the wind is of paramount importance in maintaining a sense of direction. A person can feel the direction of wind with his hands, face, and body, and he can also observe the fresh snowdrifts and constantly check for any change in the direction of wind. Older Nunamiut were very specific in pointing out to me the importance of using the wind as a reference *in extremis*. For example, one day I was out hunting in January and night fell before I started home. I built a fire and had a cup of tea, waiting for the moon to rise. Instead, a heavy fog rolled in. Using the wind and an occasional glimpse of a mountain top, I covered eight miles in only half an hour more than it would have taken if I could have seen the landscape. At times I could not even see my feet.

Geological Resources

The four primary rock types that occur in the northern Brooks Range are limestone, sandstone, shale, and conglomerate. There are many other rocks and minerals in addition to these basic types (Porter 1962). Those that the Nunamiut are aware of are considered here.

They have no explicit ideas about the nature of the rocks they use, nor do they talk about the nature of the geological formations beyond the analogy, mentioned above, that the land crushed up like the sea ice to form mountains. Some Nunamiut derive great pleasure in rolling large rocks down steep mountains. One summer afternoon, a 60-year-old Eskimo and I spent over an hour rolling rocks weighing up to 400 pounds down a small mountain into a lake in the valley below.

Pebbles of chert and flint were picked up from river gravel. A man would break a pebble in half and, if the broken face were flat, he knew it would chip evenly when he tried to make a scraper, arrowhead, spear point, or a straight or crooked knife.

The Nunamiut say that they once used slate for all kinds of tools, even whale harpoon heads which they traded down to the coast. At some unknown time in the past, it is said that the Nunamiut themselves learned how to use flint and chert. Slate stays sharp for a while, but becomes dull and breaks easily. Flint and chert are much superior, and the use of fine, chipped implements was supposed to have raised the Nunamiut standard of living.

The Nunamiut traded in jade from the Kobuk Eskimos until

the late 1800s. Jade was most highly valued for making adzes for felling spruce trees and for knives, whetstones (for slate and, later, steel), labrets, and beads.

One informant made a vague reference to obsidian or "rock you can see through," found in only one place high in the mountains 10 or 15 miles west of the Killik River in the northern Brooks Range, but no living Nunamiut has even seen such a deposit. Both Porter and Campbell (personal communications, 1961) state that the occurrence of obsidian in the Brooks Range is very unlikely, and that obsidian was most probably traded in from elsewhere, but my informant said this was not the case.

An iron oxide, probably hematite, occurs in three known places: the Killik River valley, near the head of the Sagavanirktok River, and a few miles east of the Chandler River just north of the Brooks Range. Iron oxide occurs elsewhere in the Brooks Range but is not used by the Nunamiut. Hematite is ground down, mixed with water, and applied to such wooden objects as snowshoes, sleds, and tool handles. Nunamiut like the dark red color, and one man said hematite preserves wood. Hematite was sometimes traded to the coast.

In one tributary of the John River, called Wolverine Creek, black slate occurs in the form of pebbles which the Nunamiut use as whetstones for steel knives. This "Eskimo" whetstone is preferred by some Nunamiut over commercial whetstones because the former "eats only a little metal" in the sharpening process.

Small chunks of pyrite are found in the Killik River valley and recently have been used to start fires. In the old days fire bow-drills were used for this purpose.

An asphalt-like lignite, or possibly an oil shale, occurs at the base of a mountain near the range front a few miles west of the Anaktuvuk River. In the old days the lignite was said to have come from the sky. A few families have used it for fuel. One or two Nunamiut believe that if a chunk of lignite is left in the house overnight it will suck a person's blood. Others say they have never heard of such a thing and leave it in the house overnight with no fear.

A few Nunamiut have learned about gold prospecting from some of the first white men who traveled through their region, but so little gold occurs in the northern Brooks Range that it has proven unprofitable to try to mine it there. Because the Nunamiut know that gold is valued by white men, some Nunamiut keep their eyes open and bring home strange-looking rocks, hoping they are salable.

A fine white sand found in the lower Colville River was collected and used as a friction agent in finishing scraped skins. A white slate was sometimes used for finishing particularly fine skin work. In the old days, a mud clay was collected from cutbanks in the Colville River and mixed with ptarmigan feathers, animal blood, and seal oil. The mixture was then shaped into a pot by hand and placed next to a fire to dry.

Salt licks occur away from the main valleys of the Brooks Range, up in the mountains. Occasionally, mud from a salt lick was collected and boiled with meat to give it a salty flavor. More important, however, is the knowledge that mountain sheep frequent salt licks and are easy to hunt there.

Soapstone, used for shallow lamps, was traded in from the Mackenzie River Eskimos and beyond. Local sandstone was sometimes ground out to be used as a lamp.

A little copper was reported to have been traded in to the Nunamiut from the Coppermine Eskimos living far to the east of the Mackenzie River.

Climate

Next to caribou, the Nunamiut are more concerned about the weather than any other aspect of the environment. People are forever talking about the wind, how cold it is, and the conditions of snow. When a person wakes up in the morning, the first thing he does is to look outdoors at the weather or to ask someone about it. The state of the weather may determine his actions for the day. If there is plenty of meat in the house and a man had been thinking of going out into the countryside to search for caribou and other animals, bad weather may put him off. If there is no meat in the house, he may have to go out anyway. Firewood and water, however, must be collected regardless of the weather.

Wind is often the main part of the weather that a Nunamiut wants to know about. In the major valleys of the Brooks Range the wind usually blows only up or down the valley, roughly north or south. In the small side valleys, and high in the mountains, the wind can blow from any direction. On the north slope, the Nunamiut told me that there are northwest, west, and east winds in addition to north and south winds. At times the wind can be very unpleasant; especially in the spring, the wind may blow steadily for an entire month. While spring winds do not prevent people from working outdoors, walking and dog sledding may be very uncomfortable. When a person has to face the wind, he is forced to keep his head down or to touch his face every now and then with his hand to keep it from freezing. When walking sideways or with his back to the wind, a person has to watch his balance at every step to keep from falling down with a sudden gust of wind over the uneven terrain. A dog that is thin or very hungry may refuse to pull a sled into the wind, even when beaten. When the wind picks up loose snow and swirls it around any object above the level of the ground, travel becomes more and more difficult. The snow stings a man's face, blinding him for moments. The struggle never ceases. In the middle of winter, severe winds are infrequent, but when they arrive, dogs and men alike are hesitant to venture out into the country. A man must remove his mitten to shoot and in a cold winter wind he has only a few seconds to fire at his target before he must warm his hand. In the old days, one or two Nunamiut were renowned for their skill and endurance in traveling and camping in the face of severe winter winds, but most Nunamiut stay indoors if they can. While spring winds may be very cold (from our point of view), they are not so chilling as the winter winds, and the Eskimos do not hesitate to travel by foot or sled, uncomfortable though it may be at times.

The wind does have its more pleasant aspects, and life in the Arctic without wind would be inconceivable. Early in the winter of 1960, I traveled south from Anaktuvuk Pass with three or four Nunamiut about 25 miles to the confluence of the Iyenatuk and the John rivers. We arrived in the late dusk of early evening. For an hour or two we were very busy taking care of the dogs, unloading our gear, and setting up camp. Then, shortly before going to bed, my 60-year-old companion and I stood outside the hut for a moment to look into the night, to make sure the dogs had not sensed a wolf or a grizzly, and to accustom ourselves for a moment to being in this place. All was very still except for the wind. Our camp was well protected and we could feel no wind ourselves, but two miles across the valley the north wind howled resonantly across the face of a mountain. "Good old Iyenatuk," sighed my companion. For years he had hunted and camped at Iyenatuk. To hear the sound of the north wind seemed to give him a sense of security in returning to a familiar location. The wind can be exceedingly harsh, but at rare moments, even a man who has struggled for decades to wrest a meager living from the frozen valleys of the Brooks Range may be touched by the friendly note of the alive-like wind.

In a more practical way, a hunter is often happy to have wind. A steady breeze carries a hunter's scent away from animals; sometimes even the sound of walking may be obscured by it. After a fresh snowfall, walking and traveling may be very difficult, but in the northern Brooks Range the wind usually blows the newly fallen snow away in a few days and forms a hard crust. The summer is often a windy time, but of course it is not so cold. Nunamiut often welcome a stiff breeze in July, which blows the mosquitoes away. Otherwise, wind in the summer evokes little comment. The importance of the wind to the Nunamiut in maintaining a sense of position and direction has been discussed.

In fall, winter, or spring, one of the first questions asked of a hunter or traveler returning home is what the snow conditions are. There are a great many terms for snow: snow in the air, new snow, crusted snow, old granulated snow, very old granulated snow next to the ground, snowdrifts, snow piled up near the bottom of a hill or cutbank, snow overhangs, and a general term for snow to be gathered for water.

New snow, for the moment, is disliked. Walking and dog sledding are then very difficult. The first strong winds blow most of the new snow away, often exposing the ground in unprotected places. In a few small valleys and those areas protected from the wind, snow builds up and often remains soft all year. Travelers go out of their way to avoid such places.

Snow gradually becomes crusted by the action of the wind. Before thinly crusted snow is strong enough to support a man on snowshoes, it can be worse than new snow. When a walker breaks through, he may get his snowshoes caught under the thin crust. Before long, however, the crust becomes thicker and harder with the continuing wind, and eventually it is strong enough to bear the weight of man, sled, and dogs.

Old granulated snow is used for melting into water. It is much preferred to new snow because of its greater density. Old snow can be easily found by digging underneath the hard crust. Snowdrifts, and snow that piles up near the base of a hill or cutbank are often evenly packed. Such snow is easily cut into blocks and used for the overnight, snow-block houses.

The first snow in the fall of the year usually occurs some time in September. Fall snows are often light and rarely do more than a few inches fall during one night. Early in the fall the wind blows the snow around constantly but rarely causes a good, hard crust to form. There may be little snowfall during the winter, but the wind continues to move the snow around a great deal. After snow has been redistributed by the wind and allowed to settle, the needed crust begins to form. Often during the three or four months of winter, snow conditions are quite stable, greatly facilitating any kind of travel. In the spring it is not uncommon to have a heavy snowfall. The wind blows the new snow away from open country, but in protected areas in the spring, travel may be exceedingly difficult. Once a good trail is made and traveled frequently, any fresh snow is usually packed down in a very few days.

Most of the snow falls in the spring and autumn of the year. When there is less snow during the autumn, the Nunamiut say it is more difficult to make a living. Trails are hard to make over the uneven terrain and animals are more difficult to hunt and trap. When there is little snow, it is hard to insulate a house carefully by packing snow around the base of it. The Nunamiut, especially the oldtimers, liked to have a thick snow cover in the fall, even though they preferred to have little or no snowfall in the spring.

Alapaa! (cold!) is one of the most frequently heard expressions among the Nunamiut. During the winter, the temperature usually ranges between $-10°$ and $-30°$ F. If there is little wind, such days are considered very pleasant, if, of course, a person has adequate clothing. When the temperature drops to $-40°$ F and below, a Nunamiut begins to think it is really cold. One informant told me that one early December morning he started walking along a river in the timber. It was so cold that he could not breathe comfortably. He climbed high into a small side valley where it was much warmer. Should the temperature rise to $0°$ F or above in the winter, the weather is thought to be too warm. Caribou skin clothing is too hot on such days, and boots sometimes get wet because so much heat is created walking in the warm snow (relatively speaking that is). In the middle of winter, the sun never rises above the horizon, and the temperature remains fairly constant through-

out the day, making the selection of clothing easier than in times
of seasonal change.

In the spring, the temperature rises with the appearance of the
sun. But as the sun rises higher in the sky, the temperature fluctuates considerably during the day, making a selection of clothing
more difficult, especially footwear. In the early morning of a
typical spring day, the temperature may be well below 0° F. If a
hunter plans to leave the house long before the sun rises, he
usually puts on a pair of all-caribou winter boots. By the early
afternoon the sun may have warmed up the air and the snow so
much that his boots become wet with sweat and melted snow.
Then in the evening the temperature drops and his outer boots
freeze (usually not the caribou skin socks or the feet). By walking
and shuffling around constantly, a hunter can at least prevent his
feet from becoming numb with the cold or freezing altogether.

Break-up in the late spring, usually in early May, is very impressive. High in the mountains where the warm sun reaches the
snow, the first trickles of water begin. Down the larger creeks, into
the small rivers feeding the major river of the valley below, the
water slowly eats its way into the soft snow. Sometimes, if the
weather is still a bit chilly, the snow may absorb the first waters,
completely staunching the flow. Then, as the weather continues to
warm, the trickles grow larger and the snow melts the instant it is
touched by the water. In some of the larger tributaries of the
major rivers of the Brooks Range the snow is very thick, and the
first trickles may be transformed into a raging torrent for a few
days. On a still evening in May, a Nunamiut woman suddenly
remarked about the roar of the water down Giant Creek, a short
distance south of the village. It is a dangerous time, and children
are warned not to play too close to even a small creek during
break-up. The thick snow becomes so soft in the warm weather
that a man can fall up to his waist in snow. Many years ago, a
Nunamiut family lost their umiak and all its contents in break-up
when it was sucked into a field of quicksand-like snow.

In a very few days, the worst of break-up is over. In late May,
much of the ground is still covered with snow and the wind can
still be very chilling. Once in late May I was sitting with two
Eskimos behind a stone blind a mile or so above the village,
watching for caribou. The wind was so chilly that day that we all
had on caribou skin parkas.

During the first two weeks of June, most of the snow is finally melted by the sun and the warm air. The ground defrosts 12 to 18 inches, down to the permafrost, and becomes wet and spongy as only those who have struggled over the Arctic tundra in summer can appreciate. A few permanent fields of ice and snow remain throughout the summer. High in the Brooks Range a few glaciers still exist, all of which appear to be receding.

The summer is a time of relief from the steady work required of winter living, but a few Nunamiut become bored with summertime. Many days the weather is just too hot from a Nunamiut's point of view to do anything. Mosquitoes rise on warm days, especially during July, making it even worse. Summer temperatures range from 32° to 70° F or slightly above. I have seen it snow in the middle of July and Nunamiut say that snow may fall any time in the summer, but it usually melts in two or three days. Rain seems to fall mostly in June and August. Rain is uncomfortable in the Arctic, and the Nunamiut dislike it, although a hunter is rarely deterred by rain alone from going out into the countryside. A thunderstorm is thought to occur when the north wind sneaks in under the south wind and makes the air boil. The only positive feeling about heavy rain is that it ensures a good crop of roots and berries in August and early September. The June rains were very heavy during the last summer I spent in Anaktuvuk Pass, but the berries in August were marvelous. Sometimes a hunter spends a half hour or more in a berry patch gorging himself, if the country appears to be empty of animals.

The dropping temperatures and shortening days of late August and early September presage the long winter ahead. Many Nunamiut look forward to the fall and winter, hoping for good hunting and trapping. Freeze-up occurs in late September or early October.

Silya is the general term for air, weather, and atmosphere. Immanent in the atmosphere is *silyam iñua,* the power or spirit of the air. This iñua is a vague one. While people are aware of it, they are not so immediately concerned or conscious of it as they are, say, of the grizzly iñua. Gazing up into the distant sky when the weather is turbulent, a Nunamiut may say *silyaqpaq imma* (the big or actual weather up there somewhere). Generally the Nunamiut take the weather for granted; they accept it for what it is, just as they do most of the elements of their environment. On a given day, a shaman may have tried to call the south wind in order to pull the caribou up to the mountains but, as a whole, people do not try to coerce the weather. It would be unthinkable, or futile if ever considered, to try to force the weather to be warmer or more stable season after season. A few Nunamiut see oscillation in the severity of the weather from one season to the other. If there is a heavy snowfall in the spring, there will be little rain the following summer. If the summer is cold and nasty with occasional snow, the following winter will be mild. The Nunamiut are very aware of the relationship of the weather to many elements of the fauna and flora.

The Nunamiut like much of their weather, harsh though it may be at times and marginal as whites often consider it. After the daily effort demanded by winter comes to an end, a warm day in May when a person is able to stand still outdoors visiting, without feeling the cold, or a warm, mosquito-free day in August evokes all kinds of comments about how pleasant the weather is. People recall nice days decades back, when they lay on the tundra near a pure mountain stream, roasting fat ribs and boiling big pots of strong tea with lots of easily obtainable firewood. Many days in the winter too can be very pleasant. On a clear, windless day, traveling, hunting, and working outdoors can be very comfortable. Many winter days I have sat for hours on a hillside with one or two Nunamiut over a pot of tea, watching the countryside for animals —talking, joking, and trying to learn a little ethnography. On still winter days, women often pause in their wood-collecting to chat for a few minutes before returning to the endless chores of the household.

Flora

Of the plants occurring within the range of the Nunamiut, the cloudberry, blueberry, cranberry, crowberry, and a parsnip-like tuber called *masu* (*Hedysarum alpinum s. lat.* after Porsild, 1953 and 1957) are important as food sources. Willow, alder, birch, spruce, cottonwood and, on the coast, driftwood (pine, spruce, and cottonwood) are important for fuel, tools, traveling equipment, and house building. *Ivaroq* ("moss," a generalized term for tundra growth) is important for house construction and hygiene. A few infrequent roots and some greens were exploited sporadically as minor dietary supplements. One or two leaves were boiled for medicinal purposes, specifically to relieve an aching back or joint. Green willow bark was sometimes chewed to relieve backaches. Grass is sometimes used to make insoles.

On the tundra and the northern part of the Brooks Range, willows are the only trees, except for an occasional alder and a scrub dwarf birch. But willow can be used for many things— house and tent frames, much of the frame of a kayak, floors, mattresses, crosspieces on a sled, snowshoe frames (in rare instances), drum beaters, deadfalls, toothpicks, toys, and so forth. In the old days, willow roots were used to make small baskets. Of paramount importance is the use of willows as fuel. A large household (say, of ten persons) often uses fifty pounds or more of willows in a single day. People are constantly exchanging information about the supply of dead and green willows in different localities.

Other trees that occur in the middle and southern Brooks Range are important to the Nunamiut, and most older persons can specify exactly where to find birch, alder, cottonwood, and straight-grained spruce.

Cottonwood is valued for carving masks and making toys. In the old days, cottonwood bark was dried, ground, and mixed with tobacco so the latter would not be used up so fast.

Birch is highly valued for its tough resiliency and was used for the shafts of bear spears, bows, parts of sleds, walking sticks, buckets, and many other items. Today, birch is used primarily for snowshoes. The Nunamiut never made birchbark canoes but did make baskets from strips of birchbark. This skill was probably learned from the Koyukon Indians, possibly via the Kobuk Eskimos.

Alder is valued mainly for its bark which is shredded, boiled, and applied to the inner side of scraped skins to give it a dark red color. In the old days, people used alder for pipe stems. A gnarled alder crotch makes the best handle for a scraper.

Spruce is readily available within a day's travel from the village of Anaktuvuk Pass and is valued for its lightness and rigidity, although it splinters easily. Sleds, drum frames, and house frames are among the items made from spruce. Spruce logs are used to a limited extent for firewood. Many children like to chew spruce gum. In the old days, spruce was also used for buckets, arrows, dishpans, many parts of the frames of kayaks and umiat, and so forth.

Although many Nunamiut are familiar with the timbered regions of the middle and southern Brooks Range, they generally prefer to stay north of the timber and on the north slope. In the old days, a trapping expedition of several men sometimes ventured deep into the timber all the way to the southern Brooks Range, for as long as two or three months. In occasional years Nunamiut used to travel with their families down as far as Bettles at the confluence of the John River with the Koyukuk River in the southern foothills of the Brooks Range. At present, many Nunamiut camp for two or three months with their families in the northern fringes of the timber along the John and nearby rivers in the middle Brooks Range in order to hunt and trap.

In spite of familiarity with timbered regions, they sometimes express uneasiness and even fear about living there, mainly, in the old days, because this is the type of country where Indians roam. Even today a few Nunamiut fear the Indians. Another source of fear is the grizzly bear, because bears are so difficult to see in the timber. Time and time again I heard Nunamiut complain about the lack of visibility in the timber. One time an older Eskimo and I traveled by dog sled for five days in the timber in the late spring just before break-up. We saw fresh evidence of three grizzlies. Our reaction was not fear but readiness; we had hunted together before and merely kept our rifles ready on top of the sled, without a cartridge in the chamber. Had we come close to a grizzly, our dogs would have given us plenty of warning before we could see the bear ourselves. Although dogs are invaluable for sensing a bear and keeping it at bay, giving the hunter ample opportunity to squeeze off two or three good shots, dogs also infuriate bears, so that only the death of the bear or its quarry ends the encounter.

The lack of visibility in the timber also makes caribou hunting more difficult, that is of course, as the Nunamiut are accustomed to hunt caribou. In the spring, the snow in timbered regions often accumulates, since valley floors are protected from the wind, and travel can be exceedingly difficult in deep, soft snow. Two Nunamiut men spent one summer in the timber and they told me they could find so little food that they almost starved to death. Thus it is easy to see why the Nunamiut prefer to base their activities north of the timber.

Most berries were gathered in the late summer and eaten raw on the spot, or boiled, or stored with seal oil in sealskin pokes. *Masu* tubers are eaten raw, roasted, or allowed to age in sealskin pokes. Hall (1961) estimates that in precontact times, plants constituted 5 per cent of the total diet. At present, with the availability of imported food, plants constitute less than 1 per cent of the total diet.

The Nunamiut seek plants primarily for a change in diet; they do not stress the nutritional motive. While there is some nutritional value in the edible Brooks Range plants, Stefansson has demonstrated convincingly that plants are not a necessary part of a well-balanced diet. In addition to adding variety to the diet, collecting the plants provides a certain amount of recreation for the collector and, perhaps more important, prestige for being observed as an industrious worker.

The mention of plants in folktales is rare, and the only superstition I encountered in connection with plants was about a large mushroom which, if touched, was supposed to cause a person's hand to fall off.

Plants are considered to be *iñuroat* (living things) but different from animals. Plants apparently do not have iñua, like other forms of life. The Nunamiut believe that plants are bisexual, since this characteristic is observed in most forms of life, but admit that they have never seen a difference.

Birds

In various publications (1953, 1954, 1958, 1960), Dr. Laurence Irving has presented a great deal of very carefully collected zoological and ethnological information about the birds of the Brooks Range and adjacent areas. I shall therefore make only a few observations about the general conceptions the Nunamiut have about birds and consider individually a few of the more important species.

The Nunamiut divide birds into two basic categories: *tigmiagruitch* (small birds) and *qaugatch* (large birds). Sparrows, redpolls, longspurs, plovers, sandpipers, phalaropes, chickadees, jays, larks, robins, warblers, and so forth are typical of the small birds. Hawks, owls, loons, geese, and ducks are typical of the large birds. Many Nunamiut, as Irving has pointed out, are amazingly aware of bird life. Their classification and naming of birds and their awareness of bird behavior reflects a knowledge developed beyond what is necessary for the exploitation of economically important birds.

During the late spring and summer they spend many hours in the countryside, hunting for caribou, ground squirrels, marmots, and other game and have the opportunity—which many Nunamiut take —to observe the migratory and nesting habits of birds. In some years Nunamiut have observed a few migratory birds flying north in the fall and south in the spring. One of them has theorized that this aberration in normal migration habits is a result of certain geographical and climatic factors. He thinks that in the spring some birds fly up the Mackenzie River valley, west along the Arctic coast, and then south through the Brooks Range.

SMALL BIRDS. The boys hunt with slingshots and rocks such small birds as the snow bunting, longspur, sparrow, redpoll, rosy finch, pipit, warbler, thrush, robin, chickadee, jay, swallow, lark, woodpecker, phalarope, sanderling, dowitcher, sandpiper, and plover. In the old days, a few small birds were snared in their nests and eaten, mainly as a novelty and change in diet. Today, when a young boy brings home a small bird he has killed, he is usually praised for his skill in hunting. A parent often identifies the bird and teaches the child its name. A boy or girl may play with the dead bird for a while as a toy before an older person throws it out or puts it into the stove. Small birds are of little shamanistic or magical significance. A few small birds, however, are the subject of folktales. One of the best examples is the story about the northern phalarope.

> Once in the very early days, two birds came together as husband and wife in a country far to the south, where it is summer when it is winter in the Arctic. In the spring, the couple came to the Arctic. The bird couple settled down alone somewhere on the seashore, no one knows exactly where. The husband liked to hunt by kayak and was a very good hunter. Every day he paddled out onto the sea and always found many animals such as seals and bearded seals which he speared and brought home without fail. The wife was also very busy in the spring. Both the husband and wife worked very hard. The couple did not know what kind of people they were, but they lived by hunting.
> One day the husband paddled out on a quiet sea to hunt. He came home very late in the evening with no animals. His wife asked him why but he answered that he had not seen an

animal all day. From then on, he left home every day by
kayak, disappeared on the sea, and returned home late in the
evening. He always returned from the east. Before long the
couple were running low on food. Every now and then the
husband brought one seal home, but one seal does not last
very long. He continued to hunt by kayak every day but he
told his wife that the animals must be frightened, since he
had killed so many.

He always returned home very tired. The wife wanted to
have sexual intercourse, but he was always too exhausted.
She asked him why he could find no more animals, but he
replied that the animals had become afraid of him. Finally,
during the long nights after her tired husband had fallen
asleep, she began to think differently, that perhaps the
trouble might not be that the animals were scared.

One morning the husband paddled out onto a smooth sea;
the weather was very nice and he paddled on and on. His wife
left the house and started walking to the east. She followed the
shoreline, walking in the sand near the water so her husband
could not see her tracks. After walking some distance, she
came to a small bay. She looked around carefully and could
see a small hump on the other side of the bay. She started
walking toward it. As she came closer she could see smoke
coming from a little house. Then she left the shore, went inland a short way, and hid herself from view. She could not
see anyone, but because of the smoke she figured that someone
must be in the little house. She began to think that her husband must be meeting someone there. As she approached,
she could see a great many dead seals and bearded seals lying
nearby, some of which were skinned. She was scornful to see
that some of the unskinned bearded seals were lying in the
open sun without cover. The woman wanted to see if there
were any people in the house. Then suddenly she rushed in.
Aha! there were two women. She asked them if they had her
husband in the house, and they replied vehemently that they
did not. But the woman was sure her husband had found
these two other women. Her heart was broken. The women
were tending a large pot of boiling meat over a fire in the
middle of the house. They offered their visitor something to
eat. The wife thought that she was stronger than both of the

women. She stood there looking at the huge pot of boiling meat and figured she might fool them by saying there was something funny in the boiling water. Then she said, "Look at that in the middle of the pot, there is a funny little man who can stand that hot, boiling water. Quick, take a look." The two women stood up excitedly; she grabbed them both, shoved them into the water, and cooked them to death. Then she dragged the bodies over to the sleeping skins, laid them down as if they were sleeping, and rushed out of the house, laughing to herself. Maybe today, she thought, her husband would come home with many animals from the sea. She hid behind a small knoll near the little house so that she could watch for him.

Early in the evening, the woman heard someone singing a song. The singing became louder and louder. Then the husband appeared paddling slowly over the smooth sea. He was paddling steadily ahead, but he was dragging many animals in the water behind him. The woman learned the song he was singing. She thought the two women must be named in the song. The man paddled on, but slowly, because of the load on his line. Finally the front of his kayak touched the gravel bar near the house. The man suddenly became very angry because no one came down immediately from the little house. He shouted that he should beat his two wives who were so lazy. He really wanted to beat them, and his wife hiding behind the knoll was scared. She almost jumped up but thought that she had better sit still and listen for a while. The husband went into the little house and began to cry. He moaned, wondering who had killed his two wives—the two women who had loved him so well. The woman was frightened, but she knew that she had to leave for home before long.

As soon as she returned home, she began to get ready for her husband. She was very busy because she knew he would bring home many animals. Late in the morning, the husband left the little house, paddling his kayak through the water. Very late that evening he came home with a very heavy load on his line. The woman was happy, her heart felt very warm. She told her husband she was surprised that he brought so many animals home, but she could see that his face was red and swollen. She asked him why and he replied that he had

had a very difficult time paddling a very long way to find animals. Then his wife knew for certain that he was mourning for his two wives.

Then for a long time they lived together. Every day when the man went out to hunt by kayak, he brought home many animals. Finally, late one evening while they were lying in bed, the woman began to sing the song she had heard her husband singing. She sang only in a whisper, but her husband heard her. He remained silent; then the woman began to sing louder and louder, and he recognized his own song. "Where did you learn that song?" he demanded. "In my own mind," she retorted. The man became very angry because he knew his wife had killed his other two wives. Suddenly he wanted to kill her and he jumped out of bed to look for a knife. The woman flew up into the air and turned into a short-eared owl. He was a northern phalarope and he shouted at her from below, but she laughed at him from above. The northern phalarope was too small and weak and he could not reach her. His wife shouted to him, "I'll never return. You fooled me many times, now you can look for another wife. I am happy now anyway." And away she flew.

The seals which the man speared every day are the insects which the northern phalarope finds on the water for his food.

DUCKS, GEESE, AND EIDERS. During May, ducks and geese migrate north through the Brooks Range in great numbers. The northward movement is much more pronounced than the southward flight of fowl in the late summer. Also, ducks and geese seem more prone to stop in May than in August on the lakes where Nunamiut used to spend their summers. In the old days Nunamiut set foot snares of sinew or baleen just below the surface of the water where ducks and geese might land. Bolases were also used. Today only a few Nunamiut try to shoot ducks and geese with shotguns, partly because shotgun ammunition is very expensive in the Brooks Range and partly because Anaktuvuk Pass is not a very good location for hunting ducks and geese. In the old days when the Nunamiut frequented the Arctic coast, they used snares and bolases to catch eiders during the late spring and early summer when they are numerous.

The Nunamiut value ducks, geese, and eiders very highly for their meat and especially for their fat. The Eskimos who have wintered on the coast told me that they always tried to catch as many eiders and other large birds as they could, to store in ice cellars for use through the winter. The skins of ducks, geese, and eiders were sometimes used for insoles of boots and for some articles of clothing. When a coastal Eskimo did not have enough caribou calf skins for a summer parka, he sometimes substituted duck skins.

One August day, I was sitting in the tent with the family I was living with, drinking tea and visiting. Suddenly we heard a mother duck with her ducklings traveling through the willows and summer tundra streams near the tent. A 4-year-old boy immediately grabbed his slingshot and rushed out of the tent. His mother dashed after him, followed by the rest of us, and held him back, telling him that the ducklings were only babies and could not be eaten. The little boy struggled but he was finally restrained. There seemed to be a definite feeling on the part of the boy's parents that the ducklings would some day grow larger and be more valuable. His elders were also very curious and struck by the sight of the duck and her ducklings struggling through the brush. The little boy, nevertheless, was admired for his zeal and we tried to assuage his disappointment by telling him what a terrific hunter he was going to become.

PTARMIGAN. From the first part of October until January, willow ptarmigan move from north to south through the valleys of the Brooks Range. From February to May, they move from south to north, mostly in two large migrations of many thousands of birds, the first in late February and early March, and the second in April. During the spring migrations in particular, ptarmigan are very easy to shoot. With a double-barrelled 10-gauge shotgun using number six shot at fifty yards, a man could easily average five to ten birds a shot for several shots. During most of the time when ptarmigan are in the mountains, they are a little more difficult to approach. Many Nunamiut still set snares for ptarmigan day after day during the lean months of the winter. During part of the winter I stayed at Anaktuvuk Pass, the caribou were very scarce. One family in particular did not leave the village to hunt and trap, and had very little money. Without extensive ptarmigan snaring, especially by the old man of the house, the members of this household would have lost a considerable amount of weight during January and February; and since other families were having a difficult time, there was not too much hospitality available.

Many Nunamiut speak of the ptarmigan as an invaluable dietary supplement, especially in the hard times which are not unusual in the Brooks Range. The only problem with ptarmigan, however, is that they have very little fat, and eating boiled ptarmigan without blubber or fat of some kind "is like eating moss." Many older Nunamiut can remember a winter when, if there had been no ptarmigan, some people would have starved to death. One old Nunamiut could remember a winter during the early 1900s when there were no caribou to be had. Fortunately his uncle had obtained a large supply of seal blubber from the coast. Two or three families managed to stay alive in the Colville River near Umiat by snaring ptarmigan all winter in the willows.

There are few references to ptarmigan in folktales but, as pointed out earlier, the ptarmigan iñua was once the personal helping spirit of a shaman.

LOONS. Although loons are not as good to eat as ducks, geese, and eiders, the Nunamiut used to hunt them in the summer a good deal with bows and arrows, bolases, and even with spears from kayaks. Sometimes a man could kill enough loons to make a whole sled load; they are sought for the large quantity of meat and fat they yield. The bill of the yellow-billed loon is sometimes used for decoration on a headband for dancing. The neck skin of the loon is very tough and can be used for the insole of a boot. In the old days, a whole parka was sometimes made from the neck skins of loons.

One day late in August, a Nunamiut family and I were camped several miles from the village, hunting for summer caribou skins for clothing. There had been a slight north wind for several days. We were very anxious for a south wind which would pull the caribou up from the north slope to the mountains. Late one evening, as we were returning to our tent after a day of trapping ground squirrels and looking for caribou, two or three red-throated loons flew some 2,000 feet above us. In the still evening inside the large valley, their screeching was very audible. My companion turned to me and said that tomorrow there would be a south wind. Somehow, he pointed out, the red-throated loon always knows in the summer when the wind is going to change and flies screeching through the sky. The next morning, the south wind was so strong that we had to build a willow windbreak to protect our tent.

HAWKS AND OWLS. Nunamiut used to catch hawks and owls with baleen snares, either in their nests or on a high knoll where they were likely to land. These birds were only rarely eaten; their meat is generally disliked and they are difficult to catch in large enough numbers to be worth the trouble for food alone. The feathers of most larger hawks were used for arrows and frequently traded to the coast. Irving (1960: 50) reports:

> Paired feathers were preferably matched from corresponding feathers of the right and left wings. If tail feathers were used, matching parts were used by preference in pairs. I did not learn the principle or practical reason on which this practice was based. I also asked whether left wing feathers were preferred for convenience of attachment by right-handed arrow makers, as Bridges (1949) [Bridges, *Esteban Lucan, Uttermost Part of the Earth,* 1949, New York] relates to have been the case among the Ona Indians of Tierra del Fuego. I could find no comparable discrimination among the Nunamiut.

In the old days, a shaman tied an eagle feather or two to his drum beaters to help him work up his power. Large feathers were often used for some kind of decoration for a dance.

Hawks and owls evoke admiration and, in a sense, envy on the part of Nunamiut. Many of these self-sufficient birds stay in the Brooks Range all winter and appear to be able to "make a good living" with their speed and strength in killing small animals and their mobility in searching for food.

RAVENS. Aside from the mention of "Mr." Raven in many folktales, there is much discussion about this bird. Many Nunamiut abuse the raven in discussion as an eater of carrion and feces. Ravens often spring a trap by eating the bait. The funniest thing I saw in the time I spent with the Nunamiut was one midwinter day when an old Eskimo returned from checking his traps. In reply to a question about his luck, he said in resignation that he caught two ravens, one, graphically reaching for his thigh, by the leg, and the other, even more graphically grabbing his pursed lips by the thumb and forefinger, by the goddamn beak.

Ravens often raid caches, and the best protection is to put up mock snares. Nunamiut pointed out to me that when Mr. Raven sees those snares he will back off in fear.

Ravens are ubiquitous. Climbing up the highest mountain, work-

ing one's way up the narrowest ravine, walking along a muddy
cutbank, on the coldest windy day, in the hottest summer heat,
ravens are to be seen circling endlessly. One older Nunamiut
claimed the raven as his friend. One day standing beside his tent a
raven flew by. He shouted for the raven to come to him. The raven
circled twice as the Eskimo shouted repeatedly. His deceased uncle
was named *tulugak* (raven) and he often said that Mr. Raven was
his uncle. He never suggested the bird as a possible source of
shamanistic power or help in any way, nor was there any restriction on his killing ravens. The man merely asserted his affinity for
the bird.

Many of the stories about Mr. Raven portray him as a trickster,
a very common motif in much of North American folklore. While
the Nunamiut have probably learned many of these trickster tales
from other peoples, the stories have become well integrated into
their verbal tradition. Some of the stories about Mr. Raven, however, are not so complimentary and place him on the receiving end
of a prank. The following story is a good example and is more
typical of the sentiments commonly expressed by the Nunamiut
about ravens.

> One time in the very early days, Pacific Loon was Mr.
> Raven's partner. In those days, both Mr. Raven and Loon
> were white; they had no coloring of any kind on their parkas.
> The two partners hunted during the day and spent many eve-
> nings talking, joking, and making a lot of fun together. One
> day while Mr. Raven was out hunting, he saw a fireplace
> where some person had camped on the shore of a lake. Mr.
> Raven returned to his camp and said to Loon, "Partner, I
> have found something for you and me. Our coloring is light
> and in the summer any animal or enemy can see us easily
> from a long distance. We ought to do something to our
> parkas." His partner the loon was happy to hear Mr. Raven.
> He often had difficulty in chasing fish; because he was so
> white he frightened them away. Loon believed that Mr. Raven
> was right about wanting to add color to their parkas. "How?"
> asked Loon. "We can use charcoal," replied Mr. Raven, "and
> we can make all kinds of fancy trimming for our parkas."
> Mr. Raven told Loon where the fireplace was, but Loon com-
> plained that he could not walk very far on land. His leg was
> crippled and he traveled only by kayak. Mr. Raven gave Loon

complete directions how to find the fireplace and flew up into
the air. "Watch where I land," cried Mr. Raven, "it is not far."
Loon got into his kayak and paddled slowly toward the fireplace. He was very happy. He smiled to himself and thought,
"I will paint Mr. Raven all black because he wants to fool
me, his partner."

As Loon approached the fireplace, Mr. Raven was sitting
there waiting for him. Mr. Raven picked up a piece of charcoal and tested it on his parka. It made a dark color all right.
Mr. Raven called out to Loon, "Come over here, there is
plenty of charcoal." When Loon's kayak touched the shore,
he climbed out and walked slowly up to the fireplace. Then
Mr. Raven told Loon, "Let me color your parka first, but you
will have to shut your eyes until I finish. Then after I finish
coloring your parka, you may color mine." Loon closed his
eyes, and Mr. Raven proceeded to color his parka. He worked
slowly, marking Loon's parka very carefully with the charcoal. He put some very fancy trimming on Loon's parka. "My
gosh, partner," said Mr. Raven, "You are going to have a
beautiful parka. Someone will like it very much." Finally he
finished coloring the parka. "All right, open your eyes," he
said. Loon opened his eyes and looked around very slowly,
"My gosh!" he said, "My parka is very nice. Thank you,
partner." Then Loon told Mr. Raven, "Now, you must not
open your eyes until I am finished." Mr. Raven was so
happy, he really wanted to have a nice parka. Loon marked
Mr. Raven's parka very slowly, very carefully with the charcoal. Finally Loon said, "All right, partner, take a look at your
new parka." Mr. Raven turned around and said, "That is very
nice, the trimming is very pretty, but I think you better
darken the whole thing a little more." "I will," said Loon,
"Shut your eyes and this time I'll finish it." Loon began marking Mr. Raven's parka very carefully with the charcoal. Mr.
Raven thought to himself, "Loon is doing all right. It's good
to have a nice-looking parka for hunting, so the animals and
even enemies cannot see me." For a long time Loon colored
Mr. Raven's parka. "My gosh! Your parka is beautiful. I have
only a little more to do . . . all right, now, open your eyes."
But Loon's heart was very warm because he knew he had
colored the parka entirely black; he knew Mr. Raven would

not like it. Mr. Raven opened his eyes and turned around but he could see no fancy trimming; he became angry, "You are a damned fool, I know I should not be that black." But Loon, he just laughed. Suddenly Mr. Raven grabbed a handful of ashes and threw them at Loon, but Loon dived quickly into the water. Just before Loon entered the water, the ashes hit him on the back of his neck. Mr. Raven tried to throw more ashes; Loon kept on laughing and laughing and diving every time Mr. Raven tried to throw ashes at him. Mr. Raven ran along the lake shore but he could not swim; he tried to call Loon back, but it was hopeless.

That is why the Loon has a funny-looking coloring on his neck, like ashes. The loon is laughing to this day about how he fooled Mr. Raven. They quit visiting together and were no longer partners. They had become enemies.

Fish

The Nunamiut are very aware of the habits of the fishes that occur in the waters of the northern Brooks Range. Fish, however, do not play as important a role in Nunamiut economy as many outsiders think. Salmon occur in large numbers in the territories of the Kobuk Eskimo and the Koyukon Indians and are exploited by them, but they are rarely to be found in the rivers near which Nunamiut ordinarily camp. The fishes that do occur are not numerous enough or of sufficient nutritional value, notably in their lack of fat, to constitute a significant food source, even if Nunamiut made greater efforts to catch them. Fish are generally less important than moose, mountain sheep, and ptarmigan as dietary supplements or as an emergency carry-over when caribou are scarce. Dogs, it is said, become thin and weak if fed on Arctic fish alone. The Nunamiut value fish primarily for the variety in diet and, on rare occasions, as a needed food supplement, but they should not be underestimated as a food source. In a year when caribou are scarce and a few families are camped near good fishing sites, fish may constitute 10 to 20 per cent of the diet. They are eaten boiled, fried, roasted, frozen, slightly tainted by the sun (but not rotten), or dried. Fish oil, whatever quantity is produced, is skimmed off a boiling pot of fish and mixed with any kind of fish eggs. In normal years, fish probably accounted for 10 per cent or less of the diet. Today, only a few families make an effort to catch fish in any quantity. One never hears of fish warding off starvation, as do mountain sheep, moose, and ptarmigan. Some Nunamiut do not even like fish or become tired of eating it after a very few days.

In January 1961 I joined an extended family for two weeks to go north to Tulugak Lake to catch a variety of round whitefish. After we had been there for three days, the older man of the family said he was tired of eating fish and that we would leave in two or three days. The next day I saw 35 caribou about four hours' walk from the house. I decided not to hunt them alone and returned to the family. The next day, three of us went after the caribou and got four animals apiece. With that we stayed two weeks, catching a much larger number of fish than we had expected. Nunamiut just do not feel healthy when eating nothing but fish, even with plenty of fat, which in fact we did have. We had to have red meat if we were going to stay in that place.

Lake trout, various whitefish, Arctic charr, ling, grayling, and one or more herrings are the fish the Nunamiut commonly exploit. Whitefish, herrings, and grayling are usually caught with nets, fish traps, or hooks. In the summer or the winter, nets are stretched across the outlet of a lake. A net or fish trap is placed in a small creek along which small fish may be driven with willow flails. Lake trout, ling, and charr are usually caught with hooks or spears, either in open water in the summer or through holes chopped in the ice in the winter. The Nunamiut know of the shee and various salmons, but seldom catch them because they are so rare in their region. Dried salmon is sometimes traded in from the Kobuk Eskimos. The sucker, pike, flounder, blackfish, and smelt are known but are rarely caught by the Nunamiut for food. Blackfish and smelt are well liked, but the Nunamiut rarely have the opportunity to fish for them. Arctic charr run along lake shores in June and are easy to catch in large numbers. In January, a variety of round whitefish leaves several lakes in the northern Brooks Range. Ling may be caught any time. Lake trout and grayling are easy to catch in spring, summer, and early fall, but not during the winter when they are too "lazy to bite."

Because fish are difficult to observe all the time, the Nunamiut were unable to figure out where some were at a given time of year. One variety of whitefish, for example, is known to migrate from the Beaufort Sea up the Colville River to some of its tributaries and return, but they seem to disappear from sight during part of their stay inland. Some Nunamiut believed that these fish disappear into the ground for a short time.

The size of lake trout has given rise to some fantastic stories. One lake trout in Chandler Lake was said to have been as long as three kayaks, over fifty feet, and capable of swallowing a whole caribou.

In the rivers and creeks of the headwaters of rivers draining the Brooks Range, a dwarf charr occurs (Walters 1955: 275), which the Nunamiut call "old man fish." This fish is only occasionally used for food but arouses a great deal of curiosity by its small, stunted shape and exotic coloring.

There is a short folktale about the pike and the sucker.

> Once in the early days, a pike and a sucker were both traveling on a river in kayaks. They were carrying forked spears shaped like the bones in their bodies. When they met on the river, they immediately fell into an argument and became very angry at each other. The pike accused the sucker of being lazy. The sucker replied that he was not lazy, that he was in very good physical shape, and capable of obtaining his own food and, further, that the pike was a poor hunter and was forced to live on bones and rocks. The pike was very proud and they began to fight each other with spears. The sucker was faster and speared the front part of the pike's kayak. The pike was slower and managed to spear the back part of the sucker's kayak. That is why we find forked bones in the front part of the pike, and forked bones in the back part of the sucker. The sucker won the fight and after that the pike never accused the sucker of being slow or lazy.

Insects

Some of the stories the Nunamiut tell about insects are briefly related here.

> One time Mrs. Louse was very busy making sealskin trousers. Several lice were living on a human being's head and those living on the back of the person's head wanted to walk up to the forehead to have a big dance with some friends. That is why the trousers Mrs. Louse were making were so fancy, so that Mr. Louse could be very proud.

> If a louse is killed with the teeth, he says, "I'll be back again, I'll come alive again." But if a louse is killed with a fingernail, he will be dead forever.

During the winter, the mosquitoes and their parents live in one round room. Late in the spring, the young mosquitoes get tired of staying in the same place, but their parents say, "It is too cold yet, we will let you go in a little while." Finally the parents open up the room; all the mosquitoes are very happy and they spread out over the whole country. But the weather soon turns cold again, and all the mosquitoes have to return to the room. When they all come home, the parents remark, "My! You all must have lost a great many people [i.e. mosquitoes]," but they reply, "Maybe four or five during the whole summer, but you never know."

When mosquitoes first appear in the summer, people should not use seal oil for five days or the mosquitoes will become angry. After that time, it is all right with mosquitoes to use seal oil.

If a person grabs a mosquito and it flies away when he opens his hand, the mosquito laughs, "Ha Ha! I got away from five guys," meaning the five digits of the hand.

When I asked if there were any stories about gnats, my informants replied that there was none, perhaps because nobody was interested. This is typical of most of the insects, with the notable exceptions of lice and mosquitoes which are such pests.

Sea Mammals

Some Nunamiut know very little about sea mammals, while others, having lived on the coast for a winter or more, are quite knowledgeable about many of them. As pointed out elsewhere, most Nunamiut over the decades have relied almost exclusively on trade contacts with coastal Eskimos to obtain the products of the sea. I have spent very little time on the coast of northern Alaska and have shot only one bearded seal with a coastal Eskimo near Point Barrow. Thus I have relied almost entirely on informants' statements for the following information.

The mammals that occur in the Arctic Ocean near the north coast of Alaska include Pacific harbor porpoise, ribbon seal, Pacific killer whale, northern fur seal, gray whale, narwhal, white whale or beluga, harbor seal (or commonly, spotted seal), polar bear, walrus, bowhead whale, ringed seal (often known as the common seal), and bearded seal. Arctic fox, lynx, and possibly other essentially land mammals have been seen on the sea ice, but cannot be said to be indigenous there.

PACIFIC HARBOR PORPOISE. The Nunamiut say that the Pacific harbor porpoise is known only to the coastal Eskimos.

RIBBON SEAL. Some Nunamiut have heard of the ribbon seal, but say they occur only in western Alaska. According to Bee and Hall (1956: 225), the coastal Eskimos rarely shoot a ribbon seal.

PACIFIC KILLER WHALE. The Nunamiut claimed never to have harpooned a Pacific killer whale, which is known to be very dangerous to the coastal Eskimos who hunt them.

NORTHERN FUR SEAL. There appears to be no knowledge among the Nunamiut of the northern fur seal. Bee and Hall (p. 220) report that coastal Eskimos take northern fur seals only rarely.

GRAY WHALE. The Nunamiut know very little about the gray whale, only that the coastal Eskimos hunt them occasionally.

NARWHAL. My informants did not know anything about the narwhal, although Bee and Hall (p. 160) report that some coastal Eskimos know of them.

WHITE WHALE OR BELUGA. According to the Nunamiut, belugas are very rare at the mouth of the Colville River; only those that are "lost" would occur there. The Nunamiut know that belugas are smaller than walrus and were speared from kayaks (umiat were too slow) before rifles were used. I found no one in Anaktuvuk Pass who had ever hunted beluga, which were said to occur primarily at the mouth of the Mackenzie River and in Kotzebue Sound.

HARBOR SEAL (spotted seal). Harbor seals have been reported by the Nunamiut to travel as far as twenty miles up the Colville River. The Nunamiut speared them from kayaks and by crawling up to them on the ice. Rifles, of course, have been used since about 1890. In the summer it is difficult to hunt harbor seals, since they sink after they have been shot, because they are not very fat in the summer.

POLAR BEAR. Some Nunamiut have hunted and killed polar bear. The easiest way is to find one eating a seal carcass. If a hunter knows how to creep on the ice, he will have no trouble getting within rifle range. Sometimes water freezes in the fur of a polar bear and a small-caliber, low-velocity rifle is inadequate. For the same reason, and also because of its size, a bow and arrow alone was considered inadequate for hunting polar bear. The method employed by Nunamiut was much the same as that used for grizzly. One or more hunters approached a polar bear on the ice and angered it by shooting arrows into it. When the bear charged, the hunter placed the butt of a 7- or 8-foot spear firmly on the ice. As the bear approached the hunter, it reared up to grapple the man. By holding the spear carefully, the man forced the angered animal to run itself through as it lunged forward.

A few Nunamiut have observed to their amazement that a polar bear will eat the blubber of a whole seal but not touch the meat. When a polar bear does this, they say, it suffers diarrhea for a while, but with such a good meal it does not mind.

Polar bear liver should not be eaten or, it is said, a man will lose his hair. One informant knew a man several years ago who did eat polar bear liver. Afterward he lost all his hair, but within a year or two it grew back.

Polar bears have been known to venture inland. A very few have been shot over the past few decades near the Brooks Range.

WALRUS. The Nunamiut shoot only an occasional walrus. A few appear each decade near the mouth of the Colville River. Nunamiut living to the west or to the east have hunted walrus more frequently and find them easy to kill, if one knows the thin part of the skull to shoot at. Even a Winchester .25-35 is adequate if the bullet is aimed properly. When walrus occur in large numbers on the ice, they can be dangerous and may upset an umiak. Nunamiut sometimes talk about the great size of the walrus and the tremendous amount of meat there is in a bull.

BOWHEAD WHALE. While the coastal Eskimos have for perhaps centuries exploited the bowhead whale, only those Nunamiut who have moved to Point Barrow or east to the Mackenzie River have hunted this huge mammal. In the early spring, whenever a south wind blows, the Nunamiut say that the coastal people are praying for the south wind to open up leads. Then the whales can pass through, giving the hunters a chance to attack them. When there is heavy snowfall in the early spring, whales are supposed to be numerous in late spring.

The news of a whale catch travels very fast to Anaktuvuk Pass and has for many decades. The Nunamiut crave *muktuk* (whale skin) and consider whale blubber to be better than any other kind. White men who are connoisseurs of blubber concur. To eat boiled caribou meat and fresh whale blubber is about as fine eating as a Nunamiut can imagine.

One Nunamiut has a story he likes to tell about two coastal

Eskimos who once sat on a bowhead whale tongue floating in the
ocean like a raft. Nunamiut who have never seen such a thing
listen in amazement and wonder how such a gigantic animal could
exist.

RINGED SEAL (often known as the common seal). Common seals
seem to occur in endless numbers everywhere along the Arctic
coast. According to the Nunamiut, common seals have ventured as
far as fifty miles up the Colville River. In open water, seals were
speared from kayaks and are now of course shot with rifles. Since a
summer seal will sink if killed, because it has so little blubber, the
best technique is only to wound the animal. When it struggles back
to the surface for air, it can easily be speared or, immediately after
shooting, the hunter may throw a line with a multiple (usually
four) pronged hook at the seal. If one of the prongs catches on the
skin, the seal is easily taken.

When hunting seal on the ice, one must crawl in such a way that
his body appears as one gray mass; the seal will then think the
hunter is merely another seal. If the hunter sticks out an elbow or a
knee, the seal will know the hunter has legs and is after him. Also
a hunter should watch the seal's head, but must not let the seal
know that he is doing so. While a seal is sunning on the ice, it will
raise its head every few seconds to look around for polar bears.
When a seal does raise its head, the stalker should stop. A good
seal hunter can sometimes predict when the seal will raise its head.

Seals have very large, brown, almost human-looking eyes. One
Nunamiut told me that when one is close to a seal and about
ready to shoot, the seal will discover that it is too late to escape; it
will rise up, open its mouth in a threatening manner, and grimace
as if it were very disgruntled about being shot.

Common or ringed seals are greatly valued for their blubber
which was, and is to a lesser extent, used for cooking, eating,
waterproofing clothes, heat, light, and medication. The skins are
used for rawhide line, summer waterproof boots, pokes and, in the
old days, pants and parkas.

BEARDED SEAL. Bearded seals are much like common seals except that they are fewer in number, much larger in size, and more
difficult to hunt. They are hunted as are the common seals, but
they do not occur in the Colville River. Bearded seals are much
more valued than common seals. They weigh several hundred
pounds, and their meat and blubber are considered far superior.

The skin of a bearded seal is used for spring and summer boot soles and for rawhide line by the Nunamiut.

Land Mammals

The mammals within the inland range of the Nunamiut include: dusky shrew, Arctic cinerous shrew, tundra saddle-backed shrew, brown lemming, Alaska varying or collared lemming, red-back vole, tundra vole, narrow-skulled or singing vole, marten, ermine, least weasel, mink, red squirrel, muskrat, river otter, beaver, tundra or gray wolf, coyote, wolverine, red fox (occurring in red, cross, and silver or gray phases), Arctic fox, snowshoe hare, Arctic or tundra hare, lynx, porcupine, Arctic or Parry ground squirrel, hoary marmot, grizzly bear, black bear, moose, musk ox (until the middle 1800s), Dall sheep, and barren-ground caribou. The Nunamiut classify these mammals in a slightly different way; that is, they lump all three shrews into one category, and any variations noted in size, coloring, and so on are described. Although there is a general word for the red fox, the Nunamiut almost always make a terminological distinction based on the color phases. Thus three terms exist: for the silver and black, the cross, and the red phases. The Arctic white fox has a separate name. While different phases are known to occur among grizzlies, there is no reflection in the terminology. There is a generic term for wolf, but the Nunamiut distinguish three phases, the gray or "real" wolf, the blue or black phase, and the reddish phase. Both lemmings are subsumed under one term meaning "from the sky" or "drop down from the sky." The three voles are subsumed under one term with any noted difference described. The remaining land mammals are classed as we class them.

Mammals are divided into two broad categories, *aŋutit* (edible mammals) and *pishuqaat* (inedible mammals, or literally, they are sought [for their furs]). Aŋutit include caribou, mountain sheep, moose, grizzly bear, black bear, beaver, ground squirrel, marmot, Arctic or tundra hare, snowshoe hare, and porcupine. One informant mentioned that the lynx should be included among the aŋutit because it is edible but, according to the way he learned it, the lynx is included among the pishuqaat. Many aŋutit are sought for their skins also. Such pishuqaat as wolves, wolverines, and foxes are sought only for their skins and are not eaten except in extreme emergency.

Like all forms of life, mammals are considered *iñuroat,* living things. Iñuroat, as pointed out elsewhere, includes all mammals, birds, fish, insects, plants and, of course, man. Dead willows and rocks are considered nonliving or dead. Unlike man, animals were not considered to die from old age; they die from being killed by other animals or from accidental causes such as a fall.

Nunamiut say that animals are more sensitive in the winter than in the summer, when the noise of the wind and the water obscures their hearing. The varied colors of the summer tundra make it difficult for them to distinguish between a man and a large rock, and the many odors of plants and animals then interfere with an animal's sense of smell. In the winter, on the other hand, almost all flowing water freezes, and when there is no wind it is very still. A footstep in the snow can easily be heard, even by a man, over a mile away. The whiteness of winter makes foreign objects stand out visibly and most summer smells are absent.

SHREW. The Nunamiut regard the shrew as a pesky, active little animal that constantly tries to steal food from people. Shrews are not considered very intelligent. I was told that about ten years ago two Nunamiut were lying on a hill watching a herd of caribou. A shrew appeared three or four feet in front of the two men; they did not move because they did not want to scare the caribou. The shrew moved toward one of the men and suddenly ran into his parka: only a stupid animal would do such a thing because it could have been killed instantly. Nunamiut have little use for shrews but nowadays trap them for biologists either with mouse-traps or in five-gallon cans.

One Nunamiut likes to tell a story about a coastal Eskimo who found a frozen shrew while hunting inland. He put the shrew into his mitten, where he kept his chewing tobacco, to take home to scare his wife. He forgot about it, and when he felt like chewing tobacco later, by mistake he put the frozen shrew into his mouth. He started chewing, but could not get any flavor. Suddenly he remembered the shrew in his mitten and he spat it out on his hand. There it was, pink and clean, with all the hair chewed off.

Theoretically a shrew may have an iñua, but one informant said it had none.

LEMMING. Lemmings do not occur in large numbers in the Brooks Range, but the Nunamiut are familiar with them. In the old days lemmings, especially the whiter ones, were thought to fall

down from the sky with snow. They are much more common north
of the Brooks Range where they are faced with less competition
from voles and shrews (Bee and Hall 1956: 77–80, 92). The
fluctuation in population, especially of the brown lemming, occurs
in three- to five-year cycles and is carefully noted by coastal
Eskimos; the population change in the Brooks Range is much
smaller (ibid.: 92) and most Nunamiut take little note of lemmings. They are considered rather stupid animals which are unable
to see very well. To a Nunamiut, visual acuity is such an important
index of general intelligence that any animal, or person for that
matter, that cannot see well is likely to be regarded as stupid.
In the early 1900s lemming skins were in demand for cleaning
telescope lenses, but otherwise Nunamiut have had little market
for the skins. Children occasionally kill lemmings with rocks,
slingshots, or toy bows and arrows.

VOLE. Voles, or "mice" as they are called locally, are very
common in Anaktuvuk Pass and elsewhere in northern Alaska.
Since the Nunamiut have settled permanently in one location, the
vole population has increased considerably in the village and may
become a health problem in the future.

Voles are thought to be unintelligent but they will run quickly
for their holes if attacked. At least, it is said, they know enough to
try to save themselves. The Nunamiut observe voles collecting
roots and plants for their "winter supply." In digging moss for a
house once, I came upon a large pile of *masu,* the root Nunamiut
frequently collect in the late summer. A few Nunamiut nearby
joked that after collecting so much food each fall, the voles, just
like people, have a great deal of fun all winter in their karigi, the
large underground holes they make.

The Nunamiut have two short stories they enjoy telling; one
is about two voles who were playing on a see-saw. All of a sudden
one exclaimed "Oh! I touched the sky!" They were playing under
a willow leaf.

The other is about a village of voles.

One of the vole women was about ready to give birth, but
the babies would not come. The vole husband went to a vole
shaman in the village and offered him a new parka and pair of
boots if he would help his wife. A parka, made of the ear skin
of a caribou calf, and a pair of boots were very valuable to the

vole people in those days. With the prospect of receiving such nice gifts, the vole shaman was happy to help the woman. He began to sing and dance, working up his power to aid the mother, and shouted, "Have the babies come out yet?" "No! not yet!" was the reply. Again and again the shaman sang and danced, trying harder to help the vole mother with his power. Then five baby voles were born; the parents shouted "Thank you very much!" The vole shaman asked the names of the five babies. Shortly afterward, he received his payment of a new parka and pair of boots.

MARTEN. Rausch (1951: 174) reports that marten are rare even in the northern fringes of the timber in the middle Brooks Range and nearby regions. Nunamiut say that they occur only in the more heavily timbered regions of the Brooks Range. The Nunamiut obtained most of their marten skins in trade from Kobuk Eskimos and used them for trimming boots and hats or traded them on to the Arctic coast. In the old days, a few venturesome Nunamiut trappers made excursions far enough into the timber to set spruce-log deadfalls for marten. Snares were never used, probably because a marten would chew his way loose.

The Nunamiut do not consider the marten to be very clever; it is similar to the ground squirrel in that respect. A marten, however, can learn how to avoid traps if exposed to them two or three times before getting caught.

ERMINE. Ermine, the larger of the two weasels present in Arctic Alaska, occur frequently within the range of the Nunamiut and during the late 1940s and early 1950s they trapped as many as forty or fifty a year (Rausch 1951: 175). Today, as other sources of income have developed, primarily from sporadic odd jobs, Nunamiut no longer try very hard to trap ermine. In the old days, one or two Nunamiut sometimes spent months trapping them and traded the skins to coastal Eskimos. One Nunamiut heard that ermine trapped in the Brooks Range were traded as far as Siberia. The Nunamiut themselves have little use for these skins.

The ermine is considered to be a stupid animal, similar to the vole, but, the Nunamiut observe, they are at least smart enough to make a living by killing ptarmigan and other small animals.

LEAST WEASEL. Least weasels are less common than ermine within the range of the Nunamiut, and they are rarely trapped.

During the early 1900s when there was a demand for least weasel skins, Nunamiut considered the price of twenty-five cents to $1.50 to be a good price for such a little skin.

The least weasel is considered as unintelligent as the vole and ermine, but it knows enough to run to its hole when threatened, and is fast enough to outrun even a good rock thrower. Occasionally a Nunamiut kills a least weasel with a stick or catches one in a trap set for ermine or voles.

In July of 1959, two Nunamiut young men and I saw a least weasel in the Savioyok River valley about two miles from the pass over to Giant Creek. It stood up on its hind legs and looked at us curiously. In a second or two, our dogs rushed the animal and it disappeared. My two companions were surprised to see a least weasel, a rare occurrence and worth a good story back in the village.

MINK. Mink tracks have been reported at Hunt Fork, Chandler Lake, the upper Savioyok River valley (Rausch 1951: 175–76), and north of the eastern Brooks Range (Bee and Hall 1956: 211), but no specimens have been collected; they have not been observed by Nunamiut on the tundra. Most of the mink skins the Nunamiut obtained were traded in from the Kobuk Eskimos. The Nunamiut who have trapped in the timbered regions of the Brooks Range say that mink are not very intelligent, rather like ground squirrels and marten. Like the marten, a mink can learn to avoid traps if it manages to escape once or twice before getting caught.

RED SQUIRREL. Red squirrels occur normally only in the timber. One red squirrel was collected by Rausch (1953: 126) in the summer of 1952 near the summit of Anaktuvuk Pass in a stand of willows some thirty miles north of the spruce. Another red squirrel was seen in Hunt Fork River about ten miles south of the north/south divide of the Brooks Range a few miles north of the timber (Bee and Hall 1956: 262). The Nunamiut had little to say about red squirrels. They know the animal occurs in the timber, but apparently have never utilized them. Nowadays they collect them on odd occasions for biologists.

MUSKRAT. Bee and Hall (ibid.) suggest that muskrats might have occurred occasionally north of the Brooks Range. More commonly, of course, they occur in the timbered region of the southern Brooks Range. The same authors (p. 262) report that Indians and Eskimos at Bettles have claimed that muskrats range as far up the

John River as Hunt Fork, still ten or fifteen miles from the northern fringe of the timber. According to the Nunamiut, muskrats are found only in deep timber, not even in the northern fringes of the spruce; only trappers who have traveled far into the timber have ever encountered them. Generally muskrats are not considered very intelligent, definitely less so than beaver. Muskrats can easily be lured to bait and shot from a blind. One Nunamiut boasted that the oldest living Nunamiut woman at Anaktuvuk Pass (now about 65 years old) was quite proficient in her younger days in shooting muskrat. In one season in the southeastern Brooks Range she sometimes shot fifty to a hundred muskrats, either with a .30-30 or .25-35.

RIVER OTTER. Before the late 1950s, river otters rarely if ever occurred in the northern Brooks Range or north slope of Alaska (Rausch 1951: 177, 1953: 114; Bee and Hall 1956: 216). Recently, however, the Nunamiut report that a population of them has developed in the Chandler River just north of the range front where fish are numerous. In the early days, it was said that Nunamiut did not know how to catch river otter, but they had heard that the Koyukon Indians used bows and arrows. The Nunamiut have come to consider the otter much more intelligent than other small animals. I found only one Nunamiut who had had any luck in trapping them. He set steel traps in open water where it would be impossible for an otter to smell or to see readily. Even then he managed to catch only a few. A good otter pelt was worth as much as $60 in the early 1960s, but nowadays, with increasing opportunities for sporadic employment, few Nunamiut would seriously consider expending the effort required to maintain a good trap line for otters in the Chandler River.

BEAVER. The beaver normally occurs in the small lakes and creeks of the timbered regions of the southern Brooks Range. Rausch (1953: 138) reports that two Eskimos found a beaver dam several miles north of the timber in the upper Ikiakpuk Creek, one of the tributaries of the John River. Other Nunamiut told me of a beaver dam at Hunt Fork, ten or fifteen miles south of the northern fringes of the timber. Rausch (1951: 185) suggests that beaver dams are absent in the upper Savioyok River valley but may occur farther south. There has been evidence of beavers north of the northernmost dams. Rausch (1953: 138) reports that an adult beaver was seen in the willows just south of Anaktuvuk Pass in the summer of 1953. One summer in the early 1950s, two or three Nunamiut saw a beaver at Tulugak Lake near the northern range front of the Brooks Range. In the summer of 1959, John M. Campbell and I saw fresh willow cuttings chewed in characteristic beaver fashion among the willows just south of Anaktuvuk Pass. Evidence of beaver north of Hunt Fort is unusual, and Nunamiut often refer to an animal out of its customary range as being "lost."

Beavers are considered to be very intelligent animals and extremely difficult to catch. Several Nunamiut have attempted to trap them, but the animals are so clever that only two or three persons have had any luck. The Nunamiut regard the beavers' habit of warning other beavers of danger by slapping the water with their tails as "very helpful" and a typical example of the cooperation found among beavers. One Nunamiut has an idea that he thinks might work in catching beavers. He would fasten a trap to a long spruce log and tie a swatch of green willows near the trap, then chip a hole through the ice in a lake where beavers occur. The log would be placed in the hole with the trap and green willows submerged. Each day the trap would have to be checked and the new ice chipped away from the hole.

Once a Nunamiut saw a beaver that had been caught by freeze-up and was unable to escape under water. The Eskimo clubbed it with no difficulty.

While the Nunamiut have trapped a few beaver now and then, over the years they have obtained most of their beaver pelts from the Kobuk Eskimos. The skins are greatly valued even today for trimming on boots and parkas, and in the old days were used for hats and whole parkas.

WOLF. The wolf population in the Brooks Range has fluctuated considerably over the decades. From the early 1900s to about 1920, wolves were few, probably because of the scarcity of caribou. When the Nunamiut returned to the Brooks Range in the late 1930s, they found the wolf population had increased, as had the caribou population. By the middle 1940s, wolves were very numerous, and the Nunamiut were taking 50 to 100 a year. In 1951–52, the wolf population reached what Rausch (1953: 111) considers may have been an all-time high for northern Alaska.

The United States Fish and Wildlife Service of Alaska moved in to reduce the wolf population with strychnine-poisoned baits and by shooting them from small airplanes; a great many were killed, and they are still being shot from the air, which has kept the wolf population at a very low level. This has worked a hardship on many Nunamiut who had relied heavily on the bounty (at present $50 per wolf) for a large part of their cash income. The Nunamiut also value wolf skins highly for parka ruffs, boots, and even full parkas and trousers. When Nunamiut have a surplus of wolf skins they sell them to other Eskimos and whites, for as much as $50 for a good pelt.

Nunamiut have continued to trap wolves in the early 1960s, but often fewer than twenty a year are taken. Most Nunamiut, however, are very familiar with the wolf and consider it to be the most intelligent of all the animals. A human being has a difficult time trying to fool a wolf. A young wolf is easy to hunt because it is not familiar with the ways of man, but an older wolf, which has encountered man several times, is most difficult to approach. It seems to be very sensitive to what man is like and how he hunts. Even the best wolf hunters of Anaktuvuk Pass admitted that it is almost hopeless to try to hunt a really experienced wolf.

An inexperienced hunter usually thinks it will be easy to hunt them. One novice figured that wolf hunting must be similar to mountain sheep hunting, a good example of the analogical thinking so common among the Nunamiut. Each time this hunter approached a wolf, however, it saw him and ran away; obviously the technique of approaching mountain sheep did not work for wolves. The hunter realized that he had to learn to think more like a wolf if he was going to have any luck. He had to learn to guess how a wolf would respond when frightened by the sound, smell, or sight of man. The most effective approach, the hunter learned, was to arouse a wolf's curiosity and entice it to him. The hunter began to practice howling like a wolf. He found that if he sat still he could often arouse a wolf's curiosity to the extent that it would come within rifle range. Wolves are especially easy to call during the mating season between the middle of March and the middle of April.

Another method commonly used by Nunamiut wolf hunters is to find a carcass that a wolf or wolf pack has partially eaten. The patient hunter hides on the leeward side of the kill within rifle range and waits. The moment a hunter fires, the wolves disperse in all directions and it takes a good rifleman to kill three or four of them.

A hunter walking along a valley once suddenly spotted a wolf that had already seen him. He immediately ran away from the wolf as if greatly frightened and hid behind a knoll. The wolf, said the hunter, must have felt very proud; it walked up on a hill to see what kind of strange animal it had frightened; it must have been terrifically surprised when a bullet came tearing through his body.

One hunter saw a wolf in open country where there was no place to hide. He stuck his rifle above his head to look like caribou antlers and scratched the snow as if he were trying to get at the lichens and grasses. The wolf advanced with the idea of a caribou in mind, and the hunter shot him.

Hunting wolves on foot takes skill and endurance. Physically, emotionally, and mentally, a good wolf hunter commits himself to his task day after day in the often unrewarding pursuit of this intelligent animal. Most Nunamiut, especially today, rely heavily on steel traps; they must be particularly careful to deodorize all traps, gloves, and bait, or the wolf will sense the hand of man. Even when a Nunamiut sets a trap to the best of his ability, an occasional brilliant wolf fails to be deceived. In the old days, the Nunamiut set snares for wolves.

Because bounties are paid on wolves of any age, many Nunamiut have become skilled wolf-pup hunters. Wolves bear their young in May and possibly early June. Dens are usually located along river cutbanks, and the pups do not grow large enough to leave until the first weeks of July. Hunting parties of two or three Nunamiut, sometimes four to six, check the dens they have seen in previous seasons and scour the countryside for evidence of new dens. Sometimes, if the pups have not grown too large, a Nunamiut catches a wolf pup alive, which he can sell at double the bounty price.

Wolves are to be found in almost any kind of terrain, from river bottoms to mountain ridges. They occur singly, in small packs of three to six, in larger packs from six to ten or more, and very occasionally in even larger packs. Many Nunamiut seemed to think that the smaller packs constitute a "family" of wolves, i.e. mother, father, and offspring. Larger packs of six to ten or more are thought to be composed of two related families. Packs of one or two families appear to be stable groupings. Larger packs do occur, but Nunamiut do not consider them to be stable; perhaps several wolves had happened to come together to hunt for a while, but sooner or

later they would be forced to separate into smaller packs in order
to hunt more effectively. Medium-sized hunting packs of six to
ten are probably the most efficient for hunting in the Brooks Range.
For a description of how wolves hunt caribou, see p. 311.

COYOTE. The coyote occurs rarely in the Anaktuvuk Pass region,
but the Nunamiut definitely know of the animal and have hunted
it. The skin is valued by the Nunamiut for children's parkas because it is thin—much thinner than that of a wolf. In fact, Nunamiut figure that a coyote must feel very cold in the winter and perhaps that is why there are so few in the far north.

Nunamiut profess to know little about coyotes, since they do
not occur regularly in the Brooks Range. They know that pups are
born in May; the time of mating is unknown but is assumed to be
from the middle of March to the middle of April, like the wolf.

Perhaps less than one coyote a year is caught in a Nunamiut
wolf trap. A few Nunamiut have seen coyotes; they are reckoned
to be similar to wolves although easier to hunt. One Nunamiut
chased a coyote for several hours until he finally managed to get
within rifle range and shoot it. Because coyotes occur so irregularly
in the northern Brooks Range, a few Nunamiut think that they are
lost when they wander up north, and that is why they are easier to
hunt than wolves.

WOLVERINE. A solitary scavenger and hunter of small animals,
the wolverine occurs throughout northern Alaska. Compared to
other animals in Alaska, little is known about wolverines. They
tend to travel in the lower terrains of the regions through which
they pass, but they do not hesitate to ascend any mountain. The
cubs are born in the first part of April. Nunamiut are not sure
about the location of wolverine dens but suspect they must be
fairly high on low mountains; they do not know the mating habits
of this animal.

The Nunamiut value the wolverine more highly than any other
fur-bearing animal. A good wolverine skin lasts for years, losing
hair and fading very slowly. A wolverine skin can be traded anywhere in the Arctic at any time for $50 for a good pelt. For a man's
parka ruff and for the inner circle of a woman's parka ruff, a strip
of good wolverine is almost essential; a person would not feel
properly dressed without a suitable ruff.

The Nunamiut consider the wolverine to be a very intelligent
animal, perhaps next to the wolf, and pound for pound certainly
the toughest animal alive. Today wolverines are caught by the

Nunamiut in steel traps, but a wolverine knows enough to chew his foot off after it freezes in a trap. A man has to check his traps frequently to avoid losing wolverines. Rausch (1951: 176) states that the Nunamiut catch three to six wolverines in a normal year and twelve to fifteen in an unusually good year. This still is the case today.

In the old days, wolverines could not be snared because they would chew through the snare. Heavy rock deadfalls, one of which is still in use today, were built. For a description, see p. 95.

A man rarely sees a wolverine. A hunter many years ago spotted one; he began crawling on all fours like an animal obliquely toward the wolverine. When he got within rifle range, he opened fire killing the animal. In late June of 1960, two young Nunamiut and I were walking in the upper Savioyok River valley when we suddenly noticed a wolverine clambering over the rocks of a low talus slope. Our dogs were after the animal like a shot. Fortunately we managed to mortally wound it with rifle fire before the dogs reached it and were badly hurt. The wolverine, shot through the neck and one paw lay on its back as the dogs snapped warily at the tough little animal. Our dogs had suffered only minor cuts around the muzzle by the time we climbed up to where the wolverine lay. We finished it off with several blows from heavy rocks. My companions were quite startled to see a wolverine in the summer, and one of the young men thought there might be a den in the area. The other young man was impressed with the difficulty we had in killing it with rocks. In the early spring of 1961, a Nunamiut trapper was driving a sled along a river in the timber when his dogs scared up a wolverine. The animal made for a spruce tree and climbed up. The Nunamiut shot it with no difficulty. In general, however, few wolverines are shot. No older Nunamiut has shot more than three or four in an active hunting life of forty years.

The Nunamiut relate an incident of a wolverine killing a polar bear. Several years ago on the coast, a polar bear and a wolverine met and came together in a terrific clinch. Using everything he had, the wolverine dug his way through the chest of the polar bear, apparently mutilating the heart or aorta before the bear was able to inflict a mortal blow. The polar bear rolled over dead and the wolverine walked away. In spite of the large size of a bear, perhaps a drawback in this instance, the toughness and ferocity of a wolverine bring this account within the bounds of plausibility.

The wolverine is the subject of a Nunamiut folktale:

A young married couple was living in the mountains, no one knows exactly where. The young wife bore a son, their first child. The new father and mother were very happy and loved their son very much. They had enough food because the father was a good hunter. The son grew quickly and within a year he was big enough to go out hunting and to bring home meat. He grew stronger and learned more and more how to shift for himself. Finally he was capable of leaving home. The family was alone and the son wanted to learn about other people. He wanted to find a wife; it was no fun to be alone all the time, he wanted something more than just hunting. His father and mother finally told him where he could find people. The mature son set off one day, and he did not return.

Soon, the couple had another son. Similar to their first son, their second grew rapidly, became a hunter, and began to feel lonesome. Just as the first son, the second longed for a wife. His parents finally told him where to find people and he too left home. He did not return.

Again, the couple gave birth to a third son. Just as his two elder brothers, he grew up in only one year, became a hunter, and began to think of a wife. He left home and did not return.

The couple had a fourth son, no different from the first three. He too did not return home.

Then a fifth son was born to the man and wife. When he grew up, his father decided to kill him to prevent him from leaving home. The father dug a pit in the snow and placed a sharp-pointed stick in the bottom, so that when his son fell into the pit, he would impale himself; but it was of no avail. It is an excruciating thing to want to kill one's own son. In the evenings, the father hung a snare in the doorway, but the son always knew what was going to happen and he managed to avoid the danger. Once the father sneaked up on his son with a bow and arrow and took a shot from behind, but the young man managed to jump out of the way. The father shot only once; he did not try a second shot. Another time the father tried to spear his son, but it is a hard thing to spear one's own son. The young man became exceedingly unhappy with his father's continued attempts on his life. His father never told him about his four brothers.

One day, the father went out to hunt, and the son spoke

with his mother. "I had better not stay at home any longer, my father is constantly trying to kill me. Do you know where I could find people?" His mother felt that she should not tell, but her son insisted on learning the whereabouts of people. His mother knew that if her son left, he would never return. Finally one day his mother said, "We know where people are, but it was a long time ago." Then the young man's mother told him how to find people. After learning where to go, he told his mother, "I had better go now, maybe life will be easier without the attempts of my father to kill me. I will return if I can manage it." As her son left, the woman called out, "Don't be like your brothers. Your four brothers went to the place where people are and they never came back."

Then the son left. As he walked along, he watched very carefully trying to see what had happened to his brothers. Something must have gone wrong and he wanted to avoid the trouble his brothers had encountered. He thought to himself that he would indeed return home after finding people.

The young man walked on and on. He made camp before he saw any sign of people. The next day he continued walking but he was careful not to make a big circle and then discover himself back home. He made a point of walking straight ahead.

That evening, he was following a river when he saw some kind of house near the bank. He looked at the house intently for a moment but could see no light. He thought to himself, "There must be no one in that house because there is no light." He continued walking downstream. Before long he saw another house. This time he could see a light shining through the skylight. He left the river and walked up to the bank where the lighted house was. He walked cautiously because he thought someone might see him, but no one seemed to be inside the house. He made a noise with his feet just outside the door, but no one came out to look for him. Finally he decided to find out for himself if anyone was home. He was hungry because he had carried so little food. He was so hungry. He pulled the door open and there before his eyes was a beautiful young woman sitting on the floor combing her long black hair. He stood still for a moment, absorbing this vision of loveliness. The young woman looked up at him enticingly and asked, "Are you hungry?" "Yes!" stammered the young man. The woman continued combing her hair and smiling warmly, she asked him again, "Are you hungry? Help yourself." Near the flickering lamp by the woman's side was a large dish of freshly boiled fat meat. "Help yourself," smiled the woman, "there is lots of fat meat here." Everything looked so nice. The young man took a piece of meat with his knife. BOOM! In an instant the beautiful young woman and the glowing lamp disappeared. The young man could not move, he was caught under a heavy rock. Then he realized why his brothers had not returned home, they had been caught by this rock. Although he could not move at all, he did not feel any pain and he was fully conscious; he did not forget what was happening to him.

While he was lying under the rock, the young man heard footsteps coming up the river. They came closer and closer. Finally he could tell there were two men. One of them said to the other, "My age [the fact of being old, and the respect it entails] has caught a wolverine, young boy." Under the rock, the startled young man thought to himself, "So I am a wolverine! That man out there just told his companion, 'My age has caught a wolverine.' " The two men pulled the wolverine out from under the rock. He could not move in the slightest, but he could remember everything that happened. He could see himself being carried along by the two men. They took him to the house where there was no light. There was no wolverine there; the house without a light had not caught one. They arrived at a village and the older man, the owner of the light and the beautiful young woman, took him, the wolverine, inside his house. The man was carrying a strange-looking knife.

The wolverine remembered coming to the good-sized village where the house was. Inside, he saw the old man's wife. He looked down at the floors and he noticed how neat and clean everything was. Then the old man and woman invited many people to their house, so happy were they to have another wolverine. The old man held the strange-looking knife in his hand and spoke to the wolverine, "There are many good things in this house. You may have anything you like and then you may return to your home. Take something, whatever you like." The wolverine thought he had better take the knife, which had been chipped very carefully from the best flint. Then the old man and woman gave him food to eat. After refreshing himself, the old man told the wolverine, "We will keep your parka. We will give you an old, wornout parka, but it will be good enough to get you home." "Well," thought the wolverine, "that will be all right since I have the knife. Perhaps my parents can make another parka."

The next morning, the young wolverine took the old, dirty, wornout parka and his bright, new, sharp, shining knife and started to leave the house. The old man told him, "We are glad to have strangers. We always give them what they want and take their parka." The wolverine walked out into the camp and saw many people around. He would have liked to stay, but the people told him that he had better return home because they were a different people. The old man told him not to tarry on the way home and to return directly to his parents. He always told strangers not to linger and to go straight home.

The wolverine set out walking up the river, following the tracks of the two men who had trapped him. He easily recognized the countryside near the house where his body had been caught by the heavy rock. He stopped for a moment but he could see no light nor could he hear anything. He walked on until he saw the first house where there had been no light. He stopped to listen but heard nothing. He could recognize his own tracks and saw that they were altogether different from those made by the people in the village. In the evening, he made an overnight camp. Early the following morning he kept right on traveling. Finally in the distance he could see his parents' house. Toward evening he arrived. He rushed into the house and his parents recognized him immediately. His father and mother were jubilant to have their son back again, but they asked him what had happened to his parka. The son told his parents about everything that had happened. His father looked at the flint knife and said, "We are glad to have a good knife. It is difficult to make a new parka, but we will see about it later."

As the young wolverine had been returning home, he had seen animals up in the mountains. He did not hunt them, however; he followed the advice of the old man and did not fool around on the way home. The young man stayed with his parents for years. When they grew old, he hunted for them and took care of them. His parents learned from him that they were wolverines and figured that their first four sons had probably been caught in a rock deadfall just as their fifth son had been. They realized that they were wolverines and that sometimes members of their kind get caught in deadfalls. The beautiful young woman, combing her hair, smiling warmly, and offering the young man what he wanted means that young women can easily tempt young men. When the young man saw the first house there was no light. He continued walking until he found another house, the one with light where the meat had been cooked with the lamp. People who keep their floors clean, keep a good light burning, and have good meat to eat and to offer to visitors will have luck in catching wolverines [implying that only those persons who work hard at hunting and keeping the house in order and are generous with their food will have good luck]. The son who returned to his parents was the fifth son, and [in the old days] Eskimos never took more than five wolverines in one year.

RED FOX. The Alaska red fox occurs frequently throughout the Brooks Range, most commonly in the red phase, less so in the cross, and only rarely in the silver or black phase.

Foxes are often to be found in broken terrain, especially on small hills and riverbanks. In a year when foxes are numerous, the Nunamiut believe there must be many voles and other small animals around. Bee and Hall (1956: 183) note that coastal Eskimos also assert that a high population of Arctic foxes on the coast follows a high population of lemmings.

The Nunamiut had little use for foxes themselves and rarely made efforts to trap the animal until the advent of outside demand in the middle and late 1800s. Foxes are considered to be very clever little animals and are wary of man. If a fox encounters a snowshoe trail, it will run alongside it for a long way trying to find the end of it, rather than take the risk of jumping across. One older Nunamiut said that in his younger days when he saw a fox in the morning, he knew that fox was going to be his. By nightfall he could run it down. A fox leaves a clear track in the snow, of course, and mile after mile, a hunter walks in steady pursuit. Finally, it is said, a fox becomes so tired of running that it becomes lazy, and a man eventually can come within rifle range. Sometimes if a man is well hidden when he sees a fox, he can attract the animal to within shooting range by making a squeaking sound with his lips. Foxes are reputed to be very curious. A Nunamiut and I were once sitting on a high knoll watching for caribou. About 400 yards away we spotted a fox. My companion started making a squeaking sound like a vole or mouse. The fox perked up its ears and began darting stealthily toward us. Just as it came within rifle range, it stopped in its tracks and in a moment bolted away. My companion burst into laughter saying that the fox must have finally sensed our "human stink."

The year I lived among the Nunamiut many foxes suffered from rabies or severe distemper. The Nunamiut use the same word for either affliction—*kinnaq* (crazy). To call something or someone kinnaq is an extreme statement. A few Nunamiut explained that foxes go crazy when they become too numerous. Perhaps, informants theorized, foxes begin fighting over the same food; before long, a few become so hungry that their brains deteriorate and they wander about aimlessly. A fox that cannot recognize a human being is considered to be in the last stages of life. In January 1960 I shot a diseased fox at Tulugak Lake: early one afternoon I was carrying home a load of round whitefish from the lake when I spotted a fox trotting slowly around the corner of the house only about fifty yards away. I immediately threw the heavy sack of fish to the ground and jerked my rifle out of its case. By that time the fox had come within two or three yards. As the fox did not charge, I held the gun as a club, waiting. The fox approached to within five feet and stopped still. It sniffed curiously and peered at me with misty sunken eyes before trotting off slowly. The moment it was far enough away to give me a second shot should I need it, I fired. The animal, along with other diseased foxes Nunamiut had shot, was sent to the Arctic Research Laboratory at Point Barrow.

ARCTIC FOX. The Arctic fox occurs only sporadically in the Brooks Range (Rausch 1951: 172); it is commonly found along the Arctic coast, the low coastal plains, and sometimes on the sea ice (in search of the remains of seals from polar bear kills). The Arctic fox prefers open terrain and occurs locally along the Arctic coast in greater numbers than does the red fox in the foothills and valleys of the Brooks Range (Bee and Hall 1956: 181–85). Rausch (1951: 172) suggests that the Arctic fox occurs in the Brooks Range in some years because of a high population of them on the coast, resulting from a high in the lemming population. One Eskimo told Rausch (ibid.) that an Arctic fox wandered as far as the southern Brooks Range in 1910.

The Nunamiut catch Arctic foxes in the mountains only occasionally; they give rise to no particular comments except that they are "lost." While they were on the Arctic coast from the early 1900s to the late 1930s, many Nunamiut trapped Arctic fox intensively, in some years making large sums of money. The decline in the demand for them in the middle and late thirties was one of the factors contributing to the return of several Nunamiut families to the Brooks Range.

SNOWSHOE HARE AND ARCTIC HARE. The snowshoe hare occurs rarely in the northern Brooks Range, and biologists have little information of the animal in the region. The Arctic hare is perhaps a little more common. Nunamiut have reported the presence of both hares in the northern Brooks Range and north slope in occasional years. The Nunamiut used sinew snares for hares but had to check them diligently in the early morning before the hare could see well enough to chew the snare. Even bright moonlight, it is said, enables a hare to chew his way out of a sinew snare. Hare skin was sometimes used for a patch on a mitten or a parka because of its warmth and ease of handling. Neither hare is significant as a food source, and only a few skins have been traded to the coast over the years.

The Nunamiut consider hares to be rather stupid animals. Informants laughed about the inane appearance of one or two hares sitting on the snow blinking their big eyes in the bright spring sun: maybe two hares had a good time exchanging the news.

LYNX. Lynx commonly occur in the more heavily timbered regions of the Brooks Range. When snowshoe hares are numerous, lynx may be found in the northern fringes of the timber where Nunamiut often hunt and trap. On rare occasions lynx have been reported on the north slope (Bee and Hall 1956: 217–18). A Nunamiut reported that hares were very numerous north of the Brooks Range from 1915 to 1917 and that lynx poured over the mountains by the hundreds in pursuit. A few lynx were seen to venture out onto the sea ice. Nunamiut do not think a lynx could catch a seal, but they admit it is a possibility. Like the Arctic fox, the lynx in 1915–17 ventured onto the ice to find the remains of polar bear kills. In the timber, one informant's father saw a lynx jump from a spruce tree onto the back of a small caribou.

The Nunamiut rarely make a special effort to catch lynx. A trapper who happens to be in the timber for a season might decide that he would like to have a lynx parka made for him or, if lynx appear to be numerous, he might decide to exploit them. Several Nunamiut have learned to build a small log house with beaver castor as bait and either a steel trap or a triggered door to catch the lynx. In the old days, lynx were easy to snare. They frequently travel up and down mountains and by chopping down several long spruce trees in a series up a mountainside, a lynx can often be guided right into a snare. They are not considered very intelligent; they do not even know enough to chew a snare. Above all, Nunamiut think of the lynx as a very lazy animal. When a hunter sees a lynx in open country he can often run it down. When a man approaches, a lynx will run very fast for a short distance and stop to catch its breath; it usually sits still until its attacker becomes an obvious threat again. After a few hours, a man can usually get within shooting range.

PORCUPINE. The porcupine occurs most commonly in the timber, but individuals not infrequently wander to the northern Brooks Range and north slope. The year I was there, two porcupines were killed near the village of Anaktuvuk Pass. A Nunamiut rarely sets out specifically to hunt porcupines, although when they are fat they are very good to eat. The Nunamiut never indicated that traps or snares have ever been set in the past for porcupines. Rather, when a man happens to see a porcupine, he clubs it with a stick or, if necessary, shoots it. Sometimes a man might wait near a meat cache if he suspects that the same porcupine has raided it night after night. In the summer of 1961 two or three Eskimo dogs tangled with a porcupine just outside the village. The dogs failed to harm the animal but they returned to the village with beards of porcupine quills stuck in their muzzles. Two men spent several hours extracting the quills with pliers. Dogs, it is said, never seem to learn about porcupines.

The Nunamiut consider the porcupine to be a rather unintelligent slow-moving animal that cannot see very well. About the only thing it knows to do is to hide in rocks. In the old days, the belly skin of a porcupine was sometimes used for decorating boots. Quills were collected and woven together into a belt and sometimes traded to the coast.

ARCTIC GROUND SQUIRREL. Ground squirrels occur frequently throughout the Brooks Range and adjacent areas; they thrive on almost all edible plants in the Arctic. They prefer to live in broken, well-drained terrain but may occur anywhere from river cutbanks to high mountain slopes, as long as there is a food source. Ground squirrels suffer predation from ermine, grizzlies, man, gyrfalcons, golden eagles, a few other large birds, and occasionally from wolves. In small local areas, intensive trapping may reduce the population but, as a whole, the animal appears fully able to maintain its numbers in the Brooks Range. The ground squirrels enter hibernation in the latter part of September or early October and emerge in late March or early April. They are very fat when they emerge from hibernation and are highly valued by Nunamiut for meat and fat as well as for skins. Ground squirrels breed in late April or early May; they lose their fat, and their skins become scarred with fighting, so that the Nunamiut do not seek them in the late spring and early summer. Then in late August or September, when the skin improves and the animal fattens itself before entering hibernation, they are again hunted. The skins of ground squirrels were sometimes used by Nunamiut for parkas but were more often traded to the Arctic coast where demand was high.

Nunamiut observe that ground squirrels which live in high rocky places are smaller than those living where food is more plentiful. Also, ground squirrels living among lighter-colored rocks are lighter in color than those living among dark-colored rocks, dirt-colored cutbanks, or on the dark side of a mountain.

The Nunamiut do not consider ground squirrels to be very intelligent animals, but they can learn to avoid sinew snares and small steel traps if they escape once or twice before getting caught. In checking traps set for ground squirrels, two Nunamiut and I once found in a trap a ground squirrel that had been killed and mutilated by another squirrel. My companions had seen this happen before and thought it was a strange thing that, rather than trying to help one of its own kind out of trouble, one ground squirrel would sometimes kill another.

In the old days, shamans were afraid of ground squirrels: if a shaman ate a ground squirrel's head, he might die. Once many years ago, a visitor who was a shaman was about to enter a house. The woman of the household had placed two or three ground squirrel skins underneath her sleeping skins out of sight. As the shaman stood at the door about to enter, he suddenly looked up into the air and made a shrill chattering noise like a ground squirrel. He refused to enter until the skins were removed. I could discover no particular reason for this fear; the fear is there, passed down from shaman to shaman, from generation to generation.

HOARY MARMOT. The marmot occurs throughout the Brooks Range usually in small, localized colonies high on rocky mountainsides and in talus slopes. A few marmot occur north of the Brooks Range in the foothills where boulder fields and rock taluses may be found. The golden eagle (Rausch 1951: 179; Bee and Hall 1956: 38) is the greatest predator of marmots. Foxes (Rausch: ibid.) and, according to the Nunamiut, wolves, constitute other threats. Those marmots living on the sunny side of a mountain or among light-colored rocks are said to be lighter in color.

Like the ground squirrel, the marmot depends on hibernation to carry it through the long winter. Marmots enter hibernation about the middle of September; biologists (Rausch 1951: 178) are not certain when they emerge from their dens. Nunamiut say that when gulls appear in the Brooks Range marmots see them and know it is time to come out of their holes. Irving (1960: 79–80) records the first appearance of the two most common gulls in the Brooks Range between the first and third weeks of May. Hence, it would seem that marmots emerge about the first part of May. They are very fat shortly after emerging and one or two Nunamiut in the old days were known for their love of marmot fat. In May, they dropped everything they were doing for a week or two in order to trap as many marmots as possible. Today Nunamiut often trap marmots from July to early September. Summer may be a hungry time, and the fat meat of marmots is a welcome supplement. Marmots are greatly valued for their skins, which are made into parkas and blankets. A marmot parka is very warm and windproof in the winter and waterproof in the summer. The fur is rich enough in natural oils that rainwater can easily be shaken from it. A good marmot pelt is worth from $6 to $8 in trade.

The Nunamiut do not consider the marmot to be an especially intelligent animal. They are easy to catch as far as skill is concerned but difficult in the amount of labor required. Marmots, it is thought, always expect danger from above and do not fear animals approaching from below. When a marmot sees an eagle or other animal approaching from above, it gives out a frightened whistle, warning other members in the colony. When a marmot sees an animal below, it often whistles in a more relaxed way. According to the Nunamiut, the reason a marmot evinces little fear from animals below is that the marmot must figure that such a predator as the wolf cannot run as fast uphill as it can downhill. When a hunter approaches a steep rocky slope in the mountains where he thinks a colony of marmots might live, he may try to locate a marmot by throwing a stick into the air. A marmot's curiosity is easily aroused, and it often whistles, in the relaxed way mentioned above, at an unusual though unfeared sight. By walking carefully, a man can often come within fifty yards of a marmot and shoot it.

Rock deadfalls, similar to those for wolverine (p. 95), are considered an almost foolproof way to catch marmots; a Nunamiut once remarked "marmot life is funny" because it is hard not to catch a marmot if a trapper plugs all the holes of a den but one and then sets a good rock deadfall. In the old days, another method was to dig a hole down to where a marmot was known to hibernate in the fall and then to fill it with loose soil. After freeze-up, the loose soil could easily be removed and a fat marmot had for the evening meal.

GRIZZLY BEAR. In the Brooks Range, the adult male grizzly bear weighs between 300 and 600 (or possibly 700) pounds. According to Rausch (1953: 95–107), the grizzly found in the Brooks Range must be considered conspecific with others in Alaska, including the grizzly occurring on the Kodiak, Afognak, and Shuyak islands, which reaches 1,200 and possibly 1,500 pounds and is one of the distinct subspecific races of grizzly bear.

In the Brooks Range, the grizzly is widely distributed. Many are found in the foothills north of the Brooks Range and even down on the coastal plains within fifteen or twenty miles of the coast (Bee and Hall 1956: 190). Grizzlies seem to avoid the actual coastline, possibly fearing polar bears. In the mountains, grizzlies roam for the most part in the valleys but are capable of climbing any mountain. At present there is little danger that the number of grizzlies in the Brooks Range will be reduced. The Nunamiut usually kill four to ten grizzlies a year but do not make concerted efforts to hunt the animal. Grizzlies range far and have no difficulty in avoiding regions where they are likely to be hunted.

Most grizzlies in the Brooks Range enter hibernation very late, about the last of October. Dens are usually dug high in the mountains. A few do not hibernate and Nunamiut have shot them in November and December. These bears are thought to have forgotten to dig holes in the fall and are forced to forage during the winter. One grizzly killed by a Nunamiut in December had suffered severe frostbite on the paws. I trailed a grizzly in late November of 1960 several miles. In each footprint of the left rear foot was a speck of blood. I found the animal's sleeping place of the night before where it had merely lain down for a few hours under a light cover of willows. No effort had been made to prepare a warm place to sleep. The grizzly's feces were very scanty, and it obviously was having trouble finding food. A few Nunamiut feel that a grizzly which forgets to den cannot survive the winter. One Nunamiut laughed that the grizzly has a nice wife in June and July when the animal mates, but in November and December after hibernation the mighty grizzly has no wife to make him any boots.

Grizzlies normally emerge from hibernation in the first part of April. At that time they are very fat and their pelage is excellent, usually a very dark brown. On rare occasions grizzlies have been known to leave their dens in early spring when it is still very cold and wintry. Any water the animal touches freezes in its fur. Such bears are greatly feared by the Nunamiut, since an icy coat prevents the penetration of small-caliber bullets.

During April and May, grizzlies are highly desired for their meat, fat, and hides, but during June and July grizzlies are poor and their hides are worthless. Nunamiut figure that grizzlies become thin and ragged because of the energy they expend in mating during the early summer. During August their condition begins to improve as they eat the abundant vegetation of late summer, fat ground squirrels, some fish, voles and other small animals, and carrion. During September and October Nunamiut greatly value any grizzlies they manage to kill for their excellent hides (though lighter in color than in the spring), their meat, and their large quantities of fat.

The Nunamiut talk a great deal about the grizzly. Fundamentally, the Nunamiut do not fear the animal, although the risks of

the moment are fully appreciated. The Brooks Range grizzly is a
very powerful animal, but it is not considered to be really intelligent. Grizzlies do have acute senses of hearing and smell, but they
appear to have little visual awareness, the most important criterion
of intelligence to a Nunamiut. If a grizzly takes a good look, it
seems to be able to see very well, but generally it does not bother
to look around very much until after it has been threatened. When
a grizzly is frightened, it looks all around, trying to locate the
source of danger, defecates a great deal (a source of uproarious
humor to a Nunamiut), and runs with great speed from the danger,
usually up the side of a mountain if it can.

The Nunamiut consider the grizzly bear an easy animal to hunt
as far as rudimentary skill is concerned. To kill a grizzly, nevertheless, is held to be a physical challenge and a source of egotistic
satisfaction. In the old days, various techniques were used. The
favorite method was for two or three men to locate a grizzly and
anger it by shooting arrows into it. When the grizzly charged, the
hunter in front of the others placed the butt of a 7- or 8-foot spear
firmly on the ground and let the bear run himself through as he
attempted to grab the man. A young hunter, it was said, could out-
maneuver a large, cumbersome bear by jumping to the side as the
bear lunged at him. Another trick was to bend down and run
underneath and between a bear's hind legs as it reared up to em-
brace the hunter. Another method sometimes used in the old days
was for two or three hunters to find a grizzly's den. After digging
away the cover at the entrance to the den, the men taunted the
bear until it attacked, when it was speared. Grizzlies were sometimes caught in caribou snares. In the old days, a trapper set snares
specifically for grizzlies, usually in the timber. A strong, bearded
seal rawhide snare was set where a grizzly might travel, and heavily
counterweighted with a spruce log.

Today, Nunamiut hunt grizzlies with rifles. A hunter tries to
approach as close as possible; he then shouts loudly so that if he
only wounds the bear, it will not run in his direction. A gun of any
caliber is considered suitable, even the .22 Hornet, although heavier
calibers such as the .243 Winchester and the .257 Roberts are preferred. Nunamiut often hunt with dogs, and this greatly reduces the
fear of grizzlies. With good dogs, a man feels fairly safe with only
a .22 Rimfire, although a heavier caliber would be desirable. Most
white hunters would probably consider the preceding sentence

foolhardy, but many white men hunt with oversized guns and rely on firepower rather than careful placing of shots and knowledge of the animal. Nunamiut men greatly enjoy hunting grizzlies and take real pleasure in killing them, aside from their economic value. Eskimos as well as whites love to tell bear stories.

Women and children are afraid of grizzlies and often speak in fear of the animal. One summer during my stay at Anaktuvuk Pass two women and one small child went several hundred yards out of the village to collect berries. Before long they saw a grizzly ambling their way. The women set up a terrific screaming and several men ran up to the berry patch, filling the air with rifle fire. The bear got away. For several days afterward the child was asked about her experience; she gained considerable prestige from her experience and will have an amazing tale to relate to her grandchildren.

Parents sometimes discipline their children by saying there is a grizzly outside. Many an evening I have seen rambunctious little children halt their play with surprising suddenness when some adult knocked on the floor and said in a hushed, tense voice, *Aklaq takanna!* (grizzly out there!). A parent is usually disciplining in earnest when he makes such a warning; an uncle, on the other hand, often makes such a warning in pure jest.

BLACK BEAR. Black bears range almost exclusively in the timbered regions of the Brooks Range where the Nunamiut encounter them only infrequently, mainly because black bears are usually in hibernation when Nunamiut travel in the south. A very few wander north of the timber and in June 1951 a Nunamiut killed a black bear in the mouth of Giant Creek, a mile or two south of the village of Anaktuvuk Pass (Rausch 1951:171). In the old days, the Nunamiut occasionally hunted black bears in the timber; a bow and arrow were considered adequate. Nunamiut sometimes set snares specifically for them. Most black bear meat and fat were obtained in trade from the Kobuk Eskimos. The hides were sometimes traded in and used for bedding as a "status symbol," reflecting the owner's position of wealth. The winter I lived at Anaktuvuk Pass, one family obtained some black bear meat and fat in trade from the south, and they took great pleasure in offering this rare treat to any visitors. Black bear meat is good eating.

The black bear, relatively speaking, is little known by the Nunamiut. It is considered quite a different animal from the grizzly, much less dangerous and much less likely to be aroused or angered.

The possible presence of black bears in the timber in the spring is not a source of fear to the Nunamiut.

MOOSE. Moose occur regularly in the timbered regions of the Brooks Range, the type of country where moose customarily range. Older informants' grandfathers did not remember moose north of the Brooks Range (that is, before 1870 or 1880). Their fathers (1880–1900) remarked that they killed an occasional moose in the Colville River valley and elsewhere. Since 1900, many older Nunamiut have observed moose, singly and in pairs, traveling up from the timber, through the Brooks Range, and down to the Colville River valley and other large river valleys as far east as the Canning River. In the heavily willowed areas of the Colville River, one may see dozens of moose from an airplane in an hour. The moose the Nunamiut observe traveling from south to north along the Anaktuvuk/John River and other valleys are young—frequently a young cow and her yearling calf. The willows in the upper reaches of a few valleys above the timber in the middle Brooks Range have been largely destroyed by moose. In late April of 1961, an older Eskimo and I traveled up the Kivik River from the Hunt Fork River to the base of Nahtuk Mountain in the middle Brooks Range. The upper part of this valley had recently been inhabited by moose. The biggest green willows we could find were year-old shoots. My companion referred to the valley as "dead," having been "killed" by moose. No fresh evidence of moose was to be seen. After moose had finished browsing in that valley, they moved on to another.

Some Nunamiut figure that moose have been moving north over the past fifty years because food resources in the south have become exhausted and the big moose chase the smaller ones out.

Although moose may be found in the northern Brooks Range during the fall, winter, and spring, they usually move from south to north in the summer. The Nunamiut take three to ten or more a year. A good-sized moose is traditionally equated with ten caribou in terms of meat. A few Nunamiut have trapped for a season in a region where they had to live on moose. After a month of nothing but moose, a hunter will look long and hard for mountain sheep or caribou for a change in diet.

Because the caribou is a migratory herd animal and is sometimes totally absent from a hunting region for months at a time, moose have sometimes saved many lives in the old days. When caribou became scarce and no other alternative presented itself, several hunters might travel for several days into the timber where moose customarily occur. It was a gamble; if no moose or only thin ones were found, the return trip could be exhausting without good food.

Some time ago [I was told], probably in the early 1880s, a small group of families was living at Tulugak Lake. It was late winter and there had been no caribou for some time. Hunger eventually forced people to eat their caribou skins and sealskin boots. Only essential clothing and bedding were retained. One or two older people died. One day a young hunter burst into camp and reported that he had found a dead moose recently killed by wolves. The remains of the moose were brought into camp and carefully rationed. That moose enabled the people to live until the ground squirrels came out of hibernation around the end of March. They then lived on ground squirrels until the ptarmigan migrated in April. Finally, much later than usual, the caribou surged north through the Brooks Range, enabling the people to resume a normal diet. Without the moose, most of them would have starved.

The Nunamiut do not regard the moose as a very intelligent animal. It is a huge, usually lone animal, easy to hunt. Only when a moose senses a man from a long way off or is already traveling away from him at a fair speed is a hunter likely to lose it. In the old days, a common way of killing a moose in the summer was for one hunter to drive it to another hunter or two. Several arrows were normally required to kill a moose. In the winter, hunting moose is more difficult because they can hear so well, better than most animals, it is said. If a man knows how to move quietly, he can kill moose. When a moose grows old, it can be called like a caribou, that is, by making a low, vocalized breathing noise.

MUSK OX. According to the data assembled by Bee and Hall (1956: 255), musk ox were numerous on the north slope of Alaska in the late 1700s and early 1800s. According to Nunamiut informants, there were three known places where musk ox were hunted: above Umiat, in the lower Anaktuvuk River, and in the Colville River—all north of the Brooks Range Mountains. Musk ox did not migrate and they were always fat. Their skins were highly valued by the Nunamiut for clothing, bedding, and shelter, and they were often hunted. It was very difficult for a lone hunter to kill musk ox with a bow and arrow. The technique they used was as follows. When several hunters spotted a small herd, they spread out as far as possible and released their dogs. In fright, the musk ox gathered in a circle with the bulls facing outward and the cows and calves in the protected center. They would not stampede, and the hunters could sometimes kill an enitre herd with spears. From what present-day Nunamiut have heard from their fathers and grandfathers, hunting pressure greatly reduced the numbers of musk ox during the early 1800s and drove many animals to the east. Hornaday and Brower (1911: 755) figure the last musk ox on the north slope of Alaska were killed in 1858. During the middle 1800s, Nunamiut heard there were musk ox near the Mackenzie River delta in Canada, and in the very late 1800s, an old Nunamiut, Jessie Ahgook, told of hunting musk ox farther east in the Coppermine River; he said the meat was very similar to that of mountain sheep.

Musk ox were not considered particularly intelligent. While their response to danger (gathering in a defensive circle) was effective against wolves, it was a help to a human hunter with dogs and spears. A herd was recognized to have a leader or dominant male. Sometimes, it was said, the leader would rip up a tussock from the tundra with his horn and toss it playfully to the others. I collected a fragment of a story about musk ox:

> A hunter observed a young girl during her first period of menstruation. When he went out to hunt musk ox, both the hunter and the musk ox turned into stone. The hunter's father was not turned into stone, however, and he beat the girl to death with a stick.

While only one living Nunamiut at Anaktuvuk Pass has seen a musk ox, many older Nunamiut are familiar with the animal, and Rausch (1951: 193) reported that when several Nunamiut saw the skull of a musk ox, they had no difficulty in recognizing it.

DALL SHEEP. Mountain sheep are distributed widely throughout the Brooks Range and occasionally in the foothills north of the mountains. Mountain sheep occur singly and in flocks, rarely exceeding twenty in number. They appear to be more common in the west than in the east (Bee and Hall 1956: 256). During the summer, mountain sheep remain very high in the Brooks Range, feeding on "sky meadows"—the highest patches of vegetation in the mountains. Lambs are born in late May and the first part of June and remain in the high pastures with their mothers, away from the threat of wolves. Also, according to the Nunamiut, mountain sheep avoid mosquitoes in the summer by staying high where there is likely to be a breeze. Skins are good in the summer, but the animals are not very fat.

During August, when the mosquitoes disappear, mountain sheep often graze in the lower parts of mountains, especially near salt licks and around the heads of creeks. In the late summer and early fall, sheep skins are excellent for mittens and other articles of clothing and the animals are heavy with fat. A few Nunamiut make concerted efforts to hunt them at this time of year but, because of the difficulty of sheep hunting generally, many hunters do not bother unless driven by hunger or a desire for prestige.

After rut in very late October and November, the rams lose most of their fat, but ewes often remain fairly fat all through the winter. During the late fall, winter, and spring, sheep graze wherever they can find food, but tend to keep to the upper parts of mountains. The wolf is a constant threat to mountain sheep but certainly does not menace sheep numbers (Rausch 1951: 193). Wolverines and golden eagles account for a few sheep kills among the younger animals but, except for local hunting pressure, mountain sheep seem to have a secure pasturage in the Brooks Range. On occasion a Nunamiut has seen a lone sheep cross a major valley from one mountain to another. Mountain sheep stay in lower areas only briefly, and Nunamiut think that they must feel wary so far from their home environment. In the spring the sheep are very thin and are hunted only when caribou are scarce and other meat is not readily available.

The Nunamiut consider mountain sheep to be more intelligent than moose or caribou. The sheep can see extremely well, almost, according to one Nunamiut, as if they had telescopes in their eyes. And sheep are constantly looking below them as if checking for wolves and man. They rarely look upward, however, a fact which good sheep hunters exploit. Mountain sheep cannot hear very well, especially in the summer when the wind and the water make so much noise anyway, and hunters of sheep worry more about being seen than being heard. Sometimes, asserted one experienced sheep hunter, a man has to walk five miles or more out of his way completely around another mountain to avoid being seen if he really wants to get sheep. The following personal incident illustrates the seeing ability of sheep as well as a means of evoking comments from informants.

One early afternoon in January I was walking up a small creek between two high mountains looking for sheep. As I came around a slow bend, the side of a mountain came into view. I scanned the mountain quickly and perceived a faint patch of yellow, different from the snow. I sat down with my telescope and brought it into focus. There were some nine sheep. I looked at them for a minute or two, letting my eye adjust itself to the telescope. Suddenly I was aware that the sheep were looking at me. Strange, I thought; at this distance they appeared to be two miles away. Checking a map later with an Eskimo who had once walked this creek confirmed my guess—they were just a few hundred yards over two miles away. I stood up to find a better place to sit. When I again brought them into view, the sheep had bolted about fifty yards. They paused for a moment and then quickly climbed to the top of the mountain and disappeared from sight. I told two or three Nunamiut how amazed I was that sheep could see so much better than humans, but they assured me that they had had similar experiences. One sheep hunter pointed out that sheep which had been shot at became very wary of man.

Sheep that have never seen man, on the other hand, can be approached to within bow and arrow range, especially in the summer. Above all, a sheep hunter must remember and constantly strive to get above sheep. Sheep have even been known to charge upward toward a hunter when he started shooting from above. Once a man places himself well, sheep are easy to kill.

Mountain sheep meat is considered by some Nunamiut to be the best meat in the world. A few white men agree. A month or two on lean meat, however, and some Nunamiut, especially younger people, have difficulty getting used to the rich, fat meat of sheep. A few older Nunamiut laughed about coastal Eskimos who had never eaten sheep. When they first tried it, they usually vomited. After a while, though, they usually became "worse" than Nunamiut in their craving for sheep. And among Eskimos, a craving can become a morbid obsession.

Mountain sheep are difficult to hunt generally, and they do not constitute a major part of the Nunamiut diet, especially today. In the old days, one or two isolated families have lived off sheep for the better part of the winter. A few Nunamiut shot mountain sheep with bows and arrows, but snares were more reliable if a family wanted to remain in a sheep area for some time. By using snares, set in the fashion described for caribou, the hunter avoided being seen by sheep and thus frightening them away. Sheep would continue to graze in the same region for months. In the old days, a few dogs were trained to help a party of men drive a flock of sheep over a cliff. A gun is a sure way to kill several sheep in a hurry, but continued use of guns in one region soon frightens the remaining sheep away. Today, two or three Nunamiut still make real efforts to hunt sheep, especially in August and September, and mountain sheep, along with moose and ptarmigan, should be considered an important food supplement and, in rare instances, a lifesaver.

Dogs

The subject of dogs among the Nunamiut would make a book in itself. Here I will try only to explain what the Nunamiut think of their dogs and to give some notion of their significance for the existence of these Eskimos.

Unlike most mammals that Nunamiut observe, the females of dogs come into heat at any time in the year. There is some effort to breed selectively, but extreme care is not taken. The Nunamiut speak of crossbreeding dogs with wolves in the old days, and the family I lived with said that in 1957 or 1958 one of their bitches in heat ran off with a wolf for three days. The family had kept one of the pups and it did appear to be half wolf. The eyes had a different slant and its coat, particularly along the back, looked in color and form like a gray wolf's.

From three to as many as fourteen pups are born in one litter; Nunamiut feel that a bitch can care best for four to six pups. Women are responsible for raising the pups. In the winter a caribou skin is propped up for protection against the wind and a piece of caribou skin is even put down for a floor. In the old days, and until a decade ago, a bitch with pups was often allowed in the house. Training began very early; when a pup started to eat the wrong food it was beaten and spoken to harshly. Severe beating is very rare. Ideally a young pup should be fed some meat and a little meat broth two or three times a day. If pups are fed only once a day, they will develop voracious appetites and require more meat to keep them fat when they became adult.

When a dog is a year old it is put to work, but it does not reach its prime until its third year. A dog is usually good for eight to ten or even more years if well fed and cared for; when it becomes a burden on a household it is shot.

In the old days, dogs were larger than they are today. The reason given for this is that more care used to be given in the raising of pups. The Nunamiut have traded dogs in from Siberia, which were said to be very large, and spotted dogs from the Kobuk Eskimos. Gray is the most preferred color, since it blends in well with the countryside; white is valued for the same reason. Black dogs are more noticeable and are more likely to frighten game.

Dogs are very highly valued as economic assets. A man is often judged by the number, power, endurance, and size of his dogs. Today, from six to ten dogs are tandem hitched in pairs to one sled. In the old days from one to six dogs were hitched alternately along a single tow line. A man, or more commonly, a woman, led the dogs, often helping by pulling on a trace. Those were the tough days, they say. Today the lead dogs are half-heartedly, but sometimes carefully, trained.

In the winter a man and dogs can cover amazing distances with heavy loads. The longest trip I ever took was with a 65-year-old man. He drove one sled with eight dogs loaded with 300 pounds, and I drove another with six dogs and 250 pounds, 50 miles in one day. Good dogs are really appreciated, and one learns how exasperating lazy dogs can be. The spring I lived at Anaktuvuk Pass one man with no load and a team of 14 dogs traveled over 100 miles, with no stop longer than a break for tea, in less than 24 hours. Another Eskimo and I with 13 dogs sledded over 1,500 pounds of meat for 1,000 yards. With such mobility, endurance, and power, it can readily be seen how crucial dogs are to the Nunamiut way of life. In the winter they contribute over 90 per cent of the power used for transportation of goods and about 50 per cent of the effort for traveling (this latter figure varies a great deal; some hunters walk extensively, others tend to use dogs whenever possible).

In the summer, the Nunamiut use their dogs far more than do most maritime Eskimos. By making a saddlebag or dog pack from bull caribou hide, meat and camping equipment are easily trans-

ported over the treeless tundra. A travois was never used and probably would not be practical in the terrain. A dog can pack 50
pounds or more for a short distance, say a mile or two, but should
not be made to carry 30 pounds or more for a whole day over a
20- or 25-mile trail. Although this is much less than a winter sled
load, summer travel by dog pack still permits a great deal of mobility, but a hunter rarely can bring home more than 200 pounds
of meat from a long trip. Meat can be scarce toward the end of
the summer and dogs may become thin. If a thin dog is forced to
carry a heavy dog pack, he will be a poor sled dog the coming winter. Nunamiut are very aware that working a dog too hard for a
while renders it weaker for later use. Still it is difficult to balance
one's needs, and the exigencies of the day or season often leave a
man no choice but to overwork his dogs.

In the early 1800s when Nunamiut used to hunt musk ox, dogs
were used to help round them up and force them into a defensive
circle. Also in the old days, a few good dogs were trained to help
drive mountain sheep over cliffs. As far as I can determine, dogs
were never used for herding caribou in any way. But this use of
dogs for rounding up sheep and musk ox suggests one way in which
the domestication of reindeer in the Old World could have begun.
Man and dogs can learn to work very closely together, but it remains exceedingly difficult to imagine that caribou could become
domesticated in the Brooks Range.

A dog is named early and learns to respond to its name quickly.
Many of the names given to dogs are specifically dog names and
are passed down "bilaterally" from forebears. Sometimes dogs are
given human names, especially when a childless couple raises and
keeps them in the house.

As a boy approaches his middle and late teens he gradually
acquires the use of some of his parents' dogs and the partial responsibility of tending them. Over time, a young man comes to
regard several of them as his own by virtue of his management of
them and his contribution generally to the household. When he
leaves the parental home upon marriage, it is usually agreed that
he take some of the dogs he has used. He also frequently assumes
joint responsibility and ownership of the dogs presented to the new
couple by the wife's parents. There are no invariable rules about
these matters, and they are usually determined by the needs and
economic well-being of the households involved.

At death, a person's spouse has first claim on the deceased's rights in the dogs, that is if the deceased is not too young, in which case the deceased's parents or siblings may claim the dogs. The surviving spouse may be very old, of course, and incapable of actually using the dogs himself; if so, the deceased's sons and daughters and their families may receive the dogs. Co-residence and common locality often determine which children receive most of the dogs, although theoretically each child has an equal claim unless the deceased specified otherwise before he died.

Contrary to some popular opinion, an Eskimo does not have an entirely mechanistic or utilitarian attitude toward his dogs. One rarely sees the petting and fondling of dogs that occur among white men, but I often saw Nunamiut men in their sixties tap dogs on the top of the muzzle out of affection. The family I was living with had one especially good-natured dog. He never chewed things up, never growled or became angry or jealous, and always pulled hard on his harness. The members of the family often spoke of this dog in very affectionate terms and they treated him well. He was getting on in years, and in the spring of 1961 he had to be shot. The younger children were very sad, although they did not cry. The older members commented on the dog's death but did not seem remorseful.

On the other hand, many Nunamiut, men and women alike, take out their feelings of frustration and aggression on dogs by speaking harshly to them and beating them, sometimes for little reason. Some Nunamiut are quite aware that dogs function as a limited psychological escape valve. I watched one Nunamiut beat his dogs with great energy and extreme white man's profanity (which he only vaguely understood) several times during a day's travel and then brag to me that night that he only beat his dogs with a willow stick or a rope whip, and not with a board or heavy stick like someone else we knew. Young men often brag about how they prevented their dogs from chasing caribou, with powerful verbal threats and frenzied lashing with light whips or willow branches.

A man is sometimes judged by his dogs in other ways. A team that a man has trained and driven for some time is said to reflect his personality. If a man is gruff, hard-spoken, and mean, his dogs are vicious and likely to fight and snap at people. A man who is quieter and more industrious has mild-mannered but hard-pulling dogs. Dogs provide an excellent means of expressing egotism; men brag a great deal about the speed and endurance of their dogs, always claiming to be able to out-travel everyone else. Rather than saying he is better than somebody else, which can breed ill-feeling, a person merely says his dogs are better than someone else's.

Dogs, interestingly enough, are not thought to have iñua. There are a few stories about dogs. The following one is considered highly improbable by informants.

> One time, an old bitch had four male pups, one of which was a human being. The three dog-pups had faces like human beings, and the man-pup had a face like a dog. The bitch and her offspring traveled to Point Barrow. The man-pup married an Eskimo, returned to the mountains, and had several children. The children married Indians and returned to Point Barrow.

Dogs do not appear to play much of a supernatural role. They are generally considered to be dirty, and people rarely touch them any more than necessary. Dog feces are considered to be one of the most disgusting substances in existence. I once saw a woman cutting some thawed meat. Some dog feces had been frozen with the carcass and when she touched and smelled them, she retched violently several times.

In some years, the Nunamiut have great difficulty with rabies and distemper. The year I lived in Anaktuvuk Pass, over a fourth of the dogs died, either from severe distemper, some nonviolent form of rabies, or both. Most of the dogs that survived were greatly weakened. Life became difficult with reduced and weakened dog teams. Hauling heavy loads of meat and firewood turned into arduous tasks. In the memory of older Nunamiut, every now and then fatal epidemics among the dogs have occurred. A few always seemed to survive, and in a year or two a man could build his team up again; but meanwhile mobility was reduced, and people had to pull and push their sleds themselves until new dogs were born and trained.

Without the dog, Nunamiut life could not exist as it does today or has in the past; households could not stay together in large encampments for more than a few days, if at all. Only caribou occur in large enough numbers to support more than a very few isolated

families in the Brooks Range, and caribou range over great distances during the year. Since so many caribou have to be killed
so far from any one encampment, only the transportation provided
by dogs permits the continued existence of Nunamiut society.
Without them, families would be forced to split up and forage on
all the elements of the fauna and flora in order to eke out the
barest living; the only alternative would be to move out of the
Brooks Range.

9. The Caribou

Aᴄᴄᴏʀᴅɪɴɢ to Hall and Kelson (1959: 1017–20), the caribou that occur in northern Alaska are classified as *Rangifer tarandus stonei,* barren-ground caribou, which is one of perhaps 23 or more subspecies that have been established for *R. tarandus.* In the past, a few persons have maintained that Old World reindeer and New World caribou constitute two species—*R. tarandus* and *R. arcticus* respectively, with several subspecies each. Now such biologists as Rausch, Hall, Ellerman, and others maintain that *R. tarandus* is one holarctic species and that a separate specific term, *R. arcticus,* for the New World varieties, is invalid.

One way of determining a species, according to many biologists, is to investigate the possibility of obtaining offspring from the hybrids which result from the crossbreeding of the two varieties in question. If 10 or 15 per cent or more of the hybrids are sterile, then it is likely that they are of two species. At present the data are insufficient for complete certainty on this basis about the status of caribou and reindeer.

Palmer (1934: 36) reports that caribou and reindeer can be very easily crossed. He states further: "Developing a larger and stronger animal through transmission of the rangier size and stronger bone of the caribou to the reindeer should result not only in a heavier meat producer but also in an animal that will be a better breeder, more rugged and vigorous, and better able to shift for itself on the range." While this statement is not conclusive, it does indicate that experiments were conducted in the 1920s and 1930s, with a suggestion that the hybrids of reindeer and caribou are "good breeders." In what percentage of the cases this is true, we do not know.

The Nunamiut are fully aware of the differences in size, structure, and appearance between wild caribou and domestic reindeer, and they have different names for them.

Rangifer is the genus including caribou and reindeer generally, a member of the family Cervidae (deer), of the superfamily Cervoidae, of the suborder Ruminantia (ruminants), of the order Artiodactyla (even-toed ungulates). In Alaska and the western Yukon, *R. tarandus stonei* appear to migrate in two or three major herds, back and forth through the Brooks Range from the north slope of Alaska to the southern Brooks Range and beyond. The southern range of these herds extends in some cases to the northern edge of the Yukon Flats, and the northern range to the Arctic coast. In earlier decades there were caribou in most of Alaska, but today the great majority of caribou occur only in northern Alaska.

These terms are in common usage among white men for caribou: calf (male and female), yearling (male and female), young bull (immature and just mature), bull, and cow.

The following are the common terms among Nunamiut:

tuttu, (one) caribou, male or female

tuttuk, two caribou

tuttut, three or more caribou

tuttugaruitch, a herd of caribou (from ten to several hundred)

tuttupauragatat, a huge number of caribou (as during a migration)

ivilauq, a caribou fetus, male or female

nogaq, a calf, male or female

shiokalaq, a calf, male or female, in the last part of its first year (after it separates from its mother) and the first part of its second year (the second summer after it is born)

aŋayukliakruq, a yearling (a male or female caribou from its second summer to the following spring)

nukatagaq, a general term for young bulls

nukatagauraq, a young bull from the summer following the spring when it ceases to be an aŋayukliakruq

nukatagaluq, a young bull older and larger than a nukatagauraq

nukatagaq, generally a young bull, but specifically larger and older than a nukatagaluq

nukatagaruaq, a large young bull, just smaller than a mature bull

pagniq, a mature bull (the term for bull may be modified by a number of suffixes indicating small mature bull, large mature bull, etc.)

pagnigoichiaq, an old bull

pagnigoichauraq, a very old, skinny bull (bulls are thought to live longer than cows; some Nunamiut think that bulls may live 30 years or more)

kolavauraq, a young cow; a female caribou in the spring when it ceases to be an aŋayukliakruq and before it first conceives (in unusual cases a female caribou may conceive during its second year, but generally not until a year later)

kolavaq, a cow (if a female caribou does conceive in its second year, it is theoretically a kolavaq; a female caribou is not called a kolavaq until

it does begin to bear young or attains the age at which most female
  begin to bear young, i.e. the third year)
kolavagoichiaq, an old cow, thought to be about 20 years old or more
kolavagoichauraq, a very old, skinny cow
tikitagauraq, an odd, shriveled up, stunted caribou of either sex

Each of these terms can be greatly modified by suffixation, infixation, and description.

The caribou is a large, heavily-built deer. It is considerably smaller than an elk but larger than a mule deer. A mature, fat bull (in September) weighs as much as 350 pounds live and as little as 280 pounds live when it is thin (February). Woodland bull caribou in British Columbia have been reported to weigh 600 pounds live. A mature, fat, not pregnant cow weighs between 150 and 220 pounds live. A one-day old calf weighs from 9 to 16 pounds, 18 to 30 pounds in two weeks, and by six months anywhere from 60 to 120 pounds. Young bulls have longer, thicker necks and longer legs than mature cows, but the two are easily confused when observed from a distance.

The pelage of caribou ranges from fairly dark brown in the late summer to light tan or buff in the late winter. The hair is much longer in winter than in summer; on the underside of the neck it is very long and yellowish-white in color, as is most of the underside of the body.

Semipalmated antlers occur in both male and female, but antlers of the male are much heavier and take the brunt of the fighting during rut. For example, the brow tine in the male is large and well developed (see quote below); in the female it is only a prong, or slightly developed. Murie (1935: 17–18) aptly characterized the antlers as follows:

> Caribou antlers are distinctly unlike those of other members of the deer family. Those of the full-grown buck are generally composed of two heavy main beams, each leading back from the forehead almost in a line with the rostrum, then sweeping upward with a more or less noticeable angle nearly half its length and curving forward near the tip; a pair of brow tines, either one or both flattened into a broad vertical "shovel," often reaching forward nearly to the nose; a pair of bez-tines, longer than the brow tines, and bearing lesser points near the tip; usually a small point or back tine at the posterior

angle of each main beam; and near the tip of the main beam, usually palmated, a series of points projecting from the upper edge.

The two even hooves of each foot of the caribou are large and broad, with the dewclaws often touching the ground or snow. On ice, the dewclaws rarely touch. Each hoof is rimmed, enabling a caribou to maintain excellent footing on ice, rocks, or other difficult surfaces, yet is broad enough, and slightly concave, to enable the animal to travel across the wet summer tundra. Although susceptible to hoof rot and occasional sprains in sharp rocks and crevices, the hooves of caribou may be considered a very functional adaptation to Arctic terrain.

Their sight is not remarkably good, but with good light against a background of snow, a caribou can see a man walking a mile away. Both scent and hearing are acute; caribou perhaps rely more on scent than on hearing in sensing danger.

The Nunamiut described an ability of caribou to sense the trails of animals and man which I have not encountered in the literature. In the winter, but not in the summer, a caribou is said to be able to sense the presence of a man's or other animal's footprint with its feet. It will stop, look at the ground, and sniff. One informant attributed this sensitivity to the caribou's feet themselves. It could be that, as with any experienced man, the packed trail or even one footstep of a heavy animal can be sensed by the difference in the feel between normal and disturbed snow conditions.

The general size, fatness, condition of skin and pelage, and "grade" of meat are the physical conditions of caribou that determine their desirability for Nunamiut. In time of hunger, of course, any animal that can be taken is taken, but the more meat and fat the better. Here, let us assume that there is no crisis of hunger.

The larger the caribou, the more it is desired except when the consideration of skin, rut, or fatness is paramount. The size of caribou may be determined from the terminology given above.

In large young bulls and mature bulls, the fat cycle is as follows. During the early summer after a long winter and the northward migration, bulls are rarely fat. Toward the end of the summer (August) they begin to accumulate fat, noticeably along the back, on the rear of the hindquarters, around the large intestine and some other internal structures (kidneys, peritoneum, etc.), which reaches a peak in September. As rut begins in late September and October the fat gradually diminishes. During the initial stages of rut, the fat is still edible and even desired by some people for the slight flavor of the rut. By the end of rut, what little fat is left is stinkingly inedible. During the months of November, December, and January, bulls are usually very skinny and shot only for their excellent skins and large quantity of meat. In February they begin to fatten a little, but not as in the fall. During the early spring (March, April, and the first part of May), bull caribou are more or less fat and highly desired. By late spring and early summer, most of their fat seems to wear off, perhaps because of the traveling during migration.

The cows, after giving birth and during the summer while nursing, are very thin. Sometimes even the bone marrow is inedible. During the fall they begin to fatten, as their calves have ceased to nurse and the strain of traveling comes to an end. When forage is readily available, cows are usually fat all through the winter and are highly sought by hunters. Older Nunamiut sometimes complain of younger hunters' lack of ability in winter to distinguish between a fat mature cow and a skinny young bull. Caribou are very sensitive in the dead of winter, and a person rarely has a chance to shoot more than four or five animals in a small herd. In the spring the cows lose fat as the fetus grows. The exertion of spring migration while carrying a large fetus reduces a cow's fat even more. Unpregnant cows in the spring during the early stages of migration are sometimes very fat.

Calves, yearlings, very young cows and bulls, very old cows and bulls, and stunted or diseased caribou are very rarely fat in any season. The tongue of any caribou in any condition is said always to have enough fat for one good meal.

In the summer, after the winter fur has been shed and the warble flies have left, all caribou are desired for their skins. Summer skins are thin and the hair is short and dark. They are excellent for most articles of clothing and other small items. Calf skins especially are desired for parkas; cow skins for socks, mittens, and pants; and bull skins for boots and other moderately heavy items.

In the fall, skins become thicker and the hair longer. Early fall skins of all kinds may be used as summer skins are. Sometimes a woman clips the fur if it is a little heavy for clothing.

By winter, caribou skins are thick and the hair is very long. Calf skins in the winter are of little use. Winter cow skins are satisfactory for making trousers and for parts of shelter. Winter bull skins are highly valued for bedding, kayaks, and other heavy items.

After late February or early March, when the larvae of the mature warble fly leave marks and holes on the skin and the long winter hair starts to shed, all skins are considered worthless. They can be used to lay over the top of a pile of meat or on the door of a permafrost cellar, but otherwise are of little use. The skin of a fetus in the later stages of pregnancy is very thin and was formerly used for underwear and other delicate items. Fetus skins are not used today.

Since they eat enormous quantities of meat, Nunamiut like to have it as good as possible. Almost any meat can be made edible, but the following comments indicate Nunamiut preferences for the condition of meat in different caribou.

ivilaut: caribou fetuses, are greatly relished by most Nunamiut, especially by young children. Some of the Nunamiut in their late teens and twenties, who have eaten too many fetuses when they were young, do not care for them, and refer to them as *migiaganaktoq* (it can, or will, be vomited). After a few years, most people come to like them again. Boiled caribou fetus meat is soft and white, similar to chicken.

nogaitch: calf heads are considered good eating, but the texture of the rest of the meat is softer than the meat of more mature animals and is not eaten unless nothing else is available. A few people enjoy eating soft calf meat for a change, but otherwise feed it to the dogs.

shiokalut: are essentially calves and are not desired when larger caribou are available. The meat is still soft, and the animal has very little if any fat.

aŋayukliakrut: yearlings are desired only if they are fat, which is rarely the case. Yearling meat is no longer soft, and the texture is almost like that of a mature caribou. When meat and skins are plentiful, yearlings are not taken.

nukatagaurat: a very young bull has a little fat in the fall, and the meat is almost like mature caribou. Very young bulls are not taken when other animals are available.

nukatagalut and *nukatagat:* in the fall, young bulls are fatter than very young bulls and are sometimes taken. The meat is almost as good as that of mature bulls.

nukatagaruat: the meat and fat of large young bulls are almost the same as of mature bulls.

pagnigitch: many Nunamiut consider good bull caribou meat (in the fall and the early and middle spring) to be the best eating there is. Meat from the breastbone and ribs especially is liked, followed by the head, vertebrae, pelvis, kidney, heart, abdominal muscles and, last on the list, "steaks and roasts"—the tenderloin, shoulder, and hindquarters. When bull caribou are thin, they tend to be tough, and other meat is preferred. Although some people like the slight tinge of early rut in their meat, toward the end of rut, the meat smells so that only very hungry dogs and ravens will eat it. When mating season is over, about the first of November, the meat loses the odor of rut and becomes edible. In spring (and sometimes fall) bull intestines are cleaned and boiled to make chitterlings, which came to be my favorite fat. A few young Nunamiut do not like the delicacy, partly because they feel that white men think it is disgusting. Little do they know.

kolavat: in the summer, the scrawny meat of cow caribou is used only for dog food, but in the late fall and throughout the winter, cows are greatly desired for their excellent meat and fat. A few Nunamiut like cow better than bull. In the late spring, a cow is more desired for its fetus than for its meat.

A brief list of terms for the parts of the caribou may be useful. I have tried only to indicate the larger features, particularly the ones that are mentioned frequently. These anatomical terms apply also to the human body, except those marked with an asterisk.

amiq, skin
aqaagoq, stomach
aqaaviñiq, muscles covering the abdomen
auq, blood
auqquñ or *augavik,* blood vessels
iŋaluat, intestines
iri, eye
ishigaq, foot
ivalu, back sinew
kassiq, shoulder
kiguuñ, tooth
kiŋaq, nose
kiiŋaq, face
koyapikquq, backbone
kuchik, pelvis
kunivauŋ, diaphragm

*mamauñ, udder
mapsha, pancreas
*mitqoq, hair or fur
*mumiq, back leg
*negaruk, antlers
nigaviq, thigh
niqi, meat, or muscle generally
niqipiaq, "real" meat, or muscle generally
niuq, leg
nuukik, tendon, ligament, and cartilage
oqaaq, tongue
pamiok or *pamialuk,* tail (also human coccyx)
patiq, bone marrow
puvuk, lungs

302 THE NUNAMIUT ESKIMOS

qaqishaq, brain
**qaunaq*, fat, i.e. fat that congeals, such as the back fat of a caribou
**qovulugoq*, dewclaws
qonashiñiq, neck (also, as my first name is "Nick," Qonashiñiq came to be one of my nicknames)
qukik, hoof (also human fingernail)
saqigaq, breastbone
shaaqoq, generally, the front part of the body

shauniq, bone
shiuñ, ears
taaqtuq, kidney
talliq, front leg (also human arm)
tiŋuq, liver
tulimaaq, rib
**tunnuq*, fat, a general term for animal fat
uuliutiq, tenderloin
uumañ, heart

Population and Migration

Throughout the literature on caribou there are a great many fragmentary, often confusing, and often contradictory statements about the population and distribution of caribou in northern Alaska. Population estimates range from 100,000 to 1,200,000 with the more credible ones ranging between 300,000 and 600,000.

Rausch (1953: 139–40) thinks that the caribou in northern Alaska occur in three separate herds: one migrates back and forth from the Kobuk and Noatak river territory, through the Brooks Range, to the upper Kuk, Utukok, and Kokolik river areas. The second herd seems to migrate through the central Brooks Range (Killik, Anaktuvuk/John, and other valleys), wintering in the headwaters of the Kobuk, Koyukuk, and Chandalar rivers; passing through the Brooks Range in the spring, this herd summers east and west of the Colville River. The third herd appears to migrate northwest–southeast, wintering along the Porcupine and lower Chandalar rivers, and summering in and around the Romanzof mountains.

In spite of a general pattern in distribution and migration, caribou have been observed north of, south of, and in the Brooks Range in all seasons of the year. Rausch's three herds of Alaskan barren-ground caribou is best thought of as a tentative hypothesis, in the light of which variations in caribou migration may be considered. Membership in these herds is most likely very fluid; in the past hundred years or more any one of the herds may have been absorbed into another herd, greatly depleted, or shifted hundreds of miles to another region.

Nunamiut hunters observe only isolated segments of caribou migrations. As a result, most of them have little perspective and can only say that sometimes caribou migrate and sometimes not, sometimes through this valley and sometimes through that, sometimes early and sometimes late. A very few older, more reflective Nunamiut have observed and hunted caribou for decades and have developed an overall conception of their migration. These Eskimos point out that, although there is a great deal of variation, there appears to be a general pattern of migration in the Brooks Range.

In the very late spring and early summer (June and July), most of the caribou are on the north slope, generally west of Anaktuvuk Pass. A few big bulls remain in the timber of the middle and southern Brooks Range throughout the summer. In July and the early part of August, when the mosquitoes are at their worst, many caribou move from the north slope to the northernmost mountains west of Anaktuvuk Pass, and others travel north to the Arctic coast, where there are fewer mosquitoes. In late August and early September young ice begins to form on the innumerable puddles and rivulets in the flat tundra of the northern part of the north slope. When a caribou breaks through the thin ice, the water is very chilling and painful to its feet. As the formation of young ice creeps from north to south, most of the caribou leave the flat regions of the north slope and head for the low foothills where footing is better. After freeze-up, the flat tundra becomes solid and caribou can again walk there in comfort.

By late August, or sometimes in early September, dependent on the weather, thousands of caribou have gathered north of the mountains. They never stay very long just north of the Brooks Range because, according to one informant, of the changing sun. In the middle of a clear day, caribou avoid traveling in order not to become overheated. When the sun is low, or when the sky is overcast, they are able to travel comfortably. During September, most of the caribou pass through the valleys of the Brooks Range to the southern part of the range and beyond. Many small herds may migrate as late as October, and a few stragglers are known to drift south as late as December. A few small herds spend the entire winter on the north slope.

According to the Nunamiut, the caribou used to migrate south of the Kobuk and Selawik rivers and even south beyond the Kotzebue area. Older Nunamiut observers of caribou now think that caribou never travel south of the Selawik River, and that most of them probably remain north of the Kobuk River in the winter.

During the winter months, caribou feed in small groups, usually above the timber. The wind blows the snow away from the exposed mountainsides making it easier for the animals to paw at the lichens and grasses. The snow piles up in the timbered river bottoms, and it is generally colder than up in the mountains. Wolves often travel along rivers, another reason why caribou tend to remain high in the mountains. On relatively warm days, caribou may descend to a river for a short time or, in traveling from one group of mountains to another, may have to cross rivers; otherwise they keep to the higher parts of their range. Most of them wander around the high country of the southern Brooks Range and beyond, but a few caribou find pockets in the northern Brooks Range which are havens from the wind and have enough lichens, sedges, mosses, and grasses to attract a number of them. In January 1961, I observed thirty caribou feeding on the low rolling hills along the major east branch of Itigamalukpuk Creek at 68° 17′ north latitude, 151° 15′ west longitude. And flying over the north slope in winter, one occasionally sees small groups of them feeding. Nunamiut say that caribou living on the north slope during winter are rarely fat.

During the winter months when caribou are feeding in small groups, they move around in the countryside in ways that are considered unpredictable by the Nunamiut. Wolves, when numerous, are a major factor in the winter movements of caribou, but less so during migration. A pack of five or six wolves may cause two or three hundred caribou to move a hundred miles or more. Man, too, in his hunting, causes caribou to move around, although hunting pressure is usually more localized.

During February in the southern Brooks Range and beyond, the small groups of wandering caribou come together to form larger and larger groups, for as yet unknown reasons. Finally in March, a slow steady migration to the north begins. The herds in spring migration are smaller and more drawn out than in the fall. Cows, near yearlings, and young bulls follow. By the first of May most of the cows and young bulls are on the north slope. During May, several herds of as many as 300 big bulls travel north through the main valleys, while a few remain behind to spend the summer in the timber. In August, small herds of big bulls travel from the timber to the north slope.

The routes of migration traveled by caribou according to the

Nunamiut are as follows, with the Anaktuvuk/John River valley as a point of reference. From the Anaktuvuk/John valley to the west, the Chandler, Okokmilaga, Killik/Alatna, Nigu or Alashuk rivers, and Howard Pass and the Akutuk and Niyoktun valleys (both within 30 miles west of Howard Pass), serve as migration routes. An older Nunamiut indicated that valleys farther west might also be used as migration routes, but he had never been there. From the Anaktuvuk/John River valley east, the Shanin/North Fork (of the Koyukuk), Ulu (Itkillik), and the headwaters of the Sagavanirktok and Ivishak to the headwaters of the Chandalar River serve as migration routes. The Canning River is possibly to be included, but east of the Canning, the migration assumes a different pattern: caribou travel in a more northwest to southeast direction, following the coast north of the Brooks Range front at times. The Nunamiut I talked with knew very little about caribou east of the Canning River. A few have hunted caribou south of Barter Island and Herschel Island, and north of the upper Yukon within Alaskan territory, but I was not able to evoke any real conception about the nature of eastern migration.

Theories for the cause of caribou migration include need for shelter, need to drop calves on the tundra instead of in timber and deep snow, reaction to insects, response to hormone secretion, search for food, and instinct. According to the Nunamiut, the caribou leave the north slope during the early stages of freeze-up because of the thin ice forming over the puddles and creeks. They try to get away from the discomfort caused by breaking through the thin ice, and the foothills of the Brooks Range provide better ground for walking. In response to questions why the caribou moved north in the spring, I could obtain no answer. A few Nunamiut figured that caribou migrate from the south by force of habit, or maybe, like people, "had a lot of fun" coming together and traveling in large groups. Maybe, it was said by one Nunamiut, caribou migrate in order to find better food. Generally, however, informants stated that, although they had a good explanation for the southward migration, they had none for the northward migration.

It bears repeating that while many Nunamiut, especially older ones, have an idea how caribou normally migrate, they are aware of seemingly inexplicable aberrations. Because observation is limited, many Nunamiut simply admit that they can know only so much about the movements of caribou. When they do appear, hunters kill as many animals as possible, but the older people know that they may have to rely on other members of the fauna to tide them over in times of stress.

Rut

When a male caribou reaches its fourth year (nukatagaluq), it is able to procreate. Informants did not know if a male caribou in its third year (nukatagauraq) could procreate, but knew that it could at least "have fun" in mounting other caribou. Sexual connection for nukatagaurat, however, is not established. The large, mature bulls drive nukatagalut, nukatagat, and even nukatagaruat (large young bulls) away from the females. These young bulls sometimes put up a strong fight, but usually get the worst of it, receiving gashes on the neck, back, and sides. Even at the age of 6 or 7 years, a bull is likely to be driven away by the stronger, more mature bulls. Mature bulls spar constantly, but hard fighting is rare.

As early as the first part of September, the testicles of male caribou begin to swell and remain swollen for almost two months. The actual period of mating, however, appears to last only for two or three weeks in the last part of October and very early November. During this time, a bull may mate as many as six times in one day, "if it is lucky." During the rut, bulls run around, "sweat," eat very little food, but swallow a great deal of snow. By the first of November, when rut is over, bulls have lost most of the fat they gained during the summer. Nukatagalut especially become very skinny, with all their chasing around and fighting in vain.

Calving

Calves are dropped on the north slope in the last part of May and the very early part of June. Single births are most common. A few Nunamiut have heard of twin births, but never a triple. About three fourths of the mature cows appear to calve. Nunamiut estimate that the average healthy cow gives birth to about twenty calves during its lifetime. Soon after a newborn calf is dry, it can walk and trot after its mother, and a man can easily catch one, but within a very few days a calf can outrun a man. Should a cow be separated from its calf for a short period of time, it seems to be able to find and recognize its calf with no difficulty. When a cow and calf are pursued by a man, wolf, or other predator, they often try to hide or camouflage themselves by standing motionless in a willow patch. A calf will frequently obey its mother to the death.

In late August 1960, when I first started hunting calves for clothing, two or three Nunamiut told me to shoot the mother first, since her skin was also good, and then kill the calf. Even if killing the mother frightened the calf away, before long it would return, giving the hunter another chance. During August 1960 I was once several hundred yards above a small herd. An older Nunamiut was in position and shot several cows and calves as they passed by on their way south. One cow–calf pair stopped to hide in a willow patch. The Nunamiut was hunting with a .22 Rimfire so as to damage the skins as little as possible. He walked slowly toward the cow and calf but they stood motionless. He shot the mother twice, and the calf did not move; he then shot the calf.

When calves are born, cows are spread out over the north slope in small groups. When the calves are able to walk easily behind their mothers, larger groups are formed. Before calves are a month old, they are traveling extensively with the herds over the north slope in search of forage. At the age of three months or so, a calf is already supplementing its diet with grasses, lichens, and sedges; they are probably weaned in September or, by the latest, in October; calves follow their mothers for almost a year, until the latter are about ready to give birth again.

Relationship to the Environment

In their southward migration through the Brooks Range, caribou travel, as one would suspect, by way of the major, U-shaped valleys transecting the Brooks Range from north to south. When frightened, however, a herd or part of a herd does not hesitate to ascend a mountain rising 2,000 or 3,000 feet from the valley floor, and then, a mile or two later, descend. In the spring of 1961 I watched a herd of 300 caribou descend in half an hour from the top of a mountain to the valley floor 3,000 feet below, down a mountainside and talus slope averaging about 45°. During migration, and at any other time, a hunter must constantly keep his eyes open for the appearance of caribou anywhere.

During the winter, caribou are usually found in small groups feeding in high, rolling terrain—seldom on the valley floor. In the summer they are sometimes found high in the mountains but are more likely to be seen in lower country and, of course, on the north slope. In winter or summer, during migration or quiescent periods of feeding, when they are frightened they almost always run away from and up from the source of danger. Nunamiut hunters are very cognizant of this response of the caribou and make the most of it. A good hunter takes great care to work his way around and above a feeding herd or to place himself just above the probable line of travel of a moving herd. A few good hunters often prefer to hunt alone because they can avoid the mistakes of others. Most hunters, however, prefer to hunt in groups of two or three. If possible, the best marksman tries to place himself above the herd and let the other hunters drive the herd toward him. Sometimes the other hunters can predict where the caribou will run when they are frightened a second time.

Wherever caribou travel, they mark the land. A few caribou will make little impression on the land except when crossing a loose talus slope, but in numbers, especially during migration, caribou plow the ground up. In a wet area, the mud soon becomes knee deep; in a swath several hundred feet wide, not a square inch is spared. In crossing a loose talus slope, a herd of caribou makes a path that lasts over a hundred years. Caribou trails across loose shale usually erode in a few years, as do trails over the soil on low hills and across gently sloping mountainsides. On high flat areas, which caribou herds have traversed, water collects and in some instances appears to remain in permanent puddles. One compensating note is that caribou droppings fertilize the soil.

In crossing rocky areas, a caribou sometimes gets its foot caught between two rocks and it may even die there, or it may wrench loose and hobble about for a few days before dying. An occasional caribou breaks a leg falling on a rock, and a skinner sometimes sees a leg bone with a healed fracture.

Caribou do not hesitate to enter lakes and swim many hundreds of yards; they often enter a lake to cool off after becoming overheated, to avoid mosquitoes in July, or to escape from a wolf or a man. Caribou may pause before crossing a river, but they rarely turn back. In some years, late summer rains may cause rivers to rise, making them impossible to cross in some places. Larger rivers during breakup are dangerous, and conceivably a caribou could drown in soft, water-saturated snow. According to the Nunamiut, when the caribou are migrating north in the spring and come to the Colville River, many cross it and head west.

There are several days during breakup, however, when caribou cannot cross this river, and considerable numbers of them, varying from year to year, are diverted to the east. In the summer, caribou sometimes pause for a while to cool off on *aufeis* (semipermanent ice fields) or on residual patches of snow.

CLIMATE. Caribou appear to be well adapted to the extremes of Arctic climate where temperatures drop to perhaps $-70°$ F. They actually appear to suffer more from the heat of summer than the cold of winter. When they run for hours to avoid mosquitoes on a July day, with a temperature as high as $70°$ F, they pant and easily become overheated, but the effects do not appear to be as severe as in a horse that becomes seriously overheated in a high, dry, southwestern United States climate.

Nunamiut say caribou like to travel into the wind during the summer in order to avoid mosquitoes and to be in a better position to sense any danger; they are not "lazy" to travel back and forth over the same country as the wind shifts. In the winter, caribou often stand with their tails to the wind, like many domesticated ungulates, or seek shelter in a protected valley. The low temperatures of winter do not seem to harm them or to make life difficult, and summer rains do not seem to affect them. Snow is the most difficult aspect of the climate caribou have to contend with. In the early fall, snow is usually blown free enough, or is loose enough, that food may easily be had. In the winter, a hard crust of snow makes feeding difficult. In January 1961 it rained lightly at Hunt Fork, about forty miles south of Anaktuvuk Pass; the water melted the surface snow which then froze. Two or three older Nunamiut commented that caribou would have a hungry time if they could not get through the icy sheet. In past years, caribou have been known to lose fat because of winter rains that froze. Deep snow can also be dangerous to caribou when predators approach. Several years ago, a Nunamiut hunter approached a small herd which was feeding near a creek bed where the snow was soft and deep. The hunter was on snowshoes and when the caribou suddenly became frightened and tried to run across the deep snowfield, the hunter had no difficulty in keeping up with them. He was able to shoot several—as many as he could skin and transport at the time.

In the winter, when the herds have broken up, one rarely sees a group of fewer than fifteen or twenty individuals. When there are less in a group, they seem to be uneasy, searching for other caribou, and are usually very difficult to approach. Caribou rarely occur singly in the winter when their increased sensitivity of sight, hearing, and smelling seems to emphasize their gregariousness. The smallest group I recall seeing in the winter, which was undisturbed and apparently "happy" or in what I would call a state of "psychological" equilibrium, was fifteen. This group did not display erratic behavior of any kind nor did it appear to be seeking the company of other caribou.

In the summer, on the other hand, a caribou appears to be a different animal, seemingly stupid and often unaware of or unresponsive to danger. Single animals, or only two or three caribou, appear to be in psychological equilibrium. Some of the pranks related by Murie (1935), indicate the insensitive state of caribou in the summer. He told of one man who took a picture of a sleeping cow caribou, then walked up to it and, with the help of others, tied it down with rope. Perhaps the insensitive state of many caribou in the summer is due to the climate, at least indirectly. The noise of running water and wind, the various odors of summer flora, and the multicolored tundra of summer render a caribou less sensitive to its environment.

Lichens and grasses form the major part of the caribou diet, supplemented by mosses, sedges, willows, dwarf birch, and a scattering of other small plants. In the summer, many of these plants are green, and the caribou stomach contents are very green in color. In the late summer, caribou sometimes eat cloudberries. When rainfall is heavy in the early summer, green plants grow abundantly, and caribou are noticeably fatter in the late summer than after a summer of little rainfall. In the winter, when fresh green plants are unavailable, lichens, dead grasses, willows, and other plants are the basis of the caribou's diet; the stomach contents are usually a dark reddish color.

To whatever extent the quantity of lichens and grasses varies on the Arctic tundra, the fatness and health of caribou, and eventually their numbers, also vary. When reindeer are introduced and maintained in an area, caribou must go elsewhere. Or should caribou become too numerous and overgraze a region, they are forced to alter their distribution and ultimately their migration habits in order to find food. Otherwise, as may happen in the future if the caribou population keeps on growing, caribou may continue to try to find food in overgrazed areas, resulting in a loss of weight and an increased susceptibility to disease because of their weakened condition. An interesting study, requiring careful observation over a considerable period of time, would be to determine the relationship of lichens and grasses with caribou in terms of population, distribution during the year, and migration.

The caribou interacts closely with many elements of the fauna. In this section, only its relationships with animals other than man are considered.

According to Murie (1944: 53), on the basis of fecal examination, caribou constitute slightly more than 40 per cent of the wolf's diet. In general wolves prey on adult caribou during the fall, winter, and early spring, and on calves in the late spring and summer. A lone wolf hunts caribou by approaching a herd or small group and giving chase. The animal that lags behind, usually crippled, old, or diseased, is taken. Wolves in twos or threes or in larger packs often cooperate; one or more circle around a herd and attempt to drive them toward a ridge or other hiding place from which the rest of the pack may burst. An older Nunamiut once observed a pack of wolves attempting to hunt caribou in this fashion. They were unsuccessful. A healthy caribou appears to be able to outrun most wolves. A few older Nunamiut have noticed that some wolves can run much faster than others in chasing caribou.

Wolves have no difficulty in catching calves shortly after they are dropped. Within a few days, however, a calf is able to give most wolves a real run for their money. The selection process of the weaker calves being taken by predators begins within weeks after birth. Throughout the year wolves eliminate the weaker caribou from the herds. During the late 1950s and early 1960s, there were few wolves in the Brooks Range, and trapping for bounty and the program of shooting and poisoning have kept the wolf population very low. Because there are so few wolves to cull the herds, weak and sick caribou are eating plants which healthy caribou would otherwise eat.

Although coyotes occur rarely in the northern Brooks Range and north slope, they are found in larger numbers in the timbered regions of the Brooks Range. Little is known about coyote predation. Newly born calves could easily be had by coyotes but the latter are very rarely in the calving area. In the timber, a caribou is considered fairly able to protect itself from coyotes; only two or more working together could have much luck. Coyotes depend largely on smaller animals and carrion, and only rarely, it would seem, manage to kill a caribou.

Wolverines have occasionally been reported to drop onto a caribou from a cliff and kill it. Such an incident is very unusual and certainly does not constitute much of a threat. I once heard (from non-Eskimos) that a wolverine can run a caribou down and kill it. No person doubts the strength and endurance of a wolverine, but the absence of such an incident from the accounts of Eskimos and biologists alike does not lend credibility to such a story.

Grizzly bears too have been reported to kill caribou by dropping on them from some height. Grizzlies have been known to take calves shortly after they are dropped. Other than that, they do not appear to hunt caribou. Caribou evince fear when they see grizzlies, but have little trouble avoiding them.

Lynx rarely hunt caribou; only, according to Murie (1935: 9), when rabbits are scarce and the lynx are desperate. As mentioned earlier, a Nunamiut's father once saw a lynx jump from a tree onto the back of a small caribou.

The grazing areas of mountain sheep and caribou sometimes overlap. I have seen several hundred caribou pass over mountains where sheep had previously grazed. When caribou appear, if sheep are there, they probably tend to absent themselves. Caribou are on the move so much, however, that their invasions of the mountain sheep's range are only temporary. Sheep are usually left in peace, at least by caribou, and sheep often feed on plants in places where caribou are unlikely to go. I once saw five sheep feeding on a "sky meadow" about 4,500 feet above sea level, just above a long talus slope where caribou would have had an exceedingly difficult time with footing.

To some extent, as Murie (1944: 140) has pointed out, caribou function as a "buffer species" for sheep in absorbing the brunt of wolf attacks. Murie speculates, because the caribou enable a larger wolf population to survive, that when caribou are absent, the wolves remaining in the same locality turn in full force on the sheep. In the Brooks Range, this relationship may be skewed slightly by the wolves' tendency to follow caribou herds to a greater extent than elsewhere.

Although the ranges of caribou and moose overlap, because the habits of the two animals are so different, they rarely come into competition. Caribou are constantly on the move and seldom remain in one area for more than a few days. Moose do travel great distances occasionally, but they are usually restricted to willow patches and the lower areas of the timbered regions where they are able to find adequate forage. Only in traveling does a moose leave the timber or willow brush, and then only for a short time. I once saw a cow and calf at 2,500 feet above sea level just south of the summit of Anaktuvuk Pass, up in the foothills near a mountain. I have not seen evidence or heard of a moose at a higher altitude in the Brooks Range.

The destruction of willows by moose has been described. While willows are recognized not to be the caribou's primary food, two older Nunamuit seemed to think that when moose "kill" a valley, caribou tend to avoid the region since there are no willows to eat.

Caribou are not affected by the presence of the large numbers of moose in the heavily willowed parts of the middle Colville River north of the Brooks Range; they do not linger in river bottoms in their travels.

In the early 1930s, some 60,000 reindeer were herded near Wainwright and Point Barrow (Rausch, 1953: 141). Too many reindeer were kept in too small an area and overgrazing resulted, forcing caribou to seek other range. Because close herding could not be sustained, many reindeer became scattered and mixed with caribou; others were exterminated.

The reindeer is shorter than a caribou, has a lighter, sometimes spotted pelage, and has more rounded hooves and a straighter, fuller face. In skinning, the leg skins of a caribou are much easier to pull off. How much hybridization has occurred is not known, but is felt to be deleterious to the caribou (Rausch 1951: 190; 1953: 141). Reindeer no longer exist on the north slope, except for a few as members of caribou herds. The worst effects are probably over, although how much range is damaged is unknown.

Golden eagles (and possibly an occasional bald eagle) occur in small numbers in the Brooks Range and occasionally prey on very young caribou calves. Most calves taken by eagles are probably two weeks or less in age (Murie 1944: 162). Older calves have been observed fending off eagles with their forelegs. The Nunamiut state that eagles are much more likely to prey on the lambs of mountain sheep. In fact, a Nunamiut tells a story about a very small boy whose mother made him a beautiful mountain sheep parka. That summer he wandered out a little way from camp. There were eagles nearby, and when the little boy's parents discovered he had wandered out, they ran after him, fearing that an eagle might mistake him for a lamb.

One day in the spring of 1961, I was hunting a small herd of about 200 caribou which were migrating north. Ptarmigan were also migrating. As the caribou approached a willow thicket, a flock of ptarmigan suddenly rose, making a terrific noise in the air with their wings. The herd panicked and ran for some distance. After sensing that there was no danger, they resumed their migration.

When men or wolves approach a caribou herd, ravens may be present, which often become alarmed at the approach of a predator and fly around restlessly, screeching. Caribou may be warned or diverted for a moment.

Small animals and fish do not appear to have a direct relationship with caribou, but Murie (1935: 43) reports that wild Norwegian reindeer have been known to eat lemmings, mice, and fish.

During July and the first part of August, mosquitoes greatly annoy caribou, and they will run for miles on a still day trying to avoid the insects. Even when there is a breeze, mosquitoes can still alight on the lee side of a caribou. Sometimes a cow runs so far and so fast that it loses its calf; at nightfall, when mosquitoes settle to the ground, both cow and calf wander about looking for each other. They seem to be able to recognize each other immediately.

In July and August, mosquitoes drive caribou to the northern part of the north slope and to the foothills of the Brooks Range. In August 1961, a 60-year-old Nunamiut and I walked 25 miles north of Anaktuvuk Pass to hunt caribou. When we came to the range front of the Brooks Range where the Anaktuvuk River flows out onto the north slope, we could see about a hundred caribou five or six miles to the west, just north of the mountains. "They will be back," said my companion with calm assurance. We set up camp. About noon the next day we spotted a herd of about sixty caribou standing on a mountainside in the general area where we had seen caribou the day before. My companion said the caribou had sought the high ground to get away from the mosquitoes. He said we could wait until about six o'clock in the evening before they would come down, after the mosquitoes had settled. After a

long afternoon of drinking tea and talking, we walked to the
bottom of the mountain. Shortly after six o'clock, the caribou
slowly began to descend. We shot over twenty, with fine summer
skins, ideal for clothing. We skinned and butchered until the early
hours of the morning. My companion said he had utilized the
reaction of caribou to mosquitoes and had obtained summer skins
in this way for years and years. The limit on the number of caribou
we shot was the number we could skin. Long before all the caribou
were out of rifle range, the Nunamiut said that would be enough.

Caribou are usually very meek and easily frightened by man.
According to the Nunamiut, the only time they can be dangerous
to man is when huge swarms of mosquitoes force a large herd to
run around in circles on a hot day. Should a man get into the
middle of such a maddened herd he would be trampled. At any
other time, caribou avoid man even when frightened. Once in the
fall I was sitting on top of a hill when two Nunamiut frightened a
herd of 500 caribou directly toward me. The herd came within ten
yards but veered to one side. No actual danger was present. Bulls
in rut can be a little dangerous if slightly wounded or irritated, but
the Nunamiut do not seem to fear them.

While mosquitoes pester caribou considerably in July and
August and cause a great deal of local movement, there is no basis
in the old contention that mosquitoes cause caribou to migrate.
For one thing caribou migrate after mosquitoes have decreased
in number; second, this supposed cause of migration has never
really been observed; and third, such reputable biologists as Murie
(1935) and Bee and Hall (1956) deny that such a causal relationship exists.

During July and August, warble flies lay their eggs in the hair
of the caribou. When the larvae hatch, they drill through the skin
and travel to the back and upper sides of the caribou. By spring
most caribou are infested with hundreds of the larvae. In the late
spring, when the larvae mature, they bore through the hide, leaving
a large hole behind, and fall to the ground. During egg-laying time,
warbles are a source of annoyance to caribou, but not to the extent
that mosquitoes are. When a caribou hears a warble fly approach, it
becomes tense and tries to avoid it by shaking its antlers or running
off at full speed for several hundred yards. In the spring when most
caribou have a hundred or more warble larvae on their backsides,
they seem to suffer no outstanding ill effect. A few weak and
stunted caribou sometimes become very heavily infested with

larvae, lose a great deal of weight, and become easy prey for predators.

Nostril flies lay their eggs in the nostrils of caribou. When the larvae hatch, they make their way to the animal's soft palate and neck. In the spring the larvae grow large and are probably a source of some irritation to the caribou. The larvae are edible, and when they are boiled with the meat they resemble a soft, spongy nut. Nunamiut sometimes tease their children by saying that if they eat boiled nostril fly larvae, the grizzly bear will never catch them. This is done in jest, and no real meaning is attached.

A bladderworm, *Taenia hydatgena,* appears in caribou liver at times. To what extent this worm affects the caribou is unknown. Bladderworm-infested liver is not eaten, but the rest of the animal is considered safe by whites and Eskimos alike in northern Alaska.

Caribou are also subject to a tapeworm, *T. echinococcus,* in the lungs, which appears to restrict breathing in severe cases. It looks like a large, dark cyst, and is usually less than four inches in diameter.

Hoof rot occurs among caribou, as it does among other ungulates. Rausch (1953: 144) considers the hoof rot found in caribou probably a *necrophorus* infection. In any event, the weaker animals, which have been susceptible to it, straggle behind and are easily brought down by wolves.

Other very rare parasites and diseases have been observed in caribou over the past fifty years.

In general caribou appear to be healthy animals, the weakened and sick animals being eliminated quickly from the herds by predators and the strenuous migration.

A man, of course, generally keeps his dogs tethered. The yowling of poorly disciplined dogs, however, frightens caribou and may divert them for miles from a previously selected migration route. Sometimes dogs get loose from their masters and chase caribou. A dog rarely if ever catches one unless it is wounded, but I have twice seen dogs run down a wounded caribou and dispatch it in an instant.

The Effect of Man on the Population and Distribution of Caribou

The numbers and distribution of caribou in northern Alaska before 1800 are not easily determined. Archaeological evidence

(Bee and Hall 1956: 234–35) indicates that caribou have been present in the Brooks Range for more than a thousand years and that they have been hunted either by Eskimos or other peoples for that length of time or longer. It is highly likely that the Arctic regions of North America were populated with caribou from the Old World by way of Siberia. That there were Nunamiut hunting caribou in the Brooks Range by 1700 is certain from the historical and ethnohistorical evidence. I am not in a position to speculate about earlier dates. The population of caribou during the 1700s is also open to question but seems to have been adequate to support the Nunamiut population, whatever that was (probably from a few families to 1,500 people between 1700 and 1800).

During the 1800s, when such white men as explorers, trappers, prospectors, miners, traders, and whalers ventured up to northern Alaska, caribou proved to be a valuable supplement to the supplies that they brought along. By the late 1800s, the whalers in particular were abusing the caribou resources. The encouragement by whites of Eskimo market hunting, and the extensive hunting by whites themselves, resulted in a noticeable decline in the caribou population in northern Alaska and possibly in a change of migration patterns.

By 1905 or a little later, hunting pressure declined markedly with the almost complete cessation of whaling and the emigration of Nunamiut from the Brooks Range. The availability of trade goods on the coast also tended to lessen coastal Eskimos' need for caribou.

But the damage had been done and, according to the Nunamiut and most historical sources, the caribou population in northern Alaska was very low during the early 1900s. To what extent north Alaskan caribou had shifted to the east, if at all, is unknown.

After 1900, the herding of reindeer was a source of increasing competition for range until the 1930s, when reindeer were scattered and killed or mixed with the wild caribou. The reindeer industry impeded the recovery of the caribou population before the 1930s, particularly in northwestern Alaska.

Since the 1930s, the pressure of white hunting has continued to decline. Fewer trappers, prospectors, and miners frequent the Brooks Range now than in the past. Increasing numbers of scientists now travel through the Brooks Range, but few do any hunting, and those who do, take very few caribou. This decline of white

pressure on the caribou, together with the reduced pressure from
the lowered numbers of Eskimos hunting caribou, the near-
extinction of wolves in northern Alaska, and the recovery of parts
of the range (to what extent is unknown) from the overgrazing of
reindeer, has resulted in a considerable increase in the caribou
population from the 1930s to the present day.

Bee and Hall (1956: 234) report:

> The decline of the Eskimo population has reduced hunting
> pressure on the caribou but the availability of guns and
> ammunition has offset the effect of the smaller number of
> hunters. Localization of Eskimos, who live in fewer villages
> than formerly on the Arctic Slope, has resulted in heavy
> hunting pressure in the immediate vicinity of villages.

This statement is supported by a graph (1956: 235) in which the
hunting influence of Eskimos with guns on the number of caribou
in northern Alaska is considered to start in 1825 and rise sharply
during the following decades until the early 1900s, when the
influence lessens only slightly. I would seriously qualify this assertion. During the late 1800s, there is no question that the extensive
market hunting by Eskimos and whites using guns greatly lowered
the caribou population. Bee and Hall feel that since 1900 the
decreased numbers of Eskimos have been offset by their use of firearms. Before the use of guns, Eskimos were very successful in
obtaining caribou by means of drives, both into corrals and into
lakes, by bows and arrows, and by snares. Older Nunamiut say
that during the 1800s, the Nunamiut living in the Brooks Range
(who numbered at times several hundred) were able to kill all the
caribou they needed for clothing and food. In the interior of
northern Alaska today, there are only a hundred Nunamiut who
depend heavily on the caribou as a source of food, clothing, and
bedding. Such inland villages as Bettles, Shunagak, Kobuk, Arctic
Village, and Wiseman, some of which are very small, take few
caribou, relatively speaking, and depend to a larger extent on
moose, fish, and trade foods. The changed economy of these native
villages precludes the extensive exploitation of caribou. The villages on the coast, such as Barter Island, Point Barrow, Wainwright,
Point Lay, and Point Hope, depend more on sea mammal hunting
and employment, and exploit the caribou to an even lesser extent
than in precontact days. With the reduced hunting pressure on the

caribou in northern Alaska by Eskimos during the past few decades, with the cessation of reindeer herding, and with fewer
wolves, the caribou population as a whole has increased. The
problem most likely to develop now is overpopulation. As long as
the wolves are kept at a low level, the number of caribou will continue to increase, resulting in damage to the range from overgrazing
—and tundra vegetation recovers very slowly. As caribou are less
able to find adequate food, their general health declines. If more
wolves were permitted to roam the Brooks Range, they would
eliminate the weaker and diseased animals, resulting in smaller,
healthier herds, more in balance with the food resources.

From the Nunamiut point of view, in Anaktuvuk Pass the
problem in the future as far as caribou are concerned is too many
hunters in one area. While I do not think this constitutes a threat
to the caribou population as a whole, for reasons stated above, the
Nunamiut at the Pass are likely to experience increasing difficulty
in obtaining all the caribou they need, even though there are
plenty of caribou in northern Alaska.

Among the Nunamiut at Anaktuvuk Pass in 1960, there were 32
hunters who provided for 96 mouths (including their own) and
about 200 dogs. Of the 32, only 20 were the major hunters of their
households. As well as I could determine from questioning hunters
and spending a year among these Eskimos, in a normal year the
hunters account for about 1,000 caribou of all ages and both sexes.
Seven or eight of the best hunters account for between 70 and 100
caribou apiece, while the remaining 24 hunters shoot between 5
and 70 caribou apiece. Although I obtained no precise data, on the
basis of what I heard about hunting in northern Alaska, I would be
very surprised if the total number of caribou shot in one year by
whites, Indians, and Eskimos other than those of Anaktuvuk Pass
reached a thousand, and this number is not likely to be surpassed
in the near future. Conservative estimates of caribou population
range between 300,000 and 600,000. Thus hunting accounts for a
small fraction of 1 per cent of the caribou population each year.
If the lower estimate of 300,000 is taken, in view of the fact that
about three fourths of the mature cows give birth each year, then
probably no fewer than 75,000 calves are born each spring. The
caribou is a long-lived animal, with life estimates of between 20
and 30 years. Thus, at present, the number of caribou is more a
function of the resources of the range and control of predators

than of hunting pressure as a whole. Locally, however, in the environs of Anaktuvuk Pass, hunting pressure is increasing, making it more and more difficult for hunters to obtain the caribou they need. By 1980, from the 1960 population alone, there will be at least 25 hunters added to the present 32. This does not include teen-age hunters who will be born between 1960 and 1965. Barring a serious epidemic, no more than six to eight persons are likely to die between 1960 and 1980. Between 15 and 20 marriages are likely to take place between 1960 and 1980 (or else there are going to be a large number of highly frustrated young people, which may come to be the case in these times of change and insecurity). If the birth rate (net) continues at four to six a year, a conservative estimate, by 1980 between 55 and 60 hunters will have to provide for 200 or more mouths and presumably 300 or more dogs. This means that between 2,000 and 2,500 caribou or more will have to be taken each year at Anaktuvuk Pass. While a harvest of this many caribou from the total population in the Brooks Range would probably do the herds more good than harm, the sensitivity of caribou to the presence of that many hunters would lessen the village's chances of obtaining all the caribou it needs. Already in the early 1960s, several of the better hunters were beginning to complain about the difficulty of hunting with so many persons in the field on a given day and the incessant yowling of poorly disciplined dogs. Caribou are accessible from any one location in the Brooks Range for brief periods each year when the heavy seasonal hunting must be done. During 1960–61, one man who hunted only from the village, told me he went for six months from fall to spring without killing a single caribou. Fortunately he had done well that fall. By 1980, if the present mode of life continues and everyone remains in the village, each hunter's opportunities will be reduced. It may happen, however, that some of the younger Nunamiut may decide to leave Anaktuvuk Pass in the next few decades and seek employment in such places as Point Barrow (which has its own population problems), other Eskimo settlements along the coast, or Fairbanks and other cities. Also, as the opportunities for sporadic employment increase as Anaktuvuk Pass becomes more and more a Brooks Range center for transportation, communication, scientific research, and tourists, the Nunamiut may become less critically dependent on the caribou.

Over the past several decades, many Nunamiut have been very

aware of the fluctuations of caribou population within the Brooks Range. In response to questions about the possibility of changed migration routes, I could elicit no satisfactory answers. A few Nunamiut believe that from 1905 to 1930 some caribou could have shifted to the eastern Brooks Range or beyond. Generally, however, Nunamiut feel that the actual number of caribou was greatly reduced, owing to the unnatural hunting pressures of the late 1800s. One old Nunamiut who died a few years before I first went to Anaktuvuk Pass had a theory that the number of Nunamiut in the Brooks Range fluctuated with the number of caribou. From his adult children I learned that he figured when caribou were plentiful, the Nunamiut were able to obtain large numbers of them, and the human population increased. Finally, however, there were so many people catching so many caribou that the herds were reduced and starvation and emigration ensued. A few families could manage for a while in the Brooks Range, and some Nunamiut maintained their inland identity while living temporarily elsewhere before returning inland when the herds increased. This theory seems true in the light of the past hundred years; before that there is not enough evidence to know.

Nunamiut conceptions of the reaction of caribou to the presence of man greatly affect the way a Nunamiut hunts them. According to several Nunamiut, the factors that determine these reactions are the season, the climate of the season, the terrain, and the number of caribou in the group. The means by which caribou sense man are scent, sound, and sight, in varying degrees of sensitivity depending on the season and climate.

In the summer, a caribou cannot hear a man's footsteps very well because of other noises. When hunting caribou in the summer, a Nunamiut avoids making unnaturally loud noises with his feet but otherwise does not go out of his way to walk stealthily. Also in the summer a hunter may talk in a very low voice when he is within several hundred yards of caribou, something he would never do in the winter. In approaching a group of fifteen caribou with four Nunamiut in January of 1961, even at a distance of a mile, we spoke very quietly, which would never be necessary at that distance in the summer.

In the summer, the sight of man rarely frightens caribou. Often a caribou seems to regard a man more as an object of curiosity than as a source of danger; only when one sees a man running toward him or walking very fast on his long legs is it likely to be frightened. A man has no difficulty in walking obliquely toward a caribou in the summer, stopping or hiding behind a rock if the animal becomes restless. Once a caribou is thoroughly frightened, it usually only trots away rapidly in the summer—it rarely dashes off at full speed. While Nunamiut hunters do not go out of their way to avoid being heard and, to a lesser extent, being seen, they do try to avoid letting caribou get their scent. Even though a caribou's sense of smell seems to be less acute during the summer, several times I saw a more experienced hunter tell his companions to watch their wind.

In the summer, a single caribou feeding or wandering aimlessly about is usually very easy to approach. Even when a lone caribou senses a man, it often only trots off a short distance, quickly loses its fright, turns around to look at the man, and eventually shifts its attention to something else. A small group of caribou is a little more difficult to approach. If a hunter scares one of them, it runs off a short way, frightening the others. After stopping and looking around, if only one caribou is again frightened, the others are also likely to be frightened and the whole group may leave for good.

Caribou in large groups, from fifty to a thousand or more, often appear to be lulled into the security of the group, especially if they are feeding, and are very easy to approach. In a large group, one caribou may look up at a man, but since the other caribou continue feeding, it often returns to its lichens and grasses. When several caribou of a larger herd become frightened, they may run a short way, frightening part of the herd. Sometimes a large herd is frightened in waves, parts of the herd running and stopping in ir-regular alternation, so uncertain are caribou of danger in the summer. Mosquitoes and warble flies make caribou restless, but are likely to divert their attention from man.

In the winter, caribou are much more sensitive to man. On a cold, still day they can hear exceedingly well. Several Nunamiut commented that caribou can hear the crunching noise of a man's snowshoes over a mile away. When caribou hear a man walking in the winter, they look intently in the direction of the noise. If a hunter stops walking and squats down to look like a rock, the caribou may lose their fear. Frequently, however, against the white background of snow, a caribou seems able to see that a man is

danger, and when the hunter tries to come closer, even though he
is still several hundred yards away, caribou often run away in
fright. When caribou have been pursued recently by men or wolves,
they are more wary and frighten very easily. A few Nunamiut have
tried using, with some success, large overshoes made from caribou
hide with the fur on the outside. On a cold, still winter day, it still
remains exceedingly difficult to approach a herd within rifle range,
much less within the range of a bow and arrow. Thus it can be seen
why snares were used so extensively in the old days. Nowadays,
when two or three hunters with high-velocity, small-caliber rifles
cooperate, they are often able to kill the caribou they need.

As with sound, a caribou's sense of sight is more sensitive in the
winter than in the summer. Sight, however, is rarely the sense by
which a caribou first learns of danger; it does not normally scan
the countryside the way a man or wolf does. Nor does the sight of
man alone always send a caribou off in panic. Two or three times
I remember being seen by caribou but not until I made a noise did
they become frightened. My Nunamiut teachers stressed that even
if one is seen, often it is a man-like noise or smell that really
frightens caribou.

According to many Nunamiut, the scent of man is almost certain
to send any caribou off in panic. Some caribou, it is said, run
away in fright the moment they smell man, even without having
seen or heard him. A few Nunamiut indicated that when a man is
sweating and is wearing old, dirty clothes, he is much more likely
to be smelled than when he is clean.

During the winter, caribou are much easier to hunt on windy,
snowy days, even though it may be unpleasant to be outdoors. If
a hunter watches the direction of wind carefully, he can usually
avoid being smelled or heard. On a cold windy day the air is
sometimes filled with snow, enabling a hunter to approach the
animals without being seen. Older Nunamiut talked about hunters
with bows and arrows who could sometimes approach caribou on
windy days in the winter close enough to shoot.

In the old days according to informants, some hunters were such
skilled runners and could cooperate so closely that several men
could spread out over a valley and, as coyotes run down a deer in
the western United States, take turns in running a herd of caribou
around until they tired and the hunters could come close enough
to use their bows. I do not doubt the Nunamiut ability to run,

especially in the old days, but caribou can run very fast for very long distances. Still, almost anything is possible, and the presence of several hunters in a large area might well confuse caribou, enabling men to use brains as well as brawn in bringing the animals down.

On a relatively warm winter day (say, $-10°$ to $+32°$ F) Nunamiut notice that caribou cannot hear as well as on a cold, still day. Scent and sight, however, do not seem to be impaired. One reason why caribou cannot hear so well on a warm day is that snow does not crunch so loudly underfoot as on a colder day. Another reason indicated by informants is that caribou are simply not so alert on a warmer day. One warm day in January 1961 two Nunamiut and I approached a small herd of caribou about six miles east of Tulugak Lake. I was amazed that we had so little difficulty in getting within rifle range and taking four animals apiece.

In the winter, caribou usually occur in small groups of twenty or more scattered over the country feeding. Occasionally, however, caribou feed singly or in very small groups of two, three, or more. Such caribou always appear to be looking for other caribou and are more wary of predators, including man, than are caribou feeding in the security of a larger group. In approaching a small group of restlessly traveling caribou in the winter, the hunter had best place himself in the line of travel and wait. If he tries to stalk such a group, it is very likely to sense him and run away. Sometimes a very skilled hunter can call a lone animal or a cow and calf by making a low, heavy breathing sound like a caribou.

During the fall migration, a cow and her calf invariably take the lead, regardless of the size of the herd. The cow picks her way slowly, sniffing the air, listening, and looking around. The moment she senses danger, she stops, and the entire herd stops. As she intently checks for danger, the other members of the herd either lower their heads to graze or vaguely test the air. Should the lead cow suddenly decide that danger is present, she bolts ahead with the entire herd following her in panic. The fission of a herd often occurs at such a moment if some other cow and calf take off in another direction, followed by a part of the herd. Once the migration has begun, a herd, even when frightened, attempts to maintain its general direction of travel.

There seems to be no pecking order in the choice of a lead cow. As one starts to wander off she has to look out for danger herself, since no other caribou is in front of her. When the animals behind her see there is a caribou leading the way, they follow confidently, without having to watch for danger.

During the spring migration as well, a cow and her near-yearling calf take the lead whenever a herd of any size begins to travel. In May and August, the only two months when bulls travel great distances without a cow in the herd, one of the bulls assumes the lead. How long one individual caribou retains the lead is unknown, not even older Nunamiut had an answer for that. I have seen a herd of caribou feeding and as they started to move away, a cow and calf assumed the lead. Then a few hundred yards later, the herd stopped and began to graze again. A minute or two afterward another cow and calf took the lead simply by moving ahead until the other animals were behind them. Within a herd, a caribou is less alert than when alone. A caribou in a herd may hear or see something that would send the leader off in panic, but remain relatively undisturbed.

During the fall migrations, the Nunamiut strongly emphasize the need to avoid frightening the leader of the first herds. While later herds are likely only to ascend mountains to escape danger, if the first herd of the fall migration is frightened and turns back, the whole valley may be avoided by caribou for the duration of the migration. During my time at Anaktuvuk Pass, I never saw a herd turn back, but I heard about incidents in the past when overanxious hunters rushed up to the first herd and frightened it completely out of the Anaktuvuk River valley back onto the north slope from whence it traveled south by a different route.

When the first herd or two have been allowed to pass, hunters may approach herds during migration and shoot to the limits of their ability to skin and handle the meat. During the fall migration, several thousand caribou pass through Anaktuvuk Pass (if that is a route) in one day, but this may last only for two or three days, after which small herds may or may not follow. Once the hunters allow the first herd to pass and avoid scaring the leaders of subsequent herds, it is only necessary to remember that a herd's response to danger is governed by the terrain. Thus, if a hunter is near the base of a mountain, or three quarters of the way up from the river toward the mountains, he is likely to have the best opportunity to kill.

During the spring, the migration is more drawn out. Herds are greater in number and smaller in size, usually never more than a few hundred animals in one herd. Again hunters have to be careful not to frighten the first herds, which usually appear in March. This may be hard for young hunters, according to the older Nunamiut, because by February food can be very low. Once the first herds pass, spring hunting is usually a more leisurely affair, since the migration may last for months.

Attributes of Caribou

Like all animals, the Nunamiut believe that the caribou (tuttu) has a soul or spirit (*iñua*)—the *tuttum iñua*. In the older days, when a man killed a caribou he was supposed to cut off its head after skinning the animal. Then the iñua was able to return to the other caribou and to tell its relatives (generally) that it had been freed from its body; that is, it was said to "bring the good news" to its relatives. Here we see the implicit notion that caribou are essentially well disposed toward men and do not go out of their way to avoid being caught. The act of cutting off the head to send the tuttum iñua back to the caribou is a way of saying "thank you," as it were, for the meat and hides. If a person should find a dead caribou he should cut off its head so the iñua could return to its "people" and become the life force of another caribou. The iñua is glad to be released. There is no vengeance or retribution for failing to cut off a caribou's head; the note, rather, is on affective cooperation between man and caribou. If the head is not cut off, the tuttum iñua does not become angry, it is merely forced to remain in the dead body where it is uncomfortable. Caribou are peaceful animals, unlike, for example, the grizzly which easily becomes angry at man.

I have already pointed out that seal and caribou meat should not be boiled together in the same pot and that a woman should not scrape or sew caribou skins near a fishing place. A caribou spear should not be used to kill seals, nor should a seal harpoon be used to dispatch snared caribou. If these injunctions were broken, a person, either the offender or someone close to him, might have bad luck in trying to catch the particular animals involved. This avoidance of mixing products and objects associated with land and sea was never so highly developed among the Nunamiut and adjacent peoples as among the Eskimos farther to the east, especially between Baffin Island and Coronation Gulf in Canada (Weyer 1932: 367–70). The cult of the Sea Woman or Sedna does not occur among the Nunamiut. The various restrictions on the handling of animals and implements associated with land and sea were not correlated to any season as such. For instance, many Nunamiut used to travel to the coast in the spring and remain there all summer hunting seals and fishing. But there was never any restriction against hunting caribou or any other land animal during that time, just so long as a seal harpoon was not used and other contaminative acts were avoided. The restriction on sewing caribou skins near fishing places was not a restriction of midwinter, summer, or any other time in particular, but a restriction coming into force only when the activity of fishing took place.

The folktale below illustrates many of the moral attributes of caribou which the Nunamiut used to believe in and to some extent still do, and are similar to those emphasized in the creation myth of Aiyagomahala and in the moral values stressed by informants. Ikiashuruak, the name of the man in the story, is best translated as "Big Lazy."

The Story of Ikiashuruak and the Caribou

In the very old days there lived a man named Ikiashuruak. He was very lazy and refused to go out hunting very often. Whenever he did go hunting, he always had bad luck. The caribou could see him and they saw that he lay in bed too much, not like other men. A lazy person is repulsive to caribou, and that is why caribou were shy and ran away when Ikiashuruak hunted them. The men who woke up early in the morning, straightened their houses, and kept their floors clean were the hunters who always were able to catch animals. Ikiashuruak knew he was a filthy person, but he did not care. When he returned from hunting, he would lie down for an entire day—that is why his bladder was so big—he would not even get out of bed for a whole day or more to urinate.

Finally one day his wife told him to get out of bed and try to live right. But Ikiashuruak was tough-minded and refused to listen. Nevertheless his wife made him feel very ashamed. He began to think that he might not remain with his wife forever. He felt a sad longing for his little boy who was still too young to hunt, but his wife made him feel so ashamed and sorry for himself that he thought he might have to leave.

One morning, Ikiashuruak took his bow and arrow and his spear, and went out into the country to look for caribou. After walking some way, he spotted a herd. He tried to come near them, but they were so shy and sensitive that he could not get close enough to shoot. Ikiashuruak was a long way from home. He decided that he might as well keep on walking. He knew he might become very tired and weak, but he did not care even if he died. Then he walked and walked. After some time he became tired and weak, but he was a long way from home.

Up ahead of Ikiashuruak, a caribou had stopped and was waiting for him. He was very tired. He was still too far away to shoot, but he knew if he could get a little closer he could kill the animal. Just before he was going to shoot, the caribou brushed its head with its foreleg and turned into a man. The man spoke, "Do not shoot. Come, live with us, and learn about the caribou life. We will give you food. You cannot return to your family now, you would starve to death if you tried to return home." Lazy Ikiashuruak believed what he heard. It was kind of nice, what the caribou said. Ikiashuruak was very hungry and knew that he would never make it home. He put down his bow and arrow and his spear. The caribou-man told him what to do and Ikiashuruak joined the herd.

The herd traveled until evening when they stopped and began feeding. The caribou-man said to Ikiashuruak, "Shut your eyes and dig with your left foot. Then open your eyes and maybe your foot will be in the right place." He did what he was told, and sure enough, he found lots of good food—fat, dried meat, and boiled meat. Ikiashuruak ate and was satisfied. When it was time to sleep, the caribou gave him a blanket, but they never told him what kind of blanket it was. From that time on, Ikiashuruak stayed with the caribou.

One day Ikiashuruak saw several men hunting caribou. The caribou-man told him how to run because he was so slow. The caribou-man instructed him not to look at the ground, but to keep his head up like other caribou. Some of the hunters Ikiashuruak saw were dirty men trailing filth in their wake. Caribou never came close to old bedding. The caribou-man told Ikiashuruak about everything he saw; all the dirt on the floor of any house in the camp. Some men never cleaned their arrows or spears after killing an animal. A few men even left their arrows and spears on the dirty floor for everyone to step on. Caribou never came close to such men because they could see their filthy habits.

Ikiashuruak lived with the caribou for a long time. One of his sons had grown big enough to hunt, but he could not return to his family.

Ikiashuruak saw many snares. Some of them were dirty and caribou avoided them, but the clean snares always caught caribou. Caribou even knew about persons who were nervous and acted funny, and who easily became angry at people. Caribou knew about good and bad living among people, and lazy Ikiashuruak saw everything that people did.

Finally the old caribou-man said, "It is time for you to return home. Your three sons are grown now, maybe you will be caught by one of your sons. If you remember to do what I say, you will return to your human form. When you feel yourself caught in a snare, brush your head with your foreleg, and you will become a man." Ikiashuruak believed what the caribou-man told him. He very much wanted to return to his family, but he had no idea when it would be time to be caught in a snare. One day the caribou crossed a river. Ikiashuruak remembered seeing a snare and suddenly he was caught. The caribou-man said, "Remain here until your son comes, but be sure to brush your head." When his full-grown son approached, Ikiashuruak brushed his head, stepped forward, and asked his son where his two brothers were. His son recognized him and both of them cried, they were so glad to come together after such a long time. Ikiashuruak also asked about his son's mother, his wife. She was still alive.

Ikiashuruak's son took him home and he found everyone in his family happy and in good health. His wife began to cry and gave him a good kiss [Eskimo style, of course].

Then Ikiashuruak told everyone what he had learned. The caribou, he said, can easily see people from another life. Everyone should wake up early in the morning and keep the floors, campsite, snares, arrows, and spears clean all the time. Ikiashuruak told people that no one should be angry or nervous or act funny toward anybody and that everyone should think well of others and be helpful to them. People should act this way because other animals can see them easily. Good people can always catch the animals they need, and from that

time on, the Nunamiut believed what they heard from Ikiashuruak and tried to stay clean and lead a good life.

As do many human beings, the Nunamiut attribute human
characteristics to things that are not human. Nunamiut anthropomorphic ideas about caribou are an important part of their general
conception of the caribou and how to hunt them. This anthropomorphism is not excessive but is tempered with empiricism or, as
the Nunamiut say, "You have to see something before you can
know anything about it." The Nunamiut do not make a sharp distinction between their anthropomorphic ideas about caribou and
the knowledge that results from empirical investigation. Many of
the anthropomorphic characteristics which the Nunamiut attribute
to the caribou are in fact substantiated by the observations they
are able to make. This is well exemplified in the following incident.

One summer day in August of 1960 I was walking along a mountain ridge and saw fresh caribou feces. As I crossed a small rise, a
bull caribou came into sight. It stood looking at me. I quickly sat
down and drew a bead. The first shot was low in the neck, only a
flesh wound. It was about 350 yards and I had not held high
enough. But the caribou only turned and started to walk away. I
raised my sights and shot the bull through the chest. When I arrived at the camp where our tents were pitched, I asked one of the
more experienced hunters what was the best thing I could have
done if the caribou had been 500 yards away, a very difficult shot
even with a good telescopic sight. He answered as follows:

> In approaching a lone caribou or a very small group of
> caribou, especially in warm weather, the hunter must make
> the caribou think he is merely another caribou, or at least not
> after them. He can do this by turning his face to one side and
> not letting the caribou see the hunter looking directly at them.
> The hunter can see the caribou, however, by looking out of
> the corner of his eyes, or around the edge of his parka ruff.
> Then, in trying to come within range, the hunter should walk
> at an angle toward the caribou, never directly toward them.
> Thus the caribou will think the hunter is either feeding or
> traveling, and at least not a menace. In the winter, it is more
> difficult to fool a caribou, but if a hunter is skilled enough, he
> can learn to kneel down and stick his snowshoes or rifle along-
> side his head to look like antlers. A caribou may look at a
> hunter for a long time, not quite certain whether the hunter

is a caribou or not, but at least not a wolf. A hunter can also scratch the snow with his mittens as if he is trying to get at the lichens and dead grass, and a caribou may think he is feeding.

By attributing human characteristics to caribou on the basis of previous experience, a man can often manage to trick the animal. One could argue that men and caribou share some common sensitivities. And man, as the more intelligent of the two, may use this fact to his advantage. Most Nunamiut hunters are very practical about learning from their experiences with animals, and they do not allow their empirically derived knowledge to be obscured by anthropomorphic notions. I often heard young hunters comment about a hunting experience in which they learned about some reaction of an animal which they had not expected.

Older Nunamiut who have hunted caribou for decades sometimes regard the caribou as a strange, peculiar animal. As a Nunamiut sees it, from his perspective developed on the basis of cumulative experience and the ability to relate and compare experiences, the actions of caribou often seem stupid and even totally unreasonable at times:

> Caribou are usually easy to hunt. They are dull and slow-witted in the summer, and during a migration are easily taken if the leader is allowed to pass. Even in the winter, an experienced hunter can approach within shooting distance. Individual caribou may turn up in any location at any time of the year, but a caribou is always better off in a group of its own kind rather than wandering off alone or in twos and threes. Some caribou just do not seem to plan ahead or to think about what they are doing: a caribou will run for miles on a hot summer day to avoid mosquitoes, overheats itself by running, thereby attracting more mosquitoes. Furthermore, it is rather odd that a cow would risk losing its calf by running to avoid mosquitoes. But the caribou is a harmless animal and never becomes angry or shows displeasure with man. Even when one cuts the spinal cord between the skull and the first vertebra of a wounded caribou, it does not really appear to be angry, quite unlike a grizzly, wolf, or wolverine, which all fight vehemently to the very end.

When caribou do not migrate in the way they normally do or are absent for several months from a valley, I observed no feeling

among the Nunamiut that the caribou were upset or angry in any
way. Indeed, one could pray or, in the old days, invoke shamanistic help to bring the caribou, but if the caribou did not come, it
was because the prayer or the shaman was weak, not because the
caribou were angry or disgruntled.

Sometimes a Nunamiut expresses sympathy for caribou, but not
so much that it prevents him from killing as many as he can, but he
always waits until he is sure a caribou is dead before skinning it.
The idea of running a knife down the foreleg of a caribou while it
is still alive and feeling the animal quiver is abhorrent to a Nunamiut. One older Eskimo expressed some qualms about killing
calves before the fall migration. When the time came, of course, in
order to obtain clothing material, he shot calves and talked no more
about it. In fact, I learned from him the customary Nunamiut
method of killing a wounded calf without further marking its skin:
to strangle it by pressing its head up and back. While Nunamiut
gain prestige in the eyes of their fellows by shooting a large number
of caribou and are proud of it, I never sensed the feeling, found
among a few whites, of power from killing. Although the Nunamiut
freely expressed the feeling of challenge and excitement during a
hunt, they bragged, rather, of their marksmanship and their skill
in approaching animals.

One could argue that the Nunamiut could survive without caribou, and that other elements of the fauna and flora would be sufficient to enable a society to exist in the Brooks Range north of the
timber. Such an assertion is incorrect. One or two isolated families
can live through a winter by exploiting fauna other than caribou.
While this has occurred in the past, such subsistence groups do not
constitute a society, at least as far as the Nunamiut are concerned.
Such extreme isolation is only an interim during which a family is
fervently hoping for better times, thinking about when it can join
the rest of *the people* wherever they may be (probably on the
coast), or waiting expectantly for the return of caribou so that *the
people* can return to the mountains.

When caribou were very scarce from 1905 to 1920, a dwindling
number of families continued to eke out a living in the Brooks
Range and north slope. Most of the Nunamiut had migrated either
to large population centers or to good trapping regions along the
coast. With the decline in caribou population, that part of the in-

terior of northern Alaska normally occupied by the Nunamiut was
no longer capable of sustaining a society. By 1920, when the last
Nunamiut family had left the northern Brooks Range, the limit
of human isolation had been reached and was probably as extreme
as any place in the world where people living under natural conditions manage to maintain a sense of well-being.

By the late 1930s the caribou population in the Brooks Range
had recovered and was again adequate to support social life. Several families returned to the Brooks Range. These families had
the opportunity to go elsewhere—Aklavik, Barter Island, Point
Barrow, Wainwright, Point Lay, Point Hope, Kotzebue, Fairbanks
—and many Nunamiut did go to these places. But enough families
returned to the Brooks Range to constitute a society there, when
the caribou population increased, since the remaining fauna and
flora were intact, trade was available, and the Nunamiut were under pressure (notably because of the decline in demand for Arctic
fox and other fur animals in the late 1930s) to leave the north
Alaskan coast.

We can regard the sources of trade for coastal goods or substitutes and the presence of flora and fauna other than caribou within
the inland domain of the Nunamiut to be adequate as required but
insufficient to support societal life. The number of caribou varies
over the years and, on the basis of evidence, appears to be the primary factor in determining whether or not a society may exist in
the northern Brooks Range and north slope of Alaska. As the
caribou population has fluctuated, so have the welfare and eventually the numbers of people. For the Nunamiut Eskimos, the judi-
cious exploitation of caribou is critical to their existence. Few
societies are so singularly dependent upon one natural resource
and, as one would expect, the survival of the Nunamiut in their
customary territory is precarious. At times they have been forced
to vacate their land, almost becoming extinct through death and
assimilation; but by virtue of a specialized cultural adaptation—
the essence of which, as I see it, is the cognitive processes of scientific empiricism, supernaturalism, and anthropomorphism—the
Nunamiut have managed to perpetuate themselves as a society in
the Brooks Range.

APPENDICES

Appendix A

Distribution of Nunamiut and Adjacent Groups in Arctic Alaska

"NUNAMIUT" literally means "inhabitants of land," or inland people, in contrast to coastal people or "Tagiokmiut," a general term meaning "inhabitants of the sea [coast]." The coastal Eskimos call the Nunamiut "Nunatagmiut," but the latter call themselves Nunamiut. Many Kobuk Eskimos live inland, but they are not considered Nunamiut by Nunamiut because of the many differences in way of life.

The suffix *miut* means "inhabitants of." This suffix, however, may be used in a general sense, e.g. "Tagiokmiut," inhabitants of the sea (coast) or, in a much more specific sense, "Tulugakmiut," inhabitants of Tulugak Lake. This lack of distinction in terminology about the kind of grouping may lead to confusion in discussing the distribution of Nunamiut bands. For example, the Killikmiut were those Nunamiut who lived primarily in the Killik River valley and constituted one of the four major groups of Nunamiut. When inland population was low, the Killikmiut might be represented by only one small band which hunted and trapped in the Killik River valley. At times during the 1800s, the Killikmiut became too numerous for hunting and trapping in one valley, and several families formed bands in the Okokmilaga and Chandler river valleys, where they were known as the Okokmilagmiut and the Natvakvagmiut respectively. Most Okokmilagmiut nevertheless considered themselves to be Killikmiut. If a band had resided in the Okokmilaga River valley continuously for many years, its members would no longer have identified themselves as Killikmiut or felt like returning to the Killik River in particular when they ran out of meat. Then the Okokmilagmiut would have become one of the stable, major groupings of Nunamiut. Instead, the Okokmilaga River valley was only one of the temporary locations resulting from overpopulation in the Killik valley. Also the Okokmilaga valley was not that good a place to hunt and trap, and an Okokmilagmiut returned to the Killik River or went elsewhere as soon as he could, population allowing.

The Nunamiut bands and adjacent groups indicated on the map are those that were recognized as the more stable settlements and the more important transitory bands.

337

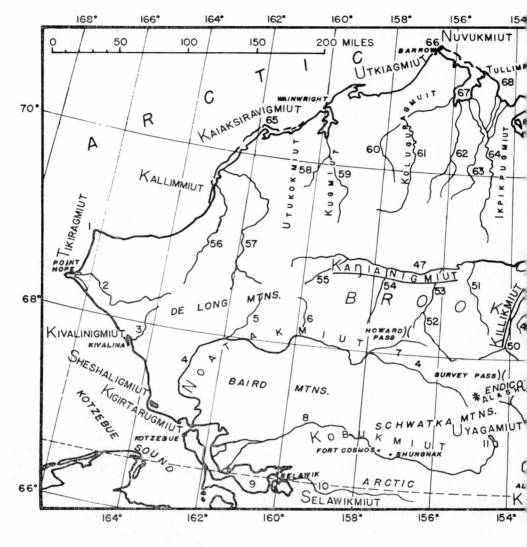

Fig. 1. Distribution of Nunamiut and adjacent groups in Arctic Alaska. Maj

KEY

1. Cape Lisburne
2. Kukpuk River
3. Kivalina River
4. Noatak River
5. Kugururok River
6. Nimiuktuk River
7. Aniuk River
8. Kobuk River
9. Selawik Lake
10. Selawik River
11. Walker Lake
12. Kanuti River
13. Alatna River
14. Koyukuk River

15. John River
16. Tinayguk River
17. Dietrich River
18. Chandalar Lake
19. N. Fork Chandalar R.
20. Chandalar River
21. E. Fork Chandalar R.
22. Wind River
23. Yukon River
24. Porcupine River
25. Sheenjek River
26. Coleen River
27. Firth River
28. Kongakut River

338

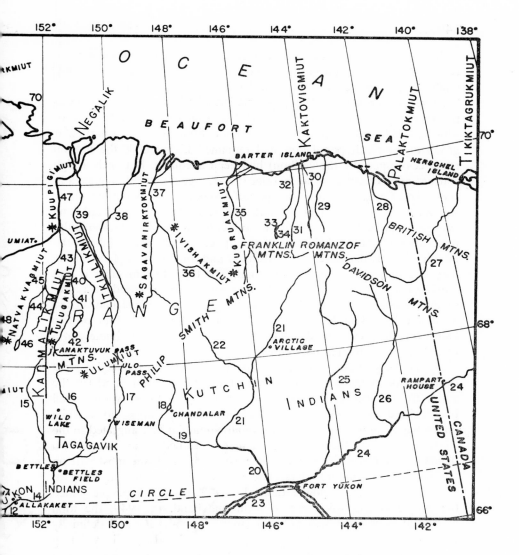

Nunamiut groups are underlined, temporary Nunamiut groups are asterisked.

29. Jago River	43. Anaktuvuk River	57. Kokolik River
30. Okpilak River	44. Siksikpuk River	58. Kaolak River
31. Hulahula River	45. Chandler River	59. Ketik River
32. Sadlerochit River	46. Chandler Lake	60. Nigisaktuvik River
33. Schrader Lake	47. Colville River	61. Meade River
34. Peters Lake	48. Okokmilaga River	62. Topagoruk River
35. Canning River	49. Okpikruak River	63. Oumalik River
36. Ivishak River	50. Killik River	64. Ikpikpuk River
37. Sagavanirktok R.	51. Kurupa River	65. Icy Cape
38. Kuparuk River	52. Nigu River	66. Point Barrow
39. Itkillik River	53. Etiviuk River	67. Dease Inlet
40. Nanushuk River	54. Kuna River	68. Cape Simpson
41. Kanayut River	55. Nuka River	69. Teshekpuk Lake
42. Shainin Lake	56. Kukpowruk River	70. Cape Halket

During the latter 1800s and the early 1900s, the Nunamiut were composed of four major groups. When population was low, each group might be represented by only one band. One region may even have been vacant for a while. When population was high, such a people as the Kaŋianigmiut might be represented by four or five bands, each of which could have become a stable band, identifying itself as a particular group of people if population had remained high and if the natural resources (especially the caribou) had been adequate. But such a high concentration of bands of normal size (50–150 people) could not exist in such a small area for a very long period without experiencing hunger or starvation, as happened in the late 1880s. Nunamiut had lived long enough on the upper Colville River to identify themselves as Kaŋianig-miut—literally "the inhabitants of the upper Colville River [above the mouth of the Killik River]"—to develop and thus merit a place on the map as a major grouping of Nunamiut. The thing to remember is that the Kaŋianigmiut, just as any other major grouping, could be represented by only one or two bands (in which case everyone had all the meat, fat, and skins he needed) or, for a short time, by four or five bands (in which case the decimation of caribou resulted ultimately in a reduction of the human population).

By the early 1900s, Nunamiut population had been reduced a great deal, and often there were only two or three Nunamiut bands in the entire Brooks Range. During the winter of 1913–14, only one small band existed on the Colville River, and one family trapped for a while on the Sagavanirktok River. By 1920, all Nunamiut had migrated to the coast. In the late 1930s, several families returned inland where two bands were formed, the Killik people who resided for the most part on the Killik River before 1949, and the Tulugak people, residing at Chandler Lake and Tulugak Lake. In 1949, the Killik people joined the people at Tulugak Lake to form one band. In 1949, the total Nunamiut population was only 65 (Ingstad 1954: 26) and definitely not too large for everyone to live together as one band, especially during the seasonal migration of caribou. During the early 1950s, most Nunamiut moved to Anaktuvuk Pass as a result of white influence, although two families continued to base their camp at Tulugak Lake until 1960 when they finally moved to the Pass. At present the settlement at the Pass has ceased to be "a shifting aggregation of households" and has become a permanent village in the sense that all Nunamiut regard the village as the place to which they always return after a few days or a season spent hunting and trapping elsewhere.

During the latter 1800s and early 1900s, the major groupings of Nunamiut and people living in adjacent regions were as follows:

1) The Kaŋianigmiut included the Nunamiut who lived along the

upper Colville River (above the mouth of the Killik River) and its tributaries such as the Nuka, Kuna, Etivluk, Nigu, and Kurupa rivers. When population was especially high, several Kaŋianigmiut formed a band on the Aniuk River in the Noatak River drainage. Here Noatak-miut could easily join Nunamiut to form a band. At times the distinction between Noatakmiut and Nunamiut could become blurred. Generally, however, a Kaŋianigmiut looked to the east for many, though not all, of his relatives and traveled north to the mouth of the Colville River to obtain coastal goods from the Point Barrow Eskimos. Many Nunamiut never hunted sea mammals. A Noatakmiut living in the upper Noatak River looked west for many of his relatives and traveled primarily to Kotzebue and secondarily to Icy Cape for coastal products from the Point Hope and other coastal Eskimos. A few Noatakmiut established Camps at Kivalina and Sheshalik in order to hunt sea mammals themselves.

2) The Killikmiut included the Nunamiut who lived in the Killik, Okokmilaga, Okpikruak, and Chandler rivers. Some Killikmiut ranged as far as Survey Pass and the upper Alatna River where they were known as the Alashukmiut.

3) The Kaŋmalikmiut included the Nunamiut who lived in the Anaktuvuk (previously called the Kaŋmalik River) upper John, Nanushuk or Anaktuvaurak, upper North Fork, upper Tinayguk, and upper Wild rivers. Tulugak Lake on the upper Anaktuvuk River was perhaps the most frequented campsite in this area, and people often speak of the Tulugakmiut. When the Nunamiut were few in number, the Tulugakmiut might be the only band in the entire area. When population was high, each of the regions indicated might become the habitat of a band.

4) The Itkillikmiut included the Nunamiut who lived on the Itkillik River, in Ulu Pass, and on the upper Dietrich River.

In the latter 1800s, before the drastic decline in population, the Nunamiut were beginning to form bands farther east, which in time might have become major groups. In the past, Nunamiut families have camped in the Kuparuk, Sagavanirktok, Ivishak, and Canning rivers, but they were only brief residents in these regions and did not develop a full sense of territoriality there: they were still Itkillikmiut, Kaŋmalik-miut, Killikmiut, or Kaŋianigmiut. If whaling and other activities had not disrupted the Nunamiut, many other families no doubt would have settled east of the Itkillik River and formed stable bands there. Al-though a few Nunamiut have traveled east of the Canning River and established camps on the Jago, Hulahula, Sheenjek, the East Fork of the Chandalar and the Coleen rivers, as far as I could determine, no Nunamiut bands were ever established in those areas.

In the old days, a very few Nunamiut families from the upper Colville, Killik, Anaktuvuk, and Itkillik rivers camped in the lower Colville River below Umiat, where they were known as the Kuupigimiut.

Now let us turn to the people who lived in regions adjacent to the Nunamiut.

The Kobuk Eskimos included those who lived primarily along the Kobuk and Selawik rivers. The Nunamiut considered the Selawikmiut to be the same kind of people as the Kobukmiut, and the Kobukmiut as distinctly different from themselves. The Kobuk people on the upper Kobuk and Selawik rivers traded more frequently with the Koyukon Indians than the Nunamiut ever did, and the Kobukmiut near the sea could easily join relatives and friends on the coast as the Noatakmiut did. Generally, however, the Kobuk Eskimos were more self-sufficient in their own country than either the Nunamiut or the Noatakmiut. Giddings (1961: 128) states that while Kobuk Eskimos did obtain coastal products in trade, notably blubber and seal rawhide line, they could find substitutes within their own country. Interestingly enough, this is not true for the Nunamiut.

The Noatakmiut include the Eskimos who lived primarily along the Noatak River. Those living on the upper Noatak River were considered by the Nunamiut to be very similar to themselves, especially the Kaŋianigmiut. The Noatakmiut living on the lower Noatak River sometimes established camps at Sheshalik and Kivalina for months at a time when they hunted sea mammals. In the late 1700s and early 1800s, Kivalina may have been a hunting camp of the Point Hope Eskimos.

The Utukokmiut include Eskimos who lived in the upper reaches of the Utukok River and adjacent regions. The Nunamiut also regarded the Utukokmiut as very like themselves. In the middle 1800s the Utukokmiut were expanding rapidly in population, and many stable inland bands were becoming established. These people journeyed to Icy Cape to obtain coastal products from the Point Hope Eskimos. But when the whalers came in the late 1800s, the opportunities for obtaining employment and trade goods permanently reduced the inland Utukok River population.

Similar to the Utukokmiut were the Kugmiut, the Eskimos who lived along the tributaries of the Kuk River. An inland population was developing there which also obtained coastal products from the Point Hope Eskimos at Icy Cape, but the whaling industry also attracted the Kugmiut permanently to the coast.

The Point Barrow Eskimos (the Utkiavigmiut and Nuvukmiut) and the Point Hope Eskimos (the Tikiragmiut) were (and are) the two dominant coastal groups along the north Alaskan coast between Cape Seppings just north of Kivalina and Herschel Island. Such groups as the

Kallimmiut, Kaiaksiravigmiut, Tullimanirkmiut, and Kaktovigmiut were settlements emanating from Point Barrow and Point Hope. With time, many of these settlements and others along the north Alaskan coast have become permanent and have established their own sense of locality. Coastal Eskimos occasionally made expeditions inland to hunt caribou and to trap. The Ikpikpukmiut and the Koluguragmiut are good examples. These two groups were primarily Point Barrow Eskimos who had moved inland for a short time to hunt and trap.

Barter Island was primarily a trading center but has now become a permanent settlement composed of Alaskan coastal and inland Eskimos. A few Mackenzie River and Coppermine Eskimos have lived there at times.

The Nunamiut refer to the Eskimos living to the east of Barter Island generally as the Kaŋmalyaluitch. The Nunamiut generally disliked and feared these Eskimos who spoke a strange dialect and had odd customs. An eastern shaman in particular was a source of great fear.

Between the heads of the Kobuk and Noatak rivers just north of Walker Lake, I have indicated a group called the Uyagamiut by the Nunamiut. The history of this settlement was described earlier.

The Kutchin Indians known to the Nunamiut lived in the drainage of the Chandalar River and its tributaries, the Sheenjek and Coleen rivers. There has always been great antipathy between them. They avoided contact with each other in the mountains except for sporadic raiding but did trade occasionally at Barter Island.

The Koyukon Indians of whom the Nunamiut were aware lived primarily in the Koyukuk River drainage. Those Koyukon who camped along the lower John and Wild rivers were known by the Nunamiut as the "Tagagavik," travelers by canoe.

Nunamiut Trading Contacts

Negalik, an island in the Colville River delta, was the principal site for trading between the Nunamiut and the Point Barrow Eskimos (the Utkiavigmiut and the Nuvukmiut). Here the Nunamiut obtained through a system of partnerships the basic staples which they needed to supplement the resources available in the Brooks Range. The Itkillikmiut, Kaŋmalikmiut, and Killikmiut were especially dependent on trade at Negalik. Many Kaŋianigmiut traveled to Negalik to trade, but a few might join a Noatakmiut trading party and obtain coastal products from Kotzebue. Kaŋianigmiut could also join Utukokmiut or Kugmiut to go down the Utukok and Kuk rivers to obtain goods from the Point Barrow Eskimos at Icy Cape.

Enterprising Nunamiut sometimes went east from Negalik to Oliktok and Barter Island where they met and traded with Mackenzie River

Eskimos and occasionally a few Coppermine Eskimos. At Barter
Island the Nunamiut also met the Kutchin Indians, who journeyed up
the tributaries of the Chandalar River and down the Hulahula River
for trade.

The Kaŋmalikmiut traded with the Koyukon Indians on the John
River, either at Hunt Fork or farther south, even as far south as
Bettles.

The Killikmiut traded with the Kobuk Eskimos just south of Survey
Pass at the head of the Alatna River.

Kotzebue (formerly known as Kiŋalik) was the most active trading
center in indigenous Arctic Alaska. Here there was contact between
North Alaskan Eskimos and Western Eskimos as well as between in-
land and coastal Eskimos. Such North Alaskan Eskimos as the 1)
Kaŋianigmiut and occasionally other Nunamiut; 2) Point Hope Eskimos
or Tikiragmiut; 3) Utukokmiut, 3a) Kugmiut; 4) a few Point Barrow
Eskimos; 5) Noatakmiut; 6) Kobukmiut, and 6a) Selawikmiut met such
Western Eskimos as the 1) Malemiut (generally from that part of
Seward Peninsula near the mainland) including the Kigirtarugmiut (from
Kotzebue), Kanagmiut (Buckland River), Kiwalikmiut (Kiwalik River),
and Kugrukmiut (Kugruk River); 2) the Kinugmiut (generally from the
western part of Seward Peninsula) including the Shakmalyagmiut (from
Shismaref) and the Kinikmiut (inhabitants of Cape Prince of Wales);
3) the Kaviagmiut (generally from the southern part of Seward Penin-
sula); and 4) the Unaligmiut (from the southern part of Seward
Peninsula and the area around Norton Sound). Eskimos from Big
Diomede Island, Little Diomede Island, King Island, and eastern
Siberia also traveled to Kotzebue to trade.

Just north of Howard Pass in the Nigu River valley, the Noatakmiut,
Kaŋianigmiut, Killikmiut, Kobukmiut, and Utukokmiut used to come
together for trading. The Nigu River was probably the most active site
of inland trade of which the Nunamiut were a part. Sometimes Nunamiut obtained coastal products from the Noatakmiut.

A few Killikmiut and other Nunamiut sometimes traveled down the
Ikpikpuk River directly to Point Barrow to obtain coastal goods.

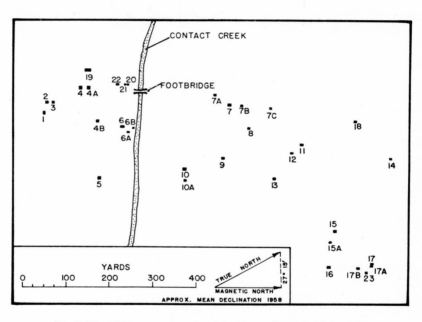

Fig. 2. The 1960 summer camp of the Nunamiut at Anaktuvuk Pass

Appendix B

The 1960 Summer Camp of the Nunamiut at Anaktuvuk Pass

DURING the summer of 1960, 96 Nunamiut were camped in 28 tents at Anaktuvuk Pass, comprising 18 households in which there were 15 conjugal couples. In some instances, a family and a household are identical, but this is not always the case. Other tents or buildings in use during the entire summer included: 4B, the winter house of Homer and Rebecca Mekiana, which served as the post office; 19, the church; 20, the cabin of Arthur O'Connell, trapper and trader; 21, his storehouse; 22, a cabin built by O'Connell and used by visitors; and 23, the tent of the writer. During the summer of 1960, visitors stayed either in O'Connell's cabin (22), in a Quonset hut just less than a mile northeast of the village, or in a tent pitched near or in the village. During the winter, all the members of each household move into one sod house in the village and spend varying periods of time in other sod and log houses scattered within a fifty-mile radius of the village, hunting and trapping. The summer is usually the longest period during which all the Nunamiut are camped together in one location.

In the summer of 1960, residence by household at Anaktuvuk Pass was as follows:

HOUSEHOLD 1:

> Ben Ahgook, aged 40, son of Jessie and Myrtle (d. 1953) Ahgook, m. to
> Elizabeth Ahgook, 34, adopted daughter of Elija and May Kakinya, actual daughter of Morry (b., Killik River; d. 1958) and Minnie (d. 1941) Maptirak
>
> Jacob, 12
> Vera, 4
> Dorothy, 2
>
> All live in Tent 1 and live together in the winter.

347

HOUSEHOLD 2:

Justice Mekiana, 32, son of Homer and Amilia (d. 1943, daughter
of Morry and Minnie Maptirak) Mekiana, m. to
Ethel Mekiana, 25, daughter of Jessie and Myrtle Ahgook

Myrtle, 6
Kenneth, 4
Rachel, 2

All live in Tent 2 and live together in the winter.

HOUSEHOLD 3:

Zacharias Hugo, 28, son of Old Hugo and Hetty (d. 1938)
Iñualurak, m. to
Doris Hugo, 24, daughter of Homer and Amilia Mekiana

Margaret, 3
Roy, 1

All live in Tent 3 and live together in the winter.

HOUSEHOLD 4:

Homer Mekiana, 55, a coastal Eskimo b. at Point Barrow, m. to
Rebecca Mekiana, 43, daughter of Old Hugo and Hetty Iñualurak;
of their children the following live with them in Household 4

Cyrus, 9
Kendon, 6
Patrick, 4
Donald, 2

All live in Tent 4 and live together in the winter. Also members of Household 4 are:
Joseph Mekiana, 18, son of David (d. 1938) and Rebecca
(now m. to Homer Mekiana) Paushana, who lives in
Tent 4A
Rachel Mekiana, 18, daughter of Homer (now m. to Rebecca) and Amilia (d., as mentioned, 1943) Mekiana,
who lives in Tent 4A

Both live with their parents and half-siblings in the winter;
Joseph and Rachel are *qataŋun* (step-sibling) to each other.

HOUSEHOLD 5:

Thomas Rulland, 25, son of Frank and Vera (d. 1953) Rulland, m.
to

Ruth Rulland, 22, adopted daughter of Elija and May Kakinya, actual daughter of Jessie and Myrtle Ahgook

Dorcas, 1

All live in Tent 5; in the winter of 1960–61, this couple and child lived as part of Household 7 and, for a short time, of Household 1; they plan to build their own winter house.

HOUSEHOLD 6:

Old Hugo Iñualurak, 75, b. upper Wild River, first cousin of the late Morry Maptirak, whose wife Hetty d. 1938, who lives in Tent 6B

Sarah Hugo, 48, unmarried daughter of Old Hugo and Hetty Iñualurak; her adopted son is

Cris, 7, actual son of Homer and Rebecca Mekiana

Elizabeth Hugo, 25, unmarried daughter of Old Hugo and Hetty Iñualurak

The last three live in Tent 6. Also members of Household 6 are:

David Mekiana, 16, son of David and Rebecca Paushana, who lives in Tent 6A, who lives much of the time in Household 6 during the winter and part of the time in Household 4

Jack Morry, 14, son of Peter (d. about 1940, son of Morry and Minnie Maptirak) Morry and Maggie (now m. to Amos Morry) Morry, who lives almost all the time in Household 6 but occasionally in Household 8

All members of Household 6 live together in the winter unless otherwise indicated.

HOUSEHOLD 7:

Frank Rulland, 60, b. Killik River but Kobuk Eskimo in origin, m. for one year to Puya, sister of Simon Paneak, d. 1926 before giving birth to any children; who then m. Vera, sister of Elija Kakinya, d. 1953; of their (Frank and Vera's) children, the following live in Household 7

Jane, 33, whose illegitimate children are:

Samuel, 8
Lauralu, 7

Johnny, 30, who lives in Tent 7C
Lazarus, 27, who lives in Tent 7B
Joshua, 23, who lives in Tent 7A
Ada, 21
Rosanne, 18

All, unless otherwise indicated, live in Tent 7 and live together in the winter.

HOUSEHOLD 8:

Amos Morry, 40, son of Morry and Minnie Maptirak, m. to
Maggie, 36, daughter of Old Hugo and Hetty Iñualurak

Hetty, 4

All live in Tent 8 and live together in the winter.

HOUSEHOLD 9:

Billy Morry, 45, son of Morry and Minnie Maptirak, m. to
Olive Morry, 38, daughter of Old Hugo and Hetty Iñualurak

Lulu, 13
Hetty, 6
Stanley, 3
Minnie, 2

All live in Tent 9 and live together in the winter.

HOUSEHOLD 10:

Clyde Hugo, 46, son of Old Hugo and Hetty Iñualurak, m. to
Ellen Hugo, 37, from the coast

Daniel, 16, who lives in Tent 10A
Martina, 14, who lives in Tent 10A
Harry, 10
Patrick, 8
Willie, 4
Charlie, 2
Delmer, 1

All, unless otherwise indicated, live in Tent 10 and live together in the winter.

HOUSEHOLD 11:

Robert Ahgook, 32, son of Jessie and Myrtle Ahgook, m. to
Rhoda Ahgook, 38, daughter of Morry and Minnie Maptirak

Minnie, 4
Jimmy, 2

All live in Tent 11 and live together in the winter.

HOUSEHOLD 12:

John Hugo, 37, son of Old Hugo and Hetty Iñualurak, m. to
Dora Hugo, 36, daughter of Morry and Minnie Maptirak

Anna, 15
Henry, 9

Also a member of Household 12 is:
Alice, 5, adopted at birth by John and Dora Hugo from
Clyde and Ellen Hugo

All live in Tent 12 and live together in the winter. Also a part-
time resident of Household 12 is:
Larry, 11, son of Billy and Olive Morry, who recognizes
them as his parents and who lives some time in Household 9

HOUSEHOLD 13:

Jack Ahgook, 27, son of Jessie and Myrtle Ahgook, m. to
Molly Ahgook, 26, daughter of Homer and Amilia Mekiana

Esther, 2
Ada, 1

All live in Tent 13 and live together in the winter.

HOUSEHOLD 14:

Jessie Ahgook, 78, b. upper Noatak River, m. Myrtle Ahgook, b.
upper Colville River and d. 1953, who lives much of the time
in Household 14, but also some time in Households 17 and 11
Noah Ahgook, 22, adopted son of Jessie and Myrtle Ahgook,
actual son of Old Hugo and Hetty Iñualurak, m. to
Leila Ahgook, 20, daughter of John and Alice (see Household 15)
Morry

Charlie, 2
Richard, 1

All live in Tent 14 and live together in the winter except for
Jessie Ahgook who may live elsewhere for a while.

HOUSEHOLD 15:

John Morry, 47, son of Morry and Minnie Maptirak, m. Alice (d. 1953) Morry, daughter of Simon Paneak and his first wife, d. 1924

Riley, 18, who lives in Tent 15A
Mark, 16, who lives in Tent 15A
Ina, 14
Susanne, 9, who lives occasionally in Household 11

All, unless otherwise indicated, live in Tent 15 and live together in the winter.

HOUSEHOLD 16:

Elija Kakinya, 64, b. near Demarkation Point of Colville River parentage, m. to
May Kakinya, 67, b. at Chandler Lake; of their adopted children, the following live with them in Household 16:

Abe Kakinya, 26, adopted son of Elija and May Kakinya, actual son of Morry and Minnie Maptirak, m. to
Marie Kakinya, 27, daughter of Old Hugo and Hetty Iñualurak

Betty, 2

All live in Tent 16 and live together in the winter.

HOUSEHOLD 17:

Simon Paneak, 60, b., Killik River, m. to
Susie Paneak, 45, adopted daughter of Elija and May Kakinya, actual daughter of May Kakinya's sister and husband

Robert, 21, who lives in Tent 17B
Raymond, 19, who lives in Tent 17B
Mabel, 17, who lives in Tent 17A
Roosevelt, 14, who lives in Tent 17A
George, 11
Alan, 4

All, unless otherwise indicated, live in Tent 17 and live together in the winter.

HOUSEHOLD 18:

Jonas Ahgook, 43, son of Jessie and Myrtle Ahgook, who is unmarried; he lives in Tent 18 and lives in his own winter house in the winter

Appendix C

Calendar of Seasonal Activities

SEPTEMBER

Fall (*ukiuxaraq*) begins, light snowfalls, freeze-up by late September in some years.

Caribou migrate to the south, mountain sheep very fat, marmot and grizzly fat with good pelts, some fishes still running.

Preparation for winter: intensive hunting of caribou, occasional hunting for grizzly, mountain sheep, and moose, trapping for marmot; skinning, transporting, and caching of skins, meat, and fat; making and repairing sleds, snowshoes, traps, and snares. Daily work of collecting firewood, ice, water, cooking, keeping the house clean, and repairing material possessions, which continues throughout the year.

Families move from summer tents to winter houses; men of each household hunt independently; formerly all households came together to form bands in order to corral herds of caribou; by late September, many households that used to summer on the Arctic coast had returned to the mountains.

OCTOBER

Fall, freeze-up often in early October, windy, some snowfall.

Many caribou still migrating southward, few fishes available; in late October and early November, grizzlies, marmots, and ground squirrels go into hibernation, southward movement of ptarmigan begins.

Activities much the same as in September; in addition, the preparation of skins and making of clothing, some ptarmigan snaring.

People usually remain in the village to continue winter preparations before winter trapping begins; formerly, all households that summered on the coast had returned to the mountains.

NOVEMBER

Fall becomes winter (*ukiuk*), increasingly cold, often little snowfall.

Caribou scattered in small groups in the timber and elsewhere, moun-

tain sheep sometimes available, southward movement of ptarmigan continues, fur-bearing animals have rich pelts.
Sporadic hunting of caribou and mountain sheep when necessary, serious trapping begins, some ptarmigan snaring.
Men leave the village to set up trap lines; then many households spread out over the countryside in groups of two, three, or four to hunt and trap; in some years when caribou are very plentiful, many families stay together for singing, dancing, visiting, and story-telling.

DECEMBER

Winter, cold.
Caribou are scattered and not very fat, some ptarmigan available, but except for fur-bearing animals which are rarely eaten, faunal resources are meager.
Sporadic hunting, extensive trapping, manufacturing of items to sell and trade.
Households largely dispersed, as in November; today, all households make an effort to come together at the end of December for communal eating, singing, and dancing at Christmas and New Year's.

JANUARY

Winter, cold.
Fauna as in December, round whitefish begin to leave several lakes.
Activities as in December, in addition, some fishing.
Households remain dispersed, occasionally singly, but usually in clusters; today some families tend to remain in the village hunting and trapping nearby, others habitually prefer to range farther afield.

FEBRUARY

Winter, cold.
Fauna as in December and January, some fishes available, northward movement of ptarmigan begins.
Activities as in December and January, in addition, ptarmigan snaring.
Households usually still dispersed.

MARCH

Spring (*upinaxaraq*) begins, very windy, heavy snowfall at times.
Spring migration of caribou to the north slope begins, some fishes and ptarmigan available; by the end of March or early April, the pelts of many fur-bearing animals are no longer desirable.
Intensive caribou hunting, skinning, transporting, and caching of meat and fat, some ptarmigan snaring.
All households (today) return to Anaktuvuk Pass to cache meat for the

summer; formerly, all households came together to form bands and corral herds of caribou, with communal eating, singing, dancing, and visiting with friends and relatives.

April

Spring, warmer, though windy and snowy at times.

Caribou migration continues; about the middle of April, grizzlies, marmots, and ground squirrels come out of hibernation; by the end of April and on into May, large birds migrate.

Intensive caribou hunting continues, hunting for grizzly, trapping for marmot and ground squirrel; with the long days, men dogsled logs from the timber up to the village.

All households returned to the village, although the men spend many hours on the trail before breakup bringing in the last loads of meat and logs; formerly, feuding and warfare most likely.

May

Spring, the wind may still be very chilly; by the middle or end of May, breakup occurs.

Many caribou still drifting north, grizzly, marmot, and ground squirrel available, large birds migrating.

Continued hunting of caribou, hunting for grizzly, trapping for marmot and ground squirrel, shooting and snaring of large birds.

Settlement as in April; formerly, those families planning to summer on the coast traveled to Umiat by sled, then down the Colville River by open skin boat; feuding and warfare possible.

June

Spring becomes summer (*upinagaaq*), rain.

Few caribou in the mountains, a few moose travel north, some fishes running, many birds available.

Wolf-pup hunting, some shooting and snaring of water fowl and fishing, otherwise little hunting; opportunities for sporadic employment with summer influx of visitors.

People move into summer tents; today all Nunamiut stay at Anaktuvuk Pass, with no snow or ice, mobility is greatly reduced during the summer months; formerly many Nunamiut summered on the coast fishing, hunting birds and occasional caribou, and trading with coastal Eskimos; some Nunamiut stayed inland in small household clusters to fish, trap ground squirrels, and hunt for summer caribou skins.

July

Summer, warm, although a snowfall of three or four inches is still possible.

Fauna much as in June, some birds already begin moving south.

Occasional hunting for summer caribou skins, some bird snaring and fishing, some moose hunting; continued opportunities for sporadic employment.

Settlement as in June, only a few men leave the village for more than a day's walk to hunt.

August

Summer, rain.

A few caribou to be found in the mountains, moose still traveling north, mountain sheep fatten, birds returning south, some fishes available, berries and roots ripe.

Hunting for summer caribou skins, mountain sheep hunting, occasional moose taken, trapping for ground squirrels, berry and root collecting; some opportunity for sporadic employment.

Settlement as in June and July.

Glossary

Aiyagomahala	the creator of the Nunamiut
akutaq	"Eskimo ice cream," made from caribou back fat and ground meat
Anaktuvuk Pass	the village in the central Brooks Range of Alaska where the remaining mountain Nunamiut now live (correctly *anaqtuvik,* the place or location of caribou feces: *anaq,* feces; *-tu,* of caribou; *-vik,* place or time of)
iñua	the person of [the antecedent]; the animating, essential life (or existing) force of [the antecedent]; soul; spirit
iñuk	a person; a human being
iñupiaq (pl. *iñupiat*)	a real person; an Eskimo
iŋilagaan	a long time ago; early days
ipani	some time ago; personal remembrance
itchaq imma	very early days
itkilliruich	[virtually (but not quite)] Indians; term of derision applied to the Kobuk Eskimos by the Nunamiut; the infix *-ir-* is a noun qualifier meaning "not quite, largely similar to, etc."; in this instance a Nunamiut avoids calling another Eskimo categorically an Indian
itkilluich	Indians (generally)
karigi	communal or ceremonial house

Kayaktuaguniktuu	[literally] clever at handling a kayak; after Aiyagomahala, the most important giant in the annals of Nunamiut ethnohistory
kinnaq	crazy; deeply neurotic or psychotic; rabies; severe distemper
-miut	inhabitants of [the geographical region specified]
muktuk	whale skin
nunamiut	inhabitants of land; the term by which the Nunamiut designate themselves
oivaksat	"native prophecy" (see p. 18, and especially pp. 56–57)
tannik	white man
tannikhlugo	to wash; to bathe
ulu	an Eskimo woman's semilunar knife
umiak (pl. *umiat*)	open skin boat
umialik	[literally] having an *umiak;* a rich man

Bibliography

Allen, Henry T.
  1887 *Report of an Expedition to the Copper, Tanana, and Koyukuk Rivers, in the Territory of Alaska in the Year 1885,* Washington.
American Friends Board of Foreign Missions
  1912 *Mission Work of California Friends,* Richmond, Ind.
Bancroft, Hubert Howe
  1890 *History of Alaska,* San Francisco.
Barrow, Sir John
  1846 *Voyages of Discovery and Research within the Arctic Regions from the Year 1818 to the Present Time,* New York.
Bee, James W., and E. Raymond Hall
  1956 *Mammals of Northern Alaska on the Arctic Slope,* University of Kansas, Museum of Natural History, Miscellaneous Publication No. 8, Lawrence, Kans.
Beechey, F. W.
  1831 *Narrative of a Voyage to the Pacific and Beering's Strait to Cooperate with the Polar Expeditions Performed in H.M.S. Blossom in the Years 1825, 1827, 1828,* London.
Brower, Charles D.
  1942 *Fifty Years Below Zero,* New York.
Campbell, John M.
  1961 Personal communication.
Cantwell, John C.
  1887 "A narrative account of the exploration of the Kowak River, Alaska," in *Report of the Cruise of the Revenue Marine Steamer "Corwin" in the Arctic Ocean in the Year 1885,* Washington, pp. 21–52.
  1889a "A narrative account of the exploration of the Kowak River, Alaska," in *Report of the Cruise of the Revenue Marine Steamer "Corwin" in the Arctic Ocean in the Year 1884,* Washington, pp. 49–74.
  1889b "Exploration of the Kowak River, Alaska: Ethnological notes," ibid., pp. 75–98.
Cook, James, and James King
  1784 *A Voyage to the Pacific Ocean, Undertaken by the Com-*

mand of His Majesty, for Making Discoveries in the Northern Hemisphere, 3 vols., London.

Dease, Peter W., and Thomas Simpson
    1838   "An account of recent Arctic discoveries," *Journal of the Royal Geographical Society of London, 8,* 113–225.

Dufresne, Frank
    1946   *Alaska's Animals and Fishes,* New York.

Franklin, Sir John
    1828   *Narrative of a Second Expedition to the Shores of the Polar Sea in the Years 1825, 1826, 1827,* London.

Giddings, J. L., Jr.
    1956   "Forest Eskimos," University Museum Bulletin, 20 (2), University of Pennsylvania, Philadelphia.
    1961   *Kobuk River People,* Studies of Northern Peoples, No. 1, College, Alaska.

Great Britain, Admiralty
    1854   "Papers Relative to the Recent Arctic Expeditions in Search of Sir John Franklin and the Crews of H.M.S. *Erebus* and *Terror,"* London.

Hall, Edwin S., Jr.
    1961   "Eskimo-Aleut Ethnobotany," Senior Essay, MS, Yale University, New Haven.
    1962   Personal communication.

Hall, E. Raymond, and Keith R. Kelson
    1959   *The Mammals of North America,* New York.

Healy, M. A., et al.
    1887   *Report of the Cruise of the Revenue Marine Steamer "Corwin" in the Arctic Ocean in the Year 1885,* Washington.
    1889   *Report of the Cruise of the Revenue Marine Steamer "Corwin" in the Arctic Ocean in the Year 1884,* Washington.

Heinrich, Albert
    1960   "Structural features of Northwestern Alaskan Eskimo kinship," *Southwestern Journal of Anthropology, 16,* 110–26.

Hornaday, W. T., and Charles D. Brower
    1911   "The musk-ox in Alaska," *Bulletin,* New York Zoological Society, No. 45, pp. 754–55.

Hulley, Clarence C.
    1953   *Alaska 1741–1953,* Portland, Ore.

Ingstad, Helge
    1954   *Nunamiut,* New York.

Irving, Laurence
    1953   "The naming of birds by Nunamiut Eskimo," *Arctic, 6* (1), 35–43.

1958   "On the naming of birds by Eskimos," *Anthropological Papers of the University of Alaska*, 6 (2), 61–77.
1960   *Birds of Anaktuvuk Pass, Kobuk, and Old Crow,* Bulletin 217, Smithsonian Institution, Washington.
Irving, Laurence, and Simon Paneak
1954   "Biological reconnaissance along the Ahlasuruk River east of Howard Pass, Brooks Range, Alaska, with notes on the avifauna," *Journal of the Washington Academy of Science, 44* (7), 201–11.
Jarvis, D. H., et al.
1899   *Report of the Cruise of the U.S. Revenue Cutter* Bear *and the Overland Expedition for the Relief of the Whalers in the Arctic Ocean, from November 27, 1897 to September 13, 1898,* Washington.
Jenness, Diamond
1957   *Dawn in Arctic Alaska,* Minneapolis.
Kelsey, Rayner W.
1917   *Friends and the Indians,* Philadelphia.
Kotzebue, Otto von
1821   *A Voyage of Discovery into the South Sea and Beering's Straits, 1815–18,* 3 vols., London.
Leffingwell, Ernest de K.
1919   *The Canning River Region, Northern Alaska,* U.S. Geological Survey, Professional Paper 109, Washington.
Lent, Peter C.
1960   *Caribou Investigations, Northwest Alaska,* Project Report, Phase III Progress Report, College, Alaska.
Linton, Ralph
1936   *The Study of Man,* New York.
Lomen, Carl
1954   *Fifty Years in Alaska,* New York.
McLenegan, S. B.
1887   "Exploration of the Noatak River, Alaska," in *Report of the Cruise of the Revenue Marine Steamer "Corwin" in the Arctic Ocean in the Year 1885,* Washington, pp. 53–80.
Mendenhall, Walter C.
1902   *Reconnaissance from Fort Hamlin to Kotzebue Sound, Alaska, by Way of Dall, Kanuti, Allen, and Kowak Rivers,* U.S. Geological Survey, Professional Paper 10, Washington.
Murdoch, John
1892   "Ethnological results of the Point Barrow Expedition," in *Ninth Annual Report,* Bureau of American Ethnology, pp. 19–441.
Murie, Adolph

1944   *The Wolves of Mount McKinley,* U.S. Dept. of Interior, National Park Service, Fauna Series No. 5, Washington.

Murie, Olaus J.
1935   *Alaska–Yukon Caribou,* U.S. Dept. of Agriculture, Bureau of Biological Survey, North American Fauna No. 54, Washington.

Osgood, Cornelius
1940   *Ingalik Material Culture,* Yale University Publications in Anthropology, No. 22, New Haven.

Palmer, L. J.
1934   *Raising Reindeer in Alaska,* U.S. Dept. of Agriculture, Miscellaneous Publication No. 207, Washington.

Porsild, A. E.
1953   "Edible plants of the Arctic," *Arctic,* 6 (6), 15–34.
1957   *Illustrated Flora of the Canadian Arctic Archipelago,* National Museum of Canada, Bulletin No. 146, Ottawa.

Porter, Stephen C.
1961   Personal communication.
1962   "Geology of Anaktuvuk Pass, Central Brooks Range, Alaska," Diss., Yale University, New Haven.

Pospisil, Leopold
1964   "Law and societal structure among the Nunamiut Eskimo," in *Explorations in Cultural Anthropology,* ed. Ward H. Goodenough, New York.

Rasmussen, Knud
1927   *Across Arctic America,* New York.

Rausch, Robert
1951   "Notes on the Nunamiut Eskimo and mammals of the Anaktuvuk Pass region, Brooks Range, Alaska," *Arctic,* 4 (3), 147–95.
1953   "On the status of some Arctic mammals," *Arctic,* 6 (2), 91–148.

Ray, P. H.
1885   "Ethnographic sketch of the natives," in *Report of the International Polar Expedition to Point Barrow, Alaska,* Washington.

Schrader, Frank Charles
1901   *Preliminary Report on a Reconnaissance along the Chandalar and Koyukuk Rivers, Alaska, in 1899,* Washington.
1904   *A Reconnaissance in Northern Alaska across the Rocky Mountains, along Koyukuk, John, Anaktuvuk, and Colville Rivers, and the Arctic Coast to Cape Lisburne in 1901,* U.S. Geological Survey, Professional Paper 20, Washington.

Simpson, John, R. N.
1855   "Observations on the western Eskimo and the country they

inhabit," *from* Notes taken during two years at Point Barrow, in *Further Papers Relative to the Recent Arctic Expeditions in Search of Sir John Franklin,* Parliamentary Reports, 1855, and reprinted, 1875, in *Arctic Geography and Ethnology,* Royal Geographical Society, London, pp. 233–75.

Simpson, Thomas
    1843   *Narrative of the Discoveries on the North Coast of America,* London.

Smith, Philip S., and J. B. Mertie
    1930   *Geology and Mineral Resources of Northwestern Alaska,* U.S. Geological Survey, Bulletin 815, Washington.

Spencer, Robert
    1959   *The North Alaskan Eskimo,* Smithsonian Institution, Bureau of American Ethnology, Bulletin 171, Washington.

Stefansson, Vilhjalmur
    1919   *My Life with the Eskimo,* New York.
    1922   *Hunters of the Great North,* New York.
    1943   *The Friendly Arctic,* New York.

Stoney, George M.
    1900   *Naval Explorations in Alaska,* U.S. Naval Institute, Annapolis.

Stuck, Hudson
    1920   *A Winter Circuit of our Arctic Coast,* New York.

Walters, Vladimir
    1955   "Fishes of western Arctic America and eastern Arctic Siberia," *Bulletin of the American Museum of Natural History, 106,* article 5.

Weyer, Edward M.
    1932   *The Eskimos,* New Haven.

Index

Abandonment, 122

Acculturation. *See* Change

Adolescents and adolescence, 91–92, 108–14, 135

Adoption, 53–54, 118–19, 140 f., 146–47

Adultery, 29, 59, 63, 68, 117, 148, 184, 219, 243–46

Adz, 87 f., 201, 232

Aesthetic sensitivity, 229–30

Affection, 105 ff., 111 f., 134, 137 f., 148, 156–57, 183; to dogs, 292

Afognak Island, 280

Afterlife, 56, 213–14. *See also* Death; Mourning; *Iñua;* Shadow

Age, and social role, 61, 72, 105–22, 137. *See also* Sex, and social role

Aging, growth, and death, 216–18

Ahgook, Jessie, 21, 186 f., 286

Air (atmosphere), 199, 238; spirit of, 238

Airplanes, 25, 26, 177, 187; wolves killed from, 101

Aiyagomahala (mythical giant), 29–32, 33 ff., 39, 201, 218, 327

Aklavik (village), 20, 333

Akutuk River, 305

Alashuk River, 305

Alaska, 1–27, 163 f., 255, 261, 264 ff., 285 f., 295 f., 302, 305, 316 ff., 333; Russian fur interests and exploration, 1–3; British exploration, 3–6; Hudson's Bay Company, 6; American whaling, 3, 7–9; Russian whaling, 7; geological exploration, 7, 9, 11, 12–14; military patrol (U.S.), 7, 9; American revenue cutters, 10–11, 12; Russian Orthodox churches, 16. *See also* North Alaska; Western Alaska

Alaska, state of: school at Anaktuvuk

Pass, 26; wolf bounty, 100; authorities, 166; U.S. Fish and Wildlife Service, 265

Alatna River, 11, 15, 29, 31 f., 305

Alcohol. *See* Whiskey

Alder, 82, 85, 176, 239 f.

Aleutian Islands, 1, 7

Aleuts, 2

Alignments, household. *See* Household, alignments; Household, clusters

Allen River, 14, 45

Americans: whaling in Alaska, 3, 7–9; contact with north Alaska, 7–27; revenue cutters, 10, 12; bilateral ties among, 140; culture, 164. *See also* White man; Trade goods

Amulets, 157, 200

Anaktiktuak River, 229

Anaktuvuk Pass, xi, 13, 18 f., 24 ff., 46, 50, 60 f., 65 f., 97 ff., 112, 119, 132, 154, 158, 165 ff., 176, 181, 186 f., 192, 211, 234, 240, 246, 256 f., 261 ff., 277, 283, 286, 293, 303, 309, 313 f., 319 ff., 325

Anaktuvuk River, 13, 25, 45 ff., 96, 177 f., 229, 232, 302, 305, 314

Analogy, Nunamiut use of, 32–33, 192–93, 222 ff., 229, 266

Anatomy: Nunamiut sense of, 215; caribou terminology, 301–02

Anchorage (Alaska), 164

Anderson, Dr., 21

Anger, 194, 212, 218 f., 245 f., 254, 282, 329, 332

Anglicans, 15 f., 22. *See also* Missionaries

Animals: lived like people in *itchaq imma,* 39; *iñua,* 199–200; supernatural treatment of, 208–09, 326–27; sensitivity to human ethics, 219–20, 327–30. *See also* Mammals, land,

365

Swallow, 243
Swedish Lutherans, 16
Swimming, Nunamiut, 176
Syrup, 75

Taboo. *See* Rules
Tanana (village), 164; Indians, 44
Tapeworm (*T. echinococcus*), in caribou, 316
Taste, sense of, 224
Tea, 51, 75
Teasing, 107
Technology, Nunamiut, 76; supplemented by trade goods, 51; altered, 54; learning, 109–10, 111, 170; variations, ecological, 163. *See also* specific items, e.g.: Scraper, Bow-drill, etc.
Telescopes, 261, 287 f.
Temperature, 90, 98, 199, 236–37, 309. *See also* Cold; Climate; Seasons
Tents: canvas, 67, 70 f.; skin, 69–71, 168
Terminology: consanguineal relatives, 135–37; combined kin, 131, 136; nuclear family, 136; siblings-in-law, 132; extended family, 136; half-sibling, 136–37; step, 137; affinal relatives, 153–54; spouse exchange, 68; caribou, 296–97, 301–02
Terrain, 229–31, 321; animals' response to, 23–; knowledge of, 230–31; and caribou, 307–09
Territory, sense of, 45 f., 165–66, 167; common, 162; hunting, 165
Theft, 11, 29, 59, 122, 127, 131, 184–86, 194, 218 f. *See also* Legal disputes
Thimbles, 83
Thrush, 243
Thunderstorms, 196, 238
Timber, 72 f., 86–87, 89 f., 94, 96, 163, 181, 262 ff., 276 f., 283 f., 303 ff., 311 ff.; Nunamiut attitude toward, 241. *See also* Spruce
Time, divisions of, 28, 191–92
Tobacco, 49 ff., 240, 260. *See also* Trade goods
Toboggans, 89
Tools, 63, 76; imported, 89; making,

170, 172. *See also* Technology; and particular items, e.g.: Scraper, Bow-drill, etc.
Topography. *See* Terrain
Toys, 91, 102–03, 240, 261
Trade: to north Alaska coast, 4, 12 f., 55, 67–68, 89, 91, 99, 133, 158–59, 172, 177–79, 232 f., 249, 278; dependence on, 160 ff., 255. *See also* Partners; Spouse exchange
Trade contacts: Nunamiut with Koyukon Indians, 2; Kotzebue Sound, 2 ff., Fort Yukon, 6; Alaskan Eskimos, 6, 20; Charles Brower and Jack Smith, 22 f.; Kobuk Eskimos/ Koyukon Indians, 2, 13; Malemiut Eskimos/north Alaskan coast, 12–13; Eskimos/Indians (Kutchin), 45; Nunamiut/Indians (Kutchin), 49; Nunamiut/Siberian Eskimos, 50–51; Nunamiut/Mackenzie River Eskimos, 233; Nunamiut/ Coppermine Eskimos, 233; Nunamiut/Kobuk Eskimos, 265–83. *See also* Trade; Appendix A
Trade goods, 2–7 passim, 12, 14, 22, 50–53, 57, 90, 97, 160–61, 179, 187, 317, 333; and Nunamiut before *1890,* 52
Traders, 7, 20, 26, 187, 313; Eskimos as, 2, 5, 23, 26
Trading, 4, 13 f., 29 f., 32, 56, 98, 130, 132, 163–64, 178, 181 f.; expeditions, 61, 89, 165, 167, 177–79, 182–83. *See also* Feasts; Partners
Tradition, verbal. *See* Ethnohistory; Folktales
Trails, 236
Transportation, 290–91, 294. *See also* Dogs; Sleds; Traveling
Trance. *See* Visions
Trappers (white), 7, 14 f., 20, 23, 26, 180, 317
Trapping (Eskimo), 26, 48 f., 55, 61 f., 68, 72, 76, 90, 92–93, 95–96, 110, 115, 121, 125, 127, 165 f., 180 ff., 236, 262, 267, 278; learning, 63; women, 112; prerogatives, 166; supernaturally sanctioned rules, 208–09; expeditions, 241. *See also* Hunting and trapping prerogatives